The Prosperity Gospel in Africa

The Prosperity Gospel in Africa

An African Pentecostal Hermeneutical Consideration

Marius Nel

WIPF & STOCK · Eugene, Oregon

THE PROSPERITY GOSPEL IN AFRICA
An African Pentecostal Hermeneutical Consideration

Copyright © 2020 Marius Nel. All rights reserved. Except for brief quotations in critical publications or reviews, no part of this book may be reproduced in any manner without prior written permission from the publisher. Write: Permissions, Wipf and Stock Publishers, 199 W. 8th Ave., Suite 3, Eugene, OR 97401.

Wipf & Stock
An Imprint of Wipf and Stock Publishers
199 W. 8th Ave., Suite 3
Eugene, OR 97401

www.wipfandstock.com

PAPERBACK ISBN: 978-1-7252-6662-9
HARDCOVER ISBN: 978-1-7252-6663-6
EBOOK ISBN: 978-1-7252-6664-3

Manufactured in the U.S.A. 05/22/20

Contents

Preface | vii
Research Justification | xi
Motivation for Study | xiii

1. The Context: Africa, and the Rise and Popularity of the Prosperity Message | 1

2. The Angle: Pentecostal Hermeneutics | 23

3. The Project: Prosperity Gospel | 43

4. The Challenge: Prosperity Gospel in Africa | 114

5. The Solution: An Evaluation of African Charismatic Prosperity Theology from a New African Pentecostal Hermeneutical Perspective | 201

Concluding Summary and Recommendations | 271

Bibliography | 281

Preface

My exposure to the pentecostal experience came when I was eleven years old. I was brought up in one of South Africa's three sisters churches, all of them Reformed churches. When I was ten, my mother died of cancer and my father remarried, with a lady who belonged to South Africa's largest classical Pentecostal denomination, the Apostolic Faith Mission of South Africa (AFM of SA). I visited the church with her, was caught up in the enthusiasm and liveliness that characterized their worship services, and was baptized in the Spirit within a few months. In time I was also baptized in water. At eighteen years of age, I started attending a local university to pursue degree studies that would qualify me to become a librarian, a field that interested me.

During the July vacations of my first year of studies, after the first semester of study that started in January, I was working at a factory to earn some pocket money. As I was working shifts, in the course of the month's work I enjoyed one long weekend, beginning on a Thursday morning and lasting to late Sunday night. The daughter of friends of our family invited me to visit her on their farm for the weekend and enjoy some farm activities, like riding horses in the beautiful Bushveld. The farm was situated in what was then called the Western Transvaal (today's North-West Province), between Zeerust and Nietverdiend. We arrived on the farm on Thursday just before dark and enjoyed dinner before taking her grandmother back to the latter's farm after she had been visiting her daughter. The girl who invited me and I were sitting on the back of the bakkie that was driven by the brother's friend, with the grandmother, brother of the girl and his friend in front. The driver was going rather fast on the dirt road when he apparently lost control of the vehicle. It overturned and I was caught underneath the bakkie before it rolled over again, landing on its wheels.

I could not remember anything about the accident until I recovered my consciousness after two or three days. There was severe damage to my pelvis, facial nerves, lungs, and brain. I lost my hearing in the left ear, the left lachrymal gland that eventually affected the sight in the left eye negatively was badly damaged, and my face was paralyzed on the one side. For many weeks I was not allowed to walk around. Eventually I was allowed to leave the hospital, six weeks before the final university exams started. The university graciously allowed me to sit for the exams. Two days before I wrote my first paper I had a scheduled consultation with the neurosurgeon. He explained that a small critical operation was necessary because the damage to the facial nerve and hearing that used the same cranial canal was becoming grave. He would be doing the procedure early the following morning but he assured me that I would be able to sit for the exams the day after the operation. I studied through the night to prepare for the exams and reported to the hospital very early the next morning.

When I awoke from the operation, I saw a clock on the opposite wall and asked my father who was standing next to the bed, "Is it nine o'clock in the morning or in the evening?" The neurosurgeon who was standing on the other side of the bed replied, "If he can read a clock he will make it." What I did not know was that the operation turned out to be a major reconstruction, which caused me to be discharged from the hospital only after three weeks. I was disappointed because I lost the opportunity to complete the academic year, and eventually the university graciously wrote off my study debts for that year.

While I was in the intensive care unit after the operation, suffering from severe headaches due to the brain operation, I was arguing with the Lord about what I was experiencing. I was trying to be a dedicated believer, trusting God with every detail of my life, when an accident suddenly changed the course of my life, changing me into a regular visitor to various medical specialists who were treating me for diverse challenges. Where was the God that I served when I needed God the most?

I experienced that God was speaking in my mind, giving me the insight that Pentecostals believe God uses to reveal God's will to the individual. What I understood was that God was preparing me for the ministry. Even before I finished my secondary school career, several believers shared prophetic words with me that God intended me to become a pastor but I was not convinced that I would be suitable material for the challenges that I perceived the ministry to hold. Now I knew that I was to change the direction of my studies and my life at a critical juncture. Shortly after I consented to the voice of God I started recovering very quickly, the severe headaches eased, and the neurosurgeon jokingly told me that he thought that he was experiencing a miracle in the way I was so rapidly recovering from the operation.

The next year I enrolled for studies at the faculty of theology at the same university and eventually also completed a theological diploma required for ordination in the AFM. While I was a student I attended a congregation where the pastor invited me to become involved in ministry on a part time basis. The pastor had ties with a well-known American prosperity teacher after they had met in America during a visit by my pastor, and the American teacher was providing the pastor with copies of his many books to be distributed in South Africa, especially to ministers of the gospel. At one stage the prosperity teacher also visited South Africa at the invitation of the pastor and took some services at the pastor's assembly where he preached the standard prosperity gospel, that it was God's intention to forgive, heal, and provide prosperity and wealth to every Christian who confessed their faith in God and God's promises by claiming and confessing that they were forgiven, healed, and becoming prosperous because of Jesus' atonement.

At one stage during his teaching, he invited members of the audience to ask him questions. I responded by asking him why he thinks God would allow a young boy's mother to die from cancer at an age when the boy needed his mother the most and why God would allow a promising student to become caught up in a crippling accident if Jesus had died for believers? Did it imply that it was the young boy's fault or the lack of faith in the young student? Who was responsible for causing accidents in our world? The teacher did not answer the question but promised to come back to it at a later stage. He left for America before that stage arrived!

A next incident happened when I was a student and joining some other students of the theological college on our way to classes. The driver of our vehicle was a young fellow student who had the personality of an evangelist, always enthusiastically trying to convince somebody of something that he believed in. He was arguing vehemently, without any opposition from any student in the vehicle, that God wanted to heal every sick person and the only qualification was that the person should trust God and believe that healing was brought about as an accomplished fact, a *fait accompli*, on the cross of Golgotha. At one stage I took off my glasses and challenged him, "If you really believe what you are preaching to us, will you please pray for the affected eye and my face that is paralyzed on the one side?" I was sincere in my request because I believed that God could heal and that God wanted to do it. He was silent for a few moments and then hit me with his fist. He never spoke about the subject again where I was part of his audience!

Today I still live with the consequences of the accident that happened more that forty years ago and each day I am reminded of its effects on my body and health. In the meantime, during 35 years of ministry I prayed for many sick people, some of whom recovered and others who did not. I humbly submit that I believe that my prayers contributed to a few of them getting healed miraculously, although it is also true that others were healed, sometimes in what seemed like a miraculous way, by means of operations, medicines, or other medical means. Some of those for whom I prayed died and I attended their funerals. I still believe God can heal, but I question the link that Pentecostals had traditionally made between healing and the atonement, and I also question the direct link that prosperity teaching has been making for the past fifty years (in my experience) between prosperity and the atonement.

When I was appointed in 2017 as a research professor in a chair at the theological faculty that was established between North-West University and the AFM of SA, I started concentrating on pentecostal hermeneutics. I had been observing how important the way that we read and interpret the Bible was in the way we defined our theology and *praxis*. In 2018 I wrote on an African pentecostal hermeneutics and the influence of pentecostal hermeneutics on the practice of pacifism, and in 2019 on the way hermeneutics determines pentecostal eschatological views.[1] The time has now come for me to further my research into what has been stimulating my thoughts for a long time, related to my personal experience, prosperity theology and its impact on Pentecostalism.

---

1. Nel, *African Pentecostal Hermeneutics*; *Pacifism and Pentecostals*; *African Pentecostalism and Eschatological Expectations*.

Research Justification

THE PURPOSE OF THIS book is to describe pentecostal hermeneutics in terms of its viewpoint toward the prosperity gospel.[1]

Most of the academic literature in the field of pentecostal studies in hermeneutic and exegesis is from American or British-European origin. The African context is fairly absent in this discourse, although Pentecostalism is thriving on the continent and presents unique and relevant challenges. This book was written by a theological scholar from Africa, focusing on Africa's need for a well-grounded theological evaluation of popular prosperity theology.

Written from the science of the exegesis of Old Testament and New Testament as well as a survey of literary studies, the book is aimed at scholars across theological sub-disciplines, especially those theological scholars interested in the intersections between theology, pentecostal hermeneutic and African cultural or social themes. It addresses themes and provides insights that are also relevant for specialist leaders and professionals in this field. Believers will also find much that is helpful for them to understand prosperity theology and the potential dangers that its beliefs hold in for the church of Christ.

No part of the book was plagiarized from another publication or published elsewhere.

The author thanks the National Research Foundation of South Africa (NRF) for providing funding for this study. The views expressed do not necessarily reflect the view of the NRF.

Marius Nel
Unit for Reformed Theology and Development
of the South African Society
North-West University
South Africa

1. When the term "Pentecostal" is applied to people, the church, or the movement as such, a capital letter is used while a small letter is applied when it refers to theology, spirituality, or practices.

Motivation for Study

Introduction

It seems as if prosperity theology is proclaimed and practiced by many African Pentecostals.[1] If this is so, the question needs to be asked: what are the reason(s) for its popularity?[2] It is argued that it should be attributed to at least three factors: the origins of independent or charismatic network Christianity and its wide influence, also on African church leaders; the role played by the African traditional notion of prosperity, that should be described in terms of the African worldview and African traditional religions; and its appeal to the deep longings of every human heart for peace, health, happiness, wealth, and prosperity. The aim of the study is to research the phenomenon of the prosperity theology in African Pentecostalism in order to pose an evaluation of the theology in terms of the context of the African church from a new African pentecostal hermeneutic perspective that is in line with the way early Pentecostals read and interpreted the Bible in their praxis-driven spiritual ethos.[3] The study is not concerned with the challenges the prosperity message poses to systematic or practical theology but is rather aimed at the way a specific Bible reading practice results in an emphasis of prosperity as an integral aspect that believers may expect from God.

---

1. Interesting to note is that a similar prosperity ethic has been emerging in Islam and Buddhism at the same time (Hefner, "Unexpected Modern-Gender," 22).

2. Ntui-Abung, *Chaos of the Prosperity Gospel*, 9 argues that about 92 percent of poor Africans, Latin Americans, and those living in Third World countries are completely influenced by the movement. This is probably an overestimation of the popularity of the movement although it is true that in a glocalized world technology carries the prosperity message into the heart of each village and township where electricity is available.

3. Archer. *Pentecostal Hermeneutic*, 3.

A problem is that the prosperity movement does not use or exercise a consistent theology. It is not possible to clearly talk about a single definite theology of its own. Prosperity preachers, called "prosperity gospellers" by Ogbu Kalu,[4] differ in several aspects of their teaching among themselves although there are clearly marked trends that characterize all their preaching. To arrive at a logical understanding of prosperity theology then demands a careful analysis of the liturgies, practices, sermons, songs, prayers, and publications of practitioners.[5] The presupposition is that religious experience can be used as a significant theological ingredient in understanding God's actions among God's people; the prosperity movement as part of Pentecostalism shares its experiential preference and cannot be understood apart from its experiences.

The argument of the research is that Africans' prevailing interest in the prosperity gospel is not only connected to the influence of American prosperity teachers reaching a worldwide audience through their imaginative use of the media, including television, radio, social media and publications. It is however also related to the African worldview and African traditional religion, and its lasting influence on contemporary Africans and the way they think about prosperity, as well as their interest in prosperity in post-colonial Africa. By only concentrating on the American influence the theologian is unable to read the African context correctly.

For a long time, colonial forces subdued Africa and abused and exploited its population and natural resources, acquiring wealth for themselves at the cost of the indigenous people and at the same time impoverishing them.[6] They did not share their prosperity with those they used and abused to acquire it but shut the local work force up in hostels far away from their families, in shanty towns and squatter camps, and the most primitive of shacks on farms. One should have no reason to wonder why liberalized Africans are interested in prosperity that is connected to the establishment of a black middle class in Africa. Prosperity implies for them taking back what colonials had been stealing for centuries and that belonged to them and their ancestors as the original inhabitants (and owners) of the continent. Whenever the prosperity message is evaluated in terms of an African context all these factors must be offset. Several other studies about the African pentecostal acceptance of the prosperity gospel

---

4. Kalu, "'Globecalisation' and Religion."
5. Quayesi-Amakye, "Prosperity and Prophecy," 292.
6. Maura, "True and False Prosperity," 33.

have been published but without recognizing the African perspective on prosperity that co-determines the way African Pentecostals perceive the prosperity gospel. Only by discounting all factors can the prosperity gospel be theologically and sociologically evaluated in a just way.

In literature three possibilities of the relation between the Christian church, including the classical Pentecostal movement of which the present author is a member, and the prosperity movement can in broad lines be distinguished. In the first place, the teaching and practice of the prosperity gospel can be rejected in an offhanded manner without much further consideration because although it sounds biblical, its teaching is heretical and its adherents are viewed as victims of seduction. For instance, some view the prosperity message in continuity with Gnosticism that threatened the church of the second century, and Irenaeus then serves as an example of how the movement should be treated. Irenaeus branded the Gnostics as heretics and refused that the Christian church might have any communion with them. Such heretical teachings of the prosperity movement are then found, *inter alia*, in its emphasis on revelation knowledge, its concept of God, anthropology, and Christology.

A second way that the relation between the church and the prosperity movement can be described is in terms of ecumenical involvement with the movement but without acceptance of all its teachings. In these circles, the argument is used that the prosperity movement represents the most vibrant (or at least one of the most vibrant) movement, as a continuation of (and deviation from) the classical Pentecostal movement, the healing revivals that characterized the middle of the twentieth century, and the charismatic movement that changed the faces of some established mainline churches that accepted pentecostalization of its worship practices since the 1960s. Many classical Pentecostal denominations fall in this category, when they tolerate the prosperity message for pragmatic reasons but do not support it for theological reasons. They have firsthand experience that the established churches' criticism of revivals in the past did a lot of harm, not only to the revivals themselves but also to their own reputation in the eyes of the world, and their opposition in many instances did not contribute much that was positive. It is argued that involvement in the movement can perhaps accomplish more, without accepting everything that the movement does and teaches. However, it should also be considered that such an attitude, of cooperation without acceptance of all its teachings, gives religious and even theological credibility to a movement that requires (and critically needs!) vibrant criticism from the side of the established church. Another danger is that such an attitude may lead to participants being influenced and even absorbed by the movement and eventually accept some or even all of its questionable doctrines as well.

A third option that is accepted and pursued in the current publication is neither to affirm all the teachings not to denounce it in a wholesale manner but to provide a detailed description of the movement and its doctrines in order to lay the groundwork for a meaningful dialogue, learning from each other and trying to resolve conflicts of opinion in a spirit of love.[7] The dialogue does not preclude that some doctrines of the prosperity movement may be criticized severely and its leaders shown what the potential effects on their followers are or could be. At the same time, the positive aspects should also be highlighted, for instance, that believers are expected to give and live generously. Much of the message of prosperity is potentially valuable and its effects on adherents probably positive in terms of life transformation and its effects on their relationships, ethics, and spirituality. This approach avoids an uncompromising and highly critical stand against the movement as well as a careless acceptance of its questionable teaching because of its apparent "success" in reaching millions of people.[8]

As argued above, it is opportune to rather speak of prosperity theologies because of the diversity of perspectives found among proponents of the prosperity message. Using André Droogers' anthropological framework that distinguishes between the sacred/transcendental dimension, the internal dimension, and the external dimension,[9] Maria Frahm-Arp suggests that the transcendental refers to how people speak about or understand the sacred, the internal dimension to the way people's understanding of the divine shapes how they think about themselves and structure their churches, and the external dimension shapes theology and the experience of the divine.[10] On these grounds she then shows

7. This is also the route suggested by Bruce Barron, *Health and Wealth Gospel*.

8. The work of McConnell, *Different Gospel*, is also successful in applying such an attitude toward the prosperity gospel.

9. Droogers, *Identity, Religious Pluralism*, 665.

10. Frahm-Arp, "Pentecostalism, Politics, and Prosperity," 7–11. See also Wariboko, "Pentecostal Paradigms," who outlines five "paradigms" of prosperity, drawing on his analysis of the teachings of prominent African pastors. He notes how each paradigm, resting on a pertinent metaphor or analogy, envisages an obstacle to economic prosperity to which it proposes a solution. Frahm-Arp's clusters are contained neatly within these five paradigms and simplify Wariboko's analysis in a useful manner.

how prosperity theology developed into three different forms, leading to changes in the internal dimensions of each different type.[11] The first category, abilities prosperity, is based on the idea that if Christians live according to biblical principles and work hard, then they will succeed in whatever they choose to do. Their theology is influenced strongly by dominion theologians such as C. Peter Wagner and Cindy Jacobs, encouraging people to find God's purpose for their lives and claim their blessings. When believers do not enjoy the wealth they were hoping for, abilities prosperity theology explains this in terms of their unrepentant sins that hold them back from realizing God's blessings. At the same time, it places much emphasis on helping people to develop themselves.

A second strand, progress prosperity, is focused primarily on the community rather than the individual. Progress prosperity theology holds that any small blessing or step of progress is a form of prosperity. What is necessary, is that believers change their attitudes so that they can see things as they truly are. It places the least amount of emphasis on material gain in the lives of believers and the most on the importance of social concern projects and helping people who are in need. Their social concern projects include providing material help such as clothes and food to the destitute, and engaging in a vast array of programs stretching from how to parent children effectively to how to run one's own business successfully. The internal structure of these churches is geared to developing the community. It also promotes an entrepreneurial mindset or spirit.[12]

While abilities prosperity and progress prosperity place a great deal of emphasis on developing the individual and the community respectively, they place comparatively less emphasis on deliverance and other miracles. Miracle prosperity theology, on the other hand, is primarily concerned with explaining the way the world is and how prosperity can be achieved through miracles. Frahm-Arp identifies three subgroups defined by their core claims: those who claim that miraculous health and wealth come about when the devil is vanquished so that God can perform miracles as a result; those for whom miraculous wealth and health happen though applying God's laws of faith, as taught by the Faith gospel; and those who merge the two ideas in which miracles only happen when people have sufficient faith and, through their faith and the power of the prophet, evil is exorcised from their lives. When these things do not materialize, they explain that it

11. Although she limits her study to South Africa, it reflects neo-Pentecostalism in sub-Saharan Africa.

12. Frahm-Arp, "Pentecostalism, Politics, and Prosperity," 9–10.

is the fault of Satan or a person's sins which are responsible. Wealth is not achieved through hard work and a strict moral code but rather through God's desire to bless people with miraculous wealth, either through their own faith or by vanquishing the spiritual powers of evil that continually want to thwart God's miracles.[13] The internal structure of these churches does not offer any programs or initiative to upskill members through education and skills development. They rather offer prayer services at which people can drive out evil and become blessed, and practice their faith. They do not have any social outreach or care programs, and developing a caring Christian community is not a prominent emphasis in their theology and praxis. While progress prosperity churches see biblical teaching as the most important component of their services with learning "the Word" as the essential part of a Christian's development, miracle prosperity churches do not emphasize the importance of study of the word of God and often refer only fleetingly to it in their sermons.[14]

For this reason, the prosperity movement cannot be evaluated without further qualification. In this study I will be looking primarily at the last strand of Frahm-Arp's useful distinction between different strands or clusters of prosperity existing within neo-Pentecostal churches in Johannesburg, South Africa. Miracle prosperity theology is the most prevalent of the three categories in neo-Pentecostal churches and groups in Africa. It should also be kept in mind that the distinction is in no way water-tight; they do not represent neat typologies and many churches are a hybrid with elements from different clusters, making a careful assessment of the phenomenon a critical necessity.[15] All three clusters preach the centrality of tithing and giving generously, a key element of Word of Faith theology. Abilities and miracles prosperity teach excess giving as one of the most effective ways of proving personal faith and thereby winning God's favor and blessing while progress prosperity churches have a more measured approach to tithing, teaching that people should give generously and abundantly while not endangering their own financial position.

To be realistic, efforts at ecumenical cooperation with leaders of some prosperity movements have not been very successful in the past, with these leaders aggressively defending themselves and their financial practices, warning that their critics are opposing the Spirit of God

---

13. Frahm-Arp, "Pentecostalism, Politics, and Prosperity," 10.
14. Frahm-Arp, "Pentecostalism, Politics, and Prosperity," 11.
15. Frahm-Arp, "Pentecostalism, Politics, and Prosperity," 13.

and dabbling in the dangers of sinning against the Spirit, which is the unpardonable sin (Mark 3:28–29). Even in the light of some prosperity teachers' authoritative claims that their message and mandate come directly from God, their heretical doctrines may not be left unchallenged, infecting some Christians with ideas that are dangerous for their spiritual health. Their theology should be answered theologically and academically to such an extent that it will be possible for all who are interested to see the implications thereof, even while the theology of the prosperity movement is not developed in any systematic or consistent manner. The trends and developments of their theological endeavors as demonstrated in their teachings and practices should be monitored carefully, especially their doctrines of God's essence and God's sovereignty, the so-called spiritual death of Jesus, anthropology of humanity's deification, and the resultant devaluation of Jesus as the only Son of God and God himself. If it should find that the prosperity movement has abandoned (or in the future should abandon) the deity of Jesus Christ and the sovereignty of God, the church would need to take a strong stand against its teachings.

Why is research from a classical pentecostal perspective necessary about the impact of the prosperity message on Africa, and African Pentecostalism?[16] The message was initially preached in independent churches with historic and liturgical links with classical Pentecostalism and the charismatic renewal movement and eventually gained entrance into and influenced classical Pentecostal denominations to a considerable extent. However, to state like Paul Gifford, a leading historian of West African Christianity, that the prosperity gospel is the most pervasive and significant message preached within Pentecostal churches is not true and does not reflect the African reality.[17] It already started with the church growth movement that advertised its philosophy of ministry effectively through publications, conferences, and the media. Today prosperity preachers from Africa, the USA, and other parts of the world are reaching many Africans representing all social and economic groups with their message because in a globalized world information is shared easily and cheaply through the internet and social media. Sometimes one even finds some racial overtones,

---

16. The impact is demonstrated in a study of the Pew Forum on Religion and Public Life (2010) that shows that in most countries in Sub-Saharan Africa, more than half of Christians believe in the prosperity gospel, that God will grant wealth and good health to people who have enough faith (in Heuser, "Charting African Prosperity Gospel Economies," 2).

17. Gifford, "Persistence and Change;" "Expecting Miracles."

with the message: you can succeed like whites, and being African does not mean subservience and poverty.[18] Because of its influence in the African Pentecostal movement and its potential to harm the faith of believers, such research is necessary, timely, and relevant. Some of the bad fruit of the prosperity gospel is seen in the disillusionment of Christian believers who put their trust (and their money) in formulas and recipes that seemingly only work for others, especially the prosperity leaders who lead by example with incredulous riches and wealth.[19]

Challenging Hermeneutical Concerns in Africa: Methodology

Gordon Fee remarks that the problem of a theology of prosperity and wealth and dominion is hermeneutical.[20] The reason for his remark is that one's theological perspectives are determined, not by the Bible but by the way the Bible is read and interpreted. Because different traditions use different hermeneutical principles they formulate different perspectives on the same issue, such as prosperity.

The research into the African prosperity message and its hermeneutics is based on several forms of research. A comparative literature study is combined with auto-ethnographical observations over years, and empirical research into sermons delivered by prominent African prosperity teachers.[21]

So much has been published in the past fifty years related to the prosperity message, not only by prosperity teachers but also by theological and sociological observers, that display a diversity of opinions about the value of the movement, that it is clearly impossible to reflect all publications. I tried to consult the main works that represent the various viewpoints about the movement and the diversity found within the movement itself, and concentrated on publications with a hermeneutical interest.

---

18. Gifford, "Expecting Miracles," 22. See also Butler, Anthea. "Media, Pentecost and Prosperity."

19. Prosper, *Prosperity Gospel*, 5.

20. Fee, *Disease of the Health*, 7.

21. It is remarkable that references to prosperity in titles of sermons published on YouTube by African prosperity preachers are extremely rare, probably due to a sensitivity for the reaction by the public to the doctrine, due to the negative press it had received. However, such references occur frequently in the sermons, illustrating the various elements of prosperity theology.

As a member of an African classical Pentecostal church, the first such denomination that was established in South Africa in 1908, and speaking one of the youngest indigenous languages in Africa,[22] I have been observing and participating in the classical, charismatic, and neo-pentecostal forms of African Pentecostalism in an insider, emic way, first handedly. My position as a pastor and one-time regional leader of the AFM of SA provided many opportunities to attend meetings in various settings, listening to countless messages, and experiencing a diversity of worship services, presenting many different worship practices. It created the room to think and engage in theological and practical terms about the theme of the present research.

The empirical research is based on grounded theory, a form of qualitative research as a process of examining and interpreting data that was used to survey several messages available on YouTube from some of Africa's most prominent prosperity teachers.[23] My purpose was to elicit meaning, gain understanding, and develop empirical knowledge in order to build theory based on data and the generation of concepts.[24]

The data reveal varieties in the elucidation of doctrines, and it was possible to formulate a sensitizing concept, in addition to the main research question. Some emerging categories became clear and I sought to illuminate and define the boundaries and relevance of these categories.

Book's Plan

The argument in the book develops in the following way: The context of the study is described, which is Africa, before the angle used to research the subject is explained, which is an African pentecostal hermeneutics. Next the project is described, which is the prosperity gospel, before the challenge is described, its teaching in Africa. Lastly the solution is described, consisting of an evaluation of the prosperity message from the angle of African pentecostal hermeneutics.

---

22. Afrikaans is a language that originated in the whirlpool of social and political developments in southern Africa and reflects the various languages from which it originated.

23. The reason why the research was limited to sermons published on YouTube was to leave the opportunity for other researchers to compare the messages.

24. Bryant and Charmaz, "Grounded Theory Research," 1; for application, see Verweij, *Positioning Jesus' Suffering*, 30, 64.

1

The Context

Africa, and the Rise and Popularity of the Prosperity Message

Introduction

THE STUDY IS LIMITED to the preaching and teaching of the prosperity gospel message in Africa although it is necessary to refer to other parts of the world as far as it is necessary to throw light on the popularity of the message in Africa. To begin with, it is necessary to say something about the origins of Pentecostalism in Africa to understand where prosperity theology comes from. African Pentecostalism drank insofar as the prosperity gospel is concerned from several traditions and the prosperity message consists of a culturally mediated adaptation of imported theology.

A synthesis of American materialism characterized by profligate consumption as a status symbol of wealth and self-worth[1] and African spirituality with its emphasis on ministry to the holistic person explains the attraction of the prosperity gospel for Africans. The success motif fits well with Africa's traditional religious imagination of fertility, abundance, and wholeness. Prosperity Pentecostalism thoroughly

---

1. See Jürgen Moltmann, "Destruction and Healing," who refers to the "Western standard of living" that can only be sustained at the expense of others: at the expense of the people in the so-called Third World, at the expense of coming generations, and at the expense of the earth.

contextualized Christianity in Africa, amid poverty and marginalization of poor Africans.[2]

Conrad Mbewe, a prominent representative of Evangelical Reformed Christianity in Lusaka, Zambia, calls the prosperity gospel the United States' number one export to Africa,[3] and argues that the route of imported prosperity theology is mainly via Nigeria. He states that prosperity theology originated from mega-churches in the USA and then found ready soil in West Africa, and specially in Nigeria. Having given it an African flavor, it was then exported across Africa at a phenomenal rate.[4] It led to a unique imbrication with African traditions.

The mechanism through which this syncretistic phenomenon came about is through its appeal to traditional African spirituality and worldview. Neo-Pentecostal pastors have in effect become the modern witchdoctors who offer spiritual protection and deliverance from bad luck, childlessness, joblessness, illness, failure to attract a suitor for marriage, to rise in a job, or get a contract, etc., according to Mbewe. That Africans are reluctant to challenge charismatic preachers who become involved in abuse of their members may stem from the age-old tradition of not speaking out against a powerful *sangoma* or chief. Some of the neo-Pentecostal pastors do not hold themselves accountable to anybody or any church or ministry board. At the same time, they appeal to Africa's upwardly mobile youth by way of gifted and strong charismatic leadership; a very dynamic, expressive, and exuberant worship style with contemporary high amperage gospel music; mostly urban-centered mega-size congregations; a relaxed and fashion conscious dress code for members; and an innovative appropriation of modern media technologies, including the effective use of print and electronic media, for the dissemination of their message.[5]

---

2. Gifford, "Expecting Miracles," 24.
3. Quoted in Hinn, *God, Greed*, 158.
4. Mbewe, "Nigerian Religious Junk!"
5. Asamoah-Gyadu, "Learning to Prosper," 66. In an attempt to affirm its contemporaneity, neo-Pentecostalism consciously and unconsciously dissolves the perceived divide between the sacred and the secular. Their creative appropriation of modern "secular" forms of entertainment enormously appeals to the sensibilities of young and upwardly mobile congregants (Gukurume, "Singing Positivity," 38). It is more flexible and emphasizes a Christian freedom to be led by the Spirit in all aspects of life.

Popularity of the Prosperity Message in Africa

The popularity of the prosperity teaching is illustrated in a 2006 survey that Pew Research undertook in various countries in Africa. The researchers asked participants if God would "grant material prosperity to all believers who have enough faith," and an astonishing 85 percent of Kenyan Pentecostals, 90 percent of South African Pentecostals, and 95 percent of Nigerian Pentecostals affirmed the statement.[6]

The independent neo-Pentecostal or neo-charismatic churches responsible for preaching the prosperity message are expanding in Africa faster even than Islam, at twice the rate of the Roman Catholic Church, and at three times that of the other non-Catholic religious traditions, even considerably stemming the growth of the African Instituted Churches in West Africa.[7] Paul Gifford labels the movement a paradigm shift amidst the new developments in African Christianity.[8] They are characterized by their reconstruction of religious geography through their construction of religious camps consisting of buying up large expanses of land and constructing a range of facilities, including auditoriums, schools, guest houses, dormitories, banks, hospitals and petrol stations, that function as alternative cities.[9] In South Africa alone, there were over 5,000 such independent denominations and groups that bore the familiar marks of pentecostal spirituality.[10] They comprised ten to forty percent of the black population, depending on how Pentecostalism is defined.[11] In Zimbabwe, 50 percent of all Christians belonged to such independent churches.[12] In southern Africa, the independent movement have a few megachurches, mostly in the hands of white leaders (like Ray McCauley of Rhema Ministries, Ed Roebert of Hatfield Christian Church, and Fred

---

6. In Phiri and Maxwell, "Gospel Riches," 24.

7. Kalu, "Discursive Interpretation," 73.

8. Gifford, *Ghana's New Christianity*, 23-4.

9. Kgatle, "Unusual Practices." Such a city was also built at the end of the nineteenth century by John Alexander Dowie, who established the city of Zion for his Christian Catholic Apostolic Church in Illinois in the USA.

10. Cox, *Fire from Heaven*, 245–46.

11. Anderson uses a wider definition that includes those Pentecostals with historical links to worldwide Pentecostal denominations, the African Initiated Spirit churches with historical links with Pentecostalism but following a trajectory of their own, and the new independent Pentecostal churches, and comes to the higher estimation (Anderson, "New African Initiated Pentecostalism," 67).

12. Banjo, "Aftermath of Eating Grass."

Roberts of the Durban Christian Centre, with Mosa Sono of the Grace Bible Church in Soweto and Kenneth Meshoe as exceptions). A positive feature of these (English speaking) megachurches was that it contributed to better ethnic relations while historic political policies of separate development led to the forced segregation between races, with multiethnic congregations promoting friendship and fellowship across racial barriers.[13] The megachurches for which Ghana and Nigeria are famous are few in number among South African blacks. Only when Nigerian, Ghanaian and Kenyan preachers began to visit South Africa in the 1990s, after the dismantling of apartheid, did the idea of a new Pentecostalism began to take off among South African blacks. It put a new emphasis on black consciousness and dignity and for that reason became an attractive alternative to the option presented by white charismatics, preaching about the realization of the African dream of prosperity for black people.[14]

In his study, Douglas Bafford draws on continuing ethnographic fieldwork with multiracial conservative evangelical congregations centered in Johannesburg, South Africa, when he investigated the trace discourses around the prosperity gospel in terms of an intertwining of theological, social, and racial arguments.[15] He also looks at some of the criticism of Evangelicals toward prosperity theology and finds that it was not only based on concerns related to the textual exegesis of those who propagate prosperity theology but it also contended that prosperity preaching was a socially unjust and abusive phenomenon that exacerbates existing racial gaps in wealth, demonstrated in the unimaginably high levels of economic inequality between middle class neighborhoods and the extended squatter camps and slums that characterize the edges of black townships.

He writes that the proclamation of prosperity theology is within the context of "charismatic" worship services led by a "prophet" or "prophetess." Prophets claim to have an extraordinary connection to and stand in a unique relationship with God, often incorporating elements from Pentecostal churches such as those that emphasize Spirit-driven, affective worship, the ability of all believers who have received "spiritual gifts" to deliver divine messages and effect healing from all types of ailments,

---

13. Ganiel, "Pentecostal and Charismatic Christianity," 137.
14. Anderson, "New African Initiated Pentecostalism," 71.
15. Bafford, "Prosperity Gospel," 1.

as well as bestowing material rewards for faithful obedience to biblical injunctions, as they interpret it.

The prophets in these churches perceive themselves as from a different order than their congregations because of their special gifts; because of their status, they are totally unchallengeable. The effect is that many of these churches are not really communities or fellowships at all, but they have rather become associations of clients of a particular "man of God,"[16] or patronages. The clients also attribute their blessings not so much to God as to the anointed "man of God."

Bafford asks the question in his research, what is motivating the increasing popularity of prosperity teachers, and how is it affecting South African communities?[17] Prosperity theology's impact extends across racial, socioeconomic, and formal denominational status with Ray McCauley's Rhema Bible Church, one of the first contemporary "prosperity" churches to establish a presence in South Africa, that attracted congregants from the wealthy,[18] while ministries to the downcast, immigrants, and the poor and jobless in urban settings are also successful.[19] In many instances, the extreme poverty of church members is juxtaposed with the affluence that the prophets themselves represent and exhibit in public to prove the success of their theology, that God wants to bless believers with prosperity. While believers experience deprivation and struggle to survive materially in the highly unequal situation that the South African social scene represents, the prophets drive (and fly) in luxury from expensive homes to the slums where their members live.[20]

16. Gifford, "Expecting Miracles," 22.

17. Bafford, "Prosperity Gospel," 1

18. Van Wyk, "Why 'Money' Gospel Followers."

19. Katsaura, "Theo-Urbanism," 232-62. McCauley was converted in the Full Gospel Church, a classical Pentecostal denomination. Akiri, "The Prosperity Gospel," remarks that most prosperity gospel churches flourish better in urban centers that are characterized by better means of communication both in terms of transport and technology, and draw their membership from the urban middle-class and urban poor. Barker, "Charismatic Economies," 416 agrees and explains, rather in generalized terms, that the prosperity gospel is especially appealing to middle class Pentecostals (illustrating the equation of Pentecostalism and the prosperity teaching made by some researchers) around the world, while the older theology of strict personal discipline characterized by its many taboos continues to be practiced by poor, working-class Pentecostals.

20. A recently released report by Statistics South Africa, in partnership with Agence Francaise de Développement (AFD), Southern Africa Labour and Development Research Unit (SALDRU), and African Centre of Excellence for Inequality

Research (ACEIR), entitled "Inequality Trends in South Africa: A Multidimensional Diagnostic of Inequality," reveals the still existing inequalities (http://www.statssa.gov.za/publications/Report-03-10-19/Report-03-10-192017.pdf). For instance, a large percentage of the population depends on the public health system to provide for its health care needs, with low levels of access to medical aid across all population groups, more especially among black Africans. Per capita expenditure is used to measure economic inequality, including the Gini coefficient, the Lorenz curve, Theil's and Atkinson indices, and the Palma ratio that assist with assessing trends in inequality over time, as well as the between-groups and within-group inequality levels in the country. Nationally, both real mean and median expenditure per annum increased between 2006 and 2011, but dropped slightly between 2011 and 2015. This reflects the overall economic climate which has prevailed in recent years. Furthermore, individuals living in male-headed households had annual mean and median expenditures higher than those living in female-headed households. The white population group had the highest annual mean and median expenditure compared to other population groups between 2006 and 2015, while black Africans had the lowest. Moreover, the annual mean expenditure of non-poor individuals was approximately ten times more than that of the poor population, while their annual median expenditure was approximately five times more. Expenditure inequality has also increased between urban and rural dwellers. The expenditure shares between groups are disproportionate relative to their population shares. The expenditure share of black Africans was significantly smaller than their large population share in the country, at 145, while the expenditure shares of whites remained disproportionately large relative to their small population share. Social grants and remittances have played a crucial role in reducing the income inequality gap between the bottom and top deciles over the years in South Africa. Measures suggested a decrease in inequality within groups between 2006 and 2015. For example, all provinces except for Limpopo and Eastern Cape reported a decrease in their respective Gini coefficients. Furthermore, individuals living in both male and female-headed households recorded a decrease in their Theil scores between 2006 and 2015. While inequality decreased for Indians/Asians, it remained fairly constant for whites and coloreds, but increased for black Africans. The Theil's index showed that the relative contribution of the within-group inequality based on sex of the household head was more or less 93 percent at all four data points. This means that inequality was predominantly driven by within-household head groups rather than dynamics between these groups. Over time, individuals living in male-headed households continued to contribute more to overall inequality as compared to those living in female-headed households. Inequality amongst black Africans was the most unequal compared to other population groups and the contribution of black Africans to overall inequality was the highest and has risen over time. The contribution of the other three population groups remained more or less the same between 2006 and 2015, although inequality within each population group increased over time. Throughout the years, income from the labor market has been the main source of household income in South Africa, accounting for over 70 percent of overall income. Additionally, labor market income is overwhelmingly the largest contributor to income inequality when compared to other income sources. Nevertheless, social grants and remittances have played a crucial role in reducing the income inequality gap between the bottom and top deciles over the years in South Africa.

Reasons for the Popularity of the Prosperity Gospel in Africa

Prosperity gospel and its popularity with the masses of Africa can be viewed as a "legitimate critique of contemporary economic and social trends, even if their solutions do not accord with dominant liberal norms," especially when viewed in terms of Africa's inequality between the haves and the have-nots.[21] The mix of poverty, the fear of slipping deeper or back into hardship, ignorance and gullibility born out of little or no education, feelings of nihilistic meaninglessness and desperation that can accompany absolute poverty, the survival instinct, collapsed social institutions, defunct public systems and services, and rampant corruption and state plundering are all factors that produce the perfect context for a dangerous co-dependent relationship between leaders of prosperity theology and their followers.[22] Fact is that the African countries in which the prosperity message had the greatest impact—Nigeria, Kenya, Cameroon, Ghana, the Ivory Coast, Uganda, and South Africa—are afflicted by poverty and disease, and struggle with high unemployment rates and political instability, have limited institutional resources to resolve health issues, and experience difficulties due to state plundering and state debt that is draining the economic basis of the countries, even more so than most other African countries.[23] Many Africans in these countries seek succor in spirituality, and the promises of the prosperity message catch their attention.[24]

Kenneth Mbugua discusses another reason why prosperity teaching is popular. He argues that its message taps into the most basic of human desires, although he adds that the solution it offers is unbiblical, misleading, and ultimately detrimental to its adherents, leaving many of them

---

21. Bafford, "Prosperity Gospel", 4.

22. Kgatle, "Unusual Practices."

23. Currently, about 315 million sub-Saharan Africans live on less than a US dollar a day, while one in three Africans suffers malnutrition, and the average life expectancy throughout the continent is 41 years, as discussed in the report of SOS Children's Villages (https://www.sos-usa.org/about-us/where-we-work/africa/poverty-in-africa; accessed 2020-01-21). More than 30 percent of African children suffer from growth disorders such as stunting due to chronic malnutrition, causing physical and mental underdevelopment in children. On average, one in eleven children dies before their fifth birthday. In sub-Saharan Africa, 59 million children between the ages of five and seventeen work instead of playing and going to school.

24. Kingsbury and Chesnut, "How Catholics are Falling."

discouraged, disillusioned, and bitter when the promises of the gospel do not realize in their personal circumstances.[25] He defines its un-biblicalness in prosperity teaching's confusion between a time when there was no suffering, before sin brought pain and suffering into a world broken by humans' rejection of God, and the time when in the new age there will again be no suffering. When it sees in the atonement of Christ the solution to all suffering, for all people and all times, prosperity theology confuses the final realization of salvation in the new age with the present world still characterized by many of the results and symptoms of the broken reality due to sinfulness. In the process, prosperity teachers miss the important teaching that suffering is only temporary, but also that it is blessed in the lives of believers because it serves to test the genuineness of our faith (1 Pet 1:3–7) and represents a sharing in the suffering of Christ, as a prerequisite for sharing in his glory (1 Pet 4:12–14).[26] To share in Christ's suffering is to share in his resurrection and glory (Phlm 3:10). Freedom from suffering is a false message, in Mbugua's opinion, because it diverts the attention from God as the sole focus of the believer's faith and hope to the things with which God is supposed to supply us. It also promises much more than it can deliver, especially in African countries with little hope for employment, especially for the youth.[27]

In the traditional African context, suffering must be understood through the lens of relationships. If a community experiences some form of suffering, it implies that one or the other relationship must have broken

---

25. Mbugua, "Suffering," 66. Mbugua does not provide empirical evidence for his assertion that many adherents of the prosperity message had become disillusioned with the message because it did not realize in their circumstances. See the sarcastic remark of Gifford, "Prosperity," 382 that only one group of Christians in Africa is actually suitable for accepting the prosperity gospel, and that is white Christians in South Africa and Zimbabwe, because it asserts that disproportionate wealth is nothing to be guilty about, but on the contrary is the sign of a true believer, providing considerable comfort and reassurance to whites that wealth is their due and had nothing to do with the unjust structures established by the policies of segregation that white colonialist governments had established.

26. Some of the blessings suffering can hold for believers, according to John Piper ("Appendix I," 115), are that it deepens faith and holiness, makes their cup of joy increase, makes others bold who witness to the faithfulness of the believer, fills up what is lacking in Christ's afflictions, enforces the missionary command, and makes the supremacy of Christ manifest.

27. For instance, the unemployment rate in South Africa in 2003 stood at 61.1 percent (https://www.statista.com/statistics/813010/youth-unemployment-rate-in-south-africa/; accessed 2020-01-24).

down, as Elizabeth Mburu explains.[28] Offending someone automatically offends the Supreme Being, arousing the anger and drawing the punishment of the Ruler. Thus angering the ancestors, for example, was bound to result in swift judgment in the form of disease or a natural catastrophe. When misfortunes visited the community, diviners were called in to find out what had offended God, whether the spirits or the ancestors. The correct response was then to offer sacrifices and prayers to obtain the blessing of the Supreme Being. In the better part of the Old Testament, God is also viewed as sovereign ruler of the earthly domain and evil powers were seen as subjected to God, leading to the opponent or accuser (the *satan*) reporting to God about his visits to earth, and the impression that Job's piety made on him and when the opponent or advocate acted to take away Job's children, wealth, and health, the opponent could only act with the permission of God (Job 1:6—2:10). Satan as an independent power did not as yet exist in the thoughts of most authors of the Old Testament writings.

Not all traditional African societies understood suffering in terms of the Supreme Being; some attribute it to witchcraft. For them, the Supreme Being is completely good and no evil can be connected with him. Evil is rather associated with lesser divinities, spirits, witches, and sorcerers. Suffering in all its forms was the direct work of malevolent spirits, with whom some human beings might be in league. The retribution theology that shapes African thinking on suffering is similar to the theology found in the Deuteronomist's historical narrative. Sin results in punishment, and repentance leads to reward.

Later it will be argued that the theology of suffering is one of the challenges of prosperity theology that should be addressed. In a context where basic survival needs of some people are not met, the gospel of health and wealth becomes attractive to people dreaming of a better future. However, it invites its adherents to seek the things that one can get from God as the source of pleasure, rather than God self.[29] In Africa, Christians need to hear about the cost of discipleship because so many Africans wrestle theologically with poverty, failure, pain, and disappointment.[30] The prosperity message's success and popularity in Africa can be ascribed to its hope engendered, vision imparted, and sense of destiny awakened.[31]

---

28. Mburu, *African Hermeneutics*, 53.
29. Mbugua, "Suffering," 69, 77.
30. Asamoah-Gyadu, "Did Jesus Wear Designer Robes," 40.
31. Gifford, "Expecting Miracles," 24.

Another important reason for the popularity of African Pentecostalism is found in its indigenizing and Africanizing of the gospel, especially in its emphasis on the continuation of biblical prophethood; a custom that also characterized African traditional religions; healing and accompanying (and much publicized) testimonies of those who are healed; ecstatic worship, including *glossolalia* and its interpretation, words of wisdom and knowledge; and Spirit-anointed preaching. The Christianity that missionaries exported to Africa was a too-cerebral and non-experiential white man's religion for most African tastes; it was perceived as a classroom religion in contrast to African religions that were essentially "spiritual" religions that provided tangible results in the form of protection from the negative effects of the intervention of spiritual forces in daily life.[32] In response, African Christians produced their own Holy Spirit movements;[33] the African Instituted Churches were part of the reaction of African culture to the dour Christianity of the early missionaries.[34] Sundkler describes the appeal of Pentecostalism and its worship practices in colonial Africa as a dynamic experience of exuberant singing, clapping and dancing and involving body, mind, will, and emotions, as "one of the few psychological safety valves" available to blacks "in a society of racial discriminations".[35]

African cultures exhibited the qualifications and elements for pneumatic and charismatic aspects of Pentecostalism and it was always

---

32. Taylor, *Primal Vision*, 21-22. Western missionaries from what Keener (*Spirit Hermeneutics*, 91) calls "desupernaturalized" Europe had declared belief in witchcraft as heretical, an idea that was unworkable in an African context. They ignored sorcery, while witchcraft beliefs fulfilled roles within societies that, if unaddressed by newer religious cultures, could persist and grow. Missionaries also denounced the widespread African culture of polygamy.

33. Quayesi-Amakye, "Pentecostalism and the Transformation," 103.

34. A salient and ironic contrast exists between the familiar image of the rather poor, Western missionary who does not care much about his clothes, outfit, and appearance, preaching wordy sermons to a congregation seated in hard pews, or that of the African Zionist, Nazirite or Aladura prophet, dressed in a white gown, carrying a cross, praying for the afflicted in the bush, on the one hand, and the exuberant appearance of the immaculately dressed dynamic Pentecostal-charismatic pastor, addressing mass audiences in beautiful megachurches in postmodern style and with air conditioning, and performing "miracles" before the eyes of cameras, using high tech media to spread the message, and celebrating the prosperity of expensive German cars and penthouses in their personal lives, in the words of Birgit Meyer ("Pentecostalism and Neo-Liberal Capitalism," 5-6).

35. Sundkler, *Bantu Prophets in South Africa*, 296-7.

a part of the traditional worldview of Africans, with reference to historical movements such as Ethiopianism[36] and the prophetic movements in white-robe wearing Zionism, Aladura, and Abaroho.[37] Pentecostal religious practices reach beyond the levels of creed and ceremony, cognizant of a cerebral religion, into the realm of "primal spirituality," defined in terms of the search for connection with the precognitive core impulse of human life that had been evident in several influential cultural movements during the last century.[38] Its resulting ritual complex "seeks to reverse estrangement, to reconstitute the divided self."[39] As a response toward social disruptions and alienation wrought by the social disruptions and alienation caused by colonial interference, black Pentecostalism sowed the seeds of resistance to a hegemonic capitalist order.[40]

Edwin Zulu mentions the fact that most people in Africa live in poverty,[41] implying that they lack basic needs such as shelter, food, education, clean water, and health care. The level of poverty in Africa creates the desire to move out of the current hopeless situation, and

---

36. Ethiopianism represents the first challenge by Africans to white representation of African values, culture and practice of the Christian faith in the modern era. It was not an ideology, theological school of thought, or a political program but rather a cluster of ideas, traditions, and assumptions about being Christian in Africa that were shared by diverse Christian leaders in the period from 1880 to 1920. Ethiopia was seen as a symbol for black pride and was used as a collective term for the entire region from Egypt to Abyssinia/Ethiopia. Other reasons were that Ethiopia had maintained its independence from foreign domination during the colonial period and the country is frequently referred to in the Bible, as Cush (Clarke, "Pan-Africanism and Pentecostalism," 157).

37. Kalu, *African Pentecostalism*. The Spirit-churches as a part of African Instituted Churches are known as prophet-healing, or "spiritual" churches, and they include Zionists (related to the work of missionaries of John Alexander Dowie's Zionist movement) and Apostolics (related to the AFM of SA) in southern Africa, spiritual, prayer-healing or Aladura (that is, "prayer" or "praying") churches in West Africa, and spiritual or Holy Spirit churches in East Africa (Anderson, "African Independent Churches," 22.)

38. Cox, *Fire from Heaven*, 117. Cox defines "primal spirituality" in terms of three dimensions: primal speech, consisting of the ecstatic utterance of "speaking in tongues" or "praying in the Spirit;" primal piety, consisting of phenomena like visions, healing, dreams, dance, and other archetypal religious expressions; and primal hope, as the millennial outlook consisting of the insistence that a radically new world age is about to dawn. See also Akiri, "The Prosperity Gospel."

39. Comaroff, *Body of Power, Spirit of Resistance*, 12.

40. Comaroff, *Body of Power, Spirit of Resistance*, 76-7.

41. Zulu, "'Fipelwa na ba Yaweh,'" 24.

consequently these people are desperate and vulnerable to any efforts that promise them relief. This provides another reason why Africans would fall for any program with promises of economic relief that comes their way, like the prosperity gospel offers. The large chasm that exists between the daily experience of most Africans and most Westerners must be kept in mind.[42] Most Europeans and (North) Americans take it for granted that their physical needs will normally be met, so they hardly connect the meeting of these basic needs with their life of faith. In contrast, most Africans cannot afford the luxury to take it for granted, and they connect it directly to their faith.

Another important reason for the popularity of prosperity theology is presented by Paul Gifford,[43] when he states that the most significant fact about the countries in Africa where the prosperity message is popular is the dysfunctional political culture that permits an unaccountable elite to appropriate wealth and power at the expense of the people. The gospel of success preached by prosperity teachers, however, seldom challenges this dysfunctional political structure because they deny that the political-economic system contributes to believers' success and blessings, rather ascribing it exclusively to God's response to their manipulative actions to force God's hand in blessing certain people. Gifford claims that prosperity and deliverance theologies are in fact Africa's biggest impediment to the development of a prosperous nation-state.[44] These teachers claim they would prosper under any political or economic regime because they have unlocked God's recipe for prosperity. However, it must be stated in categorical terms that this is not true of all prosperity teachers; many of them proclaim a message of entrepreneurship, while criticizing the corruption and state capture that marks many African governments, calling on members to make a difference by not only voting for political candidates with integrity but also to become involved in politics and elections themselves and to resist brutalizing political and economic policies. Not all preachers blame demonic forces for the activities of corrupt public officials.[45] Gifford's thesis is seriously deficient because African neo-Pentecostals are not all apolitical and otherworldly but some of them have become one of the single most important socio-cultural forces in

---

42. Ellington, "Is the Prosperity Gospel Biblical?" 29.
43. Gifford, "Expecting Miracles," 22-3.
44. As Bangura, "Charismatic Movements," 249 also discusses.
45. Bangura, "Charismatic Movements," 247.

many parts of Africa, supporting and influencing political leaders and ruling parties in a positive and critical way. At the same time, the theology that ascribes poverty to spiritual forces at work is imbibing a healthy work ethic that promotes industriousness and calling laziness a recipe for poverty (Prov 6:10–11; 10:4; 12:24; 19:15; Eccl 10:18), while it also does not incorporate a holistic ontology that fits in well with the lived experiences of many Africans and accords with most traditional African ontologies. Fact is that the neo-Pentecostal, independent movement is gradually becoming more and more involved in addressing issues of systemic corruption and poverty in Africa.[46]

Another reason for its popularity is the utilization of the "Big Man" or chief syndrome, a disease that Paul Gifford calls the curse of Africa, exemplified in the behavior of some successful prosperity preachers who amass great wealth and spend it on a lavish lifestyle while many of their members cringe in misery and poverty.[47] Some of these preachers have been using their celebrity status even to vie for the presidency of their countries, as in the case of Zambia, Nigeria, and Kenya. Gifford argues that the prosperity gospel reflects the dysfunctional political culture that permits an unaccountable elite to appropriate wealth and power at the expense of the people, with the "big men" of the African churches that mirror the "big men" of Africa's dictatorial regimes.[48] These "big men" are able to function in Africa because of the respect many Africans traditionally have for their chief or head of their tribe. The price the prosperity preachers pay for such involvement in politics is that they are disqualified from challenging hierarchical state arrangements, and this contributes to the stunting of Africa's political and economic development, in the view of Gladys Ganiel.[49] However, I do not agree with her generalization. In South Africa, at least, many of the neo-Pentecostal preachers are influencing the ruling and opposition political parties in a positive sense, encouraging and criticizing various economic and social policies, although it usually happens under the radar of the press and media.

In this sense and in conclusion, the popularity of African neo-Pentecostalism can be explained in terms of its successful focus on socioeconomic and materialist issues; in the same way, the prosperity gospel

---

46. Bangura, "Charismatic Movements," 249-50.

47. Gifford, "Expecting Miracles," 23. Reference was made already to the African respect for the chief of the tribe.

48. Gifford, "Expecting Miracles."

49. Ganiel, "Pentecostal and Charismatic Christianity," 133.

echoes and speaks to the neoliberal mentality of Africa that consists of the hope of visionary material gain with little investment.[50] It creates a psycho-spiritual reinforcement of the idea that getting rich is the highest good that one can strive for, and hence supports the widespread African cultures of patronage and entitlement by contributing on the part of these groups to a lack of vocal opposition to corruption and to the inequality that marks great parts of sub-Saharan Africa.[51]

Essence of Neo-Pentecostalism in Africa

Pentecostalism shares with African traditional religion a mystical, dualist view of the world; of the universe consisting of a visible part that portrays and reflects what happens in the invisible part, where good and evil powers constantly oppose each other. The way to promote success, prosperity, longevity, vitality, and general well-being, significant indicators in African traditional religion as well as in prosperity theology of a successful life, is through mediation and appropriation of these forces.[52] The New Testament world also used this philosophical perspective of an enchanted worldview that in neo-Platonist terms sees a visible world where events are determined by what happens in the invisible world, where good and evil, and God and Satan clash regularly. The fortunes in the different invisible battles in the spiritual realm are then reflected in the political, economic and social events that arrange people's daily lives, as becomes especially clear in apocalyptic traditions. The power of the Holy Spirit can vanquish any additional spiritual enemies and equip adherents with worldly success.[53]

However, a reductionist explanation for the role of Pentecostalism is to be avoided, as some recent anthropological studies suggest. For this

---

50. As explained in Comaroff and Comaroff, "Occult Economies," 279-303; Comaroff and Comaroff, "Millennial Capitalism," 291-343. However, that does not mean that the prosperity message is successful. Asonzeh Ukah ("Redeemed Church," 18) asks in terms of the Redeemed Church of God in Nigeria whether the church had generated the wealth it promised. His answer as a sociologist is negative, based on empirical study spanning nearly fifteen years. If the Redeemed Church had been successful in delivering prosperity, there would be fewer poor people in the church today than there were the previous year, but this is clearly not the case in his analysis.

51. Egan, *Politics of a South African Catholic Student Movement*, 63.

52. Asamoah-Gyadu, "In Search of a Better Country," 169.

53. See Geschiere, *Modernity of Witchcraft*.

reason, Naomi Haynes differs from Birgit Meyer who in an earlier study suggests that pentecostal conversion completely overhauls existing social relations.[54] In an ethnographical study of Pentecostals on the Zambian Copper belt, Haynes acknowledges that a neoliberal order brought many challenges to Zambians but does not support the idea that Pentecostalism merely serves as "a handmaiden of neoliberalism."[55] It rather provides a creative reorientation of values, allowing people to make a "good life" despite the spiritual and material dangers they face.[56] Her conclusions are supported by Ilana van Wyk who discusses the economy of giving observed at the Durban branch of a Brazilian-initiated international Pentecostal megachurch in terms of the emic meaning the givers embedded it with.[57] What may appear to outsiders as materially exploitative encouragement to "sacrifice" money to God in order to gain immediate and long-term prosperity are perceived by the contributors as powerfully meaningful. It illustrates that prosperity theology contributes to a semiotically coherent social order. It is submitted that a structural analysis of the national and global economics that condition the appeal of prosperity theology should rather be seen in conjunction with the meaning participants in the theology give to their actions, although not exclusively. At the same time, all generalizations of the movement should be avoided.

Maria Frahm-Arp also describes the spectacular rise and essence of the prosperity movement and relates it in an interesting theory to important moments of knowledge or industrial revolutions, when new forms of religion emerged to deal with the sense of alienation experienced by those marginalized by the revolution.[58] The second knowledge revolution occurred with the invention of the printing press (the first revolution occurred in 300 BCE with the establishment of libraries), and it led to the formation of Protestant Christianity. The first industrial revolution led to the rise of the Methodist Church as the Wesley brothers and others addressed the abuses suffered by workers of the new factories in the coal-mining cities of England and Wales. The second industrial revolution at the turn of the twentieth century gave rise to the Pentecostal movement as many working-class people suffered from the poverty, oppression, and

54. Haynes, *Moving by the Spirit*.
55. Haynes, *Moving by the* Spirit, 1. See also the discussion in "On the Potential."
56. Haynes, *Moving by the Spirit*, 3.
57. Van Wyk, *Universal Church of the Kingdom*.
58. Frahm-Arp, "Understanding the Rise of Cult Churches."

alienation experienced in new mass-production factories and the urbanization that it required. Each rise of a new religious tradition had in common the idea that through the power of prayer, people were able to take on new agency in their lives, to sustain their families amid the turbulence of a revolution. Another common interest is in the work and involvement of the Spirit in the daily lives of ordinary believers.

The fourth industrial revolution, states Frahm-Arp, started with the first broad-based consumer use of artificial intelligence in Apple and smartphone devices. The currency of this revolution is data, and predictions are based on analysis of the data that the public consumes. Around 2015, media reports started appearing about cult-like churches that seemed to be springing up.[59] Frahm-Arp explains its rise to ordinary people's sense of alienation as a result of the industrial revolution they are experiencing, and their lack of comprehension what the effects of the revolution on their daily lives will eventually be. Might computers soon take their jobs, doing their work? Will it contribute toward the already

---

59. Sociologist Ronald Enroth refers to three different approaches of defining the term "cult," as the sensational, sociological, and theological. The sensational definition focuses on the bizarre and dangerous behaviors of the more extremist cults, utilizing perjorative language and strong value judgments that in some cases are based on prejudice rather than correct observations. The sociological approach focuses on the broad cultural, psychological, and organizational aspects of cults, attempting to describe the cult objectively, without making value judgments. It frequently utilizes cultural standards to determine whether a group is a cult. A cult can then be defined as any religious group which differs significantly in one or more respects as to belief or practice from those religious groups which are regarded as normative and traditional expressions of religion in total culture. The sociological approach can be useful for Christians but they require something more because the most significant component of a definition of a cult is theological in nature in their own deliberations. The theological approach focuses on the actual doctrines and practices of the cults, comparing them to those of biblical and historical Christianity. Then a cult can be defined as a group of people gathered around a specific person's interpretation of the Bible. The theological approach is not only descriptive, as in the sociological approach, but also comparative and evaluative because its purpose is to determine whether those in the cults are entitled to be classified as Christians, even if they continue to insist that they are entitled, and what the effects of their participation in the cult on their well-being are. The theological approach contains judgments based upon the doctrines of the cult, and not the people in them, and they are based upon objective rather than subjective standards, that are determined by the Bible and historical orthodoxy (McConnell, *Different Gospel*, 16-17). McConnell also utilizes a fourth approach, the historical approach that examines the history of a religious movement, and particularly its founder (McConnell, *Different Gospel*, 18).

sky-high unemployment rates in Africa, especially among the youth, many of whom will probably never find salaried employment?[60]

In Africa, the prosperity message valorizes nostalgic material aspirations of the youth in an imploding economy, where lifestyles of conspicuous consumption as an embodiment of prosperity and being blessed are becoming more and more elusive for the majority of people and especially the youth, in the considered opinion of Simbarashe Gukurume.[61] While the material realities on the ground are epitomized by uncertainties and hopelessness due to the protracted economic malaise in large parts of Africa, the prosperity gospel creates a culture of self-belief and optimism, which impacts positively on adherents' lives. They are inspired to yearn for a better life and expensive high-tech gadgets, etc., leading in many cases to unfulfilled dreams and shattered hopes. In this sense, prosperity is hegemonic and counter-hegemonic in the way it endorses and questions dominant framings of social reality simultaneously.

These churches are akin to Pentecostal and charismatic churches but their message of prosperity, their way of governance through authoritarian structures and apostles, the significant role that prophets play, and their hierarchical nature distinguishes them from traditional Pentecostalism.[62] Their charismatic leaders claim to have all the answers because they are the sole receivers of divine revelation, do not bear with any form of criticism, give only selected information to chosen people, and advise (or even compel) their followers to break ties with their natural families to pledge absolute loyalty to the apostle and his ministry. They tend to attract young adults who strive to attain a modern lifestyle, with middle class patterns of distribution and consumption,[63] and teach them to spend a great deal of time, energy, and money on the church. These tendencies qualify them to be described as "cult-like" in sociological terms. In many cases they are led by educated young men, often university graduates, who have come into an experience of the Spirit through interdenominational campus organizations. These newer Pentecostal

---

60. Frahm-Arp, "Understanding the Rise of Cult Churches."

61. Gukurume, "Privatising the Millennium," 50 investigates the influence of the prosperity message in hip-hop gospel music in Zimbabwe; his conclusions are, however, also applicable to youth in other parts of Africa and can be generalized to a certain extent due to globalization of youth cultures.

62. These factors are discussed in more detail in chapter 4, and evaluated in chapter 5.

63. Meyer, "Pentecostalism and Neo-Liberal Capitalism," 13.

movements are in Anderson's informed view not fundamentally different in phenomenal terms from the other Holy Spirit movements and Spirit churches that preceded them in the African Instituted Churches.[64] The African Instituted Churches served as their bedrock that exist in continuity with modern African Pentecostalism in its various forms in terms of a shared spirituality, although many Pentecostal churches frowned upon some of the customs taken over in African Instituted Churches from African traditional religion.[65]

In South Africa, prosperity came under increasing scrutiny from the side of prosecuting authorities with the widespread publicity given to certain abuses such as the eating of grass to "be closer to God",[66] telling people to sleep and then ordering other congregants to slap those that were asleep

---

64. Anderson, "New African Initiated Pentecostalism," 68.

65. Quayesi, "Pentecostalism and the Transformation," 105. While the African Instituted Churches paid considerable attention to healing and classical Pentecostals emphasized holiness, contemporary independent and network Christianity lay great stress on material and spiritual prosperity that is expressed in taking territories or dominion, often in a semi-metaphorical way (Quayesi, "Pentecostalism and the Transformation," 112).

66. Pastor Lesego Daniel of Rabboni Centre Ministries in Garankuwa, north of Pretoria, South Africa in May 2015 asserted that the Bible taught human beings that they could eat anything to feed their bodies if he received an instruction from the Spirit that they should do so. He preached that believers' faith would change the natural substances of what they eat into solid and healthy food. By eating grass, believers would rid themselves of their sins and they would receive healing from any ailments they might have had, and their obedience to the instruction of the Spirit would result in many blessings upon their lives. Photos on the Rabboni Centre Ministries Facebook page showed the followers eating the grass as well as Pastor Daniel walking across them as they lay spread out on the floor. "Yes, we eat grass and we're proud of it because it demonstrates that, with God's power, we can do anything," one of the members, Rosemary Phetha, a 21-year-old law student, told journalists. She explained that she had been battling with a sore throat for more than a year, but it was healed after she had eaten the grass. Doreen Kgatle of Garankuwa, a 27-years old stroke sufferer, explained, "I could not walk but soon after eating the grass, as the pastor had ordered, I started gaining strength, and an hour later, I could walk again." Photos also showed dozens of people getting sick in the toilets afterwards; an image of the bathrooms showed women clutching their stomachs, while the men were vomiting in the sink. A few days later, it was revealed that dozens of church members were now ill as an aftermath of the experiment (Banjo, "Aftermath Of Eating Grass;" "Pastor Lesego Daniel's Church Members Fall Sick," *Nigerian Monitor*, 16 Jan 2014, http://www.nigerianmonitor.com/photos-aftermath-of-eating-grass-pastor-lesego-daniels-church-members-fall-sick; see also Kgatle, "Unusual Practices").

The Context

and trample on them,[67] feeding church members flowers,[68] encouraging them to drink petrol,[69] spraying people with a pesticide,[70] staging a resur-

---

67. During a service attended by a thousand people in a marquee, pastor Daniel screamed, "Sleep!" and six people went to sleep. He ordered other congregants to slap those that were asleep and trample on them, but the sleepers did not react and remained rigid and unresponsive until he ordered them to wake up. "You can leave them like this for six months. I love this, I don't want to be bored. You can even make police go to sleep when they come to arrest you," he is alleged to have said.

68. Daniel also reportedly fed members of the church flowers, and one happy flower eater declared, "They tasted like mint chocolate." "I felt fresh and good," testified another. "The different kinds of flowers had different tastes and they were nothing short of delicious," said some members. In pictures published by a newspaper, one man eating yellow chrysanthemums looked a bit anxious, but he did not defy the pastor. He bit into the flower, ended up with petals in his mouth, and then swallowed. It was not immediately clear from the pictures whether eating the flowers gave him a surge of spiritual power. The pastor motivated his unusual practices to treat his members with several kinds of dangerous and poisonous media by explaining that it was necessary for their healing process and for building their faith. It was the only way that members could be helped with their problems. He had also been captured on video praying in tongues and he interpreted it as the authoritative source for his controversial demands (Kgatle, "Unusual Practices").

69. One pastor made his congregation drink petrol, telling them that it tasted sweet, like pineapple juice. In YouTube footage, members of his congregation were seen clamoring desperately to have a drink of the petrol as the pastor instructed and encouraged them. The members exclaimed how "sweet" and "nice" it tasted, comparing it to "Iron Brew" (a soft drink) and "pineapple juice." Some of them even begged the pastor to "please give us some more." A few of the followers who consumed the petrol ended up collapsing on the floor, displaying symptoms such as breathing difficulties, throat pain, burning in the esophagus, abdominal pain, vision loss, vomiting with blood, bloody stools, dizziness, extreme fatigue, convulsions, body weakness, and unconsciousness. The video clearly showed how several members of the congregation displayed some of these symptoms (Kgatle, "Unusual Practices"). The testimony of Elly Achok Olare, a pastor in Kenya who once was a prosperity teacher, and who describes his experience of the pragmatic results of the prosperity gospel in his own life and ministry is also relevant. When things did not work out as he taught it would, he was dismayed with God, whose ways no longer made sense to him. His faith became a mirage, even though at first he kept up appearances, trying to pretend that he was not despairing, he states. He felt doubtful, hopeless, even cursed. He was angry at God for not answering his prayers and honoring his faith and positive confessions and he vowed to quit the ministry because he felt like a fraud for preaching a "gospel" that did not work. God had become an enigma, and faith a labyrinth (in Hinn, *God, Greed*, 150-151).

70. Pastor Lethebo Rabalago of Mount Zion General Assembly in South Africa sprayed the members of his church with Doom, a pesticide, to demonstrate the power of the gospel and to cure various ailments. He stated that his God can make a dangerous insecticide to be harmless and bring healing to the sick (Kgatle, "Unusual Practices").

rection from the dead,[71] and raping young girls while Timothy Omotose was allegedly ministering to them in the privacy of his own home.[72] In one instance, Pastor Paseka Motsoeneng of Incredible Happenings Church in South Africa fondled the private parts of his female congregants while praying for their bedroom and gynecological problems. He also stated on social media that he visited heaven and took selfies to prove it, and claimed to have delivered a fish from the womb of a pregnant woman.[73] Prophet Mboro Motsoeneng told the members of his church to remove their underwear "in order to attract the angels."[74] Prophet Walter Magaya was accused of sexually abusing one of his adherents.[75]

The South African prosperity preacher, Shepherd Bushiri, is a Malawian pastor known as the "prophet" at Enlightened Christian Gathering Church based in Pretoria. It is a multinational and well-financed megachurch that teaches its adherents to contribute generously to the church and its ministry with the promises of God's blessings for those who contribute generously. Bushiri was arrested by South African authorities for fraud and tax violations in February 2019, stemming from the way he managed the finances of the church. He was released shortly thereafter but the press related several stories of how he had swindled his followers for his own enrichment. In one case, the members of his church did not have any money left for their taxi fare to return home because the prophet promised them that God would bless them exceedingly and immediately if they donated all their money to the church.

Nigerian Pentecostalism have also come under increasing scrutiny as social and political stability remain elusive in the country. Some members who left the prosperity movement voiced their discontent and

---

71. https://www.iol.co.za/news/south-africa/gauteng/pastor-lukaus-resurrection-stunt-sees-accused-pair-remain-behind-bars-21480630; accessed 2020-02-10. In Rio Janeiro, Brazil, a prominent pastor, Cicero Vicente de Araújo, was accused by federal authorities of running a slave labor farm, a slave-owning scheme, and money laundering. He coerced the workers on his property to hand over their savings, paid them little to no wages, and discouraged them from speaking to their families at all. He had built up a $30 million agribusiness empire. He also pressurized up to 25,000 followers to invest at least $1,000 each as part of a Ponzi scheme, pledging high returns that never materialized (Zaimov, "Evangelical Pastor Accused of Running Slave Labor.")

72. Maxon, "Fake Pastors and Their Followers."

73. Kgatle, "Unusual Practices."

74. https://www.youtube.com/watch?v=kYc-5ieZ2iQ; accessed 2020-01-02.

75. See the lady's testimony at https://www.youtube.com/watch?v=H9J6PVbeyKE, and https://www.youtube.com/watch?v=Ay9AFoPTQto; accessed 2020-01-02.

disillusionment with the materialism and the empty hopes offered by prosperity preachers.[76] Christians and theologians from differing theological commitments criticize the movement along similar lines. At the same time and in response to these criticisms, some prosperity teachers redefined the concept of prosperity and success.[77] It is for them not anymore only about everyone enjoying the lavish riches of the prosperity gospel, whether luxury cars or designer clothes. Instead, it is defined in terms of an interdependent material hierarchy that allows everyone to advance their relative economic position, but at the same time taking care of the interests of other people, as when one person patronizes another's business, and with families taking communal care for their members.

Conclusion

In this chapter we looked at the rise and popularity of Pentecostalism, and in particular the prosperity message in Africa. Many African Pentecostals as well as other Africans were influenced directly by the prosperity gospel, and various reasons were provided for this popularity. The connections that pentecostal spirituality show with African traditional religion, leading at times to practices within African Pentecostalism that some critics describe as syncretistic; the emphasis in Pentecostalism on a holistic spirituality that links directly with primal spirituality in Africa; the role of the prophet in both traditions; and the importance of prosperity in an enchanted worldview that African traditional religion and African Pentecostalism share are some of the reasons for the widespread African prosperity teaching that relates poverty and prosperity to a visible and invisible world, influencing each other, and where spirits and ancestors play a critical role in preventing or causing natural catastrophes and personal damages.

The essence of neo-Pentecostalism was described in terms of these spirit beings that directly influence the circumstances of people living in Africa, and the necessity for mediation and appropriation of these forces for survival and a successful existence as human beings. The African pentecostal spirituality links directly with the New Testament's enchanted worldview with events in the visible world determined by what happens in the invisible world, where good and evil, and God and Satan clash regularly.

76. Marshall, *Political Spiritualities*, 239-43.
77. Haynes, "Pentecostalism and the Morality of Money," 135-6.

In the next chapter, we are looking at the angle from which the study is done, betraying the presuppositions and assumptions that all researchers have. Pentecostal hermeneutics is described historically, in terms of several phases that developed through the decades and led to important shifts and changes in its hermeneutics, before the new hermeneutic that developed in the past fifty years is described that serves as the means to evaluate the African prosperity message in the last chapter.

2
———

The Angle

Pentecostal Hermeneutics

Introduction

THE PENTECOSTAL MOVEMENT IS diverse, consisting of various parts that are historically related. Due to its diversity it also consists of a diversity of hermeneutics and it is difficult to generalize a "pentecostal hermeneutics." One can discern, however, some tendencies in the way early Pentecostals read and interpreted the Bible; followed by the changes brought about when important proponents of Pentecostalism formed alliances with Evangelicals with the purpose to obtain the approval of the community and earn some respectability from its sectarian status, a trend that still influences the better part of the classical Pentecostal movement;[1] and a new pentecostal hermeneutics that was defined since the last three decades of the twentieth century by pentecostal scholarship in conjunction with early hermeneutical tendencies of the movement. These three trends in the hermeneutical development in classical Pentecostalism is discussed in this chapter. The purpose of the discussion is to form the substructure of pentecostal hermeneutics that will be used in later chapters to evaluate the popular prosperity message that is engulfing Africa, and influencing the classical Pentecostal movement as well.

---

1. Historically one can only speak of classical Pentecostalism since the rise of the charismatic movement, the second wave of Pentecostalism; before that period, there was no reason to qualify the movement further.

Pentecostal Hermeneutics

Early Pentecostal Hermeneutics

William Oliverio argues that the ethos of early Pentecostalism rests on four core interpretive assumptions that explain its orientation.[2] The first is that Protestant Scripture served as the sole ultimate authority for Christian belief and living which functioned dialogically with the religious and general experiences of early Pentecostals to form a theological understanding of their world and circumstances. Second is a restorationist beliefs, centering on the narrative of God's plan for humankind coming to pass with the outpouring of the Spirit in the latter rain. Third is the fourfold or fivefold "Full Gospel" that served as the doctrinal grid that oriented pentecostal beliefs and living and as doctrinal hypotheses which explained Scripture and spiritual experiences. Lastly, a pragmatic naive realism formed early pentecostal rationality, integrated with an understanding of the primacy of the supernatural.[3] For Pentecostals, the supernatural is tangible, something (Someone) that can be experienced as part of daily reality.[4]

It was important for early Pentecostals to read the Bible as literally as possible,[5] taking it at face value.[6] In the process, the distance between the original context of Scripture and the context of the reader was collapsed to a large degree.[7] They searched the Bible for all Scripture references to a particular subject and then synthesized those references into a theological statement in a harmonizing and deductive way.[8]

What was important was not necessarily to find a lot of information about God and other subjects in the Bible; they rather read the Bible with the expectation that they would experience and encounter God in the same terms and ways as described by biblical witnesses. In the words of Craig Keener, "All Christians should read Scripture as people who are living in the biblical experience—not in terms of ancient *culture*, but as

---

2. Oliverio, *Theological Hermeneutics*, 231-4.
3. Oliverio, *Theological Hermeneutics*, 32.
4. Ganiel, "Pentecostal and Charismatic Christianity," 133.
5. Archer. *Pentecostal Hermeneutic*, 65.
6. Archer, *Pentecostal Hermeneutic*, 66.
7. Martin "Introduction to Pentecostal Biblical Hermeneutics," 3.
8. Archer, *Pentecostal Hermeneutic*, 102.

people living by the same Spirit who guided God's people in Scripture."⁹ Believers also learnt how to verbalize their experience of encounters with God in the language of the biblical witnesses in order to testify to the pentecostal truth.¹⁰

Jesus at the center of pentecostal theology was the theological grid that provided a firm interpretive lens for the fluid Pentecostal community and their reading of Scripture.¹¹ Because the Spirit is viewed as the Spirit of Christ, the Spirit reveals Christ in the Spirit's illumination of Scripture. Experience of the Spirit shapes the reading of the Bible, but the Bible most often provides the lenses through which the Spirit's work is perceived and acted upon.¹² For that reasons, the Spirit's revelation focuses on Christ as the fulfillment of Scripture.¹³

However, Pentecostals did not interpret the Bible in a fundamentalist manner¹⁴ because they did not ascribe authority to the Bible due to its inerrancy or infallibility, but to its utility of showing the way to a

9. Keener, *Spirit Hermeneutics*, 5.

10. Plüss, "Azusa and Other Myths," 191; Ellington, "Pentecostalism and the Authority of Scriptures," 162.

11. Archer, *Pentecostal Hermeneutic*, 137.

12. Fowl, *Engaging Scripture*, 114.

13. Several Pentecostal scholars found the writings and philosophical ideas of Paul Ricoeur useful in formulating their own theological perspectives (Joseph Byrd, J. Kwabena Asamoah-Gyadu, among others). One such concept is the idea of revelation that Ricoeur defines (Ricoeur, *Hermeneutics*, 111-52, in a chapter entitled "Hermeneutics of the Idea of Revelation"). He distinguishes between three different levels of language that are concerned with the idea, first on the level of the confession of faith, where what one prays is not divorced from what one believes; next, the level of ecclesial dogma, where a historic community interprets for itself the understanding of faith specific to its traditions; and, lastly, the body of doctrines imposed by the magisterium as the rule of orthodoxy. He rejects the "massive and impenetrable concept" of revealed truth (or truths), that is, the dogmatic propositions that are taken to be identical with the founding faith. He desires to carry the notion of revelation back to its most originary level, the discourse of faith or the confession of faith. This suggests a pluralistic, polysemic, and at most an analogical concept of revelation, instead of the monolithic concept of revelation which is obtained by transforming these different forms of discourse into propositions (Ricoeur, *Hermeneutics*, 112-3). Pentecostals argue for a concept of the word of God as revelation that consists firstly and primarily of the person of Jesus Christ, the incarnation of God's revelation to humankind. They are not interested in formulating theological doctrines in the first place but in encountering God in a personal relationship, that eventually leads to the need of words to share their testimony with others. Theological formulation of ecclesial dogma plays an insignificant role in their praxis, in line with Ricoeur's ideas.

14. Hollenweger, "From Azusa Street to Toronto Phenomenon," 8.

personal encounter with God.[15] Theirs was a distinctly non-cessationist, or continuationist approach to Scripture. Pentecostals were interested in the Bible not simply for what it taught about ancient history or ideas, intriguing as that might be, but because they expected to share the kind of spiritual experience and relationship with God that they discovered in the Bible.[16] Scripture formed an important voice in a congregational context where it exerted its power conversationally and not unilaterally.[17] Pentecostal theology flourished in the context of spirituality with song, prayer, sermon and testimony as the most important contributors to meaning, and not in the format of lengthy treatises or the development of complicated doctrines.

Early Pentecostals did not look at the Bible from the outside but they "entered" the world of the Bible, and the world of the Bible shaped their world and metanarrative.[18] Their passion for the kingdom of God was fueled by their reading of the biblical meta-narrative and not necessarily because they were socially deprived, although their social situation contributed to what themes they heard in Scriptures.[19] It is in the nature of narratives that they have the potential to engage and change readers; biblical narratives engaged Pentecostals to look for similar encounters with God. Their daily charismatic experiences altered their epistemology, giving them existential awareness of the miraculous in the biblical worldview and appreciating the influence of the Spirit.[20] Although their charismatic experiences in itself did not assist them to become "infallible" interpreters of the biblical text, yet it provided an important pre-understanding to the Bible. Normative doctrinal positions cannot be validated by exegesis alone, argues Roger Stronstad; the doctrinal positions must be livable and demonstrable within the Pentecostal community.[21] In this

---

15. Ellington, "Pentecostalism and the Authority of Scriptures," 170; Yong, *Spirit-Word-Community*, 44.

16. Keener, *Spirit Hermeneutics*, 5.

17. Long, "Living with the Bible," 72. Cox, *Fire from Heaven*, 200-201, e.g., writes that Pentecostalism is less concerned with systematic comprehension and rightness of logic and more with breaking out of the constraints and limitations of everyday life, ignoring grammar and syntax and more with worship and testimony, emphasizing moral and emotional values alongside cognitive matters.

18. Pinnock, "The Work of the Holy Spirit," 246.

19. Archer. *Pentecostal Hermeneutic*, 28.

20. Ervin, "Hermeneutics: A Pentecostal Option," 24.

21. Stronstad, "Pentecostal Experience and Hermeneutics," 25-6.

manner, the community validated the understanding of Scripture. Their own experiences of the supernatural affirmed and supported the truthfulness of the supernatural components of the biblical story and suggested a broader approach to knowing the truth because the Spirit who had inspired the Bible moved in them to reveal the meaning of Scripture as well.[22] Narratives were understood literally, taken to be repeatable and expected, and the experience of biblical characters were seen as to be emulated.[23] The enchanted worldview of the biblical narratives was accepted and applied to interpret reality. Pentecostals accepted that they lived within the larger narrative world of the Bible, a world where the supernatural and eschatology were real.[24] Their charismatic experience was perceived as an important part of New Testament experience, and it provided a much more adequate starting point or preunderstanding for engaging the text than does the lack of such experience.[25]

Although the Bible served for them as the standard to define faith and practice,[26] their angle to define doctrine was on the basis of their experiences with the God who utilized the Bible to reveal Godself through God's Spirit. Pentecostals confessed that while careful study of the Bible could help counter the unbridled subjectivism of popular charismatic excesses, a study that did not lead to living out biblical experience in the era of the Spirit missed the point of biblical texts. Study of a "Spiritless Word" as rationalism would never suit the pentecostal sentiment. Pentecostals understood and utilized doctrine in a fundamentally different way from most other traditions which were grounded in rationalist models. For Pentecostals, doctrine was not essentially *generative* in function; it was rather descriptive because they utilized doctrine to describe and verbalize lived experience. Formal deductive doctrinal statements were for Pentecostals an attempt to organize and understand described

22. Their view of "illumination" goes beyond the Reformed concept to allow an element of divine revelation (Waddell, *Spirit of the Book of Revelation*, 127).

23. Nel, "Pentecostals' Reading of the Old Testament," 527.

24. In the first decades of the twentieth century, classical Pentecostalism was energized by a strong eschatological expectation of the second coming of Christ. Most of them supported the teaching that a rapture will precede the final events that accompany the end of the present world and the transition to the new world expected to replace the current planet. However, Pentecostal and non-Pentecostal premillennialists generally labored along separate lines. Eventually they would join forces, but that would take decades of careful work (Sutton, *American Apocalypse*, 31).

25. Keener, *Spirit Hermeneutics*, 6.

26. See Nel, "Pentecostal Movement's View."

experience and not an attempt to serve as proof for those things which lie completely outside the realm of experience.[27] Pentecostals based their faith first on the God that they had met and only then did they attempt to articulate their experiences in normative, doctrinal ways. Doctrine was defined experientially in terms of the Bible. Canonical texts were "measuring sticks" and not texts to be exploited for ideological agendas.[28]

By way of conclusion, early pentecostal hermeneutics can be characterized as oral, charismatic, largely ahistorical, and minimally contextual, literal in its interpretations, morally and spiritually absolutizing, pragmatic, and pastoral. Early Pentecostals were characterized by an anti-intellectuality. Their spirituality arises from the affections rather than intellectual ability, with emphasis on the individual's encounter with a living God leading to an emotional and volitional reaction and adjustment. Love, passion, desire, feelings, and emotions were emphasized in an attempt to integrate orthopathy with orthodoxy and orthopraxy. The sole rule of the intellect and its accompanying orthodoxy was rejected. Pentecostal "thinking" happened at the level of the affective, unconscious, and pre-deliberative, and left ample room for the un-determinative working of the Spirit.[29] It was aimed at and subjected to witness and worship before it entered the cognitive, deliberative world of understanding. It did not deny the significance of the intellect; it rather rejected its dominance and suggested that more was needed for the full pursuit of and construction of an epistemology. Pentecostal spirituality was also dominated by imagination rather than reason. It functioned on an epistemological level that was aesthetic rather than noetic.[30] The world was viewed in terms of the manifestation of the Spirit, the biblical witness, and the community of faith. Imagination was contrasted to the dominance of reason and order, leaving room for improvisation, play, performance, and instrumentality which stood diametrically opposite the views of mainline churches as well as the academy's formal disciplines and methodologies.

An important part of pentecostal spirituality was its sacramentality that saw reality and looked beyond reality as necessary presuppositions for engaging with the world and participating in its struggles and sufferings rather than isolating itself in an ivory tower of intellectual

27. Ellington, "Pentecostalism and the Authority of Scriptures," 150.

28. Keener, *Spirit Hermeneutics*, 107–8.

29. See in particular the discussion in the Methodist minister Asamoah-Gyadu, *Contemporary Pentecostal Christianity*, 21.

30. Smith, *Thinking in Tongues*, 81.

engagement. Pentecostal "action-reflection in the Spirit"[31] allowed for the rational pursuit of meaning but it was doubtful whether reason alone could lead to the discernment of truth. Pentecostal spirituality operated on the level of oral rather than written discourse and it was concerned with ongoing, daily revelation of truths in the life of the individual and assembly rather than the revelation of eternal truths.[32] Pentecostals operated at the limits of speech where the Spirit revealed insights and they were more comfortable with testimony, story, song, preaching, praise and speaking in unknown tongues than with definition, concept, thesis, system, philosophy and methodology that dominate scholarly enterprises. Speaking in tongues defied categorization and operated in a realm outside of reality. "*Glossolalia* is the flagship of the Pentecostal resistance to the dominance of human language and the discourse of meaning."[33] It did not reject human language but questioned its ability to capture the world fully in its manifold dimensions. Its anti-intellectualism did not allow Pentecostals to be stereotyped as rejecting academic enterprises and the intellectual dimensions of life; it rather allowed Pentecostals to be sceptic and uneasy with the exclusively purely cognitive, rational, and scientific modes of knowing. Pentecostal "knowing" consisted in terms of dynamic, experiential, and relation knowledge. Its emphasis on the affections, imagination, and the limits of speech defined Pentecostalism's anti-intellectualism. Eventually it also led to the unprecedented rise of pentecostal theological scholarship during the second part of the twentieth century.

A New Pentecostal Hermeneutics

While many differences initially separated Pentecostals from Old School Princeton fundamentalists who reacted against modernism,[34] by the

---

31. Land, *Pentecostal Spirituality*, 119.
32. Refer to the discussion of Ricoeur on revelation in footnote above.
33. Vondey, *Pentecostalism*, 138.
34. Fundamentalism is described by Gifford, "Prosperity," 373 as a reaction of white American Protestants against modern and liberal trends within Christianity, focused particularly around the issue of evolution. Fundamentalists rejected any accommodation of popular scientific theories at the cost of the "clear teaching" provided in the Bible, insisting on the "plenary" inspiration of the Bible and its historical and scientific inerrancy. Modernism is defined by Grenz, *Primer on Postmodernism*, 3 as Descartes' autonomous, rational substance encountering Newton's mechanistic world.

early 1940s they had joined together to craft the modern evangelical movement.[35] It is important to take the history seriously that made a pentecostal-fundamentalist alliance possible, as well as the ways that Pentecostalism and fundamentalism overlapped in the early decades of the twentieth century.[36] The reason for the uneasy cooperation with Evangelicals was a change in the mood of the Pentecostal movement, in the transition from the initial and second generation to the third generation, with Pentecostals aspiring for their religion to become more acceptable and respectable to the public, government, and established churches. Their sectarian status that they earned due in part to their charismatic worship practices that were regularly characterized by its loudness and expressiveness and their enthusiasm to win "souls" for Christ, earning them the contempt of other churches and frequent discrimination, eventually became an albatross around their necks. In the process, some of them accepted a church order characterized by more formal worship and order, and exchanged the orchestra used for accompaniment of congregation singing for an organ, and informal singing and hand-clapping for choirs, and impromptu preaching for a pulpit and a professional pastorate. In their zeal to become acceptable, they also adapted their theology, shifting women from leading ministerial positions, and denying their pacifist roots.[37] They also adapted a hermeneutics that was more acceptable to Evangelical sentiments.

The movement was always conservative, and in their association with Evangelical values they also accepted the more conservative hermeneutical position among Evangelicals, represented by fundamentalist,

---

Modernity is characterized by humanism, the mastery of all natural and supernatural forces, positivism that accepts science and instrumental reasoning as the sole arbiter of truth, and a worldview of a naturalistic mechanistic universe, with the material universe as the sum total of reality (Archer, *Pentecostal Hermeneutic*, 43).

35. Paul Gifford, "Prosperity," 373 defines evangelicalism as that part of Christianity that places its emphasis on a personal adult experience of Christ, consisting of the experience of "being born again," and claiming the Bible as its sole norm or guide for life and teaching.

36. Sutton, *American Apocalypse*, x-xi.

37. ". . . where pastors and congregants strive to be more respectably established, church organization tends to become less charismatic, more hierarchical, and more masculine. Some among these churches may begin to require that pastors show not only proof of gifts of the Holy Spirit but seminary credentials" (Hefner, "Unexpected Modern-Gender," 8).

biblicist and literalist streams.[38] Fundamentalism can, in the words of an interesting article of James Mensch, be defined as a specific way of reading a religious text, in this case the Bible.[39] It accepts that the biblical text presents believers with unalterable absolutes, changeless commands, deathless doctrines, and timeless truths.[40] The Bible reading practices maximized the "staying power" of the text; the price it paid was to deny the transcendence of the religion that the book depicts. The staying power of a text is its ability to keep its distinctive character, and in the case of the Bible it obviously involves faith. Legal texts have a prescriptive character, and it keeps this through a community's obedience and acceptance of the laws they promulgated. If people do not obey the laws anymore, the legal text loses its character. An information text conveys information, and it gains its staying power when people accept the information and act on it. When people perceive the information as outdated or false, the text loses its character. A literary text is unique because it does not inform, promise or command anything. Its staying power is in the depiction of a linguistic context, if and when people read it again and again. A religious text intends to excite belief in its promises, and its staying power is in people accepting those promises by acts of trust or faith.[41] There is a reciprocal

38. Their viewpoint is summarized by Conrad Mbewe, who states that what God says is found in the Book. God does not say anything more. The Bible is the manual where one finds the needed instruction for every aspect of life. He refers to the issue of divorce and Christians as an instance, and explains that Jesus solved the difficulty of Deut 24:1's reference to "indecency" by interpreting it in terms of Gen 2:24 (at Grace Ministers' Conference, Joy Lodge, Pretoria, 7 January 2020).

39. Mensch, "Hermeneutics of Fundamentalism," 1-2.

40. In the words of Bruce Waltke, *Dance Between God and Humanity*, 224.

41. Some Pentecostals love to sing the song, "Every promise in the Book is mine / Every chapter, every verse, every line." However, when all promises are taken literally and with a universal scope, without considering that some promises are determined by contextual conditions and others are historically conditioned, justice is not done to the difficulty of interpreting biblical promises. What is necessary in their interpretation is that we ask whether we can discern from the context a particular person or group to whom this promise was distinctively offered, and does it bear any evidence of being offered for a certain time period or under certain set limits of time or conditions? One must also be careful not to assume that because a proverb in the Old Testament sounds like a promise, that it is one. The proverbs of the book of Proverbs are rather wisdom sayings that apply to situations generally, without listing the exceptions that most often qualify them. Proverbs cannot be generalized and universalized into unconditional truths or into promises without qualification, as words from the mouth of God. The same is true for the Deuteronomist's concept of promises and curses which is illustrated by the retelling of Israel's history. Statements in the Bible must be carefully

relation between believers and religious texts. They define themselves in terms of the texts, taking the content of the text as determinative for their belief. On the other hand, their belief is constitutive of the sacred character of the text.[42]

Fundamentalism conflates all these characteristics, in order to maximize the text's staying power. The text is regarded as containing a promise, and the promise lasts as long as people believe that it will be fulfilled. The text commands and forbids (because it contains legal texts), and fundamentalists accept the commandments as an inherent element of the Bible, to be applied in current circumstances. Fundamentalists also read the text in an informational way, and they accept the information as timely and non-expiring. They take all statements at face value, seemingly including that the earth is flat and standing on pillars, that the earth was created in six days, that God created everything according to its kind, and more, because all statements contain the same historical, existential truth as an account in a newspaper is supposed to contain. The same is true for historical accounts found in the Bible; they are accepted as true accounts of the author who told the narratives for the sake of providing factual information about them. Because all statements are viewed as part of the Bible, and the Bible is evaluated as the infallible and inerrant words that came out of God's mouth, the exact words of Scripture is considered to be inspired by God. To change any of these words is considered to be equal to the curse found in Revelation 22:18-19, that if anyone adds to them, God will add to that person the plagues described in this book; if anyone takes away from the words of the book of this prophecy, God will take away that person's share in the tree of life and in the holy city, which are described in this book. That these words form an integral element of apocalyptic thinking about its documents and should be read in terms of its genre, and a part of the unique argument presented in the book of Revelation is not a consideration for hard fundamentalists.[43] The

---

evaluated to decide which represent promises, and then it must be established whether they are directed exclusively to certain persons or conditioned by certain qualifications (Kaiser and Silva, *Introduction to Biblical Hermeneutics*, 330-331).

42. Mensch, "Hermeneutics of Fundamentalism," 2-4.

43. In this description of fundamentalism, consideration is limited to hard fundamentalism, to emphasize the negative factors that fundamentalism may contain. However, it is acknowledged that such a hard fundamentalism has become rarer and is limited to certain fringe and radical groups within the fundamentalist fold. While many Pentecostals, including pastors, read their Bibles with a fundamentalist tendency, it is also true that most of them are not intolerant to other people, as hard

religious text is also read and reread by the fundamentalist in a way that gives it the lasting quality of a literary text. By rereading it the reader acknowledges the informational quality of the sacred text and seals it from the world, that, as a result, fails to expire.[44]

The positive benefit of such a way of reading the Bible is that it provides certainty that the text contains truth, and that all religious doctrines that are required to ground the Christian's and ecclesiastical practice can be deduced from this absolute and ultimate truth. Fundamentalists function with an admirable level of confidence in the correctness, not only of their doctrines but also their view of God. The threat of an ever-changing reality does not hold danger for them because their life is fixed and their social relations are determined by truth that is immutable.

The drawback is that it produces a certain closeness of mind and an intolerance of other people who do not share their viewpoint of the "truth." At the same time, their blurring of the religious and legal character of the sacred text implies that they base their opinions about issues like relations between Israel and Palestine, LGBTIQ+, abortion, living together without getting married, and more on what they perceive to be the "Bible's infallible opinion" about the matters. In the process they support the agenda of the conservative political grouping functioning to the right of politics, blurring the boundaries between religion and politics.[45]

Mensch asserts, correctly, that God's name is revealed to Moses as the unknowable one who is greater than anyone else that can be conceived of and greater than can be thought out by any creature.[46] God acts and exists independently of the world, as indicated by a characteristic ascribed to God, namely eternity. In contrast, a fundamental reading of the Bible depicts a God that can be explained and contained in human language and who acts according to human expectations. God is limited within and to the confines of a literal reading of the Bible. God's freedom and transcendence is limited when God is explained exclusively in terms of a

---

fundamentalists tend to be, although to a large extent they support the far right conservative political agenda.

44. Mensch, "Hermeneutics of Fundamentalism," 5.

45. As a result, the movement at times supports issues that do not focus on politically disengaged, rights-based sensitization or social justice and does not serve their members' immediate concerns, such as support for anti-abortion laws and policies that question condom diffusion (Deacon and Lynch, "Allowing Satan in?," 112, 126).

46. In the words of Anselm of Canterbury; see Mensch, "Hermeneutics of Fundamentalism," 6.

religious text, while that text was written by human beings applying the only material that they had at hand, consisting of language and concepts created by humans. When the inexpressible is expressed in words, the object of its investigation is limited to what humans can conceive and the categories that they impose upon God. While there exists no certain relation between concepts and the reality that they refer to, and the specific persons using the concept, to contain God in such a concept is equal to creating an effigy of God without having seen (or being able to see) God.

The biblicist way of reading the Bible is a redemptive-historical or revelation-historical (*Heilsgeschichte*) approach because it sees God's revelation, in deed and word, as historical, starting with the historical creation of life on earth, with an organic and progressive unfolding that incorporates the history of Israel until it culminates in the incarnation of Christ.[47] The history of verbal revelation is viewed as a stream within and conforming to the contours of the history of redemption, marked by epochal junctures. Jesus is the culmination of the history and revelation of redemption, the final goal and history's consummation as God's final and supreme self-revelation.[48] Revelation is concerned with redemption; verbal revelation is always focused on and oriented toward God's activity in history as creator-redeemer.

However, although verbal revelation documents God's activity in history, it always points also beyond history to God's aseity, or self-existence, which is incomprehensible and impenetrable for humans. Scripture is viewed as revelation in itself, not less than the revelation. Scripture is the word of God, the revelation of God, although it is concerned with God's activity in history. It is also a faithful history of the revelation of God that is redemption for human beings. It is an inerrant witness to revelation. The only revelatory access to the history of redemption is the biblical canon, and the limits set by the canon provide the boundary of what can be known by revelation. An implication is that the historical descriptions contained in the biblical narratives are faithful historiography that can be trusted by contemporary readers.

Scripture also has a primary divine authorship, even though attention is given to the instrumental role of human authors as biblical authors. The fact that there are distinguishing characteristics and peculiarities

---

47. Gaffin, "Redemptive-Historical View," 91-4.

48. See, e.g., Heb 1:1-2; 2:2-3; 3:5-6 that relates to the redemptive-historical approach.

associated with each of the different authors does not bring the unity and diversity or divine and human authorship into tension at all.[49]

The redemptive-historical view is concerned with the Reformation's hermeneutical proposition of *sola Scriptura*, that the Christian church looks exclusively to the Bible for the revelation of God and uses Scripture to interpret Scripture. The sense of this self-interpretation is based on Scripture as God's written word forming a concordant unity. Any one part located within an expanding horizon of God-given contexts serves to clarify another part, implying that all texts are of equal value in terms of its worth in formulating doctrine and life of the church. The overall unity of the Bible is found in its redemptive-historical essence.

Redemptive-historical interpretation also accepts a sense of continuity between the contemporary interpreter and the writers of the Bible (and especially, the New Testament). The whole Bible is interpreted as the redemptive-historically focused, Christ-centered revelation sufficient for the life and needs of the church in every generation.

The positive result of the redemptive-historical approach, undergirded by an exegetical method characterized by its attention to the historical and grammatical aspects of the text, ensures a more rigorously biblical focus and more biblical boundaries to the theological enterprise.[50]

An Adapted Pentecostal Hermeneutics

Kenneth Archer, professor in theology at Southeastern University in Central Florida, USA, in a significant contribution to the debate about a new pentecostal hermeneutics describes the interrelationship between the Holy Spirit as the One animating Scriptures and empowering the believing community as characteristic of this hermeneutic, conforming to some aspects of early pentecostal Bible reading practices.[51] Pentecostals believe that the Holy Spirit still speaks today, and when the Spirit speaks,

---

49. See, e.g., Heb 9—10 that signifies the relation between old and new in terms of the organic tie between type and its antitype, shadow and the reality shadowed (Gaffin, "Redemptive-Historical View," 97). The Bible is read as *Heilsgeschichte*, as indicative of the plan that God has with the creation of the world and human beings, and the whole Bible is read as a revelation of this plan, with some events serving as antitypes of other events, such as those happening in the Old Testament as types and interpreted in the New Testament as antitypes.

50. Gaffin, "Redemptive-Historical View," 98.

51. See Archer, *Pentecostal Hermeneutic*, 199.

the Spirit has more to say than just Scripture. However, the Spirit will always echo, confirm and cite Scripture. The purpose in reading the Bible is that members be equipped for ministry and witness in culturally appropriate ways, rather than for mere academic reasons. Their approach to Scripture is characterized by four aspects. Firstly, because the Spirit addresses believers in ways which transcend human reason, Scripture is not simply an object which Pentecostals interpret, but a living Word which interprets them. Secondly, pentecostal experience of the Spirit is grounded in a relational epistemology where knowing about God and directly experiencing God in an embodied manner perpetually inform and depend on one another. Thirdly, the responsibility of each believer to be a witness is grounded in a distinct belief in the priesthood and prophethood of all believers. And fourthly, Scripture is approached communally as the believers gather around the Word in the Spirit to hear what God may say to the assembly of believers.[52]

Even in contemporary times many Pentecostal leaders are sceptic about academic scholarship that is over dependent on the intellect at the cost of involving the entire person in the life of faith. Especially in Africa, professional theologians are regularly viewed with suspicion and some of them live up to perceptions by publishing their sceptic unbelief in the virgin birth of Jesus, the resurrection, and any current divine intervention, among other matters. On the one side, the pragmatism of the pentecostal worldview and spirituality finds itself in an awkward position in the academic world; on the other side, the pentecostal emphasis on signs and wonders may help reform the current one-sided emphasis on the rational in current academic theological scholarship.[53]

Classical Pentecostalism was perpetuated in the charismatic renewal of the 1960s with the experiences of Spirit baptism of Dennis Bennett, Kevin Ranaghan, and Kathryn Kuhlman in Van Nuys, California, only a few kilometers north of Azusa Street and involving their congregations in charismatization of worship. It was repeated in many other mainline established churches, representing a second wave of Pentecostalism. It was again invigorated by the third-wave neo-charismatic movement of Peter Wagner, John Wimber, and others in the 1970s and 1980s.[54] Pentecostal theological scholarship coincided with the charismatic movement

---

52. McQueen, *Joel and the Spirit*, 2.
53. As Daniels, "'Wonder and Scholarship,'" 112 also argues.
54. See especially Cox, *Fire from Heaven*, 20, 23–5, 34–42.

that also reached college and university students and stirred up questions about the relationship between a Spirit-filled life and academic scholarship. The 1970s and 1980s saw an increase in pentecostal studies and the formation of academic societies among Pentecostals.

Where the first decades of the Pentecostal movement were characterized by anti-intellectualism, its modern history is defined by academic contributions and the development of pentecostal theological scholarship, although Velli-Matti Kärkkäinen argues correctly that its fundamentalist heritage that persists to the present day still marks Pentecostalism by a strong anti-intellectualism.[55] The scholarship moved from Walter J. Hollenweger's work in the 1960s to a wave of Pentecostal historians wishing to preserve the early history of the movement. Now many scholars completed their postgraduate studies, often in an environment and at faculties that neglected or obstructed the interaction of critical scholarship and pentecostal faith and praxis. These scholars investigated the biblical sources most relevant to a pentecostal self-description, particularly Luke-Acts, cessationism, dispensationalism, Spirit baptism, and hermeneutics as particular pentecostal concerns. During the 1990s, pentecostal theological scholarship saw constructive theological research with an emphasis on the distinctives of pentecostal faith, sometimes in the form of apologetics, a theology of the Spirit-filled life, and a reconsideration of existing doctrines in a more systematic fashion.

Pentecostal theological scholarship has grown beyond the traditional historical and biblical theological conversations. The twenty-first century sees pentecostal scholarship moving into questions of scientific knowledge and methodology, physics, biology, chemistry, psychology, medicine, anthropology, sociology, and technology. The coming of age of pentecostal scholarship requires that Pentecostals engage in all scientific disciplines and the increasing exposure of the scientific world to the phenomenon of Pentecostalism. Globally pentecostal seminaries and universities, and partnerships between Pentecostal denominations and universities promise a deepening in the involvement of Pentecostals in theological and ecumenical enterprises.

55. Kärkkäinen, "Pentecostal Hermeneutics," 80. Interesting research by Cartledge ("*Glossolalia*") indicates that 24.6 percent of the people that he interviewed during his quantitative research who believe that healing will always occur if a person's faith is great enough and who believe in daily conflict with demons, tend to be anti-intellectual, preferring intuition and personal senses as way of knowing. They are mainly from the ranks of less educated people from the lower social classes and represent also younger and more immature Christians.

The new pentecostal theological scholarship operating today among the academic element of the Pentecostal movement is characterized by several determining factors that is also reflected in the hermeneutics defined by pentecostal scholarship, in distinction to the customary use of biblicist and literalist methods of interpreting the Bible among the majority of Pentecostal believers and even pastors. It is experiential, defined by the foundational dimension of an encounter with the Spirit that determines pentecostal spirituality and praxis. It endeavors to articulate this normative encounter with God. "The pentecostal experiences are at the core defined theologically."[56] It is also radically informed by the anticipation that the Spirit can be discovered in all of life and thereby directs all of life toward God.

In the second place, it operates on the principle of play rather than performance. It perceives that traditional scholarship served under the tyranny of rationalism, seriousness, and work whereas pentecostal hermeneutics emphasizes a playful orientation on the level of "pure means" or "pure self-presentation".[57] The Bible is also seen as a performative book, making it a contemporary document relevant for the present reader, and its words have a declarative use: "today it is going to be fulfilled in your life!"[58] The encounter with God's Spirit in the present leads to restlessness and the anticipation of the kingdom of God where the fullness of life in the Spirit is yet to be realized, with a way of being that is radically open to divine surprises. Although it does not reject critical reflection, pentecostal hermeneutics refuses to submit to the exclusive claims of reason's dominance. It is informed by the pneumatological focus inherent in its worldview and spirituality.

Thirdly, its hermeneutics is embodied scholarship, requiring the scholar to go beyond the mere intellectual pursuit of knowledge and to participate actively in the community of faith. Embodied scholarship implies interdisciplinary and multidisciplinary inquiry where personal experiences are connected to the community, social structure, and human concerns. The Holy Spirit speaks in the scholarly pursuits where embodiment seeks the expressions of charismatic life as well. The Pentecostal scholar is not an objective observer only; they always actively and passionately participate in an embodied way in the research.

---

56. Vondey, *Pentecostalism*, 142.
57. Wariboko, "Pentecostal Principle, 165–71."
58. Gifford, "Expecting Miracles," 20.

Fourthly and lastly, it is based on a comprehensive analogical hermeneutic, what Mark Stibbe calls a "this-is-that" hermeneutic.[59] The present is interpreted in terms of the past, the Christian life in terms of biblical narratives, and the pentecostal experience in terms of the day of Pentecost and the experiences of the earliest church.[60] Contemporary pentecostal experiences are defined by way of the principle of analogy in terms of the interpretation of Scripture. It rejects dominant perceptions of reality in favor of an alternative interpretation, the perceived reality of God, as found in the interpretation of biblical narratives. The integration of the experiential, playful, embodied, and analogical dimensions of understanding and participation in the world takes pentecostal hermeneutics to the forefront of the renewal and revitalization of the postmodern academic world. These should, however, be balanced with other theological traditions by way of dialogue. Contemporary academic pentecostal scholarship is neither anti-intellectual nor intellectual; both elements are present among Pentecostals worldwide and in Africa. And pentecostal theological scholarship still experiences to a certain extent tension with anti-intellectual strains within Pentecostalism, as several Pentecostal scholars would readily testify. The coexistence of both trends is essential if one desires to come to terms with the scope and depth of the pentecostal ethos with its emphasis on the experiential and lived reality.[61]

---

59. Stibbe, "This is That," 181–93. At the same time, its definition of "hermeneutics" as the principles used for interpretation that produce meaning was broadened to include several levels of "meaning," including the linguistic, historical, catechetical, literary, canonical, and relevant contexts. An important discussion in hermeneutics is concerned with the historicity of biblical events (see Kaiser and Silva, *Introduction to Biblical Hermeneutics*, 22–23).

60. A typical Reformed view is that an analogy based on the lives of Jesus and his apostles cannot be maintained in terms of contemporary experience because Jesus and the apostles played a unique and unrepeatable role in salvation history. This is a significant point of difference between Pentecostals defined by their restorationist and primitivist urge and most of the other Christian traditions.

61. The pentecostal perspective links with Walter Wink's (*Bible in Human Transformation*) argument when he states that the professionalism of many New Testament scholars (and theologians in general) leads them to avoid the most important issues of hermeneutics, because they belong to a professional guild of scholars determined by rigorous rules and principles of what professional theology consist of, rather than being men and women living in the heart of the living church. The concerns of the Bible have become insulated from scholars who were trained "incapacity" to deal with the real problems of actual living persons in their daily lives, while the Bible was written for ordinary people and by ordinary people, and concerns itself with practical problems in the daily lives of its audiences.

The elements of a pentecostal theological distinctive can be described as the necessity that each member of the church is able to testify of conviction of sin as a function of the Spirit, leading to a personal meeting with God, and the experience that one's sins have been forgiven, and one is born again of the Spirit, leading to the wish and opportunity to witness of salvation at every opportunity; the experience of sanctification, as preparation for Spirit baptism that leads to the transformation and empowerment of a fearful and uncertain group of disciples into a missionary fellowship that boldly carries the gospel throughout the world; with speaking in tongues as the (initial) evidence; and healings, exorcisms, and other miracles as proof that the modern church succeeds as Christ's body on earth; and an eschatological expectation of the imminent second coming of Christ, in the opinion of some combined with the rapture.

An interesting feature of the charismatic movement, the second wave, is that it did not teach that speaking in tongues is the initial sign of the experience of baptism in the Spirit, but rather that love is the sure sign of a Spirit-filled life. This is also mostly true of the independent churches, or network Christianity, that does not connect the baptism of the Holy Spirit with the evidence of speaking in tongues, but rather emphasizes the power of the Holy Spirit for healing, prophetic utterances, and divine interventions in daily life, and characterized by vibrant worship, music, and prosperity for believers.

Conclusion

In this chapter, the transition in the hermeneutics of the classical Pentecostal movements was related to three trends. Early Pentecostalism viewed the Bible as comprehensible by any person, and that all Spirit-filled believers were empowered to find the revelation of the word of God in the pages of the Bible. Most believers, including leaders, had few or no theological training and they read the Bible as literally as possible, taking it at face value, in the process collapsing the distance between the original context of Scripture and the context of the current reader. Protestant Scripture was their sole ultimate authority while their restorationist beliefs led them to expect the events described in the Bible to be re-enacted in their own experience. Their pragmatic naive realism informed their rationality and it was integrated with the primacy of the supernatural. In Africa, for instance, the indigenous concept of evil eventually was reconfigured through a process of "grounded integration," rooted in traditional beliefs about evil.[62] Early believers read the Bible to find what it says about specific subjects, looking for all Scripture references to a particular subject and then synthesizing the references into a theological statement in a harmonizing and deductive way. Their interpretation was informed by their encounters with God and charismatic experiences so that the language of the Bible determined their discourse in testimonies about their adventures with God. Their world was depicted in biblical terms because they read the Bible as immediately relevant for the interpretation of their reality. They did not ascribe authority to the Bible due to its inerrancy or infallibility, but to its utility of showing the way to a personal encounter with God. They used their experiential lens to interpret the Bible and it served their spirituality along with song, prayer, sermon and testimony. The result of their study of the Bible was not lengthy treatises or the development of complicated doctrines but the expectation that the miraculous events found in the Bible will be duplicated among them.

A second groundbreaking trend and shift occurred since the 1930s and 1940s when classical Pentecostals joined hands with Evangelicalism, especially when it accepted its more conservative hermeneutical values and principles, that the Bible presents believers with unalterable absolutes, changeless commands, deathless doctrines, and timeless truths in the "word of God" that should be read literally. All texts were placed on the same level and accorded with the same authority because all the words in the Bible came from the mouth of God and was "given by inspiration from God" (2 Tim 3:16, KJV translation).[63] All statements were taken at face value, and all statements contain historical, existential truth. All statements were ascribed to God and the Bible was viewed as the infallible and inerrant word of God.

A last trend occurred since the 1970s with the development of pentecostal scholarship which reviewed pentecostal hermeneutics and defined it in terms of the preferences found among early Pentecostals, with their experiential, restorationist and primitivist urges, and that read the text as an invitation to encounter God in the same way as in biblical times. The new pentecostal hermeneutic asserts that the Holy Spirit still

---

62. Kalu, *African Pentecostalism*, 261.

63. The term *theopneustos* ("inspire") refers to a communication which has been inspired by God, according to Louw and Nida, *Greek-English Lexicon*, 417 (2 Tim 3:16), implying that the writer of Scripture was influenced or guided by God. They correctly states that it does not mean "dictated by God."

speaks today, and when the Spirit speaks, the Spirit has more to say than just what is stated in Scripture, although it is emphasized that the Spirit will always echo, confirm, and cite Scripture. The Bible is not primarily read for academic reasons and the purpose of Bible study is not to gain knowledge about the figures, trends, and events in the Bible but to be empowered and equipped for ministry and witness in culturally appropriate ways, underlining the necessity that the Bible should be interpreted and illuminated by the Spirit, the one who inspired Scriptures in the first place. Pentecostals believe that the revelation of God through God's Spirit transcends human reason, and the Bible becomes a living word when the Spirit, while one reads the Bible, reveals God and applies the biblical words to the current situation. Their epistemology is not based primarily in the Bible but in knowing God and directly experiencing God, informing their interpretation of the Bible.

The pentecostal hermeneutics defined by pentecostal scholarship operates in distinction from the customary use of biblicist and literalist methods of interpreting the Bible by being experiential, based on the anticipation that the Spirit can be discovered in all of life. It also operates on the principle of the Bible as a performative book, with a declarative use, that the events in the Bible is to be re-enacted today. It is an embodied hermeneutic, implying that the interpreter of the Bible goes beyond the pursuit of knowledge for the sake of knowledge to participate actively in the community of faith. And it serves as a comprehensive analogical hermeneutic, a "this-is-that" hermeneutic where the present is interpreted in terms of the past, Christian life in terms of biblical narratives, and charismatic experiences in terms of the earliest church and their encounters with the power of God. It defines itself by way of the principle of analogy in terms of the interpretation of Scripture, choosing the perceived reality of God, as found in the interpretation of biblical narratives, instead of dominant perceptions of reality.

This is the hermeneutic that will be applied in evaluating the African prosperity message in the chapters that follow. The next chapter consists of an explication of the prosperity gospel, followed by an investigation of how the prosperity gospel is taught in Africa, with unique emphasis.

3

The Project

Prosperity Gospel

Introduction

IN THE FIRST CHAPTER the context of the study was described, consisting of the prosperity message and its popularity in Africa, and the reasons for it being so popular in a continent characterized by high levels of poverty and suffering. In the second chapter the angle of the study was described, which is hermeneutics from a classical pentecostal perspective. In this chapter we discuss the project, which is the prosperity gospel. The relation between Pentecostalism and the prosperity movement, especially as characterized by the Faith movement, is first described before a short history is provided of the prosperity movement.

The prosperity message originated in the non-pentecostal world of mind-cure, positive thinking, self-help, and success literature as part of the New Thought movement. Faith theology and the prosperity movement is not a product of either Pentecostal or charismatic movements, but can be traced historically to cultic sources, when E.W. Kenyon combined pentecostal spirituality and New Thought with the help of Ralph Waldo Emerson's philosophical idealism, Swedish mystic Emmanuel Swedenborg's Neoplatonic theory of correspondence, Helena Blavatsky's theosophical quest for uniform spiritual laws, Phineas Parkhurst Quimby's mind thought ideas and healing, and Mary Baker Eddy's insight of the power of the mind over the body in Christian Science. New Thought included groups such as Religious Science, Christian Science, and the Unity School of Christianity.

A new phase was introduced in the prosperity movement with the neo-Pentecostal independent churches that originated since the 1970s, centered around prominent figures that operated as prophets and apostles. This eventually led to the Network movement and a new approach to the ministry of the apostle and a way of governance that is influencing Christianity on a wide front today. The success of the impact of this movement is ascribed to the way it utilized social media and electronics.

The purpose of the chapter is to delineate the prosperity gospel in terms of its origins, historical developments and present-day appearance, in order to apply the message and the movement to the African context, asking in what way(s) does the message differ from the American version of the prosperity gospel, which forms the theme for the next chapter.

Faith Movement and Pentecostalism

The Faith movement had an impact on contemporary Christianity, as becomes clear when some statistics are compared. The world population stood at 6,010,799,000 in 2002, with 536,000,000 identified as Pentecostals/charismatics, and 1,040,020,000 as Roman Catholics.[1] Any classification of Pentecostalism is, however, risky because of its diverse branches, explaining the differences in numbers provided by demographers. It has become customary to speak of three waves (although some already speak of a fourth wave as well).[2] The first is normally referred to as classical Pentecostalism, which looks back for its origins to the beginning of the twentieth century, including Charles Parham's Bible Schools, William Seymour's Azusa Street Revival in Los Angeles, and similar incidents (not all agree that pentecostal origins in other countries go back to Los Angeles—sometimes it might have been the result of indigenous revivals). Today, there are an estimated 200 million people belonging to these first-wave, classical Pentecostal churches. Secondly, since the 1960s and 1970s some established historical mainline churches experienced a charismatic renewal that resulted in a pentecostalization of their worship

---

1. Schmidgall, *European Pentecostalism*, 3. Kalu, *African Pentecostalism* mentions that by the calculation of some no less than three quarters of humanity will be committed to pentecostal spirituality forms of Christianity in 2050.

2. As stated, due to its diverse nature there is a diversity of categorizations of Pentecostalism, but Barrett's proposal for "three waves" is used the most and is probably also the most useful typology of the movement as a whole (see Barrett, "Worldwide Holy Spirit Renewal, 2001").

services and prayer meetings, and a resultant openness to the gifts of the Spirit.³ A loose worldwide "network," which began in California in 1960, eventually influenced the Protestant, Roman Catholic, and Eastern Orthodox mainline churches, including these churches in Africa.⁴ An estimated 100 million believers in Latin America alone are involved in this renewal movement.⁵ Thirdly, there is an independent movement that originated since the 1970s with its synthesis between pentecostal theology and practice, and several other theological traditions.⁶ This last wave is sometimes denoted as neo-Pentecostalism and it concurs with the pentecostalization of Christian churches, especially in the French-speaking parts of Africa.⁷

David Barrett reckons in 2001 that there were worldwide 740 classical Pentecostal denominations, 6,530 non-Pentecostal "mainline" denominations with large organized internal charismatic movements, and 18,810 independent neo-charismatic denominations and networks.⁸ The second wave of charismatics are found across the entire spectrum of Christianity, within all 150 traditional non-pentecostal ecclesiastical confessions, families, and traditions. The third-wave phenomenon is found in 9,000 ethnolinguistic cultures, speaking 8,000 languages, and covering 95 percent of the world's total population. In 2000, there were 523 million Pentecostals in total, and in 2025 this total is likely to grow to 811 million. Of these, 93 million will be classical Pentecostals, 274 million will be charismatics, and no less than 460 million will be neo-Pentecostals. Of all Pentecostals worldwide, 27 percent are white and 71 percent are non-white. Members consist of more urban than rural populations, are more female than male, consist of more children under 18 than adults, occur more in the Third World (66 percent) than in the West (32 percent), more are living in poverty (87 percent) than in affluence (13 percent), and they

---

3. Keener, "Pentecostal Biblical Interpretation," 271. Some 150 million Catholics are part of this renewal movement (Keener, "Pentecostal Biblical Interpretation," 272).

4. Paas, *Christianity in Eurafrica*, 490.

5. Jacobsen, *Global Gospel*, 38.

6. Pretorius, "Toronto Blessing," 66–7. Oliverio describes the adherents of the second group of charismatic Pentecostals as "renewal Christians," adding to the confusion in the terminology surrounding Pentecostalism (Oliverio, "Introduction," 4).

7. Neo-Pentecostals are also referred to as neo-charismatics, Third Wavers, Independents, Post-denominationalists, and neo-Apostolics (Barrett, "Worldwide Holy Spirit Renewal," 404).

8. Barrett, "Worldwide Holy Spirit Renewal," 383.

are more family-related than individualist.⁹ "The growing churches in the non-Western world are mostly Pentecostal-Charismatic, as seen in the Pentecostal movements in Latin America, Independent Churches in Africa,¹⁰ and Charismatic movements in Asia."¹¹ While 16.7 percent of Christians living in Africa, Asia, and Latin America in 1900, it was 63.2 percent by 2010. By 2025, it will be nearly 70 percent.¹²

By the end of the twentieth century, there were already more Pentecostals worldwide than mainline Protestants, accounting for something like 80 percent of evangelical Protestantism's worldwide growth.¹³ Some estimate nearly half a billion charismatics worldwide. The charismatic branch is now second in size in Christianity only to Roman Catholicism (with many Roman Catholics being charismatics). By 2050, charismatics

---

9. Asamoah-Gyadu, "Did Jesus Wear Designer Robes," 40 argues that because of its emphasis on material wealth, charismatic Christianity in Africa has largely remained an urban phenomenon. Its message has little to offer to the many young people who are unemployed and even unemployable. In Africa, viable religion has always meant that which leads to power, strength, vitality, and abundance. North American levels of materialism exist in Africa only among the elite.

10. The reference is not to African Instituted Churches but to those churches that originated as part of the third wave (Ngong, *Holy Spirit and Salvation*, 141). Independent churches are expanding faster than Islam in Africa, at about twice the rate of the Roman Catholic Church, and at roughly three times the rate of other non-Catholic Christian groups. There are now approximately 5,000 independent Christian denominations, all born in the last forty years, all bearing the familiar marks of pentecostal spirituality, and with each church displaying its own distinctive qualities. In South Africa, they embrace about 40 percent of the black population, while in Zimbabwe, 50 percent of all Christians belong to these independent churches (Cox, *Fire from Heaven*, 246–47). In southern Africa, neo-Pentecostal churches established the International Fellowship of Christian Churches (IFCC) in 1985 under the leadership of Edmund Roepert of the Hatfield Christian Church (Pretoria) and Ray McCauley of the Rhema Bible Church (Johannesburg). There are other associations for neo-Pentecostal churches as well, such as Fred Roberts's Christian Centers, called Christian Fellowships International, Derek Crumpton's Foundation Ministries, and Dudley Daniels's New Covenant Ministries (Anderson and Pillay, "Segregated Spirit," 237).

11. Lee, "Future of Global Christianity," 105.

12. Keener and Carroll, "Introduction," 1. Schmidgall, *European Pentecostalism*, 4 states that 15 million Africans were Pentecostals, 33 million South Americans, 9,5 million Asians, 5 million North Americans, 3 million Europeans, and half a million Australians.

13. Berger, "Four Faces," 425. The Atlas of Pentecostalism (http://www.atlasofpentecostalism.net/, 216; accessed 2020-01-28) asserts that one quarter of the two billion Christians in the world are now members of a Pentecostal church, compared to 6 percent in 1980. It has become the largest Christian tradition after Roman Catholicism. It is growing at a rate of 13 million new adherents a year.

and Pentecostals are estimated to constitute one-third of Christians and 11 percent of the global population.

A movement that gained popularity during the last half century and eventually realized in the neo-Pentecostal independent church movement emphasized faith, prosperity, victory, health and wealth, and became known among its opponents by various pejorative terms, like the Health and Wealth, and Name it and Claim It movement, while others refer to the Faith, Word of Faith or prosperity gospel movement. It is connected today to international ministries of celebrities like Creflo Dollar, Kenneth Hagin, Leroy Thompson, Mike Murdock, A.A. Allen, Joyce Meyer, Benny Hinn, Morris Cerullo, John Avanzini, Robert Tilton, Charles Capps, Duncan Williams, T.D. Jakes, and Joel Osteen in the USA, and Benson Idahosa, David Oyedepo, Chris Oyakhilome, Enoch Adeboye, Mathew Oshomolowo (Ashimolowo), Nevers Mumba, Mensa Otabil, Duncan Williams, Sam Korankye Ankrah, Charles Agyin Asare, Dag Heward-Mill, and T.B. Joshua in Africa. The independence that characterizes the movement makes it difficult to fathom the extensiveness of the movement, and many macro, large and small congregations fall into this category, mostly without identifying with each other in any other way than in the message they preach. Most of the churches are independent and nondenominational and their pastors do not advertise themselves as "prosperity preachers," even though they preach regularly about finances, health, victory, and wealth. Some of the congregations are mega-churches while others constitute small groups. They are backed up by millions of people around the world who watch their favorite televangelists who proclaim a fervent prosperity gospel. Today a dozen or more of the prosperity teachers had become household names in Africa and some of them hail from the USA, including Joyce Meyer, T.D. Jakes, Creflo Dollar, Joel Osteen, and Frederick Price.

The prosperity gospel cannot be interpreted in terms of fundamentalism, Pentecostalism, or Evangelicalism although the message about holistic salvation shows affinities with theological conservatism. It is also not correct to equate the Faith movement with the charismatic movement or with Pentecostalism *per se*.[14] It thrives in diverse social situations, from

---

14. As Hanegraaff, *Christianity in Crisis*, 13 emphasizes. The sociologist, Ebenezer Obadare, is one of many who equate Pentecostalism without further qualification with prosperity theology, e.g., in stating that Pentecostal churches seem to have placed an indecorous emphasis on wealth and personal accumulation (Obadare, "'Raising Righteous Billionaires,'" 1), and then asking what the emphasis on prosperity says about

groups mostly comprised of middle class and wealthy members to congregations consisting mostly of the poorest of the poor. A Pew Research survey shows that 43 percent of all Christian respondents agreed that the faithful qualified to receive health and wealth from God, across all social divides, while nearly 75 percent of Latino believers agreed with the statement, "God will grant financial success and good health to all believers who have enough faith."[15]

Kate Bowler argues that the prosperity gospel centers around four themes, faith, wealth, health, and victory.[16] It is not only concerned with prosperity. It is the link with the other elements of salvation that makes the theology so attractive for Africans, with holistic salvation as an important element of their primal spirituality. "Seldom if ever, has there been a gospel that has promised so much, and demanded so little."[17] Faith serves as the activator or power that releases spiritual forces and turns the spoken word into reality, allowing Africans with a traditional worldview consisting of invisible forces directly influencing the visible world to appease evil forces and remain on the side of the good forces. A person's faith is palpably demonstrated in wealth, health and victory. Material reality is the measure of the success of immaterial faith.[18] Faith is supposed to be marked by victory—no circumstances can stop believers from being victorious financially and in terms of their health because their faith allows them to live in total victory on earth. Faith is calculated by the outcome of a successful life.

---

the character of Pentecostalism *per se* (Obadare, "'Raising Righteous Billionaries,'" 2).

15. Pew Research, "Changing Faiths: Latinos and the Transformation of American Religion," 25 April 2007, https://www.pewforum.org/2007/04/25/changing-faiths-latinos-and-the-transformation-of-american-religion-2/; accessed 2019-12-10. See the remark of Gifford, "Expecting Miracles," 20 that the Pentecostal churches that do grow have one thing on common, and that is their focus on achieving success. The focus on success also explains the enormous popularity that the prayer of Jabez enjoys in African churches. Although Jabez was named "born in pain," he cried out to God in his adult life to bless him and enlarge his territory, and keep him from harm so that he might be free of pain. God granted his request and he became well-known for his successful life (1 Chron 4:9–10). Bruce Wilkerson's (*Prayer of Jabez*) book on the prayer of Jabez sold well in Africa as well as in the rest of the pentecostal world (see also Quayesi, "Pentecostalism and the Transformation," 111).

16. Bowler, *Blessed*, 19.

17. McConnell, *Different Gospel*, xix.

18. Hence the remark of Folarin, "Contemporary State," 91 that the prosperity gospel is characterized by the tendency to equate material prosperity with the salvation of the soul, and material success with divine favor.

In her autobiography, Kate Bowler who did excellent post-graduate studies on the prosperity movement, states that the prosperity message is a theodicy, an explanation for the problem of evil.[19] The question that presents itself to most Christian believers one time or another is, why are some people blessed and others not? Why are some believers healed and others not? Why are some Christians prosperous while others languish in poverty? The prosperity gospel looks at the world as believers experience it, as unfair to some people, and promises a solution. It guarantees that faith will always make a way, that unlocking the spiritual laws will always lead to health and wealth. The prosperity gospel has a simple way of explaining why life as it is must be inherently just. God had established a set of principles that keeps the world in order. Examples of such laws are the laws of confession, agreement (where two or more agree in corporate prayer, the answer is guaranteed), tithing, first fruits, and seed faith and life. These spiritual laws offer an elegant solution to the problem of unfairness by creating a Newtonian universe in which the chaos of the world seems reducible to simple cause and effect. There is no such thing as undeserved pain and no tragedy can occur in the life of the believer.[20]

There is diversity in the proclamation of the prosperity message, making it possible to distinguish between a hard and soft prosperity message. Hard prosperity evaluates people's faith by their immediate circumstances, while soft prosperity appraises believers with a gentler, more roundabout assessment. Materiality is inscribed with spiritual meaning.

The desire for a good life is basic to all people, including the wish that all things would go well with them. If what is happening to a person is influenced or even determined by what cannot be seen, it becomes critical that one is able to retain the goodwill of good powers and try to appease the bad forces. In Africa, "prosperity" means for a lot of people "survival;" they need the basic necessities to sustain life. Prosperity cannot

---

19. Bowler, *Everything Happens*, xiii. The Lausanne Theology Working Group Statement on Prosperity Gospel, published in 2010 after two years of consultation, states correctly that the unbiblical notion that spiritual welfare can be measured in terms of material welfare as an integral element of this theodicy should be rejected (discussed in Heuser, "Charting African Prosperity Gospel Economies," 1). Prosperity teachers, it states, exploit the poor, distort the Scriptures, and partake in and promote greed (see Bledsoe, "Prosperity Theology," 302). It should be stated again categorically that this might be true in terms of certain individuals and groups, but it is most certainly not applicable to all of neo-Pentecostalism.

20. Bowler, *Everything Happens*, 25-6.

be equated with naked greed in Africa without further qualification.[21] The important distinction between the Western and African definitions of prosperity should be kept in mind and will be discussed in detail in the following chapters.

A Short History of the Prosperity Gospel

To understand the gospel of prosperity one should go back to the early twentieth century and the way some people thought about spiritual power. They taught that one who acts in accordance with divine principles and relies on the mind to transform thought and speech experiences blessing upon blessing in all aspects of life. The teaching was called mind-cure, positive thinking, self-help, and success literature as part of the New Thought movement. Dan McConnell as well as Jean and John Comoraff are correct in their assertion that the faith theology is not a product of the Pentecostal and charismatic movements, but can be traced historically to cultic sources.[22] The marriage between pentecostal spirituality and New Thought was enacted by E.W. Kenyon (1867-1948), at first a Methodist minister who left the church and founded several churches which he linked to the Baptist church. It started with Ralph Waldo Emerson's philosophical idealism,[23] Swedish mystic Emmanuel Swedenborg's Neo-

21. See also the discussion of an African definition of prosperity in chapter 5. Only the uninformed label all African prosperity leaders as unscrupulous manipulators who are greedy for wealth and power; many (most?) of them preach the gospel message of conversion and repentance effectively, reaching many of Africa's population (Phiri and Maxwell, "Gospel Riches," 29). Spiritual insight is necessary to evaluate the movement in a balanced way.

22. McConnell, *Different Gospel*, xx; Comaroff and Comaroff, "Privatizing the Millennium," 42. A cult is defined here as any religious movement which claims the backing of Christ or the Bible, but distorts the central message of Christianity by an additional revelation, and by displacing a fundamental tenet of the faith with a secondary matter (Lewis, *Confronting the Cults*, 4). Prosperity theology conforms to this definition. Hanegraaff, *Christianity in Crisis*, 9 includes among the cults such groups as the Church of the Latter-Day Saints, the Watchtower Bible and Tract Society, and the Church of Religious Science, evaluated from a theological perspective.

23. See McConnell, *Different Gospel*, 34-42 for a more extensive discussion of Ralph Waldo Emerson's philosophy, especially as popularized by Charles Wesley Emerson, an admirer of his views of Transcendentalism which he combined with the basic tenets of social Darwinism. Emerson provided a *smorgasbord* of the sources underlying New Thought metaphysics: Platonism, Swedenborgianism, New England Unitarianism, and Emersonian Transcendentalism. These elements were held together by proof-texting from the Bible and a quasi-Darwinian view of the religious evolution of humanity which

platonic theory of correspondence, and Helena Blavatsky's theosophical quest for uniform spiritual laws, while Phineas Parkhust Quimby (1802-1866), an American hypnotist and spiritualist, applied the mind thought ideas to healing. Mary Baker Eddy filtered Quimby's insight of the power of the mind over the body through a Christological framework, arguing in her Christian Science that Jesus did not come to the world to save the world through his death, but by teaching human beings right or correct thinking. Reality as perceived is illusory; illness and death do not exist and suffering results from mental errors. What people need, is to be re-educated. Quimby taught that all sickness and disease originate in the mind, healing can be obtained with the right thinking,[24] Jesus was an ordinary man using mind-control methods to heal, and that was Jesus' secret to success. Hypnotism is the key to all healing. He denied the bodily resurrection of Christ. Quimby became the father of New Thought, including groups such as Religious Science, Christian Science, and the Unity School of Christianity.[25]

New Thought assumed an essential unity between God and humanity; human beings' separation from God was only a matter of degree. The world should be reimagined as thought rather than substance, emphasizing the mind's power to create reality, in the same way that divine creative powers function. The spiritual world forms reality and its creation is contingent upon the mind. What is needed is a spiritual or sacred alignment with the divine within human beings that consists of a mystical connection or divinization of the human. People share God's power to create by means of their right thinking, as God created the world through God's

---

ended in the human becoming god (McConnell, *Different Gospel*, 35).

24. In the same vein, David Oyedepo teaches that Job's suffering was prolonged because he wrongly accused God instead of rebuking Satan to get out of this situation he found himself in. Oyedepo says that Job did not realize that to be sick was against God's will because he did not realize the deception of Satan. "Every sickness is an oppression of the devil, not a lesson from God." In the same manner, if someone is not experiencing prosperity, it is because they have given Satan authority over their life. God will not do anything at all unless the person invites or releases God to do it from them (quoted in Ntui-Abung, *Chaos of the Prosperity Gospel*, 23). This view of God leaves little room for the transcendent and holy God who rules sovereignly over the universe, including human affairs and the lives of individual believers. The idea that a human being can compel God to do anything is anathema when one has a clear view on what the Bible teaches about God's sovereignty.

25. Hinn, *God, Greed*, 153; Hanegraaff, *Christianity in Crisis*, 15.

thoughts or words.[26] Positive thoughts lead directly to positive circumstances, and negative thoughts are responsible for negative situations.[27]

In a time when medical treatment did not offer many solutions to health problems, New Thought initially concentrated on providing a religious alternative to healing. Through prayer and right thinking, believers could access supernatural powers to get control over circumstances that they were unhappy about. In the process some of them tried to manipulate God to produce the desired results.

Although Essek W. Kenyon did not accept the full metaphysics of New Thought, he used its ideas to produce a new theology based on the rightful use of divine principles that could unlock God's blessings for believers. He taught the priority of the authority of the Bible, the necessity of the experience of new birth for every convert, the subsequent need for sanctification, and the necessity that all believers should partake in the evangelizing task of the church. He subscribed to the doctrine of entire sanctification at a calculable moment, as John Wesley taught, that God's grace sets believers on the road to perfect love and the ability to have no inclination to sin.

Kenyon argued that the death of Christ did not only secure sanctification but also many other blessings. The Fall in the garden of Eden cancelled the guarantees that God gave Adam and Eve, depriving them of the abundant life that God had initially created them for, and resulted in poverty, disease and death. The atonement restored the lost rights and privileges and makes the believer a legal shareholder of the divine rights, notably the right to perfect health and prosperity.[28] Now the believer should demand God's blessings because they are entitled to receive what

---

26. In the words of Myles Munroe, "Praise the Lord, you create your own world the same way God created his. He speaks and things happen; you speak and they happen" (quoted in Hanegraaff, *Christianity in Crisis*, 407). See also https://www.joelosteen.com/Pages/Article.aspx?articleid=6505; accessed 2020-01-30.

27. The essential New Thought beliefs can be characterized as follows: it emphasizes the immanence of God, the divine nature of man, the spiritual character of the universe, and the fact that sin, human disorders, and human disease are basically matters of incorrect thinking. Jesus was only a teacher and healer who proclaimed the kingdom as being within a person. It increasingly stresses material prosperity as one result of New Thought. It implies a kind of monism, or oneness with the world, while it also has gnostic elements and sees a dualism of matter and spirit that underlies the universe. Spiritual healing and strength of mind and body are available only to those who share this knowledge and who has been initiated into the movement at some time (McConnell, *Different Gospel*, 39).

28. Akiri, "The Prosperity Gospel."

was given to Adam and Eve, as part of the benefits of the atonement of Christ. The ontological shift from sinner to saint in a moment signaled only the first element of redemption; the cross also signified many other benefits already granted that should be appropriated by the believer.

Human beings were primarily spirits; the physical body and the surrounding world was a material reflection of a deeper reality, the pre-existing spiritual universe. By choosing to sin, the first human beings came under the legal authority of the author of sin and which consequently led to illness, poverty, and death. Now human beings could not access nor understand God's revelation or guarantee of blessings for them. Christ's resurrection unlocked these blessings because it united humanity's spiritual nature with God's own and gave them legal authority to rule over the earth. Now it has become possible to get things legally in place so God's will can be done on the earth.[29]

Divine union becomes the starting point for the Christian life because believers had become the shareholders of all the rights and privileges God intended for them. They were supermen in the embryo; what they now needed was to learn the inner workings of dominating faith. In the words of E.W. Kenyon, "When these truths really gain the ascendancy in us, they will make us spiritual supermen, masters of demons and disease . . . It will be the end of weakness and failure. There will be no more struggle for faith, for all things are ours. There will be no more praying for power, for He is in us . . . In the presence of these tremendous realities, we arise and take our place. We go out and live as supermen indwelt by God."[30] They are bombarded by data from the senses that relate to the natural world and they must be trained to perceive revelation knowledge buried underneath. What they need, is faith that consists of the confident assurance of the fact that everything is already provided for through the operation of certain immutable laws. "Faith-filled words" brought the

---

29. Henderson, *Operating in the Courts*, 27. The argument is based on the supposition that human beings can hinder God's will to happen on earth by not complying to laws and principles that are described in the Bible, while their compliance serves to compel God to do for them what they desire, which establishes a deity that can be manipulated by human beings and that made itself manipulable by revealing such laws in the Bible. The same author explains in this regard, "God has given mankind freedom of choice and therefore he can do nothing unless we give him the legal right" (Henderson, *Operating in the Courts*, 41). A human being can limit God in God's sovereign rule over the universe because God can do nothing without humans' consent!

30. Quoted in McConnell, *Different Gospel*, 21.

universe into being and governed the world as an invisible force. The power of the spoken word is needed to carry faith to the desired results.[31]

Jesus transferred power of attorney to those who operate according to the principles he had come to demonstrate. By using his name, believers' prayers took on binding legal qualities. Whatever they demanded in the name of Jesus (John 14:14), God provided, whether it was healing, deliverance, daily needs, or speaking in tongues.[32] Faith-filled believers who had learnt to speak positively to any difficult situation in the name of Jesus became powerful conduits through which God's power could flow to the world.[33] The name of Jesus is seen in the same way as the blood of Jesus, as containing magical values to scare away demonic powers, and grant forgiveness of sins, healing, and prosperity.[34]

---

31. David Oyedepo Jnr. in a sermon entitled "Vital keys to unlocking the supernatural," states that many spiritual people are not Spirit-conscious (https://www.youtube.com/watch?v=Tgq33sC025U; accessed 2020-01-02). Although a Spirit-conscious and Spirit-driven person looks like any other ordinary person, they are not because inside them is a God-being, a God-kind of mankind, a God-model of the human being. They have become spirit like Adam at the beginning. No one could harm Adam while he was in the garden. He had the authority to give names to everything God had created but none of these creatures could threaten him, and no outside evil force was able to influence him. Adam got his authority from the Spirit of God that was his spirit as well. What believers need is that the Spirit should take dominion over their lives, that they develop their spirits to become the Spirit of God. They need the mentality of the supernatural, a mental state where the supernatural is their natural state. Then no accidents could touch them and they could not get ill. They will be untouchable and indestructible. They will do greater things than Jesus did while he was ministering on earth, as Jesus in John 14:12 promises. Jesus states that no man could take his life from him if he did not lay it down himself. In the same sense, believers are not natural and they are not exposed to natural or evil forces. They need never be limited to the natural again but they should start operating in the supernatural.

32. See the sermon of David Oyedepo, "What is in the name of Jesus," that explains the way the prosperity message uses the name of Jesus to ensure successes of health and wealth (https://www.youtube.com/watch?v=oGm9d2JNK4M; accessed 2019-12-27).

33. For fuller detail, see Kenyon, *Two Kinds of Faith*.

34. See Henderson, *Operating in the Courts*, 71-80 for a more extensive discussion of the "power" of the blood of Jesus. The impression is created that blood has a voice that calls out to God, independent of the body to which it belongs, in line with the belief in parts of the Old Testament that the blood of a murdered person literally called out to God for revenge, and that blood that was not covered with dust after slaughtering a beast also called out to God. Henderson asserts that there are several voices that reach God's ears and that believers can utilize these voices effectively to get their prayers answered. These voices serve as mediators to God's presence. Such voices include the blood of Jesus, the mediator of the new covenant, the spirit of the just men made perfect, God as the judge of all (it is not clear at all what the author intends

Kenyon's high anthropology can be described in various ways, as human potential elevated to the maximum so that humans could achieve salvation even without connecting with God through a mediator,[35] Finished Work theology, a priority on spiritual reality, the power of thought expressed in word and deed, the importance of the correct use of the name of Jesus, and the belief that the believer shares in God's creationist power, implying that they can acquire the same power that God used to create the universe and use it to attain all that God promised through the atonement. Although he did not embrace the Pentecostal movement, his relationships with and influence on some of the leading Pentecostal leaders of his day, like William Durham, Aimee Semple McPherson, John G. Lake and F.F. Bosworth, ensured that his voice was heard across the pentecostal world.

For instance, F.F. Bosworth taught that healing was believers' legal right, secured by Christ, and accelerated through spiritual effects of positive words. Confession brings believers' words into reality before the healing is seen. What was needed was that believers should act according to their positive words, as though healed already. For that reason, they should never pray that God should heal them if it was God's will because it marred God's self-imposed promise to heal all who called on God.[36]

If believers prayed but did not get healed, various reasons were given that took the focus from the minister of healing and put the responsibility squarely on the shoulders of the sick person. Thus people stayed sick because they made a negative confession, associated with people who made negative statements, did not have enough faith, or they had touched the Lord's anointed, that is, the prosperity teacher.[37] The idea of the Lord's inviolable anointed one comes from 1 Samuel 24:6, where David had the opportunity to kill the king who was trying to kill him but argued that the king had been anointed by the Lord and David was not in the position to touch him. Costi Hinn remembers a remark in a sermon that stated, "When a man is anointed by God, don't touch him! Even if that man is a devil, the office he functions within is anointed. Don't speak against

---

with this), the church of the firstborn registered in heaven, the general assembly, an innumerable company of angels, the city of the living God, and finances. The "voices" are deduced from the book of Revelation; its use to construct a logical argument is not clear at all (Henderson, *Operating in the Courts*, 69-70).

35. Akiri, "The Prosperity Gospel."
36. Bosworth, *Christ the Healer*; *Christ the Healer: Sermons*.
37. Hinn, *God, Greed*, 49.

him or you'll be cursed!"[38] A key teaching of prosperity theology is the culture of honor and reverence, stating that people who wanted a special anointing needed to come under a certain preacher's ministry, and such an anointed man of God is to be revered on an almost godlike level. This is more than the respect earned by local pastors; it consists of doing anything and everything the man of God wants in order to get what you need.[39] It implies also that the man of God could ask whatever money he wanted because he was the ultimate authority, standing between God and the needy person and mediating the answers to prayers.

In this sense, such prosperity teachers become cult leaders, having ultimate veto power to end marriages before they even began, excommunicate people even when they had done nothing wrong, and trump what the Bible said anytime by stating that God told them something directly.

John G. Lake (1870-1935), responsible for establishing the Apostolic Faith Mission of South Africa (AFM of SA) along with Thomas Hezmalhalch, taught that God intended human beings to be gods, as John 10:43 supposedly states. The inner man was nothing less than a god, governing over the world because the God-power has won over soul-force in the nature of the believer.[40]

It is true that many early Pentecostals hailed from all economic sections of society although many of them were poor and uneducated. They defined their status as citizens of a new world that they awaited with much expectation, emphasizing the imminent second coming of Christ in a premillennialist and later also dispensationalist fashion. Worldly luxuries and comforts had lost their attraction for them. At the same time, they practiced divine healing, emphasizing the importance of the material body and its restoration while still living on earth. In this way, they contradicted their eschatological sentiments; the issues of eschatological judgment, the expectation of an imminent *parousia*, and heaven and hell received very little attention, if at all.[41]

Many of them started using the terms "positive words," "faith," "prayer in the name of Jesus," and "positive thinking," following in the footsteps of New Thought and E.W. Kenyon, and it was a short step from positive confession about health to apply the principles to wealth and

---

38. Hinn, *God, Greed*, 78.
39. Hinn, *God, Greed*, 117.
40. See Lake, *John G. Lake Sermons*; *Spiritual Hunger*.
41. Asamoah-Gyadu, "Learning to Prosper," 66.

prosperity as well, claiming that Jesus' promises included the benefits of prosperity when mystical alignment with the divine is reached.

The 1940s and 1950s saw the American economy blooming, medical science making much progress, and many Americans experiencing optimism about the future. At the same time, Pentecostal evangelists unveiled laws of financial returns that secure God's blessings for those aligning themselves with these principles.[42] Truths became techniques, waiting to be applied by those equipped with the necessary knowledge. High self-esteem, health, finances, and divine power became transferable goods guaranteed by God to believers and awaiting their appropriation through faith and positive confession.

During this period another development in the form of the Latter Rain movement took place within the ranks of revival Pentecostalism. It centered on power in healing, prophecy, laying on of hands, and the restoration of the fivefold ecclesial offices mentioned in Ephesians 4:11–13, of apostles, prophets, evangelists, pastors and teachers, with the purpose to equip the saints for the work of ministry, for building up the body of Christ.[43] The movement was called the Latter Rain movement because of its assertion that the last outpouring of the Spirit that preceded the second coming of Christ would include the restoration of these five offices, what was happening then, as Joel 2:23 predicted. The relation of this movement to the New Apostolic Reformation will be discussed later in the chapter.

Now classical Pentecostalism had grown into a movement that taught its adherents to be ambitious about upward mobility.[44] At the same time, they looked for the approval of society, other established mainline churches, and the government. In the process, they made an alliance with evangelicalism (in the USA, by establishing together the National Association of Evangelicals in 1942), and as a result they started acting in ways that did not alienate themselves from other churches, as they previously

---

42. Bowler, *Blessed*, 52.

43. The early Pentecostal movement also emphasized the significance of apostles, but then in the tradition of the original apostles as eyewitnesses of Jesus' ministry and healings. This was so important for them that the early Azusa Street congregation was called the Apostolic Faith Gospel Mission, and across the world missionaries from Azusa Street established denominations that contained the name "Apostolic," and in many cases these groups also referred to themselves as "Missions" and not churches, to distinguish themselves from traditional churches.

44. According to Kalu, *African Pentecostalism*, Pentecostalism is not only a religion for upward social mobility but it also contributed to a culture that domesticized men and challenged and changed the traditional role of the sexes.

had done.[45] In order to be acceptable for their new partners they toned down the volume of their worship services, introduced Evangelicals' way of singing with choirs and organs, established a professional pastorate that was theologically trained, and accepted the evangelical's hermeneutics of the Bible as the final authority, infallible and inerrant, true and reliable in all it addresses.

Later the emerging prosperity theology would ease the tension between Pentecostals' traditional otherworldliness and a consumerist culture that developed after the Second World War where personal consumption propelled the economy forward.[46] Now the healing revival also sputtered and died, in the early 1960s, with new gains in medicine and nutrition that proved so successful that healing miracles started to dry up, and more and more believers turned to doctors for medical help.

During the 1950s and 1960s, metaphysical mind thought and mind power was repackaged into positive thinking, emphasizing a psychological cast and a cheerful and well-ordered mind. For instance, Norman Vincent Peale (1898-1993), a North American Methodist minister, wrote books with simple self-help instructions, making abstract theology into workable wisdom. By using psychological categories, he caught the attention of many Christians and contributed to the development of pastoral psychology that integrated religion with scientific methods. The pragmatism of his approach also attracted many Pentecostals who were interested in all things practical rather that the abstract theologizing that they attributed to "theologians" operating in mainline established traditions.

In his *The Power of Positive Thinking* (1952), Peale taught that God's power could be harnessed by a spirit and method by which human beings could control, and even determine their circumstances. Any person could do it, by accessing God's power through positive thinking, which directed spiritual energy toward the attainment of health, self-esteem, and business acumen. The book promises the reader the necessary formulas, recipes, patterns of thought, and the resultant release of power through the use of effective words. Positive thinking was systematized into the formula: "picturize, prayerize, and actualize." The book represents the aspirations of middle-class Americans for upward mobility in the context of consumerism, a basic ingredient of the American economy.

---

45. Robeck, "National Association of Evangelicals," 634-36.

46. Walter Benjamin, "Kunstwerk in Zeitalter" makes the provocative remark that capitalism functions as a religion, suggesting that capitalist consumer culture has developed into a new kind of undogmatic cult worshiping the secret "god of debt."

An authoritative study has not been done on the influence of positive thinkers like Peale and Pentecostal revivalists on each other, but it seems as if the two traditions at times overlapped in the post-war years. The Full Gospel Business Men's Fellowship International, under the leadership of Demos Shakarian and prominent Pentecostal businessman S. Lee Braxton, for one, was devoted to positive thinking, parading athletes, corporate giants, itinerant revivalists and politicians before their audience of new capitalists, representing an ideo-financial center to delineate prosperity theology.[47]

As the healing movement subsided in the 1960s, revival tents were traded for churches, and healing for prosperity. Wealth and health were combined to form the abundancy of life promised by Jesus for all believers. The adolescence of the prosperity gospel had arrived in the Pentecostal movement, influencing the movement worldwide. The number of faith-building ministries that were devoted to financial prosperity increased and Kenneth Hagin was established as an authority, along with Oral Roberts. Hagin was an evangelist and pastor in the Assemblies of God from 1938 to 1962. Roberts' university and Hagin's Rhema Bible Training Center, both in Tulsa, Oklahoma, influenced Pentecostals across the board. The teaching and ritual enactments of tithes and divine reciprocity turned into blessings covenants, prosperity covenants, and miracle partnerships to finance missions and eventually into wholesale prosperity with the pact of plenty, the promise of financial blessing to those who donated that proves God's faithfulness.[48] Believers were encouraged to test their financial faith and earn their own proof by parting with their hard-earned pennies. Agricultural imagery entered the discourse with "abundance" and "harvest," "seed faith," fruit, grain, and gleaming coins attempting to convince believers to trust God for more by giving more.[49]

Kenneth Copeland (1936-) completed his studies at Oral Roberts University and Oral Roberts himself launched Copeland's ministry.

---

47. Heuser, "Charting African Prosperity Gospel Economies," 3.

48. Heuser, "Charting African Prosperity Gospel Economies," 2.

49. Ntui-Abung, *Chaos of the Prosperity Gospel*, 43 speaks of the prosperity message's "fixation" on the act of giving, betraying a main motif in the movement, to generate money, primarily for its leaders. Although the motivation for giving is at times to provide in the needs of humankind and to finance the proclamation of the gospel to the world, the emphasis remains on giving for selfish motives, to qualify for receiving God's riches, and the balance statements of many of the prosperity preachers show where they spend most of the money, on themselves. A lack of accountability creates room for such abuse of donors' contributions.

Copeland accepted Hagin's teaching of positive confession, that the spoken word brought circumstances into reality. Kenneth and Gloria Copeland established their ministry in 1967 and contributed to the popularity of the prosperity gospel, along with the Reverend Frederick J. Eikerenkoetter, better known as Reverend Ike, the first black spokesperson of the prosperity message with a national platform. Reverend Ike blew new life into Peale's positive thinking with promises of material wealth, channeling mind-power toward tangible results. He preached that believers should change their circumstances rather than rely on heavenly rewards: "Don't wait for your pie in the sky by and by; have it now with ice cream and a cherry on top."[50] He guaranteed material wealth for the right-thinking Christian.

The American economy bloomed during the 1960s and 1970s, making it possible for many Americans to become prosperous. At the same time, *glossolalia* and other charismatic phenomena that characterized the Pentecostal movement were carried into the heart of established mainline churches, beginning with Episcopalians and Lutherans and eventually influencing the Presbyterians, Mennonites, American Baptists, United Methodists, and Roman Catholics who awakened to charismatic influences.

At first Pentecostals were confounded by the widespread attention to the use of holy tongues while theologians devoted new interest in the Holy Spirit as a subject for investigation. The charismatic movement within established churches had a diverse leadership and no person or idea could claim to represent the center. In this situation, the prosperity gospel became one of several solutions for an experimental generation, sharing in the new ecumenism that grew from the charismatic movement and some established churches' acceptance of Pentecostals. Prosperity teachers stood outside any organized denomination and served to stand in the gap between the charismatic world and Pentecostals. They utilized television effectively to such an extent that by 1980, the market share of prosperity gospel came close to a theological monopoly.[51]

Prosperity gospel claimed to transform invisible faith into financial rewards. It was a palpable gospel that could be demonstrated, seen and measured in the financial well-being of its participants. Kenneth Copeland preached, "The gospel to the poor is that Jesus has come and they

---

50. In Walton, *Watch This!*, 50.
51. Horsfield, *Religious Television*, 88-100.

don't have to be poor anymore!"[52] Salvation begins in the here and now, with the materiality of redemption in tangible changed circumstances. Historically, Pentecostals expected that signs and wonders would follow the preaching of the full gospel, as anticipation of God's reign. God's kingdom was not already here but it realized with people accepting the good news of Jesus Christ. A supernatural trail would follow the preaching of the authentic gospel. The prosperity gospel elaborated on this expectation by including as part of the signs and wonders that believers could expect also financial well-being. Financial abundance and good health were public and perpetual demonstrations of Christians' spiritual progress.[53] Prosperity and health were two sides of the same coin. "Full gospel" was defined as prosperity, also in Africa.[54] Sickness and lack should be refused in the lives of believers. During the 1980s, prosperity gospel exploded and became one of the foremost Christian theologies of modern living. Its emphasis on Christian self-improvement tempered its hard prosperity into a soft prosperity image.[55] Now several African American leaders also became prominent as prosperity teachers, including Keith Butler, James Hash, Frederick K.C. Price, Carlton Pearson, Ed Montgomery, Charles Harrell, Mack Timberlake, Phillip Goudeaux, and Lamont McLean.

Most classic Pentecostals were lukewarm about the teachings of prosperity teachers and their denominations did not encourage the message. Some prosperity teachers responded by stating that they were teaching the same message as the pioneers and founders of the Pentecostal movement, and the claim is true at least as far as John G. Lake was concerned, as the publication of Lake's collected works demonstrates.[56]

By the 1980s, prosperity teachers associated with Donald McGravan, C. Peter Wagner, and their institutional home, Fuller Theological Seminary's School of World Mission had risen as natural experts in increase. The faith movement's emphasis on results and the materiality

52. Copeland, *Poverty*, 10.
53. Bowler, *Blessed*, 90.
54. Folarin, "Contemporary State," 74.
55. See, e.g., the distinction that Gaiya, "Charismatic and Pentecostal Social Orientations," 63-4 makes among neo-Pentecostal churches between centripetal churches that channel human and financial resources into the church, not using it for social and human development, and centrifugal churches that tend to employ resources for such development.
56. Lake, *John G. Lake: The Complete Collection*.

of salvation easily absorbed the goal of church growth as a sign of its own faithfulness.[57] Prosperity megachurches utilized the seeker-sensitive model, minimizing "churchlike" features in their buildings such as steeples, stained glass, or crosses in favor of bricks, steel, and glass that characterized corporate headquarters and opening itself up to the criticism that it represented truth in a way that accommodated corporate pandering to keep people coming back for more. The seeker-driven Jesus was a blue-eyed white man who made life better by providing in the realization of the American dream. He was easy to follow and offered a golden ticket to heaven, and a golden ride on the way.[58] Actually, he brought heaven to the earth by providing in the desires of all believers. Going to church became as comfortable and interesting as trips to the shopping mall. Successful churches implemented proven marketing strategies and viewed their church as a product and their worshippers as consumers. Church campuses were built near freeways and interstates to make them easily accessible and each congregation tailored their product to capitalize on their target audience in their niche market, hoping to capture the largest market share, using the language of business marketing.

Prosperity leaders also cultivated transnational connections and widened their influence across the globe. David Yonggi Cho became the patron of prosperity preachers and a popular conference speaker across the world with several other international speakers with high profiles.

Prosperity Teachings

Confession is defined in the Faith movement as affirming something believers believe in, testifying to something they know, and witnessing for a truth that they have embraced.[59] The secret to confession is to know the nature and extent of the perfect redemption in Christ, to know one's "identity" and "rights and privileges" in Christ, and to confess verbally the provision of Christ in every need and problem of life. What is needed to produce the required results is to make contact with the power of God, to turn it on, and to believe that the power is coming into use and accept it by faith, acting as though it already happened.[60] "What we believe is a

---

57. Bowler, *Blessed*, 113.
58. Hinn, *God, Greed*, 155.
59. McConnell, *Different Gospel*, 135.
60. Sanford, *Healing Light*.

result of our thinking. If we think wrong things, we will believe wrong things . . . If we believe wrong things, our confession will be wrong. In other words, what we say will be wrong and it will all hinge on our thinking."[61] Positive confession flows from a positive mental attitude (PMA), based on the supposition that reality is the sum total of whatever a human being thinks it to be. Humans possess the innate ability to shape and reshape reality through the powers of their mind and their words. What we think, we actually express in words; and our words bring about in our life and affairs whatever we put into them. Faith is nothing more nor less than the operation of the thought forces in the form of an earnest desire, coupled with expectation as to its fulfilment. One does not find any reference in this way of thinking to the will of God. The believer is not concerned with pursuing God's will but is engaged in realizing own personal desires. To the degree of faith that one's earnest desires would be met is continually held to and watered by firm expectations, in just that degree does it either draw to itself, or does it change from the unseen into the visible, from the spiritual into the material, that for which it is sent.[62] It is clear that the Faith theology internalizes the deity; the human being becomes the one who creates reality by faith.

During the post-war time of revivals and tent campaigns, the nascent theology of mind-power went from being a minor theme to one of major significance. The new electrified view of faith became the avenue to wealth, happiness, and creaturely comforts alongside health and healing. Prosperity theology gained momentum and within a single generation changed the face of Pentecostalism through an expanding network of magazines, crusades and conferences, Bible schools and manuals.[63]

61. Hagin, *Right and Wrong Thinking*, 3. David Oyedepo Jnr. in a sermon entitled "Vital keys to unlocking the supernatural," states the need for Christians to change their thinking in order to change their lifestyle (https://www.youtube.com/watch?v=Tgq33sC025U; accessed 2020-01-02). They need to saturate their lives with the word of God, in the words of Phil 4:8, by thinking about the things that enable them to live a supernatural life. A favorite verse of the preacher is Prov 4:32, that what comes out of the heart is what comes out of one's life ("Keep thy heart with all diligence; For out of it are the issues of life," in the KJV, the translation that all prosperity teachers prefer, betraying their conservative hermeneutical stance).

62. Trine, *In Tune*, 32-3.

63. Mark Hutchinson ("'Fools and Fundamentalists," 234) writing about the dilemma of institutionalization in the Australian Pentecostal movement, asserts that the organizing of conferences with leading speakers from around the globe became a proposed solution to institutionalization. The organization became the materialization of the kingdom of God, and the "conference" the voice of God. In this way, locality

Evangelists looked for effective methods that would spur God to act by inventing spiritual formulas that contained real power, from silent prayer, anointing oil, anointed handkerchiefs, laying on of hands, and the prayer of faith spoken in authoritative tones that illustrate the believer's victory over the forces of evil.[64] They emphasized the power of the spoken word: talk faith-talk, not to hope that you will get it sometime but believe that you have it now, confess what you want and believe that it is yours! Faith altered reality in the present, not in the future. Act your faith, stand up and walk, throw away your spectacles. Quit trying to believe; simply believe and act on your faith!

Faith was the switch that turned on the omnipotent power of the Lord. How did God turn faith into power? Kenneth E. Hagin (1917-2003) taught the law of faith built on two overlapping instruments of power, a legal and scientific instrument. Christianity is a legal document that grants believers rights to salvation, protection, and victory through the death of Christ. Because Jesus granted power of attorney to believers, they became entitled to use God's power as their own (in Kenyon's terms). The law of faith was the contract that secured these Christian benefits, providing the warranty deed that "the thing you have hoped for is at last yours." These legal benefits afforded believers guaranteed rights and privileges, including healing, financial security, prosperous business prospects, and happiness.[65] Believers had the right to command these blessings in Jesus' name, as promised in 3 John 2, consisting of the blessings of good health, prosperity and wealth.[66] If they failed to demonstrate God's power over poverty and ill health, they fell to live beneath their legal privileges.

The law of faith served as a universal causal agent and power that actualized events and objects in the real world because of its influence in the spiritual world. Faith corresponded to natural forces like gravity and electricity and served as invisible operators of cause and effect. It subjected the natural world to its power and existed apart from humanity although it was available to believers who took God on God's word.[67]

---

is created and connected to similar glocalities elsewhere to project an image of the materialized kingdom of God (Hutchinson, "'Fools and Fundamentalists,'" 235).

64. Bowler, *Blessed*, 56.

65. Hagin, *Biblical Keys*; *El Shaddai*; *Godliness is Profitable*; *In Him*.

66. Golo, "Africa's Poverty," 368.

67. In a sermon with the title, "Understanding the laws of success," David Oyedepo Jnr. states that natural laws determine how our world operates (https://www.youtube.

Hagin and his almost automated and magical law of faith became the powerhouse behind the prosperity gospel and the foundation of the Word of Faith movement, also referred to as the Faith Movement and Positive Confession.[68] It adopted a form of Kenyon's spiritual laws based on a universe structured by God to respond to Christian invocation. Faith served as an absolute law and a universal and uniform reality that proved itself. A believer's faith would work only when they believed so hard without wavering that God would answer their prayers and meet their needs that the faith was convincing to God. The believer's faith alone had the divine right to "compel" God to give them their hearts' desires, even if God did not want to![69] "Think of it; miracles are the result of deep (sic) in the word, not sweating or crying. Once you locate the word on any issue and comply with it, you have compelled God to confirm it."[70] The mere idea of being able to compel God to do anything, or of doing certain things correctly that forces God to act in a certain mechanized way cannot be reconciled with a biblical view of the sovereignty of God. "This is heretical and even worse than that, blasphemy against God."[71]

More and more, evangelists turned to financially focused ministries, emphasizing that John 10:10's promise of abundant life also applied to believers' financial destiny. A.A. Allen, for instance, taught that the believer had received the ability to demand God to perform a miracle for them financially.[72] He also taught the law of the tithe, that God was compelled by God's word to bless the one who tithed by refunding them in a tenfold manner.[73] "When you tithe, God gives to you. When you do not tithe, God takes it away from you." Or even more bluntly, "If you do not tithe, you live under the financial curse of God."[74] Financial miracles

---

com/watch?v=vaMSUwzTKc0; accessed 2020-01-01). Some laws are higher than others. The law of gravity keeps everything on the ground but the law of uplift allows birds and airplanes to fly, and in that sense the law of uplift subjects the law of gravity because it is a superior law. In the same manner, spiritual laws are superior above natural laws, and some superior laws are superior to other spiritual laws.

68. Bowler, *Blessed*, 57; Akiri, "The Prosperity Gospel."
69. Quoted in Ntui-Abung, *Chaos of the Prosperity Gospel*, 10.
70. Ntui-Abung, *Chaos of the Prosperity Gospel*, 28.
71. Ntui-Abung, *Chaos of the Prosperity Gospel*, 28.
72. Allen, *Secret to Scriptural Financial Success*.
73. The principle of tithes in the Bible is described, *inter alia*, in Gen 14:16-20 in the case of Abraham; Gen 28:16-22 in terms of Jacob; Lev 27:30-34; Num 18:21-24; Mal 3:10-11; Matt 23:23; Luk 11:42; 18:9-12; Heb 7:5.
74. Hanegraaff, *Christianity in Crisis*, 46.

operated under a law of divine reciprocity, based on Luke 6:38. If you wanted God to do something for you, you needed to do something for God. No money, no miracle![75] Prosperity teachers seldom recommend that their adherents give to the poor, which by the way provides the context for Luke 6:38.[76]

The prosperity gospels that emerged from mainline positive thinking's amalgamation into pentecostal thinking were based on a belief in the power of Christian speech to achieve results.[77] The themes that were emphasized included affirmative repetition, visualization, mood redirection, and voiced Scripture as prayerful and effective habits. The difference was that positive thinking referred to "principles" because of its association with psychology while prosperity preachers referred to the "power of the Holy Ghost" because of their pneumatological emphasis on evaluating reality. Another difference was that prosperity preachers did not lose their affinity for concrete mediations of God's power, such as handkerchiefs, water, olive oil, and miracle oil that along with testimonies of those saved and healed formed the context of revival campaigns that characterized the period. Oral Roberts (1918-2009) referred to "points of contact" to describe such objects used as springboards to release a person's faith toward God.[78] Olive oil served as such a symbolic "point of contact" for anointing, transferring divine power to people. Prosperity teachers used olive oil also to coerce people into giving money. The preacher would make an offer for an anointed exchange, stating that it was God's anointing that people needed for healing, money, conception of children, job promotions, and more, and it was available in exchange for a monetary offering.[79] Costi Hinn questioned his father, the brother of Benny Hinn, about the practice and his father explained that there was

---

75. Hinn, *God, Greed*, 45.

76. Horn, *From Rags to Riches*, 42. The Gospel of Luke has by far the most abundant texts on material possessions because of its prejudice for poor people (Togarasei, "African Gospreneurship," 115).

77. Bowler, *Blessed*, 72.

78. Roberts, *Holy Spirit in the Now*.

79. See, e.g., the example of a service described in Phiri and Maxwell, "Gospel Riches," 23 where the preacher challenged members to each contribute the equivalent of about USD200 in Nigerian monetary terms to open themselves to the blessings promised by the preacher, with more than 300 people swarming to the front to commit themselves to the offering, netting an instant tax-free $60,000.

nothing wrong with imparting the anointing on people's lives for their obedience and giving money for it.[80]

The very influential Word of Faith variety of Hagin's prosperity gospel was built on Romans 10:17, that faith comes by hearing, and hearing by the word of God, and concludes that the cycle of hearing and speaking activated faith. To accumulate faith, believers engaged in a perpetual process of allowing God's word to filter into their hearts by hearing and speaking it out of their mouths. It was not enough to read Scripture; one should hear what one is reading because in the act of reading aloud the believer is tied to God's power through faith.[81] What is required for maintaining faith was to subject oneself to a steady stream of God's word, requiring believers to attend the meetings of the congregation where the word of God is preached that sustain their faith. Only a steady diet of the spoken word could fertilize believers' hearts. Faith-building Scriptures, called *rhema* and distinguished from *logoi* that refer to Scriptures without those qualities, were displayed in cars, homes, and workplaces to remind believers to confess the truths multiple times a day. One reached higher levels of faith by careful attention to the spiritual act of hearing. Speaking positive things became a spiritual discipline. These affirmations released power or faith that brought the assertions into reality. Hagin taught that the first confession is of Jesus' Lordship: "I believe in my heart Jesus Christ is the Son of God. I believe He was raised from the dead for my justification. I confess Him as my Lord and Savior. Jesus is my Lord. He is dominating my life. He is guiding me. He is leading me."[82]

Evangelicals did the same when they made confession a hallmark of the conversion experience but they focused on the personal relationship

---

80. Hinn, *God, Greed*, 69. Prophet T.B. Joshua in a sermon entitled, "Value processing more than result," states that faith comes by hearing (https://www.youtube.com/watch?v=obGhSHnHtYU; accessed 2020-01-04). That is why believers need to hear about hearing anointing, blessing anointing, and deliverance anointing. Jesus always responded to those who put their demands to him. He still answers people who are hungry for the word, who meditate on the word, over and over until it forms their belief. This is what the enemy does not want them to hear. Once a believer hears the promise of God, they should put a demand on it. They should put a demand on blessing anointing and they will be blessed. They should put a demand on deliverance or healing anointing, and they will be delivered and anointed. Although Pentecostalism traditionally emphasized anointing, it was always done in terms of the anointing of the Spirit, and such a mechanistic concept of healing following automatically on reading the Bible is strange to them. It is also not a concept with biblical basis.

81. Hagin, *In Him*, 1.

82. Hagin, *In Him*, 12.

with God while Pentecostals expected to share in God's power in the exercise of their faith. Believers tapped into God's power by way of their spoken words that were expected to set the Word of God into motion.[83] However, prosperity adherents added to it and proclaimed also the availability of health, wealth, prosperity, and happiness to all those who believed God for it.

With reference to Mark 11:23, Hagin taught that whatever one declares and says without doubting one shall have. It is guaranteed that we shall have what we say. Faith becomes the force that actuates believers' very words.[84] Proverbs 18:21 became a popular text, that death and life are in the power of the tongue.[85] Speech created power and faith's confessions created realities. Name it and claim it; press the success buttons.[86] Give seed money and receive a great harvest back![87] Whatever happens in your life, positive or negative, is determined by the sound that you produce. Every obstacle on your way is awaiting your sound (your

---

83. Word theology is demonstrated in a sermon by Prophet T.B. Joshua, entitled "The secret of effective prayer" (https://www.youtube.com/watch?v=vCvQ3G4ophQ; accessed 2020-01-02). He teaches that the language of prayer is in the word of God. The word is our contact with God; one cannot contact God with one's own language because God does not understand human languages. Scripture prayer is important because it is what God says Godself. When one uses one's own words in prayer, one talks but when one prays the word, God talks. To use Scripture is to take God at God's word. This is the only way to get into line with God. Scriptural prayer releases the power of God. One reads, "be delivered," and one is delivered. Or one reads, "be blessed," and one receives all the blessings. Scriptural prayer also brings Jesus onto the scene. The near magic way in which the words in the Bible is viewed is clear.

84. Hagin, *In Him*, 6.

85. Pastor Chris Oyakhilome in a sermon entitled "Use your tongue to give your life a meaning," explains that we are spirit beings, not ordinary creatures (https://www.youtube.com/watch?v=yQppu1NnbuE; accessed 2019-12-27). That implies that the only way to live to one's full potential is to live by the word of God that we were made of. What Christians need to do is to learn to speak the word. That will give their life meaning that the world cannot give them. Success is in the spirit and that is the reason why it is so important to meditate on the word until it happens in one's spirit.

86. Ayegboyin, "Rethinking of Prosperity Teaching," 79.

87. The prosperity message trades in many other slogans that include: You can have what you say; God wants you rich and healthy; your harvest will be in direct proportion to what you plant; what I confess I possess (going back to E.W. Kenyon); when you identify your word in the Bible, the more you believe and say the word, the more you become prosperous in health and wealth; poverty and sickness are not meant for children of God (Chris Oyakhilome); etc.

command).[88] The most hopeless situation will take shape at the instance of a sound drawn out of the depths of God's word."[89]

What is necessary, is that Christians learn the new language that they alone can use, the language of faith.[90] Only then will they make happiness, joy, health, and prosperity their way of daily living. As a baby has to learn to speak, so Christians need to be taught the ABC of faith. They will say, "I am not well but it is the Lord that healeth me. I am hungry but it is the Lord that provideth in all my needs." They need to learn the power of the language of faith. They need to learn to speak to the foul spirit of sickness to take his hands from God's property. "I adjure you in the Name of Jesus, lose your hold on God's property! I am healed!" That is how you get well, when you learn to speak God's language. Believers need to speak words of faith to the mountains in their lives that threaten them. They are winners and not losers, they are the head and not the tail, because Jeremiah 30:16-17 teaches that all they that devour believers shall be devoured; God will restore health unto believers. Believers need to learn the language of the Bible because it is God speaking.

T.L. Osborn taught that Jehovah Jireh (Gen 22:14; the God who provides, or explained by prosperity teachers as the God of more than

---

88. In a sermon with the theme, "Your words are powerful," Pastor Chris Oyakhilome argues that Christians were born by the word and they are the words of God (https://www.youtube.com/watch?v=ZqBtsSGrh1g; accessed 2019-12-27). Utilizing many Scripture references, Pastor Chris in his characteristic persuasive style and preaching before a large audience at a stadium, states that the government will not make you rich or successful. Success is in your spirit. When you have the consciousness—I am successful—you will be successful. You must remain committed to your source, like a fish in water. The Christian must remain committed to the word. You need to start talking the word. Don't talk your fears; talk your faith. Some sick people talk about their illnesses and its symptoms because they love sympathy. Even if you suffer from an ailment, you don't need medicine but rather change your communications and it will change your life. You can be perfectly healthy, like Jesus, because he is the vine, and you are a branch in him, sharing his health. In this way, Pastor Chris has learned to talk to his shoes, his car, his finances; he speaks words of faith that are powerful to change his circumstances.

89. David Oyedepo, quoted in Ntui-Abung, *Chaos of the Prosperity Gospel*, 41. The context of the verse, on the contrary, suggests that the advice is to tame your own tongue because of the potential for damaging relationships and other people's reputation. We need to learn to use words carefully, employing it not to hurt others. The advice in Proverbs should be read intertextually along with Jas 3:2-13.

90. In the words of a sermon of Nigerian Archbishop Benson Idahosa speaking to an English audience, entitled "Speak the way God speaks," 24 August 2013 (https://www.youtube.com/watch?v=AYci-BnWWt4; accessed 2020-01-12).

enough) guarantees believers a life of overflow. He grounds his defense of biblical wealth on three arguments: that prosperity theology is based on the cross as the solution of all human needs, including sin, disease, and poverty; that believers followed in their Master's footsteps who had an anointing to prosper; and that covenant theology as an extension of the ancient promises God made to Abraham guarantees that those who obey God according to the Deuteronomistic imperative would experience blessings.[91] Mensa Otabil, a Ghanian preacher, writes in *Enjoying the Blessings of Abraham,* that it is impossible for the person that operates under the blessing of Abraham to get poorer, since faith brings Abraham's blessings in every believer's life.[92]

Poverty does not refer to a material state for Osborn; it has spiritual dimensions because poverty is a demonic force that separated people from their godly inheritance. Poverty as an evil spirit requires more than an economic solution; it requires a spiritual solution and it happened on the cross when Jesus took on the spiritual debt of poverty. He died so that believers could be free, healthy, and rich. Believers could claim wealth as one of their rights and privileges in Jesus' name because he earned those privileges on the cross by carrying the sins, diseases, and poverty of people on his shoulders.[93]

Prosperity teachers explained that Jesus was a rich person while living on earth at the hand of several references in Scriptures: with his birth he already received expensive gifts because prosperity attached itself to baby Jesus immediately after his birth; his ride on a donkey, the equivalent of a modern-day Cadillac, with his mother demonstrated the wealth of his earthly father and his inheritance; his expensive anointing oils with the eye on his coming funeral demonstrated his prosperousness; and at his crucifixion it was confirmed that he wore valuable clothes.[94]

Some stayed with the hard prosperity message that drew a straight line between life circumstances and a believer's faith. Faith served as a perfect law; any exceptions indicated that the believer did not abide by the formulas and recipes prescribed to guarantee financial success. Specificity was needed for successful prayer, the believer should name it and

---

91. "Deuteronomic" is limited to references that are related to the book of Deuteronomy while "Deuteronomistic" is used to refer to the underlying theological-ideological motif of retribution and reward.

92. In Kroesbergen, "The Prosperity Gospel," 74.

93. Osborn, *Miracles*.

94. See, e.g., Hagin, *Midas Touch*, 42–65; Avanzini, *Wealth of the World*, 81–6.

claim it. Spiritual forces should be commanded to provide in the specific needs of believers. Charles Capps taught that one should command one's mortgages: "Be paid in full … dematerialize … depart … be gone … in Jesus' name, you will obey me!" because the Bible was more practical that most believers realized.[95]

At the same time, it is also imperative to remember that the answers to our prayers are dependent on our giving. "Our giving of finances has great weight and authority when they come into agreement with Heaven's desire and intent."[96]

The faith movement's hermeneutics includes a view of the Bible that suggests its magical value, as illustrated by Chris Oyakhilome's instruction to speak the words of the Bible. The practice cannot be overemphasized in the life of a child of God because the word of God on your lips is the way to prosperity and success, with reference to Joshua 1:8. "In other words if you would keep the word on your lips, you are sure to prosper and be successful in every area of your life, which of cause (sic), includes your physical body."[97]

The Bible provides "the principles of the kingdom" and shows how to "use them to your advantage and enjoy your inheritance in Christ,"[98] which are the rules and laws of prosperity.

The rigid rules of hard prosperity were: pay tithes; expect financial miracles on a daily basis; and think positively. Divine wealth came with an easy trigger. However, tithes alone did not guarantee that the windows of heaven automatically stayed open. One should also give "first fruits," a standard classification of donations since the 1960s. The first fruits represented the first harvest of all products of the land, including the firstborn of the herd or flock and the firstborn of human parents (Ex 23:16; Lev 19:23–25; Deut 18:3–4; Prov 3:9–10). The purpose of the feast of harvest was to express gratitude to God for the harvest that had been gathered and thereby acknowledged that it was God who had given the harvest in the first place. The aim was not to give with the intention to receive, as the prosperity message emphasized. Giving as an act of gratitude has nothing to do with giving so as to obtain something in return. One is done with the expectation of reward, the other for the purpose of receiving. Some

---

95. Capps, *Tongue*; see also Capps and Capps, *God's Creative Power for Finances*, 27-8.

96. Henderson, *Operating in the Courts*, 70.

97. Quoted in Ntui-Abung, *Chaos of the Prosperity Gospel*, 14.

98. Ntui-Abung, *Chaos of the Prosperity Gospel*, 14.

Jews asserted that the harvest feast was also intended to celebrate the giving of the Law, the *Torah*, on Sinai, which was supposed to have taken place fifty days after Pentecost. The feast lasted one day and the short duration of the feast was justified by the explanation that it took God only one day to give Moses the whole of the extensive law. A last motivation for the feast was that it was providing for the needs of priests who dedicated their lives to serving in the temple. What is important, though, is that Israelites did not give to God first, and with selfish intentions. They received the blessings of daily provision and then, as a reverence to God, offered gifts that expressed their gratitude. God did not ask them to invest in God but to honor God as the author of good gifts. Their giving was not seen as a requirement for God's blessings. It was a way to express their thanks that God had provided in their needs (but not their greed).[99]

In modern parlance, prosperity theology explains that the first part of a raise in salary is to be given to God in full. Tithes and offerings should also be accompanied by specific wishes, what Oral Roberts called, "naming your seed." The "hundredfold blessing" served as the most common calculus of God's "money-back guarantee," implying that God rewarded givers a hundred times for their original donation. Hard prosperity emphasized the contractual nature of the transaction, implying that God was unable to multiply back to those who gave incorrectly. The literal minded accepted that God would apply the laws of the harvest in response to believers' donations. In return for donating huge sums of money, one could be cured of any disease and be rewarded in material wealth several times over.[100] In this way, the audience was coerced to pay lots of money, and the Bible was abused in order to enrich mostly the leader.

A text quoted regularly by prosperity teachers to motivate their reference to a hundredfold blessing is found in Matthew 10:29–30. The context is the narrative about the rich man's disappointment because he was not willing to sell all he had to give to the poor, so that he could follow Jesus in an unhindered way.[101] Jesus then states that it is hard for those with wealth to enter the kingdom. In fact, it is easier for a camel to go through the eye of a needle than for someone who is rich to enter the

---

99. Prosper, *Prosperity Gospel*, 11-2.

100. Guyson, "Of False Prophets and Profits."

101. Making use of the literary context implies that words and verses are interpreted according to what is found in the immediate and surrounding passages, and that smaller parts are interpreted in light of the book as a whole (Ellington, "Is the Prosperity Gospel Biblical?," 33.)

kingdom of God (v. 25). The disciples express their concern that no one can then be saved. And then Peter justifies their capacity to be saved by saying to Jesus, "Look, we have left everything and followed You." In this context, Jesus assures his disciples that those who left house or brothers or sisters or mother or father or children or fields, for his sake and for the sake of the good news, will receive a hundredfold now in this age—houses, brothers and sisters, mothers and children, and fields, with persecutions—and in the age to come eternal life. It is clear that the promise cannot be understood literally. Who can have a hundred mothers or children, except figuratively? The idea is rather that leaving worldly wealth and all the things that are valued in the world behind, for Jesus' sake, is rewarded in this life by the fact that, while possessing nothing, one possesses everything (see also 2 Cor 6:10). Another part of the reward is that one receives eternal life. Jesus wants his disciples to understand that, even though they might lose much for his sake, the reward of forgiveness of sin, God's grace and love, daily joy and eternal life is worth much more than what they have lost for him.[102] Lastly, the words ascribed to Jesus mention that those who give everything will also receive persecutions, an addition to the text that prosperity preachers as a rule ignore.

Era of the Downfall of Some Televangelists

The 1980s also saw the golden age of American televangelism, with Jimmy Swaggart, Robert Schuller, Oral Roberts, Kenneth Copeland, and Rex Humbard competing for the most viewers.[103] It was an expensive medium and fundraising became a necessity for survival. Jim Bakker and his wife became the most well-known (and notorious) of its fundraisers, weeping or rejoicing openly during their television shows as financial goals were missed or met. Their Rolls Royce, fifty-foot walk-in closets, gold-plated bathroom fixtures, and air-conditioned dog-kennels became paradigmatic of the sumptuous lifestyle of wealth preachers.[104] Viewers were promised immediate miraculous returns on their donations.

---

102. Prosper, *Prosperity Gospel*, 32.

103. Kalu, *African Christianity*, 256 refers to the important influence that William Branham, a well-known faith healer during the healing revival after the Second World War, exercised on Oral Roberts and Kenneth Hagin. The first echoes of the prosperity message were heard in Branham's prophecies and sermons.

104. Gifford, "Prosperity," 383.

The year 1987 saw the downfall of Jim Bakker who was charged with committing adultery with a church secretary, using hush money from his television station to buy the woman's silence, as well as with involvement in several homosexual encounters. He was eventually defrocked by the Assemblies of God after Jimmy Swaggart led the charges, denouncing Bakker as a cancer that needed to be excised from the body of Christ.[105] Shortly afterwards, Swaggart also exposed the adultery of Marvin Gorman, a fellow preacher, who retaliated by producing evidence of Swaggart's own sexual misconduct. The Assemblies of God eventually defrocked and suspended Swaggart as well. Televangelist audiences fell by millions of viewers. The disgrace of financial mismanagement also continued to haunt faith networks, contributing to its further loss of income as Christians withdrew their financial support.

A new generation of prosperity teachers changed tactics in order to regain believers' trust by replacing the flamboyant stereotypes of the Bakkers and Swaggarts with a suave, businesslike image. Joel Osteen, T.D. Jakes, Joyce Meyer, Creflo Dollar, and Eddie Long were postmodern prophets who did not plead for financial support but rather focused on the returns. They offered "tools" to help viewers stabilize their relationships and find reconciliation in their families and marriages, and taught them to apply financial principles. They favored therapeutic soft prosperity to the previous generation's hard prosperity, suitable for a less credulous and cynical generation who lost their trust in institutions but still found it necessary to invest in personal emotion.[106] Their new version was also accepted by many classical Pentecostals and some successful prosperity teachers within classical Pentecostal denominations were even elected as leaders in various capacities among the prosperity teachers and their networks.

The downfall of white prosperity televangelists did not impact the influence of prosperity teaching in the black American church. Frederick Price established America's largest worship center in Los Angeles and prosperity theology rose with a new vitality in African American churches. These churches consisted of various categories: neo-Pentecostal groups, some of which were denominational and others independent; charismatic mainline, within black historic denominations, as a result of

---

105. Swaggart, *Confession Principle*; Kaufman, "Fall of Jimmy Swaggart," 36.
106. Bowler, *Blessed*, 123.

the charismatic movement of the previous century; and Word of Faith, as non-denominational prosperity churches, under the influence of Hagin.[107]

The influence of the prosperity gospel in the USA spread far beyond the faith movement for various reasons, as Kate Bowler explains: because the message suited the economic mood of the times; because it centered on African American migration with people shifting to the south and southwest of the USA; because interaction among megachurch leaders led to theological cross-pollinations; and because African American congregations had historically been the institutional epicenter of mutual aid and the place where debates about questions of political action, spiritual solace, and community meaning raged.[108] In a context where black religious communities were still barred from the luxury of separating spiritual and socio-economic spheres and they had to assume the task of fostering economic mobility themselves, the spiritual solutions proposed by the prosperity gospel joined up with other forms of social and economic liberation. The stark materialism and hyper-individualism that marked white prosperity theology were tempered by the emergence of the priestly and prophetic, and the social gospel with the empowering of individuals through education and vocational training.[109] Here the prosperity gospel emerged as a concordant theme that blended with other concerns that marked a society formed by racial, social, and economic inequalities.

Africa of the past few decades was more influenced by the African American Pentecostal and neo-Pentecostal movement and their leaders than by classical Pentecostalism, and for that reason some attention was also given to these churches.[110] Within black America, as in Africa, neo-

---

107. Luxmoore, "African Church Warns."

108. Bowler, Blessed, 125.

109. Luxmoore, "African Church Warns." See Marti, "Adaptability of Pentecostalism," for an interesting discussion of the relationship between prosperity theology and individualization in the North American context. It would be an interesting experiment to investigate to what extent the relationship is true in Africa; the suspicion is that the new elite middle-class African *nouveau riche* may also be implied by an acceptance of the widespread American individualism.

110. An interesting fact is that Africa is now reaching the countries that initially sent missionaries to reach Africa with the gospel, but now with their version of the prosperity gospel. E.g., the largest and fastest growing congregation in Europe is the Embassy of the Blessed Kingdom of God for All Nations, founded by a Nigerian Pentecostal, Sunday Adelaja, in 1993, and the largest single church congregation in Britain is the Kingsway International Christian Centre in London led by another Nigerian, Matthew Ashimolowo, founded in 1992 (Anderson, "African Independent Churches," 26). This is mission in reverse. African Pentecostalism is an important feature of European

Pentecostal churches and groups teaching the prosperity gospel showed the fastest growth of all Pentecostal groups.[111] A wave of independent ministries brought an emphasis on spiritual gifts, ecstatic worship, and prosperity as an expected blessing for all believers. The New Black Charismatics, as Scott Billingsley refers to them, positioned themselves as media literate and expansionist. They adopted a flexible attitude to popular culture, arguing that traditionalism is a barrier to effective evangelism. These neo-Pentecostal groups became natural allies of prosperity theology that they utilized to be relevant to a highly consumerist culture. The interaction between neo-Pentecostalism and the consumerist culture and its co-option of a this-worldly orientation can be described in terms of the metaphor of the "liquid church," with religion placing itself in society as social status, since it becomes available in the market as a "place of benediction," a "place where God is," "where miracles happen," or a "place of happy people." Neo-Pentecostalism also addresses the concerns and pressures of people living in a fast-paced world, teaching them about sex, children, marriages, and work. Their pastors look like ambassadors for unrelenting progress. T.D. Jakes became the archetypal model as he ruled the media as one of the leading preachers in the world. At first, he concentrated on emotional healing for women who were the victims of domestic violence, discrimination, rape, and divorce; later, his emphasis shifted to prosperity.

Even mainstream African American as well as African churches did not escape the influence of the neo-pentecostal prosperity gospel. Many of them started using pentecostal-flavored preaching, emotional and embodied worship, and emphasis on the Spirit, an interest in spiritual gifts, and room for the revelation of the supernatural within their worship

---

Christianity today, and that is not only because of migration of large numbers of Africans to Europe.

111. The mistake should not be made, however, to stare blindly at the enormous growth. Maxon's ("Fake Pastors and Their Followers") warning is relevant, that the growth in Africa of the prosperity message is a result of its obsession with the supernatural. Desperate people are simply miracle addicts who will do anything to get a fix. They are caught by enterprising ministers who are selling various "faith products;" in the process, the ministers get rich and the poor are impoverished even further. The mushrooming of these churches should not be confused with a sudden interest in godly living. It is rather motivated by the desire to see what God can do materially and physically for the individual. In the process, television networks, radio stations, and print media become rich. For many African women, the patriarchal society oppresses them and the church becomes the only place where they find hope. Perhaps Karl Marx's criticism of religion is relevant, that this form of religion works against the poor because it keeps them complacent and docile, and poor.

services to reach their communities more effectively. They started speaking of health and wealth within the dominant Baptist and Methodist culture although they still use clerical collars and sanctuaries in the age-old style. Their models are Clarence McClendon, Paul Morton, Ira Hilliard, and T.D. Jakes, outreaching its largely white foundations.

A New Era

The prosperity movement that emerged since the 1990s was more diverse than before, surviving the disgrace of some of its most prominent leaders. Now it became a movement with boundless confidence and growth and claimed some of the world's largest churches, also in Africa. Hundreds of small congregations thrived in the heterogeneous prosperity movement by its exposure to television, radio, books, seminars, and conferences. The movement developed a style of persuasion that fit the times, a style that was therapeutic and emotive that befit soft prosperity. The harsh reality between the spoken word and reality were softened and psychological and fiscal success was tied to each other. It was now taught that a rightly ordered mind would lead to rightly ordered finances. "Positive confession" was changed into "positive declarations," although the principle remained the same: change your words to change your life and circumstances. One should make positive declarations over one's life every day: "I am blessed, I am prosperous, I am healthy, I am talented, I am creative, I am wise."[112] At first the words build one's self-image rather than one's faith. Eventually the words will change the way one looks at oneself, leading to good spiritual health. Life's circumstances still depend on one's use of faith, and divine wealth comes to good people as the result of a chain of causality-linked thoughts. God rewards the faithful with wealth, though they earned it indirectly, by way of a carefully constructed and well-considered budget, tamed spending habits, and a cheerful attitude leading to promotion at work.

Prosperity believers want their leaders to serve as models of the message, motivating them to live well. However, their lavish lifestyles led to severe criticism from the side of the media that the leaders exploited their followers by profiting from their donations. It was argued that the lifestyle of the rich leaders was paid for by donations from desperate people who believed that giving a prosperity teacher their money

---

112. Osteen, *Become a Better You*, 109, 115, 209.

would result in their living this lifestyle too.[113] Their assets were viewed as evidence of their greed, materialism, and probably corruption. Unfortunately, these leaders seldom opened their financial situation for public view and limited their accountability so that the allegations could not be proven as false or true. Their followers also rarely acknowledged the fine line between manipulation and abundant living in their leaders' lifestyle.

A few of the leaders eventually gave up on prosperity theology. Jim Bakker wrote a book after his stay in prison in which he denounced the prosperity message as false.[114] T.D. Jakes closely associated himself with prosperity preachers and supported their ministries financially and logistically, but he rejected the "so-called Prosperity Gospel."[115] Kenneth Hagin corrected some of the abuses of the movement he established to a large extent, writing that prosperity might never mean conspicuous, lavish wealth.[116] Before his death, he warned leading prosperity teachers, including Kenneth Copeland, against seeking financial gain and corrupting spiritual truths with wrong motivations. Reinhard Bonnke, known as a good friend of Benny Hinn and Kenneth Copeland whose ministries supported his outreaches in Africa, moved to establish that he was financially accountable and transparent, selected a representative and reliable leadership team, and kept his distance from prosperity theology.[117]

Fierce criticism of the movement came from the side of Pentecostal scholar Charles Farah, in 1979 a professor at Oral Roberts University when he wrote *From the Pinnacle of the Temple* that characterized the Faith movement as a "faith formula" that presumed upon the grace and sovereignty of God and that was directly responsible for disappointment among many Christians. During the same time Gordon Fee, then Gordon-Conwell professor and a member of the Assemblies of God, published a series of articles in which he asserts that the Copelands' teaching of prosperity reflects a specific use of the Bible that does not give the plain meaning of the text. The cult of prosperity flies in the face of the whole New Testament and it is not biblical, is his conclusion. He suggests

---

113. Hinn, *God, Greed*, 57.
114. Bakker, *I was Wrong*.
115. Jakes, *Reposition Yourself*, 221.
116. Hagin, *Midas Touch*, 94-5.
117. Kennedy, "The Crusader," 53. Bonnke's ministry program, Christ for All Nations (CfaN), joined the Evangelical Council for Financial Accountability. Bonnke died at the end of 2019.

that Ronald Sider's *Rich Christians in an Age of Hunger* should serve as a "cure" for what he terms the "loathsome disease" of the prosperity cult.[118]

Jim Bakker wrote from prison after he was convicted in 1987 of sexual misconduct with a church secretary, Jessica Hahn, and illegal misuse of ministry funds that led to his imprisonment and divorce. He stated that he had lost everything but he had also learned that happiness is not in things or circumstances, but in knowing God. He warned his readers not to fall in love with the gift wrapping, but to fall in love with Jesus Christ, the Gift of eternal life.[119]

Only one of many tragic stories illustrating the disastrous effects of a conception of healing in the Faith movement that states that God intends for all people to be healthy and wealthy because the cross "guarantees" it as part of its benefits is that of Wesley Parker.[120] His father Larry tells the harrowing story in *We Let Our Son Die*. Their diabetic son needed daily doses of insulin but after a Faith evangelist had prayed for him, his parents decided to withhold the medicine, with Wesley going into a diabetic coma. The Parkers were taught that Satan was attempting to deceive them with false symptoms and they kept on confessing their son's healing until he died in a diabetic coma. Instead of arranging for a funeral service for their son, their faith required that believing God would raise Wesley from the dead. When no resurrection happened during the service, the father dismissed all those who did not have faith for the miracle. For more than a year the father held to the faith that his son would be resurrected. Both parents were convicted of child abuse and involuntary manslaughter and each was given a 25-year sentence in a federal penitentiary, suspended for a probated five-year sentence. These kinds of tragedies also play out in different parts of Africa, and not only in sick people who literally die of their faith but also those who lose all hope and faith in God when faith formulas do not work for their situations of poverty and economic difficulties.

In response to these criticisms from inside Pentecostalism, Jimmy Swaggart also renounced the message he confessed that he participated in, in two publications.[121]

---

118. McConnell, *Different Gospel*, 78.
119. Hanegraaff, *Christianity in Crisis*, 232.
120. Parker, *We Let Our Son Die*.
121. Swaggart and Solum, *Balanced Faith Life*. See also Editorial, "New Role for Swaggart?", *Charisma*, 60.

Shifts within Pentecostalism That Led to Room for the Prosperity Teaching

What caused the development within the Pentecostal movement that started as nearly an anti-capitalist and world denying movement to end in supporting partly the prosperity message? Several theories have been presented to explain the shift. The early movement started out as a movement primarily of the marginalized and disenfranchised, drawing people predominantly from the lower classes. It is plausible to refer to these people as the "disinherited" and "deprived," if the theory is correct that early Pentecostals were mainly poor and in many instances displaced. The poor represented a more conservative voice, explaining why several of the early prominent leaders, such as Charles Parham and Frank Bartleman, were speaking out against capitalism.[122]

Although it is accepted that Robert Anderson's remarks about the origins of early Pentecostalism among poor classes are not based on correct sociological observations, it is probably true that early Pentecostals maintained a strong position against material possessions and wealth until after the Second World War.[123] What caused the changes that eventually led to the prosperity message has been explained by way of three theories, as Nico Horn suggests.

A first explanation is provided by way of Marxist thinking that divides human society into a substructure (*Unterbau*) and a superstructure (*Überbau*). The substructure consists of the needs of humans, production, powers of production in the form of human labor and natural resources, means of production, and production relations. The superstructure consists of theories, ideas, conscious ideologies, and religion. The substructure serves as the determinant of the superstructure.

If the theory is correct, the prosperity message did not produce affluent Christians, but the economic structures in society produced the prosperity message. Then the claims of prosperity teachers that their gospel produced prosperity for their adherents are not correct. It was the underlying and often subconscious factors determined by economic forces that were decisive for the development of the theory.

In Africa the prosperity message is the result of a foreign message that was imported; the economic circumstances in Africa did not support the development of such a doctrine. The African situation of inequality

---

122. Anderson, *Vision of the Disinherited*, 209.
123. Horn, *From Rags to Riches*, 71.

and poverty also presents several challenges to the message. While prosperity and wealth in an American context implies expensive holidays and clothing, in Africa it might imply having the means to supply a meal, buy a bicycle, or get shoes for one's children to wear during the cold winter months. If Americans and Africans serve the same God, who is the cosmic banker with an unlimited supply of riches in God's store rooms as prosperity preachers assert, then there should be no distinction between the financial position of American and African neo-Pentecostals.[124] That it is not the case implies that the superstructure of the prosperity message is based on an American capitalist substructure, and not on a biblical doctrine or a religious experience.

The prosperity message operates within a context of neo-capitalism with its establishment of a consumerist society, and it reduces the gospel to the application of the values of this society to their version of the gospel. In capitalism, prosperity and success stand opposite adversity and disappointment and the hope of prosperity keeps the economy and society in motion. Without the prospect of profits, people's courage to work

---

124. In an African perspective on wealth and riches, Prophet T.B. Joshua in a sermon entitled, "Value processing more than result," states that deliverance, healing, and blessing cannot take place without God's processing (https://www.youtube.com/watch?v=obGhSHnHtYU; accessed 2020-01-04). There is a proper process for everything, and the processing of God is more important than the result itself. In other words, how you become rich is bigger than your riches, which is the result. How you get there is bigger than getting there. A problem that he discerns with many believers is that they want to be rich and get there without following the correct processing. Only the processing will help them to maintain the result, he asserts. If the processing is tampered with or if the processing is not God's processing, they will not be able to maintain that result. They lose their riches because they do not follow God's processing. The manner they process their lives is working against them. Processing means you stay in contact with God, you talk to him. Processing is what goes through one's heart and mind, what one thinks and says. If one's mind is positive, your prayer and words will be positive. The processing of your life is what is affecting you today. Processing that is not in line with God is witchcraft. Lying, pride, and disobedience is the fruit of such witchcraft. That is why it is so important that you are in line with God to build your career or business because it is only the supernatural that can take believers to places filled with peace. The implication is that positive confession is the process to allow God's "processing" to determine our lives. Only when we think the right thoughts can we be certain that God's blessings would follow, in a mechanical way. The use of the English language by African preachers for whom it is a second or third language creates at times some unique challenges for listeners and Africans cannot be blamed for struggling to express themselves more clearly.

hard sinks and society falls into stagnation.[125] The God of capitalism is a very wealthy "capitalist" magnate.

When prosperity teachers had to explain why their gospel works better in affluent societies than in poor societies, the Western roots of their thinking became more apparent. Kenneth Copeland says that prosperity is relevant to the individual's situation;[126] the implication is that a person in Africa would be blessed in a far humbler way than somebody in the USA. A hundredfold blessing seemingly differs between the two continents, leading Horn to observe that the prosperity gospel makes its God a partner in political and economic systems of exploitation.[127] It seems that God is a respecter of persons, countries, and economic systems.

The prosperity gospel suggests that if one stays poor it is due to the lack of faith one displays. A poor Christian is a *contradictio ad terminis* because God's intention for all Spirit-filled people is that they should be prosperous and wealthy.[128] Can such a message really provide hope on a continent characterized by ethnic conflict and warfare, epidemics raging because of the inaccessibility of large areas due to ethnic conflicts, suppression and oppression of women and their rights, and extreme poverty due to state plundering and corruption of politicians in power?

A second theory utilized to explain the shift within some parts of Pentecostalism from an emphasis on an other-worldly interest and otherworldliness to the prosperity message is based on the observation that prosperity is the dream of success of American society. Where Marxist theory claims that ideologies, teachings, and theologies are determined by the social activities and position of a specific group, deprivation theories explain that teachings, ideologies, and theologies of groups determine their situation, including their financial well-being.[129] It argues that Africans patronize Pentecostalism as an instrument to respond to the socio-economic and political challenges of an environment riddled with high levels of poverty, failed and collapsed economies, legitimacy

---

125. Crabtree, *Prosperity of a Gospel Church Reconsidered*, 6.

126. In Steele, *Destined to Win*, 125.

127. Horn, *From Rags to Riches*, 74.

128. See, e.g., the remark in Michael Okonkwo in *Controlling Wealth God's Way*, cited in Phiri and Maxwell, "Gospel Riches," 23 that "many are ignorant of the fact that God has already made provision for his children to be wealthy here on earth. When I say wealthy, I mean very, very rich ... Break loose! It is not a sin to desire to be wealthy."

129. See Kgatle, "Unusual Practices".

crises, and urban anomie.[130] Untoward structural factors lead people to seek charismatic spirituality as a solace.

Max Weber (1864-1920) argues that both entrepreneur and laborer in traditional pre-capitalist society preferred increased leisure over increased profit.[131] The traditional value system prevented modern capitalism from realizing that the other factors necessary for the rise of capitalism existed. The spirit of capitalism is the accumulation of profits and wealth as an end in itself and the duty of the individual. It is the highest value that can be reached in economics. The shift to the view in pre-capitalist society that viewed accumulation of wealth as unethical to the capitalist view is ascribed by Weber to the Protestant ethics of the seventeenth century, especially European and American neo-Calvinism, pietism, Methodism and Anabaptist sects that defined a worldly asceticism. It consisted of three principles, that every believer is called of God to a specific profession, giving religious sanction to all secular labor; an ascetic attitude towards material possessions and worldly pleasures; and an emphasis on the systematic use of time.[132] At the same time, the Calvinist doctrine of predestination and the later *syllogismus practicus* of Protestant orthodoxy implied that human beings are entirely dependent upon God who has destined some to eternal life and others to eternal damnation, with no one knowing for sure whether they are or will be saved or condemned. Calvin taught that human beings must consider themselves saved and attain self-confidence in a calling to a specific profession, by working in the service of God. This led to a peculiar ascetic tendency and an ethic of hard work.[133] Salvation is to be demonstrated by works; humans ought to show their election by living according to the standards set out in the Bible. This is the reason for the link between Protestantism and capitalism, in Weber's view.[134] Although other Protestant groups such as the Baptists, Methodists, and Pietists did not share in the Calvinist view of predestination, they had other forms of perfection of grace that served the function of the *syllogismus practicus*, with members

---

130. Kalu, "Discursive Interpretation."
131. Weber, *Protestant Ethic*, 60.
132. Weber, *Protestant Ethic*, 117.
133. Weber, *Protestant Ethic*, 118.
134. Weber, *Protestant Ethic*, 197.

constantly having to prove to God and fellow-believers their participation in the true church.[135]

In this way, salvation is directly linked to the necessity of participating faithfully in a calling to a profession, by living an ascetic life and not wasting time on anything but productive work. The Catholic cycle of sin—repentance—atonement—release—renewed sin was broken and it led to the spirit of capitalism with high productivity and an emphasis on profits. Later the emphasis would shift to the pleasures of consumption with its necessity of acquisitive activity and an ascetic compulsion to save. Once the accumulation of capital became a need in itself, Protestant asceticism became more and more of a side issue. Calvin warned that the accumulation of wealth leads to pride, anger, and love of the world that might ensnare the soul of human beings but capitalism eventually reigned supreme, creating a consumerist society.[136]

Not everybody accepts Weber's theories and some argue that the rise of late capitalism is more complicated than Weber theorizes although it seems probable that Protestant theology to a limited extent played some role in its rise. Early Pentecostals did not accept the Calvinist doctrine of predestination but they emphasized the importance of a legalistic and ascetic lifestyle as necessary elements for the attainment of holiness. In his study of the early Pentecostal movement, Walter Hollenweger finds that the position of Pentecostals changed dramatically in the third generation, around the 1940s.[137] He suggests that the same dynamics that Weber at-

---

135. Weber, *Protestant Ethic*, 145.

136. Warnings about wealth are found in Matt 6:24, that a believer cannot serve two masters; in Mark 4:19, that the deceitfulness of riches chokes out fruitfulness; in Luke 18:22–23, that it is difficult for rich people to choose Christ over wealth; in Luke 18:25, that it is difficult for rich people to enter the kingdom of God; in 1 Tim 6:10, that the love of money is the root of all evil; in Luke 12:20, that the soul is the human's most important asset; and in Mark 8:36, that one can gain the whole world yet lose one's soul if one does not have Christ. Wealth is not a sign of one's elite spiritual status, as prosperity teachers imply; having Christ is (Hinn, *God, Greed*, 188).

137. Hollenweger, *Pentecostals*, 484. This happened in conjunction with Pentecostals' desire to become respectable and acceptable, forming an alliance with Evangelicals, and shifting their hermeneutics to a more fundamentalist sentiment. Paul Gifford, "Prosperity," 374 is not correct in his assertion that Pentecostals in the 1920s took over the biblicism and dispensationalism of fundamentalism, because they did not have a theology of their own. This is historically not correct and the statement that early Pentecostals had no theology is also without any grounds. The same is true of his assertion that fundamentalists, Pentecostals, and charismatics make up the broad coalition usually described as "evangelical."

tributes to the early Protestants were playing out in the Pentecostal movement where their disciplined and ascetic lifestyle led to the attainment of riches and social prestige. Pentecostal thinking then functioned as a stimulus for success and Hollenweger sees the same dynamics at work in early Pentecostalism that placed a low value on goods and possessions and the prosperity gospel.[138] Only a part of Pentecostal churches shifted their allegiance from a theology of asceticism to a prosperity gospel of accumulation, and only after a long while.[139]

Hollenweger works with the deprivation theory, a third way of explaining the shift in Pentecostalism. Because they were poor and deprived, early Pentecostals rejected the goods and possessions that capitalism offered. The prosperity message is another reaction to deprivation, with the same goal, to overcome it with the gospel. Hollenweger explains that deprived people have two alternatives, to develop a system in which the things they are deprived of are seen as of little value or even harmful, and to be avoided, or to develop a system that will provide in what they are lacking. Early Pentecostalism followed the first route while neo-pentecostal emphasis on prosperity chose the second option.

A problem that Horn sees with Hollenweger's theory is that many people follow the prosperity teaching without being deprived in material sense.[140] Hollenweger responds to the criticism by providing a wide definition of deprivation, as the feeling of deprivation that is at stake, and not necessarily deprivation as such. Sects operate, according to some sociological theories, to overcome the feeling of deprivation. However, such a wide definition cancels its value for explaining the shift within Pentecostalism because it includes a diversity of people across all barriers.

Robert Anderson's argument makes more sense, that economic and cultural changes and challenges at the end of the nineteenth century and the beginning of the twentieth century, and its devastating effects on lower class workers, contributed to the rise of the holiness and Pentecostal movements.[141] However, when he tried to explain why many of the affluent classes associated with the charismatic movement, that they felt deprived of respect and prestige and that they experienced a feeling of

---

138. Weber, *Protestant Ethic*, 117.
139. Akoko, "Ask and You Shall Be Given," 301.
140. Horn, *From Rags to Riches*, 82.
141. Anderson, *Vision of the Disinherited*, 223.

emptiness and hunger for God before their experience of Spirit baptism, he is not convincing.

In conclusion, various attempts have been made to explain the transition from the Pentecostal to the prosperity movement and what caused it and in all cases some elements were useful. However, because the prosperity teaching exists in the dynamic relationship between people and interaction between experience, theology, and the influences of society, combined with each individual's unique experiences, the teaching cannot be explained from a social analysis only.

Network Movement and Neo-Pentecostalism

Establishment of the New Apostolic Reformation

The newest historical development in this regard is the New Apostolic Reformation (according to Wagner[142] and others), representing currently probably the fastest growing movement in Christianity, both in the West and the Majority World and consisting of a network of dynamic, innovative independent religious entrepreneurs, often called "apostles."[143] In many cases these leaders are linked to conservative politicians and they view their participation in politics as necessary to ensure a just and moral community (according to their conservative agenda).[144] Their involvement with the establishment and carrying out of political policies has to do with their objective, not to primarily save souls as classical Pentecostals purported in their isolationist theology that separated the church from involvement with the rest of society,[145] but to create a "heaven on earth" where poverty, war, violence, and disease will no longer exist. Their eschatology is realized in an intra-worldly eschatology that, in practice, breaks with the apocalyptic Christian understanding of time and brings retribution or salvation to the faithful's present moment, not leaving them only for heaven and for life

---

142. Wagner, *Wrestling with Alligators*.

143. Christerson and Flory, *Rise of Network Christianity*, 2.

144. This is happening widely in Africa, and David Maxwell, "'Delivered from the Spirit of Poverty?,'" 350 ascribes it to the use of these believers of what he calls "American Bible belt" literature and resources that made them vulnerable to the agendas of the American New Religious Right.

145. Bangura, "Charismatic Movements," 237.

after death,[146] *contra* a majority of classical Pentecostals with their premillennial expectations tainted by dispensationalism.[147]

The Network movement had its origins in the charismatic movements of the 1970s, the so-called second wave of Pentecostalism. Donald Miller calls it the new paradigm movement and they represent to him a "second reformation" or third "great awakening."[148] It rejects the overly bureaucratic rules and procedures that characterize many mainline denominations, seeks to restore the "priesthood of all believers," emphasizes unmediated communication between an individual and God and direct access to the realm of the supernatural which more domesticated forms of religion have found unseemly and magical. Miller and as well as Birgit Meyer[149] follow Max Weber's reasoning that mainline Protestant denominations have become progressively formalized and routinized over time, contributing to their eventual decline. For instance, priestly roles were institutionalized, sacred texts canonized, and access to the sacred was limited by roles and procedures, distancing ordinary believers more and more from the transforming source of the sacred. Religious institutions gradually devolved into encrusted bureaucracies characterized by low levels of commitment, partly because they were integrated with other aspects of institutional life. At the same time, the phenomenon can be explained in terms of the theory that any revival movement experiences a "second generation" that does not share the initial enthusiasm of the founders of the revolutionary movement. It is partly true of most denominations within the classical Pentecostal movement, that despite their diversity of forms most also experienced some form of mustiness in time.

Weber argues that the charismatic authority of leaders derives from the personal devotion of their loyal followers, which is typically inspired by the extraordinary abilities of the leaders to perform miracles or heroic acts.[150] These acts serve to prove that the leader has been chosen or is a special recipient of God's grace. Charisma is guaranteed by what is held

---

146. Dubarry and Müller. "Pentecostal Churches and Capitalism," 2.

147. See Nel, *African Pentecostal Hermeneutics* for full discussion.

148. Miller, *Reinventing American Protestantism*.

149. Meyer, "Pentecostalism and Neo-Liberal Capitalism," 7, who adds that the dimension of pleasure and consumption is missing in Weber's scenario of disenchanted modern capitalism with its harsh work ethic. Pleasure and consumption's value is determined by whether it leads to God or the devil, in pentecostal parlance (Meyer, "Pentecostalism and Neo-Liberal Capitalism," 16).

150. Weber, *Economy and Society*, 140.

to be a proof, originally always a miracle.[151] The charismatic leader gains and retains the charisma solely by proving their powers in practice. If they want to be recognized prophets, they must work miracles.[152] Charisma knows no formal and regulated appointment or dismissal, no career, advancement or salary, no supervisory or appeals body, no local or purely technical jurisdiction, and no permanent institutions in the manner of bureaucratic agencies.[153]

The Pentecostal movement had since its inception a charismatic form of authority. As the movement grew, it inevitably became too large for a charismatic leader to manage, and the transition to a more rational, bureaucratic organization emerged. This led to attempts to routinize and replicate the miraculous practices of the original leader, within the context of tension between charismatic independence and routinized respectability,[154] leading to a transition into rational-legal authority, in Weber's terms. Now the charismatic leader is replaced by the organization, and denominations carry on the work of the original leader, but without the charisma. Older people still remember the charisma and long for its reinstitution, leading to tensions with current church leadership and at times also schisms. The lack of charisma also makes drawing new followers increasingly difficult over time.[155]

In time another leader rises who is endowed with charisma, performing heroic acts or miracles and offering new experiences of the supernatural, and the process repeats itself. Charisma cannot remain stable, but becomes either traditionalized or rationalized, or a combination of both.[156] The routinization of charisma was inevitable under the rationalization process of modernity.

---

151. Weber, *Economy and Society*, 242.

152. A related argument is that the occurrence of miracles of several types within the prosperity movement is proof that the movement is not heretical. However, McConnell, *Different Gospel*, 50 is correct in asserting that results can never be the criterion by which the truth of an idea is proven. The numerous miracles and healings supposedly occurring in the Faith movement are not necessarily signs from God that the Faith message is the gospel of the New Testament. Even if the miracle occurs "in the name of Jesus," it still does not prove that it is supported by a biblical version of the gospel.

153. Miller, *Reinventing American Protestantism*.

154. Hefner, "Unexpected Modern-Gender," 9.

155. Miller, *Reinventing American Protestantism*.

156. Weber, *Economy and Society*, 244.

The first wave of Pentecostalism eventually routinized into denominations. The charismatic renewal that since the 1960s changed the face of some established mainline churches attempted to bring charismatic practices back into these denominations where routinization led to its loss, with varying degrees of success. Third-wave neo-charismatic leaders such as Chuck Smith, Lonnie Frisbee, John Wimber, and others broke the constraints of denominationalism through the sheer force of their personalities, and their success in accessing the supernatural, allowing them to inspire their own movement.[157] Will routinization also eventually lead to create formal bureaucracies to manage growth and exercise control over controversial practices within neo-charismatic network Christianity? Christerson and Flory see the emergence of this last movement rather as part of a larger societal shift, as will be discussed next, and the shift is away from formal organizations as the primary organizing matrix of social groups to networks of independently operating individuals associating freely and spontaneously, that might counteract the natural process of routinization.[158] Prosperity theology found its home in these networks and their rapid influence resulted in the widespread acceptance of the theology, although its first home was initially among classical Pentecostals (see discussion in the next chapter).

The enormous growth of this new networks of independent charismatic Christianity accompanies important historic shifts. The first is the decline of Protestantism, especially among mainline Protestant denominations such as Methodist, Presbyterian, and Lutheran churches. In Africa, these churches seem to exclude those who prosper, and definitely those who want to prosper from the spiritual domain, and at the same time those who favor spontaneous religious impulses.[159] Although Evangelicals showed a small growth rate in most instances, it is still smaller than the growth rate of the world population.[160] According to the World

157. Christerson and Flory, *Rise of Network Christianity*, 44.
158. See also Castells, *Rise of the Network Society*.
159. Kroesbergen, "The Prosperity Gospel," 79-80.
160. See https://www.pewforum.org/2011/06/22/global-survey-of-evangelical-protestant-leaders/; accessed 2019-11-29. Evangelical leaders identified the major threats of Evangelicalism as: influence of secularism, too much emphasis on consumerism, sex and violence in pop culture, influence of Islam, theological divisions among Evangelicals, Evangelical leaders leading lavish lifestyles, Evangelical leaders violating sexual morals, government restrictions on religion, and influence of Catholicism. Some of these threats are probably also relevant for classical Pentecostalism as well as the independent charismatic network movement, such as leaders who lead

Christian Database, Pentecostals were the only denominational group defined as Protestant that grew faster than the growth of the overall population during that time.[161]

Another historic shift that favored the growth of the networks of charismatic Christianity is the decline of denominational Christianity and the rise of independents, including Roman Catholic, Orthodox, Protestant, Anglican, and classical Pentecostal Christianity. At the same time, there is a concurrent growth of those affiliated with non-denominational independent congregations. The only major categories of Protestants that grew faster than the overall population were those not associated with denominations, the independents.[162] Affiliates of neo-charismatic congregations accounted for the largest percentage of this growth.[163]

A third shift that influenced the rise of network charismatic Christianity is the growth of Pentecostal and charismatic believers during the last quarter of a century. The spirituality represented by classical pentecostal worship, song and music, exercise of the spiritual gifts and democratic participation of all in the worship service because of the acceptance of the priesthood and prophethood of all believers have become popular with the wider community, probably due to the exposure of such practices by the mass media. Within Pentecostalism, it is the networks of independent charismatic communities that are the fastest growing, defined as those who are affiliated with a charismatic congregation that is not connected with a formal denomination. A subcategory are those networks that emphasize living apostles, prophets, and other charismatic officials as the Spirit-anointed and appointed leaders, *contra* the traditional pentecostal notion that although the offices of apostle, prophet, evangelist, pastors and teachers (or pastor-teachers) still exist (Eph 4:11), these gifts do not represent the leadership. During the past forty years, their growth rate was phenomenal, compared to most other Christian groups that shrank as a percentage of the overall population. The result is that if current growth rates continue, Pentecostals and charismatics will soon outnumber all of the other established Protestant groups taken together.

---

lavish lifestyles, leaders who violate sexual morals, and (especially in some African countries) government restrictions on religion.

161. https://worldchristiandatabase.org/; accessed 2019-11-29.

162. Not everybody agrees anymore that Pentecostalism finds its natural home among Protestants. See, e.g., the arguments in Castelo, *Pentecostalism as a Christian Mythical Tradition*.

163. The term "neo-charismatic" is used interchangeably with "neo-Pentecostal."

The neo-charismatic independent networks that originated as a third wave within the Pentecostal movement are founded on certain convictions. They do not seek to build a "movement" or to create affiliated franchise congregations using a particular name, such as traditional denominations do. They are not even primarily focused on building congregations in the traditional sense, but rather seek to influence the beliefs and practices of believers regardless of their congregation or affiliation. Their adherents also include those large groups of believers who are not affiliated with any congregation or religious group. Their stated purpose is not only to save individual souls of sinners but to influence and transform society as a whole. They do not intend to build the church, or any specific church, but their aim is rather to influence governments and leaders who are responsible for social, economic and political policies. They do not formally organize a "movement" or "denomination" but the different leaders and ministries are highly connected by networks of cooperation.[164]

This new development represents a historic shift in the way Christianity is organized and practiced, and for this reason Wagner compares it to the Protestant Reformation.[165] Wagner motivates his statement of calling it a "reformation" by stating that we are arguably currently witnessing the most radical change in the way of "doing church" since the Protestant Reformation. It is "apostolic" because the recognition of the gift and office of an apostle is the most radical of a whole list of changes from the old. It is new because of the necessity that it should be distinguished from several older traditional groups that have also incorporated the term "apostolic" into their official names.

The difference between the traditional denominational administrator/congregational leader-teacher-minister model and the "apostolic" model of leadership lies in the locus of authority found in traditional churches in groups, consisting of deacon boards, church boards, boards of trustees, presbyteries, regional leadership structures, general assemblies, etc. In the New Apostolic Reformation, trust has shifted from groups to individuals. On local level, the pastor now functions as the leader of the church instead of as an employee of the church (represented by some board). On translocal level, the apostle is the one who has earned the trust of the pastors and other leaders, and their trust imparts authority, according to Wagner. Eventually, Wagner became involved with leaders whom he saw as apostles

---

164. Christerson and Flory, *Rise of Network Christianity*, 7-8.
165. Wagner, *Apostles Today*.

and they formed two apostolic networks, Eagles Vision Apostolic Team (EVAT) and the International Coalition of Apostles (ICA).[166]

Network charismatic Christianity originated within the context of third-wave neo-charismatic Christianity. It parted ways with the older neo-Pentecostal movement when Chuck Smith of Calvary Chapel combined an apostolic ministry with popular music-inspired worship, an informal style of fellowship during services, literalist biblical preaching, and openness to the miraculous manifestations of the Spirit. In the 1970s, John Wimber joined the Calvary Chapel movement with a ministry characterized by experimentation in its engagement with the Spirit. Eventually, it led to a split between the Calvary Chapel movement and Wimber, with Wimber moving to a large warehouse that was eventually called the Anaheim Vineyard and being invited to team-teach a class with C. Peter Wagner and Charles Kraft at Fuller Theological Seminary called "Signs, Wonders and Church Growth." During the course, Wimber led participants in the practices of prophecy and healing.

Another outgrowth of network charismatic Christianity is the Kansas City Prophets that adapted the theology of the "Latter Rain" movement of the 1940s, with its teaching that a final outpouring is due during the end times just before Christ's return to the earth.[167] An important indication of this final outpouring would be the restoration of the roles of apostle and prophet in the church. The church needed prophets to guide it in its major decisions because they can only receive prophetic direction from proven prophets and apostles. Another outgrowth is the Toronto Blessing that started in 1994 with John and Carol Arnott and Randy Clark at the Toronto Airport Vineyard Church. Clark was influenced by Rodney Howard-Brown, a South African preacher whose ministry was characterized by various manifestations such as holy laughter, falling in the Spirit, shaking, and crying.

The most important distinction between third-wave neo-charismatics and the new independent neo-charismatic networks is that the independent movement concentrates on spreading its influence through

---

166. E.g., Prophet T.B. Joshua mentions that he represents an apostolic ministry in a sermon entitled, "How to be filled with the Holy Spirit" (https://www.youtube.com/watch?v=IPPehKWzdIo; accessed 2020-01-02). He explains what the apostolic ministry signifies to him: he is going to teach the audience about a core and fundamental area of the gospel, the baptism with the Spirit, from his own personal experience, backed by what the Bible teaches. The authority of the apostle is in his ability to relate what the Spirit is doing in his ministry, he explains.

167. See discussion in previous chapter as well.

networks of relationships and media-based new technologies, concentrating on the impact on politics and economies rather than the local church, representing a shift from "movement" to "networks."

Apostles earn their position due to their ability to consistently bring about miracles of the Spirit. They are highly influential dynamic leaders who exude authority and take control of the governance of networks of groups and other administrative bureaucracies. They gain their legitimacy and influence from their perceived ability to access supernatural powers to produce "signs and wonders" rather than through their speaking ability, educational credentials, or position in a hierarchy. Wagner thinks that this development is in line with the biblical leadership roles of "apostles," a viewpoint that will require further investigation by exegesis of relevant Scriptures.

In Africa these apostles discovered the opportunity to wield political power. They told their followers which way to vote in elections, and some of them even aspired to political positions of power and influence. For instance, Chris Okotie of Nigeria contested presidential elections in Nigeria, becoming the first Pentecostal pastor to run for president. He is a rich man, driving around in his white Rolls Royce with bodyguards attending to his needs. He justified his participation in politics, running four times for president, by claiming that Jesus will be a political leader at his second coming and what Okotie is doing is a microcosm of what is going to happen with Jesus' second coming.[168]

These networks of independent charismatic groups are formed by spontaneous association with "apostles" who combine and recombine for specific projects but who are functionally independent of one another.[169] Groups associate freely with the apostle (or, in some cases, with more than one network of "apostles") and they pay some revenue for the privileges of the association. Most followers of apostles are not members of traditional denominations. They often move from conference to conference (or use the internet to follow the conferences), and ministry school to ministry school, and they define their faith more by their practice and allegiance to an individual leader than by their connection with a congregation, denomination, or tradition.

Apostles are not pastors, church planters, or missionaries; they do not technically "oversee" any churches that associate with them. These churches

---

168. Maclean and Egbejule, "Gospel Glamour."
169. Christerson and Flory, *Rise of Network Christianity*, 11.

chose to be under his apostolic "covering," and the apostle influences them through the network of associated apostles of which he is the head, and they submit to his apostolic covering by using his leadership resources, attending his conferences, and sending him financial contributions.

Apostles' individual revenue streams flow directly to them, and they have full discretion over how they use them. They do not rely on a consensus-based process with other believers but justify their financial and administrative decisions by calling on direct "words from the Lord" that they received. The leaders are also distinctive in their beliefs and practices, emphasizing practice over belief, while many practices they deem important are largely absent from traditional Protestantism, such as prophecy, defined as receiving direct words from God, physical healing, and deliverance from evil spirits (called *uchawi* in Swahili: "black magic"). Most of these leaders are also postmillennial in their eschatology; they believe that the power of God is available now to usher in the kingdom of God, and that it consists of a heaven on earth in the here and now. Their postmillennial utopianism is a break from classical pentecostal theology, which is focused on building the local church through the saving of souls in order to prepare them for eternity. Due to their premillennial leanings, Pentecostals in the past did not involve themselves in a political sense in their communities.

Network Christianity emphasizes healing and deliverance of individuals from demonic forces but also deliverance of cities and nations from oppression by evil spirits by way of the waging of spiritual warfare against "territorial spirits" (called "strategic level spiritual warfare") that keep people in bondage to various diseases, practices, and immorality and also keep them resistant to Christian faith.[170] It teaches that the kingdom of God can and will be founded on earth, through the rise of apostles who will establish themselves as leaders in the "Seven Mountains of Culture,"[171] which consist of religion, education, family, media, arts, entertainment, and business.[172] It asserts that in the process of influencing and determining the future of politics and economies, Christian believers will become the largest recipients of the wealth of

---

170. See Wagner, *Wrestling with Alligators*.

171. So called by Wagner, *Wrestling with Alligators*.

172. See, e.g. the establishment of Central University College by Mensa Otabil's International Central Gospel Church (ICGC) and Covenant University by David O. Oyedepo's Winners' Chapel, as a part of the call to take territories and influence public life (Quayesi, "Pentecostalism and the Transformation," 110).

nations in the history of the world, which they will use to bring about the transformation of the world.

Understanding the Impact of Independent Neo-Charismatic Networks

To understand the impact of these networks that effectively reach and influence large parts of the global south, the "religious economies" paradigm in sociology is used. In democracies where there is no official religious state religion, a "marketplace" exists in which religious "firms" or participants compete with each other for a share of available "customers."[173] Religious economies function in the same way as commercial economies. They consist of a market made up of a set of current and potential customers and a set of firms competing with each other in a share of customers. The fate of each firm rests on aspects of its organizational structure, sales representatives, products, and marketing techniques (or polity, clergy, religious doctrines and discourse, and evangelization techniques, to use ecclesial terms).

Religious disestablishment creates opportunities for religious "entrepreneurs" (or "opportunists," as many churches prefer to call them) to compete for customers who can join in theory whatever faith they choose. Religious "goods" that these firms provide include promises of future rewards, supernatural explanations for life events, meaning, and a sense of belonging, among others.[174]

Leaders of independent neo-charismatic networks have expanded their share in the religious market because of their innovative organizational structures, unique offering of "products," and inventive marketing techniques and financing their activities, all of which leverage the power of digital communications technologies.[175]

Christerson and Flory identify three macro-level social changes that have occurred since 1970 that are especially important in explaining the rise of network Christianity.[176] The first is globalization, brought about by advances in transportation and communications technologies that have accelerated the integration of social processes and economic,

---

173. See Finke and Start, *Churching of America*.
174. See Sherket and Ellison, "Recent Developments", 365.
175. Christerson and Flory, *Rise of Network Christianity*, 13.
176. Christerson and Flory, *Rise of Network Christianity*, 15.

political and cultural systems across national boundaries. A second change is the digital revolution where advances in digital technology, especially the development of the microcomputer, smartphone, and internet that has transformed the way communication is disseminated and communicated, and which led to the expansion and democratization of access to knowledge and information. A last change is represented by the rise of networks and the associated decline of bureaucracies, from large-scale hierarchical organizations toward informed and informal social systems organized by networks of small-scale actors. Advances in information technology favors this form of organization on a global scale.

These social changes have produced changes in the religious marketplace, specifically in terms of younger consumers. Globalization led to an increase in cultural and religious pluralism, interactive media led to consumers being active participants rather than passive consumers of religious options, participating in the religious "product," and leading to discontentment with ministries and sermons of their local congregation when the blogs, sermons, and live-streamed activities of more interesting and well-known speakers or more spectacular events around the world are easily available.[177] The result is declining loyalty to established institutions, because instant access to multiple worldviews and religious products and activities means that believers now can pick and choose from a wide array of products and activities that are readily and easily available from multiple sources. To access religious "goods," it is no longer needed that one commits oneself to a particular tradition or congregation. These changes increased the potential market share for religious activities organized by networks of innovative religious entrepreneurs, *contra* the traditions represented by formal religious structures.[178] It also implies that the market share of religious goods produced by networks of religious entrepreneurs will probably expand steadily because they are more close suited and adapted to the current social context in which they operate.

---

177. See Anderson's ("New African Initiated Pentecostalism," 66) reference to the globalization of charismatic Christianity by the reference to three dimensions, the use of mass communications media to disseminate its ideas, a social organization that promotes internationalism through global travel and networking, conferences, and megachurches that function like international organizations, and a global orientation or global charismatic "meta-culture" that transcends locality and denominational loyalty and displays the same striking similarities in different parts of the world.

178. Christerson and Flory, *Rise of Network Christianity*, 17.

A New Form of Governance

Charismatic network Christianity can be distinguished from other traditions and types of Christianity by its form of governance, of apostolic network. The structure of governance that it represents connects with current market trends and it has the potential to change the way that Christianity is practiced and experience by the market of people who are religiously interested and inclined.[179] The leadership can be qualified as charismatic, in the sense that Max Weber uses the term. Charisma is a certain quality of an individual personality, by virtue of which the person is set apart from others and treated as if endowed with supernatural, superhuman, or exceptional powers or qualities.[180] The qualities are regarded as divine in origin and as exemplary, on the basis of which the person is identified as a leader.

In terms of charismatic network Christianity, these leaders are also characterized by their intentional avoidance of routinization, and they are seemingly informed by Weber's theory concerning the process of routinization. They believe that they had found a way out of the seemingly inevitable routinization process, where charismatic authority always shifts eventually to rational-legal authority.[181] They represent apostolic leadership because they accept the restoration of the fivefold gifts of ministry (Eph 4:11), a principle accepted by most classical Pentecostals although they rejected the role of apostle as having relevance for current church practice and specifically leadership. The network leaders are convinced that the role of apostle has become the key element of the growing Christian worldwide movement. The apostle is defined in terms of extraordinary leadership abilities, backed by supernatural powers.

Apostolic leadership avoids routinization by enabling the sharing of resources as well as followers, which allows each leader in the network to increase their following without having to submit to the authority of an overarching organization with its limiting rules and regulations. The network is also not dependent on an individual leader that may die or retire; the lack of any bureaucratic structures implies that its web of relationships can perpetuate. Another important observation is that apostolic leaders are free to experiment and innovate, and lead the network as they feel led by the Spirit. Christerson and Flory distinguish between vertical

---

179. Christerson and Flory, *Rise of Network Christianity*, 50.
180. Weber, *Economy and Society*, 241.
181. Christerson and Flory, *Rise of Network Christianity*, 51.

networks that are structured like a pyramid, with a head apostle at the top and other apostles below the head apostle, and non-hierarchical horizontal apostolic networks where the apostle does not expect financial contributions or participation in annual meetings or involvement in any network activities while the apostle offers advice, resources, and material support to interested ones, without establishing formal ties.[182] In vertical networks, other apostles and leaders align themselves with the lead apostle who provides them with "covering." The leaders expect that the anointing resting upon the apostle would "trickle down" to them as well. In both types of leadership control, manipulation, or legal authority over others are avoided. If you disagree with the apostle, you find another one that fits your needs better.

Network governance, representing the fastest-growing subset of Christianity around the world, can be defined as a select, persistent and structured set of autonomous firms and non-profit agencies (in this case, religious groups) that are engaged in creating products or services based on implicit and open-ended contracts to adapt to environmental contingencies and to coordinate and safeguard changes.[183] It is a subset of groups that work together for short-term projects although the alliances are not simply one-time instances of cooperation, but they operate consistently over long periods of time. It represents a distinct form of coordinating economic activity which contrasts and competes successfully with markets and hierarchies. In a world that has become a network society as a result of advances in digital communication technologies, network Christianity is highly successful because of its flexibility, scalability, and survivability.[184]

Network governance emerges, thrives and flourishes, and outperforms other forms of leadership when the situation represents uncertainty because the demand for products changes rapidly, requiring firms to reduce fixed costs and increase their flexibility. Their leaders (CEOs) realize that the need for customized products involve high human-asset specificity, consisting of people who are uniquely experienced in creating such products. Normal standardized production methods are ineffective in providing what the market requires, and a network is much more effective to establish the human assets that can provide in the market needs than a bureaucracy. They also comprehend the need to produce a

182. Christerson and Flory, *Rise of Network Christianity*, 51.

183. Jones, Hesterly and Borgati, "A General Theory of Network Governance", 911-45.

184. As discussed in Castells, *Network Society*.

product quickly to meet changing market demands and that it requires the cooperation of multiple skilled participants, while their initiatives would have been smothered in a bureaucratic organization structure. Lastly, they realize that there is a need for frequent exchanges of goods and services between firms, requiring relationships of trust that can prevent firms from committing acts of narrow self-interest at the expense of their exchange partner.[185]

The competitive advantages of networks compared with those of formal religious organizations like established denominations are that networks are free to experiment with alternative religious beliefs and practices without the constraints imposed by formal structures within denominations while individual leaders have practically unlimited access to other congregations and ministries beyond their own. They are also able to access revenue sources beyond what is possible in a congregation or ministry. This explains why prosperity theology could receive the attention in the networks that eventually influenced congregations and ministries worldwide through their exposure to the ministries of apostles. In mainline denominations prosperity theology was evaluated by formal bodies established for the purpose of defending the denomination against heretical teachings while in the networks apostles are not accountable to anybody in terms of their theological stances.

While Weber's routinization theory explains how charismatic authority inevitably devolves into a bureaucratic-legal authority once the leader dies or leaves the movement, it is these bureaucratic-legal structures that allow a movement to grow on a much larger scale than would have been possible under a single leader. The cost of establishing formal structures is, however, high in terms of a loss of passion, energy, vision, and the charisma of the original leader who sparked the movement. As far as charismatic networks are concerned, the networked form of governance resists these natural tendencies because charismatic network leaders are free to provide for rapidly changing tastes of consumers in the religious market. Networks in the global capitalist economy as well as the religious economy are more flexible, reduce overhead costs, and encourage innovative responses to shifts in market demand.

Network Christianity is successful in reaching the declining religious market because of its experience of the miraculous, the opportunities it creates for individuals' direct participation in these miraculous

185. Discussed more fully in the article by Jones, Hesterly and Borgati, "A General Theory of Network Governance."

occurrences, and its promise of social (and not only individual) transformation.[186] Especially in Africa the promise of direct experience with supernatural forces appears to be particularly attractive, because of the lure of primal spirituality on contemporary Africans. In their world, prophecy, healing, and deliverance are important ingredients because of its association with African traditional religion.[187] Network Christianity takes these activities out of the exclusive context of worship services and into the public domain.

Theologically the participation in social justice is rationalized as Christianity retaking the dominion that Satan stole from Adam in the Garden of Eden that would lead to the advancement of the kingdom of God in the world, and not only result in individual conversions. Their "seven mountains" mandate includes that Christians would saturate each other with the mountains of influence (religion, education, family, media, arts, entertainment, and business) and rise to the top of each mountain. Kingdom-oriented and Spirit-filled believers would manage the different sectors of society to effect social transformation. In the process they would generate prosperity for their nations and societies, and networks would benefit financially from their support. Network Christianity accordingly sets its aim at young leaders with the potential to lead in different sectors and "bring heaven down on earth."

Genesis, however, never depicts humanity as an autonomous sovereign, but as stewards entrusted with the care of a part of creation. Genesis 1:26, 28 states that God gave humanity dominion over some of the creation, but that does not imply that they are set on a par with God in terms of the dominion over the earth, and the universe. Human beings are being held responsible for how they handle what God has assigned to them. The problem in prosperity theology comes with the meaning attached to the Hebrew word for "dominion." Benny Hinn interprets "dominion" as follows: God created Adam a super being with dominion over the fowls of the air, the fish of the sea, and the birds.

While classical Pentecostalism tended to be premillennial, hoping for the millennium to bring the required social transformation without having any hope for the betterment of the present world, most of the networks are postmillennial, believing that God has empowered believers

---

186. Christerson and Flory, *Rise of Network Christianity*, 84.

187. Network Christianity accepts as a rule that *glossolalia* is part of the experience of Spirit baptism, although it does not accept (as charismatics also do) that it is the initial sign of such baptism and as a rule it does not occur during their worship services.

through the equipment of the Spirit to literally bring heaven to earth. When they gain power in the various sectors of society, they create heaven on earth. They rule the earth.

Their strategy to establish their dominionist theology through the spiritual reform of the different sectors of society includes "strategic-level spiritual warfare," consisting of researching the religious history of a specific area and writing a "spiritual profile" before the prophets are requested to determine the names and nature of the demonic forces that oppose revival and social transformation. Then prayer leaders or intercessors arrange prayer walks, meetings, and vigils to fight the demonic spirits, calling them by name and breaking their hold over that area. They hold evangelistic campaigns and healing services while at the same time they influence the major players in the highest levels of the different sectors to place kingdom-minded believers in influential positions.

Another factor in the network movement is the creation by technology of "new power" that is less hierarchical and more participatory than older models, leading to a change in values. People increasingly expect to actively participate and shape many aspects of their lives. They question authority and institutions and do not commit themselves to institutional affiliations. At the same time, globalization brought them into contact with other worldviews and cultures, making them more open and tolerant of differences between groups of people. The digital revolution has also democratized access to information while interactivity makes the access active rather than passive, as in the past. The process of the generation of knowledge has become open, democratic and participatory, leading to the need in the religious market for experiential consuming in which participants require their active shaping and participating in religious experiences. Richard Flory and Donald Miller call this new form of spirituality an "expressive communalism," because it combines physical experiences of the sacred with a community orientation.[188]

Evaluation of the Ministry of the Apostle

For reasons that will become apparent in the course of the following discussion, it is appropriate to present an evaluation on the ministry of the apostle from a classical pentecostal perspective at this stage. It is not the first time that the movement had to evaluate the role and influence of

188. Flory and Miller, *Finding Faith*.

apostles. During the Latter Rain movement within Pentecostalism the position of apostles caused clashes between elected leadership and the authoritative claims of the apostles to enjoy the personal revelation of God that eventually led to schisms in several Pentecostal denominations. For instance, the General Council of the Assemblies of God in the USA decreed in 1949 that the teaching that the church is built on the foundation of the present-day apostles and prophets is erroneous.[189] In 2000, its General Council discussed the matter again, in the light of the growth of the independent church movement and the emphasis in a part of the movement on the government of the church by acknowledged apostles, and decided that the teaching that the present-day offices of apostles and prophets should govern church ministries at all levels is a departure from Scripture and a deviant teaching. The White Paper of the Assemblies of God motivates its viewpoint from the damage caused by "persons with an exaggerated estimate of their importance in the kingdom of God."[190]

Like the White Paper, most classical Pentecostals agree that apostolic and prophetic-like ministries in the church exists as a part of the New Testament church, and their insights and input are important to ensure the church's charismatic guidance. Like the Azusa Street revival church that was established by William Seymour, many other denominations of classical Pentecostals used the designation "apostolic" in their names, illustrating the strong restorationist and primitivist urge that motivated the movement.[191] However, the problem comes with an individual that is identified (or identify themselves) as filling such an office, and the accompanying theological conviction that the new position should rewrite church government. Instead of a corporate decision-making process that involves a representation of the church, financial and strategic decisions are left in the hands of an individual.

In a doctoral thesis, Benjamin McNair Scott distinguishes between three types of charismatic apostolic ministries in the contemporary Christian church: what he calls Apostle Type 1, consisting of hierarchical

---

189. Quoted in Wagner, *Apostles Today*, 16.

190. Wagner, *Apostles Today*, 63.

191. Although the Pentecostal movement is still motivated by a strong restorationist and primitivist urge, it should be remembered that there simply is not enough information in the New Testament to understand in detail what some of the early ministries were and how they functioned, and what characterized the early church. Primitivism can easily function as a naïve simplistic faith if this fact is forgotten (Guinness, *Fit Bodies*, 43).

or supreme apostles in the New Apostolic Reformation churches and Apostolic Networks with authority exercised in relation to those churches that the apostles have founded and those invited to become a part, and with the apostle viewed on a par with the authority of the twelve apostles of Jesus and Paul in their dealings with the church; Apostle Type 2, consisting of non-foundational apostles who act under the authority of a local pastor; and Apostle Type 3, consisting of non-select apostles that, along with the other four ministry gifts are not reserved for a select group, because every member of the church is either an apostle, prophet, pastor, teacher, or evangelist, with the apostle's leadership gifts focused on the sake of mission.[192]

Some proponents stress the hierarchical nature of this ministry (called Apostle Type 1 by McNair Scott), and a host of charismatic celebrities advocates it: Peter Wagner, Terry Virgo, Derek Prince, Colin Urquhart, and Barney Coombes alongside churches in Africa associating with the New Apostolic Reformation, the Catholic Apostolic Church, the New Apostolic Church, the Apostolic Church, and Latter Rain denominations. They view the apostle as indispensable, and his spiritual authority takes precedence over all other ministries in the church.[193] They provide the "foundational" input without which the local and universal church will never become what God desires. They use Ephesians 2:20, 4:11-13, and 1 Corinthians 12:28 as proof-texts. This form of leadership does already have a noticeable impact on the church worldwide. The apostles mentioned in Ephesians 2:20 are equated with those in Ephesians 4:11. However, apostles and prophets did not always found individual churches within the New Testament era, and there is no indication that they had to. The church at Antioch who sent out apostles was not founded or begun by apostles, nor was it seen as vital that an apostle go there to stabilize it. If an equation is not a necessity, it becomes clear that the New Testament ministry of "apostle" was not concerned with church government, as is the case with the perception of the apostle that functions here, but that the apostle's function was rather intended to facilitate the maturity of believers.[194] These advocates are arguing for a similar ministry to offices they reject, that of a Roman Catholic or Orthodox bishop, is McNair

---

192. McNair Scott, *Apostles Today*, 294.

193. Apostles are viewed exclusively as males, and females are excluded from the movement since the apostles in New Testament times were male, reflecting the surrounding culture of patriarchy.

194. Resane, "Ecclesiology of the Emerging Apostolic Churches," v.

Scott's submission.[195] Like an Orthodox or Roman Catholic bishop, an apostle is more than a function but has become in reality an ontological phenomenon with great authority. Some of the Apostolic Network apostles have a role similar to that of the Roman Catholic pope. Their pope-like status also accorded them with authority that created space for serious spiritual abuses that some apostles subscribed to. Their position also stifles the laity's participation in the ministry, creating a new elite of apostles and prophets that undermines the priesthood and prophethood of all believers.[196] Their form of government leads to an overdependence upon these super apostles for direction and revelation, at the cost of the democratic involvement of the Spirit-filled people of God.

In terms of other perspectives on the position of apostles (called Apostles Type 2 and 3 by McNair Scott),[197] there is a valid place for it as charismatic ministries, with exegetical evidence for its continuation. It was an integral part of how the church operated through the ages, without being called by the same designation. Perhaps it is a good idea to continue calling the persons responsible for those functions by different names, such as "pioneers" or "missional leaders," because of the negative baggage associated with the term "apostle," especially in Africa. At the same time, the ministry should be grounded in Scriptural categories, carefully differentiating between originary and non-foundational apostles, and focusing on functions rather than titles. In all cases, firm accountability structures should be established among apostles

Jon Ruthven wrote his doctoral dissertation on a rebuttal of the cessationist position defended by B.B. Warfield.[198] He developed an argument that the five-fold ministry is demanded biblically, and in the process he exegeted key biblical texts which are used by cessationists to argue against the possibility of charismatic ministries. He concluded that apostles and prophets, mentioned in Ephesians 2:20 as the foundation of the church with Jesus Christ as the cornerstone, will cease with the eschatological hope expressed in Ephesians 4:13, when the church will attain the full measure of the fullness of Christ. Until then the functions that these ministries have will still be needed, even if the church called the persons associated with the different functions by different names other

---

195. McNair Scott, *Apostles Today*, 269.
196. Jackson, *Quest*, 230.
197. McNair Scott, *Apostles Today*.
198. Ruthven, *On the Cessation of the Charismata*.

than the jargon used by the authors of the New Testament.[199] Ruthven also emphasizes that 1 Corinthians 12:28—13:13 supports the view that the gift of "apostle" will continue until "perfection" comes.[200]

Ruthven disagrees with the cessationist argument that the role of apostles and prophets in the time of the early church was to establish the parameters of church doctrine, and therefore once this was done their office was no longer needed. He states that the New Testament does not explicitly hold that this was their role, nor even that this was one of them. He also disagrees with the traditional view that saw the apostles and prophets as the unique receivers and articulators of Christian revelation, a role that no one may subsequently share after they had died. The New Testament was written more by those who were not apostles (51 percent) than those who were (49 percent),[201] and although prophecy is related to inspiring Scriptures ten times in the New Testament, there are 153 other types of prophetic utterances mentioned, and their functions can be summarized as: to praise and glorify God (Acts 2:14), for edification, exhortation, and consolation (1 Cor 14:3; Acts 15:32), and the equipping of believers toward ultimate spiritual goals (Eph 4:12-13). A hypothetical case of prophecy offered by Paul in 1 Corinthians 14:24-25 shows prophecy as revealing the secrets of the heart, in order to lead toward repentance.[202] It is true that these apostles are foundational in terms of being prototypes or role models for others to follow.[203] Their task is to be continually needed until the church reaches maturity (Eph 4:11-13). He concludes that the plain sense of Ephesians 4:11-13 is that the gift of apostle will continue to be given until the church reaches full maturity, and that will only happen at the realization of the new earth and heaven.

Although Gordon Fee does not agree with Ruthven's conclusion, he adds that an integral part of Paul's understanding of an apostle's function was the founding of churches through evangelism, with 1 Corinthians 12:28 and Ephesians 2:20 referring to the ministry of founding local churches.[204] David Pawson distinguishes between five types of apostles in

199. Ruthven, "'Foundational Gifts,'" 5.

200. Ruthven, "Does the Spiritual Gifts of Apostleship," 215.

201. Ruthven, "'Foundational Gifts,'" 11-2. That is, if a conservative view of authorship of writings in the New Testament is upheld.

202. Ruthven, "'Foundational Gifts,'" 12-3.

203. Ruthven, "Does the Spiritual Gifts of Apostleship," 217.

204. Fee, *God's Empowering Presence*, 190-92. See the discussion of his viewpoint in McNair Scott, *Apostles Today*, 267.

the New Testament, with Jesus as the chief Apostle, the twelve apostles, Paul as apostle number 13, a pioneer church planter who builds new churches with new converts, and any Christian sent by the local church to do anything in terms of evangelism.[205] He adds that only the last two types are still functioning today. I agree that the twelve apostles, Paul, and other first-generation apostles held a unique role which can never be repeated due to their "originary" functions, but also that the New Testament foresees an ongoing charismatic apostolate. There is evidence both in Scripture and early Christian writings for a secondary charismatic apostolate differentiated from the "originary" apostles, and the early churches variously understood themselves as apostolic on the basis of origin, doctrine, life, and apostolic succession.[206]

It must be admitted that an individual making quick decisions solely can speed up the process of decision-making considerably, but the loss for the church is not worth the cost, that consists in fellow-believers losing their sense of partaking in decisions that determine the future of the church that is financed by their contributions and the security that a more transparent process involving more experienced, knowledgeable and educated persons, some of them financial and strategic experts, ensures more balanced decisions.

For this reason, the evaluation of the ministry and position of the apostle is discussed here; it is not motivated by the fact that someone claims to be an apostle but because the reinstitution of the position holds critical implications for the form of government of the church. While Peter Wagner and others hold that this new form of government is the product of a new revelation of God to the current church, to ensure its survival in a postmodern world, I disagree. In traditional denominations, the locus of authority is ordinarily found in groups, not in individuals, as Wagner correctly observes.[207] The church held itself accountable in various ways, demonstrating the transparency of its decision-making processes to the diverse stakeholders. Decision-making was the result of a corporate process that involved church boards, boards of trustees, or presbyteries on the level of the local government, and general assemblies or synods on a national level, with in many cases a further mechanism was built in, on a regional level, to ensure that supervision of the church's

---

205. Pawson, *Unlocking*, 877.
206. See McNair Scott, *Apostles Today*, chapters 1 and 2.
207. Wagner, *Apostles Today*, 22.

decision-making processes from the bottom (local congregation) to the top (head office of the denomination), and from the top to the bottom were responsible, accountable, and transparent.

In apostolic churches the individual is trusted and entrusted with all decisions. The apostle is supposed to be appointed by God to supervise the ministry of assemblies, in most cases a group of assemblies that associate with the apostle. The apostle has the sole privilege of taking decisions determining the financial and strategical future of the assemblies, focusing the trust in one person, and not a group of responsible persons that represent the stakeholders. In Africa there are many stories of financial tragedies that can be recounted where individuals abused their decision-making powers, investing money of their stakeholders in quick money-making schemes, leading to financial losses, or abused money to enrich themselves at the cost of poor members of assemblies. The abuse is of such widespread extent that in several countries' governments have taken or are taking steps to hold such individuals accountable for their financial spending patterns. For instance, several apostles from other African countries that are operating in South Africa are investigated by prosecuting authorities for money laundering, involvement in trafficking, organized crime, and crime syndicates.

An important problem that will cause more and more problems within classical Pentecostal denominations is that due to the influence of the independent church movements on their other Pentecostal family members, more and more assemblies within established denominations are following the same form of governance. In many assemblies, church boards had for all practical purposes been disbanded, while a small governing body was instituted, mostly consisting of confidants of the pastor, and the authority of the assembly leader ensured by limiting the decision-making capabilities of the governing body. This has been happening at times in contravention of the constitutions of the different denominations. Some of the assemblies (under pressure of their leaders or pastors) have also associated with apostles in the independent movement without the approval of their denominational headquarters. Financial decision-making is concentrated more and more in the hands of an individual, making assemblies vulnerable to financial mismanagement and abuse by the pastor. My primary problem with the institution of the apostle in the current church is not that the office of the apostle was not recognized in the early church apart from the twelve apostles but that it is carrying a form of governance into the church that allows for dictatorial abuses by an individual, while the Pentecostal movement is characterized by strong, charismatic leaders that influence the movement to a great extent.

In the independent churches where the government is the sole responsibility of the apostle, the teaching is that apostolic authority is based on the spiritual gift that the apostle possesses, the assignment or call that the apostle has received, the extraordinary character that is displayed by the apostle, the extent of adherents that follow the apostle of people who recognize and willingly submit to the apostle's authority, and the vision the apostle has received as a revelation from God, claiming to understand what the Spirit is saying to the churches right now.[208] Wagner emphasizes that the term "self-appointed apostle" is a semantic oxymoron; apostles who assign themselves would never enjoy the recognition from a considerable group of adherents that qualify the person to be called an apostle.

Who then are today's apostles, from a classical pentecostal perspective? The New Testament word *apostolos* means "messenger" or "a person that is sent," and missionaries taking the gospel to unreached areas of the world, commissioned by and with a mandate from the church, are present-day apostles.[209] Jesus designated the twelve disciples that he appointed after his night in prayer alone (Mark 3:13–19) as apostles; when he sent out seventy other disciples with a message of salvation and the power to heal and deliver (Luke 10:1–12), he called them "apostles" as well.

Classical Pentecostalism distinguishes between the gift and the office of the apostle (and prophet). Some receive the gift of being an apostle through the grace of God that qualifies them for a specific task. The church perceives that the anointing of the Spirit rests on the person, equips the person further for the external aspects of the task, and sends the person to do a specific task, in most cases to establish churches from the start in areas that have not been reached successfully with the gospel.

Peter Wagner, claiming himself to be an apostle and a teacher about the current apostolic movement, and a leader of a network of such apostles (International Coalition of Apostles, or ICA), argues that the office of a prophet differs from the gift in that the gift is received by the grace of God (*charis*, as a *charisma*), while the office is received through works.[210] The office is not given by God but conferred by people. The key indicator in conferring the office of apostle on someone is the fruit of the gift, as

---

208. The list is derived from Wagner, *Apostles Today*, 23-34.
209. Cross and Livingstone, *Oxford Dictionary*, 89.
210. Wagner, *Apostles Today*, 24.

the outward evidence that the person has actually received the gift. The office then becomes the public affirmation that an individual is recognized as having a spiritual gift, of governing the church in terms of Ephesians 4:11–12 and 1 Corinthians 12:28, and that they are authorized to exercise that gift within the church. Some have been given the gift but they have not entered into their destiny because they have not yet earned the office.[211]

Although not all agree on the definition on the current office of "apostle," the influence of Wagner's publications on the apostolic movement ensures that his definition is accepted widely. An apostle is someone who is gifted, equipped, commissioned, and sent by God (and not the church, as classical Pentecostalism argues, in conjunction with God) with the authority to establish the foundational government of the church within an assigned sphere of ministry by hearing what the Spirit is saying to the churches and by setting things in order accordingly for the growth and maturity of the church and for the extension of the kingdom.[212] The task of the apostle is to receive revelation from God intended for the wider church, to cast vision on the basis of this revelation, to birth new things, to impart blessings on others, to build and govern, teach and send, lead the church in spiritual warfare, raise up second-tier leadership for the future, and equip the saints for their ministry.[213]

In the networks, the authority accorded to the apostle by adherents requires them to vow their loyalty to the apostle and to follow the apostle's guidance in everything that is demanded. When the apostle claims a revelation from God concerning God's will for the believer, such as that all believers should be wealthy, prosperous, and happy, their words are to be trusted implicitly. In the case of a revelation that suits the desires of most people it is probable that the revelation will in any case not be critically examined by believers. The office of apostle ensures that the prosperity message is accepted by many African Pentecostals as authoritative and biblically based. John McCauley, a political scientist, speculates that African Pentecostalism has fallen under the lure of the "big man rule," a description taken from traditional politics in Africa, where a "big man" or patron has exclusive access to all resources and distributes them in exchange for loyalty of his adherents.[214] As a result, the neo-Pentecostal

---

211. Wagner, *Apostles Today*, 24.
212. Wagner, *Apostles Today*, 26.
213. Wagner, *Apostles Today*, 28.
214. McCauley, "Pentecostal Politics in Ghana," 68.

preacher has become one of the most authoritative figures on the African scene, given the widespread growth of Pentecostalism on parts of the continent. In Ghana, for instance, it is estimated that a quarter of all Ghanaians are Pentecostals, in a country where two-thirds of the population are Christian. It qualifies to be called a new kind of patron-client relationship in the informal African context.

The apostolic movement also contributes to an anti-intellectual climate, isolating itself from academic activities of the theological field and in most cases preferring not to engage in proper training for its leaders.[215] No longer does the apostle need grounded scientific exegesis to interpret difficult passages in the Bible; the direct access to divine revelation ensures that the apostle's interpretation would be the correct one, even when it is farfetched. Such a farfetched doctrine is a dominant teaching among prosperity teachers, of the generational curse, implying that the dabbling of forefathers with the occult or witchcraft is visited on today's generation by way of a curse, that needs to be lifted by way of deliverance or exorcism.[216] A related teaching is that places occupied by believers may be infested by demonic presence, and these places need to be sanctified and cleansed with a ritual to regain it for believers' use. The theology of exorcism focuses primarily on Ephesians 6:12 and 2 Corinthians 10:3–5, stating that exorcism is spiritual warfare. It teaches that every Christian needs to undergo exorcism after conversion.[217] At the same time, apostles utilize the pop theology that characterizes the prosperity message, with its different formulas and recipes guaranteeing success and effectiveness in acquiring mechanically everything that one desires. It is a reductionist theology, that reduces everything to a formula that supplies health, wealth, and personal success, and happiness. Christians write their own ticket on earth because God is in their service, providing everything they want or need. It represents a theology that is based on crypto-Christian Scientism on the one hand and spiritual magic on the other, and it requires to be rewritten from a more balanced theological perspective that leaves room for the sovereignty of God and God's whole counsel. It is suggested

---

215. Kgatle, "Unusual Practices."

216. Akiri, "The Prosperity Gospel;" see also the book by the apostle, Natasha Grbich, *Repentance*. For that reason, Comaroff and Comaroff, "Millennial Capitalism" calls the public practices of warfare, purification, prayer, and conversion the economies of the occult.

217. Folarin, "Contemporary State," 85.

that the prosperity message's older nephew, classical Pentecostalism, is in an ideal position to provide such a theological substructure.[218]

A New Form of Marketing and Financing

The networks' structure as well as the availability of new and fast digital communication technologies created new opportunities for ministry and marketing of the networks, while also creating new models of finances. Apostles provide their teaching through media with low overhead costs that access revenue from members of the network who buy into the ministry. Well-known keynote speakers at conferences ensure that millions of people around the world access the teaching wherever Wi-Fi and the internet is available, explaining the enormous influence that the networks' emphasis on prosperity theology had on a continent such as Africa.

The web enables apostles to produce visually compelling content that can be live streamed or recorded for consumption on the web. Location is not a constraint of growth anymore because the web serves as primary launching pad of these ministries, taking the apostles' teaching wherever interested parties access it. It has made the idea of apostolic covering and transferable anointing or impartation amenable to congregations and leaders across the world and because they are not accountable to the apostles, their contact is restricted to the web.

Many of the networks also provide ministry schools, sometimes called universities, that equip young people for ministry within the ethos of the particular apostle, with courses for all kinds of needs and at specific costs. In some cases, they follow the boot camp model that draws young people because of the communal living conditions, opportunities to participate in experimental and public ministries, and the chance of travel, strictly regulated by the school authorities. The model funds itself because students/interns pay to live and attend classes at the boot camp, and in most cases even the staff are responsible for raising their own financial support.

While congregations typically are high-overhead and low-revenue stream models, networks shifted to a "pay-for-service" model in which followers pay for a particular product that they wish to access, whether it is a worship CD, a DVD of teachings, a boot camp program, attending a conference online, or enjoying apostolic covering.[219] The Internet allows

---

218. See chapter 5.
219. Christerson and Flory, *Rise of Network Christianity*, 121.

for 24/7 content delivery at any place in the world. This implies that the number of paying customers can be expanded significantly beyond what would be the case in a single congregation, or even denomination. More revenue can also be generated because of the wide variety of products and services available, in contrast to conventional denominations that offer their ministry for free and then rely on and plead for financial support from members.

Conclusion

This chapter discussed the project under discussion, which is the prosperity gospel. The relation between Pentecostalism and the prosperity movement was described before the history of the prosperity movement was outlined. The prosperity message did not originate within the theology or praxis of Pentecostalism. This should be stated clearly, especially in the light of widespread perceptions established by the media that equates Pentecostalism and the prosperity movement in an unqualified manner. Prosperity theology originated in mind-cure, positive thinking, self-help, and success literature as part of the New Thought movement. Faith theology and the prosperity movement can be traced historically to cultic sources, when E.W. Kenyon combined pentecostal spirituality and New Thought. New Thought included groups such as Religious Science, Christian Science, and the Unity School of Christianity.

The teachings of the prosperity gospel were also delineated. It teaches that one can get whatever one desires in terms of health, wealth, success, and well-being by following the simple recipe that one should make contact with the power of God, turn it on, and believe that the power is coming into use. It should be accepted by faith and one should start acting as though it had already happened what one confesses and expects. One needs to confess one's faith by always using positive words because what believers express in words bring about whatever they believe. Invisible faith can also be transformed into financial rewards. Prosperity and health are two sides of the same coin. The rules of prosperity are: one should pay one's tithes, donations, and first fruits; expect financial miracles on a daily basis; and think positively. The result is guaranteed, that one will receive whatever one believes and confesses.

A new phase was introduced in Pentecostalism with the neo-Pentecostal independent churches that originated since the 1970s, centered around prominent figures that operated as prophets and apostles, and that preached the prosperity message. This eventually led to the Network movement and a new approach to the ministry of the apostle and a way of governance that is influencing Christianity on a wide front today.

The ministry, gift and office of the apostle were described because of its prominence in the new forms of neo-Pentecostalism, and an evaluation of the practice found in network Christianity was attempted from a classical pentecostal perspective. The conclusion was that classical Pentecostalism accepts that the gift of apostle is still given to individuals, equipping them to facilitate the missional nature of the church by establishing new converts to the gospel and congregations in previously unreached regions. The condition for being recognized as an apostle is the anointing of the Spirit with the gift, recognition of the local church, and the empowerment of the church in sending out the minister of the gospel to the unreached. What is important is the distinction among Pentecostals between the function and office of a prophet. It accepts that the function of the prophet is still a necessity while the whole world is not reached with the good news of Jesus Christ, but from its historical experience it does not accept that the apostle occupies an office representing a kind of dictatorial governance. For that reason, it was suggested that the designation "apostle" might as well be avoided because of many negative historical associations with the term, especially in Africa.

The chapter delineated the prosperity gospel in terms of its origins, historical developments and present-day appearance, in order to apply the message and the movement to the African context, asking in what way(s) the message differs from the American version of the prosperity gospel. This is the task of the following chapter, to relate the prosperity message to its African proponents and their unique transplanting of the prosperity message to a new context, that of Africa.

4

The Challenge
Prosperity Gospel in Africa

Introduction

IN THIS CHAPTER THE prosperity gospel is brought into focus in terms of the African continent. Where the previous chapter discussed the prosperity gospel in general terms, describing its origins and history, its teachings, and its relation to the new emphasis on the office of the apostle, in this chapter the prosperity message's presuppositions, hermeneutical angle, and other characteristics as it realizes in Africa are investigated. A part of the discussion is dedicated to the way African neo-Pentecostals use proof-texts to support and ground their unique beliefs.

What has been argued so far is that the salvation market is viewed as highly competitive and different institutions like neo-Pentecostals and classical Pentecostals but also Methodists, Baptists, etc., compete furiously for "social capital".[1] There is only one market, in the sense that there is a confrontation between the different contenders for available "believers." Different groups use marketing techniques to show their attractiveness to prospective members—their pastor is more charismatic, there occur more miracles in this church, etc.[2]

A great advantage is when a church in Africa markets itself for preaching a holistic gospel, providing in all the felt needs of members of the surrounding community. The traditional African worldview does not

---

1. Bourdieu, "Forms of Capital;" Dubarry and Müller, "Pentecostal Churches and Capitalism," 1-34.

2. Dubarry and Müller. "Pentecostal Churches and Capitalism."

distinguish between secular and spiritual, and health, relationships, or money problems are viewed in similar holistic terms.³ African primal spirituality is in line with the supernatural, enchanted world referred to in Ephesians 6:12 as well, that "our struggle is not against enemies of blood and flesh, but against the rulers, against the authorities, against the cosmic powers of this present darkness, against the spiritual forces of evil in the heavenly places." Misfortunes are interpreted spiritually in terms of its causes, effects, and solutions, and those affected seek remedy from diviners, fortune tellers, and witchdoctors previously, and now from the Christian prophet, seen as the present-day equivalent of the diviners. Prosperity theology follows African Pentecostalism in utilizing a holistic spirituality, and sharing in Pentecostalism's success in reaching a wide array of people.

Marketing of the prosperity message is also effective due to the efficient use of social media and other new technologies. Neo-Pentecostals are increasingly mobilizing new technologies.⁴ Electronic media serve as suitable sites for publishing sermons in audio and even visual form, inviting people to special events, and extending the "empires of faith." Mookgo Kgatle researched the widespread and effective use of Facebook by prophets and its impact on the emergence of the prophetic churches in southern Africa, showing its wide impact in urban society and even in rural areas.⁵ Another important role-player is TBN (Trinity Broadcasting Network) that continues to broadcast the prophets of the prosperity gospel each day of the week in different African countries, along with several other television stations. Viewers are promised material gain and

---

3. See Ganiel's ("Pentecostal and Charismatic Christianity," 136) description of an indigenous worldview shared by many Africans and that consists of their treating the spirit world as real and tangible, as a Christian alternative to the traditional spirit world, in the indwelling of the Holy Spirit and a developed demonology; an incorporation of some of the symbols and signs of African traditional religion in their gospel music and religious services; a turning of the Bible into a canon of tribal history, so that the actions of God in the Old and New Testaments are explicitly compared with the actions of God in the histories of African nations; a comparing of conditions of people in the Bible with the conditions of the poor in Africa today, and focusing on the biblical promises that God will deliver the faithful from poverty; providing women with a space where they can confront their position on the margins of society, in order to speak and act for themselves; and drawing on the pre-Christian African tradition of prophets who foretold the future and the meaning behind social and political events. See also Kalu, *African Pentecostalism*, 183.

4. As demonstrated by Hackett, "Charismatic/Pentecostal Appropriation," 258–77.

5. Kgatle, "Social Media and Religion," 1.

wealth for their financial support of the ministries and the television channel, and viewers are encouraged to touch the screen and connect with the anointed man (or woman, in some cases) of God to receive their blessing of health, wealth, or happiness.

The relation between African Pentecostalism and its American nephew, African American Pentecostalism, is also relevant for the theme. At first, the Pentecostal movement was interracial, as at the Azusa Street Revival, but eventually the practice of racial separation also affected the movement. The initial Azusa Street movement was influenced by African American spirituality, with William Seymour playing a leading role, making the eventual translating of its central tenets more easily assimilable in Africa.[6] When black and white communities parted ways and developed in parallel lines in the USA, a pervasive and growing spiritualism developed among black Pentecostals that included an early form of New Age belief in which family members sought to contact deceased relatives, New Thought ideas and concepts, influences from the divine healing movement of Charles Cullis and others, the holiness tradition of the nineteenth century, the newly discovered pentecostal spirituality, and African-derived traditions such as hoodoo and voodoo. Pentecostal leaders in African American groups promised to "smooth the rough edges of capitalism and industrialism with theologies that countered poverty, disease, and despair. They sounded the ram's horn declaring the world to be—despite all evidence to the contrary—fundamentally good and ripe with opportunity."[7] When black Americans started to move from the Northern states to urban centers in Southern states in great numbers, they began to experiment with admixtures of all kinds of new supernatural powers in all kinds of religious traditions from rural settings and from West Africa.[8] The "fluidity of metaphysical Christianity in urban African American communities" that consisted of many displaced persons was something that left an indelible mark on pentecostal practice before it was exported around the world.[9] Already these theologies were mobilized to offer a hope of escape from "poverty, disease, and despair," echoing the later interest and sentiment for prosperity theology and depicted as a coping with the rise in capitalistic inequalities, especially between

---

6. Anderson, "African Independent Churches," 38.
7. Bowler, *Blessed*, 26.
8. Herskovits, *Myth of the Negro Past*.
9. Bowler, *Blessed*, 26.

black and white people. African Americans were ripe for the promise that the world is "ripe with opportunity," and in the process they occluded systems of economic inequality themselves.[10] African-American Pentecostalism influenced the black Pentecostal movement to a great extent, including its later interest in the prosperity message.

The prosperity gospel spread widely in Africa since the 1980s, and an important initial means of diffusion was the Fire Conference that Reinhard Bonnke's missionary enterprise, Christ for all Nations (CfaN) arranged in Harare, Zimbabwe in April 1986.[11] The conference drew four thousand delegates from forty-one African countries and it influenced African Pentecostalism immensely. Bonnke had invited Kenneth Copeland as one of the conference speakers, and he taught a key seminar on "The Gospel and Prosperity." This conference as well as succeeding ones succeeded in showing the way for African Pentecostalism. Ten years later, Kenneth Hagin, his son Kenneth Hagin Jr., and Kenneth Copeland visited African Instituted Churches in Nigeria and taught them the prosperity gospel, to such an extent that their churches exploded after that into millions of members.[12] Today the doctrine is associated with many of Africa's fastest-growing churches, like the Rhema churches of South Africa and Zimbabwe (although Ray McCauley had since distanced himself from some of the radical elements of hard prosperity theology), Andrew Wutawunashe's Family Church in Accra, Ghana, Benson Idahosa's Church of God Mission International in Nigeria, and many others.[13]

A word about the extent of African Pentecostalism is necessary to explain the interest in the subject of prosperity and pentecostal hermeneutics in an African perspective. Half a century ago, David Barrett already perceived that African Christianity is transforming "Christianity permanently into a primarily non-Western religion."[14] He asserts that the influence on Pentecostalism from the side of Africa will increase in years to come in the light of the growth of African Pentecostalism.

Ben-Willie Golo is correct in his observation that although neo-Pentecostal churches are an offshoot of classical Pentecostalism, they are distinct and they are rather direct results of the general renewal

10. Bafford, "Prosperity Gospel", 9.

11. Kalu, *African Pentecostalism*, 257. Kalu, *African Pentecostalism*, 258 refers to it as a "watershed" that changed the face of African Pentecostalism.

12. Phiri and Maxwell, "Gospel Riches," 24.

13. Mashau and Kgatle, "Prosperity Gospel and the Culture of Greed."

14. Barrett, "AD 2000", 50.

movements that swept over Africa, leading to the pentecostalization of main-line churches during the late 1960s and 1970s, especially among university students and student organizations.[15] The evangelistic activities of these groups formed the basis for the spread of charismatic renewal, leading eventually to the strong movement of independent groups and networks.[16] The origins of the African neo-Pentecostal movement should be seen apart from the rest of the world since it originated in unique circumstances and with unique emphasis although there are also clear interfaces with the worldwide movement.

The pentecostalization of African Christianity has been called the African Reformation of the twentieth century.[17] It is best understood and defined through the spirituality of indigenous pneumatic Christian communities and churches like the independent church movement, and their progenitors were African prophets like William Wadé Harris of West-Africa, Garrick Sokari Braide of the Niger Delta, Simon Kimbangu of Central Africa, and Isaiah Shembe of South Africa. Their activities (and many other itinerant preachers and healing evangelists who were less known) led to the rise of Holy Spirit movements, or African Instituted Churches, across the continent.[18] It charismatized African Christianity

---

15. Golo, "Africa's Poverty," 367.

16. So Ayegboyin and Ukah, "Taxonomy of Churches."

17. Anderson, "African Independent Churches," 23. I am not convinced that it represents a reformation in the same sense as the Protestant Reformation. While not denying its significance or the ongoing influence of African Pentecostals on developments in worldwide Pentecostalism, the effects of Pentecostalism, consisting of a pentecostalization of worship practices and a new emphasis on the Spirit within the theology of the church is not so widespread or pervasive as that of the Protestant Reformation.

18. Quayesi, "Pentecostalism and the Transformation," 103-4. Pentecostal-type or Spirit-type Indigenous Churches (that forms a significant part of African Instituted Churches) account for more than 40 percent of the South African black population (Anderson and Pillay, "Segregated Spirit," 227, 233). The phenomenon of African Instituted Churches is notoriously complex; various attempts have been made to classify the phenomenon along diverse lines. Anderson's (*African Reformation*, 15-8) and Oosthuizen's (*Healer-Prophet*, 1-2) classification makes the most sense, with African Instituted Churches classified as Ethiopian, Zionist, prophet/healing, and charismatic/Pentecostal or Spirit-churches. Thirty percent of the South African population consists of the almost entirely African "Zionist" and "Apostolic" churches, including the largest denomination in South Africa, the Zion Christian Church, and other large denominations like the St. Engenas Zion Christian Church and the St. John Apostolic Faith Mission (Anderson, "New African Initiated Pentecostalism," 68.). There are also between 4,000 and 7,000 smaller church organizations of a similar type. In some parts of Africa, Spirit-churches constitute up to 40 percent of the total population

The Challenge

and fundamentally altered the character of African Christianity, shifting the center of world Christianity to the global south, and the dominant theological perspectives have shifted with it.[19] The African Instituted Churches and Zionist movement serves as religious conduits for the integration of charismatic manifestations and worship into African church life.[20] The global church is not invested exclusively in mid-twentieth-cen-

(Anderson, *Vision of the Disinherited*, 306). The Spirit (or spiritual) churches form the pentecostalization of African Christianity. The Spirit African Instituted Churches, called the African expression of the worldwide Pentecostal movement by Harvey Cox, *Fire from Heaven*, 246. African Instituted Churches exist in sixty African countries with 9,300 denominations, 65 million members, and ninety-two national councils. The continent-wide Organization of African Instituted (formerly Independent) Churches is based in Nairobi, Kenya. The African Instituted Churches originated in 1864. Previously they were normally classified as "unaffiliated" Christians; today they are described as "independent neo-charismatics" (Barrett, "Worldwide Holy Spirit Renewal," 405). In southern Africa, the majority of the "churches of the Spirit" are known as Zionists and Apostolics, betraying their respective associations with the Chicago movement of John Alexander Dowie, the Apostolic Faith Mission of South Africa and the Apostolic Azusa Street Revival. Omenyo and Arthur ascribe the growth of African Pentecostalism to neo-prophetism, and the popularity of the prophetic movement to the relevance of the phenomenon to the religious context, religious pragmatism, and its compatibility with most sectors of people, the use of a predominantly oral form of communication, providing the youth with the opportunity to exercise their gifts and talents, and phenomena such as dreams and visions in personal and public forms of religion (Omenyo and Arthur, "Bible Says!," 51). If the African Instituted Churches of the Spirit are included in the reckoning with classical Pentecostals, charismatic groups, and independent Pentecostal related groups, 56 percent of Zimbabwe's population, 46 percent of South Africa's, 36 percent of Kenya's, 30 percent of the DRC's, 29 percent of Nigeria's and Ghana's, and 25 percent of Zambia's population should be grouped as Pentecostals (Anderson, "African Independent Churches," 23). African Instituted Churches are not paradigmatic of African Pentecostalism any longer; they have been overshadowed by the fast growing new and independent churches representing the neo-Pentecostal movement which have sprung up in African cities more recently (Anderson, "African Pentecostalism," 29).

19. Jenkins, *New Faces*. See also, e.g., Hunter, "Introduction," 1-5.

20. The contribution of these indigenous pneumatic movements to African Christianity is described by Quayesi, "Pentecostalism and the Transformation," 104-5 as the mediation of a process of enculturation in Christianity at a time when the faith looked very Western (as Mburu, *African Hermeneutics*, 5-6 also argues); a dynamic soteriology evident through a successful normalization of charismatic experiences in worship; an existential soteriology through the preaching and interpretation of salvation as simultaneously encapsulating eternal life, healing, well-being, employment, and human biological fruitfulness; an interventionist theology through the articulation of a practical Christian response to evil through prayer and fasting; the employment of oral theological discourses in singing locally composed choruses and testimonies of deliverance; and an innovative gender ideology through the recognition of the leadership

tury Western biblical scholarship as in the past; the church mushrooming in the Majority World where two-thirds of the world's Christians live[21] is developing its own biblical scholarship in touch with those issues that relate to the global church,[22] and Pentecostalism as a global phenomenon is influencing the scholarship. Questions posed to the Bible in the North differ from the neo-liberation questions of the people of the South.[23] The median Christian today is a young woman with limited education from the global south; her interest is with understanding biblical narrative rather than doctrinal issues, and she is poor.

In this chapter, the theological presuppositions of the prosperity will be packed out before it is explicated in terms of Africa's unique focus and emphasis on it. In a last part of the chapter, we will come back to the proof-texts quoted by prosperity teachers in their exposition of the message, and some remarks will be made about them from a classical pentecostal stance.

Theological Presuppositions of the Prosperity Message

Although the prosperity movement did not produce any formal systematic theology up to date that is accepted by most classical Pentecostals, it is possible to discern a distinctive theological system as foundation of the teaching, although it must be noted that prosperity preachers differ among themselves in terms of some aspects of the main doctrines.[24] As noted earlier, in some aspects the prosperity movement agrees with most of the doctrines of the Pentecostal movement (and Protestantism as such). Here attention will be given to those aspects in which they differ from both the pentecostal and broader Protestant traditions.

---

of women in continuity with the recognition of women as priestesses and diviners in traditional religions (see also Asamoah-Gyadu, *African Charismatics,* 39-59).

21. "Majority World" is the self-designated term that non-Western nations of Africa, Asia, and Latin America prefer. Churches in the Majority World are more sympathetic towards reports about healings and deliverances from evil spirits or demons than Western Christianity in general (Keener, "Pentecostal Biblical Interpretation," 279; *Spirit Hermeneutics,* 88-92).

22. Keener, "Pentecostal Biblical Interpretation," 274.

23. Bartholomew, *Introducing Biblical Hermeneutics,* 544.

24. One of the reasons for a lack of systematic theologies in Pentecostalism is the urge to emphasize the experiential above the academic, and life above doctrine.

The prosperity gospel is best captured in Africa by the popular choruses that believers sing. In southern Africa, for instance, they sing the popular chorus, "Everything will double double: Your house will double double, your cars will double double."[25]

View of God

Most of the publications that appear from various prosperity preachers are concerned with the practical side of religion and how to be successful, with how to pray and believe in such a way that one gets the desired results, to be prosperous, healthy and thriving in one's relationships, profession, and personal life. The theme of success is predominant. Although the prosperity preachers differ on many points from each other, they agree about the way they view and describe God. They subscribe to almost all of the traditionally accepted Christian teachings on God, including the Trinitarian doctrine, as well as the sovereignty, righteousness, holiness, love, grace, mercy, beauty, power, wisdom, purity, justice, omnipotence, and omnipresence of God. Their theoretical confessions about God, however, differ in critically important aspects from their view of God in the application of their faith.[26] In the application of their faith they portray God as they actually view God, and it differs from the pentecostal and Protestant view in several critical aspects, necessitating that Pentecostals should view and evaluate it critically.

They view prosperity, both spiritual and material, as a promise to all believers without exception, and an integral part of the gospel of the atonement of Christ. Prosperity is thus not a gift from the hand of God to some people, based on grace. It is rather the right and heritage of all believers because God laid down certain rules and principles to govern every single thing into existence, and as the laws of gravitation, matter, and light govern our existence, there are laws in the "world of the spirit" that function in terms of salvation. When you do some things, it will necessarily and consistently bring forth the results God intended. If someone calls on the name of the Lord, they will be saved. These laws only operate when they are put to work. Salvation is a gracious gift but humans have to put the law to work in their lives before they are saved. They have to believe in Jesus and the atonement he realized on the cross before they are

---

25. Dube, Musa, "Between the Spirit and the Word," 6.
26. Horn, *From Rags to Riches*, 86.

saved. The same applies to prosperity, where God also revealed certain laws, that function by human faith. By applying these formulas, one is guaranteed in getting the results that God promised. These laws serve as God's unchangeable way of governing the world. Even an unbeliever can have prosperity if the rules concerning prosperity are applied.[27]

These rules are found in "God's word." The relationship between God and the Bible is described in almost pantheistic terms. God and God's word is one; the presence of the word is God. The *logos* ("word") in John 1 does not refer to Jesus, in Kenneth Copeland's view, but it refers primarily to the Bible. This word is the manifestation of the power of God.[28] The Bible is not a history or testimony of revelation, but the "textbook with God's laws and rules for success." The prescriptions and laws in the Bible work in an almost magical way when they are applied.[29] The existence of humans is determined by the laws found in the Bible, explaining why the Bible is identified with God in this perspective. These laws, and God, become principles that need to be applied to become successful in life.[30] For instance, if you give one dollar God will give you back a hundred dollars because the word promises that God would give back a hundredfold. If one gives a thousand dollars, one can expect to

---

27. The works of Kenneth Copeland, *Laws of Prosperity*, and Gloria Copeland, *God's Will is Prosperity* were largely used to describe this viewpoint. However, it will be demonstrated by references to African prosperity teachers.

28. Copeland, *Laws of Prosperity*, 46.

29. This is true of the Lord's Supper as well for some such teachers, as David Oyedepo explains, according to Bitrus, "Means of Prosperity," 336-8. The New Testament teaches that unworthy partaking of the communion can bring God's judgment on a person (1 Cor 11:27) but Oyedepo reinterprets the communion as a miraculous means of prosperity, stimulating massive participation and a frequent community meal in many neo-Pentecostal churches. The result is that believers are not partaking in the communion in celebration of the forgiveness of sins and for celebrating their participation in the body of Christ but for the sake of appropriating prosperity. In this way, the communion meal is changed into a magical meal with powers of granting healing and prosperity in the same way as quoting promises from the Bible does.

30. To illustrate, David Oyedepo writes, "You may say, 'Everything depends on God. He is the one who determines everything. If He wants me to live I will live.' . . . As nice and humble as this communication sounds, it is wrong. Many have died unnecessarily by talking and thinking this way . . . There are some Christians who just keep hoping that God will come into their situation and shake up everything and make things alright (*sic*). They say 'it is up to God,' they talk this way because it helps them escape responsibility" (quoted in Ntui-Abung, *Chaos of the Prosperity Gospel*, 33). When one uses biblical principles it becomes possible, not to hope that God would do some things for you, but to compel God to do it, the argument closes.

The Challenge 123

receive back a hundred thousand dollars. The person donating one car may rest assured of a supply of cars for a lifetime.[31] The idea of a hundredfold blessing is derived from Genesis 26:12–13, that states that Isaac sowed in the land while there was famine and reaped a hundredfold because the Lord blessed him. He became rich and gained more and more. He reaped an unbelievably great harvest because of his faith that led him to sow even in the midst of a drought, because he trusted the Lord's promises.[32] However, it should be noted that the text is not concerned with "giving to the Lord" as a precondition for Isaac's success. He made a good harvest because the Lord blessed him, as verse 13 explains.

John 10:10 serves for many prosperity teachers as the absolute truth against which all of Scripture should be interpreted. Jesus explains to his disciples that he is the gate for the sheep. Before him came thieves and bandits to which the sheep did not listen. Anyone who enters by him will be saved, and find pasture. Thieves only came to steal and kill and destroy. "I came that they may have life, and have it abundantly."[33] Don Gossett states that whenever he reads anything in the Bible that seems contradictory to what John 10:10 promises, he immediately stops and straightens his thinking.[34] God is a good God who does not steal from those who follow God. God gives only the best things to those who belong to God. John 10:10 serves as the hermeneutical key and theological presupposition.[35] When this key is used to "unlock" the "true meaning" of the rich young ruler who asks Jesus what he must do to inherit eternal life and who heard that he must sell all that he owns and must distribute the money to the poor (in Mark 10:17–31), Copeland interprets the text that the ruler was rich because he observed the biblical laws of prosperity from his youth. Jesus actually wanted the ruler to give all his money to the poor so that he may receive back a hundredfold; that would have made him fabulously rich.[36] What Jesus said was that the man lacked one thing,

---

31. Copeland, *God's Will is Prosperity*, 54.

32. Horn, *From Rags to Riches*, 41.

33. Seldom these preachers read verse 11 as well, that Jesus is also the good shepherd who lays down his life for the sheep. It does not suit their theology of victory, success, and provision, to have a suffering Savior who promises his disciples the same kind of suffering associated with crucifixion (Mark 8:34–38). See also Piper, "Appendix 1," 113-4 on the importance of not concealing the cost of the cross to believers.

34. Gossett, *What You Say is What You Get*, 63.

35. Horn, *From Rags to Riches*, 88.

36. An alternative way to think about the "abundant life" that Jesus came to impart

a "working revelation of the covenant."[37] Fortunately, this revelation was given to some prosperity teachers.

The concept of God used in this viewpoint is that God is a good God who intends believers to have all the best things in life.[38] For them to realize those good things, they need to carefully follow the rules, laws, recipes, and formulas found in the Bible. All people who apply these regulations in their lives and honor God in doing so will receive the prosperity promised by God, without exception. This is because prosperity is God's will for all believers. When the prosperity "principle" does not work in the life of a believer, the reason is the believer's immaturity and lack of faith; after all, the principles are "guaranteed" to work.[39] If the promises do not realize immediately, the believer should persist in intense prayer, regular fasting and positive thinking.[40] Some believers were so dazzled by the promise and prospect of earthly wealth that they did not apply all the conditions for its attainment, and for that reason they were still poor.

It must also be stated that several prosperity teachers have emphasized that believers should guard against the love for money. Money may never become a goal in itself. However, in the end they all promise prosperity to all believers who trust God. For a Christian to be poor is to be outside God's intended will and to live a Satan-defeated life because God wants prosperity for every one of God's children.[41] If God has not been meeting the needs of a believer it is because the person has not placed God first.[42] The blame is placed squarely on the shoulders of the believer, explaining the guilt complexes that many prosperity believers suffer from.[43]

---

is to relate it to God's provision to live with enough or even more than enough, in order to become a vehicle through which God provides also for others in need. The believer is entrusted with enough to build God's kingdom in heaven by investing in the needs of poor people, and not to build their own kingdom on earth (Randy Alcorn quoted in Hinn, *God, Greed*, 179).

37. Copeland, *Laws of Prosperity*, 66.

38. Not all would agree that "the best things in life" can be bought with money, or that there is any relation between money and a godly or good life.

39. Steele, *Destined to Win*, 55.

40. Akiri, "The Prosperity Gospel."

41. Fee, *Disease of the Health*, 3.

42. Gossett, *What You Say is What You Get*, 75.

43. McConnell, *Different Gospel*, 191-3. See, e.g., Kate Bowler's experience (described in her autobiography, *Everything Happens*, 16) of her conflicting emotions when she became critically ill and blamed herself for the illness due to the theology

The prosperity teachers' God is rich, also in human terms. God is the owner of a heavenly storehouse with unlimited supplies and God has given the key to believers. What believers should do, is talk about the riches of God and the promises that these riches belong to them.[44] They should speak, live and act like rich people. The power of the spoken word should be employed through positive confession that will eventually develop into the speaker's reality. Positive confession is defined by Joel Osteen as conceiving whatever is in your mind, continuing to visualize it, and experiencing that it happens.[45] If you talk about trials, difficulties, lack of faith, and lack of money, your faith will shrivel and dry up. If you confess sickness, you will become sick.[46] The right confession will eventually result in a situation where all your words will come to pass because the force of faith is released by words. Our faith formulas should not be determined by the realities around us but we should use the eyes of faith to see what God promised and speak that into reality. It is important that believers also do not trust the symptoms when they pray for healing,

---

of prosperity that she was exposed to at that time. She argued that in a spiritual world in which healing is a symptom of unconfessed sins, she looked for a solution to the puzzle of her suffering. Was it due to unconfessed sins like unfaithfulness, unexamined attitudes, or careless words, or of a lack of forgiveness? Only later did she realize that her illness represented the mystery of God's sovereign rule over the world, and in the lives of God's children.

44. Prophet Andrew Mutawunashe in a sermon on 13 November 2017 entitled, "Seven things you cannot do without" stated that you can do anything with nothing, as long as you depend on what God is saying (https://www.youtube.com/watch?v=TwX6sloQ3uI; accessed 2020-01-12). While people depend on what they can see, believers need to depend on what God said about them. They should speak about what they expect God to do, to provide in all their needs, to heal them, and to make them happy and successful. They should position themselves for a new situation that befits the new revelation that God is going to give them.

45. See https://www.joelosteen.com/Pages/Article.aspx?articleid=6505; accessed 2020-01-30. In Prosper, *Prosperity Theology*, 66 Chris Oyakhilome writes, "One of the beautiful things you can do for yourself as a Christian is to always build in your mind the right pictures about what you want in life. It pays when you activate your faith-eyes to see beyond the present horizon and envision yourself living out the very best of what God has prepared for you in this world. God never created us to suffer or live the average life where we are barely getting by. He created us to excel and flourish in all areas of our lives. However, until you begin to see yourself that way living in abundance, perfect health, victory, and success it will be difficult for you to experience it. You must first envision yourself living that dream," quoted in Ntui-Abung, *Chaos of the Prosperity Gospel*, 17.

46. Hagin, *How to Write*, 10.

but to keep on confessing healing even if the symptoms never cease or should return.[47]

In faith formulas the name of Jesus features prominently as the key to unlocking God's riches. The name of Jesus serves as a signed check from heaven on the resources from heaven, with the invitation to fill out the check with our needs and desires.[48] While the name of Jesus is not to be used like a magic charm or a rabbit's foot, it will work for us when we begin to confess and believe what that name can and will do for us.[49] Hagin confesses that God has answered all his prayers, without any exceptions at all. When he prays for other people, however, he sometimes finds that they nullify the effects of his prayer by their negative confessions.

The faith formulas are so effective that Hagin provides his readers with a little formula for faith to make it work for them: "Follow these four steps and you'll always get there because they are four certain or sure steps to deliverance, healing, answered prayers, or whatever it is that you are seeking."[50] All you have to do is to say it, do it, receive it, and

---

47. In a sermon with the title, "Understanding the laws of success," David Oyedepo Jnr. defines the "force of faith" as follows: it is the living force that comes from listening to the living word and acting on it, and which is ordained to produce living proofs of God's power to bless believers (https://www.youtube.com/watch?v=vaMSUwzTKco; accessed 2020-01-01). What is important is that one should listen to the living word, as Romans 10:17 explains, that "faith cometh by hearing, and hearing by the word of God." What believers should do, is to stop tolerating what is not supposed to be theirs, and start reacting in faith. Faith will energize them to expect the impossible from God because the word states that nothing is impossible for God to accomplish.

48. Hagin, *Name of Jesus*, 23.

49. Hagin, *Name of Jesus*, 59.

50. "Hagin, *How to Keep*, 29. One finds more realism nearer to the ground of African practice where a large proportion of the population is very poor. In a sermon of Prophet T.B. Joshua entitled, "Value processing more than result," it is stated that God sometimes can allow "foolish things in our way," later qualified as unanswered prayers and challenges (https://www.youtube.com/watch?v=obGhSHnHtYU; accessed 2020-01-04). These events can lead to doubt if the believer does not remember that they are actually meant to take you to a school of embarrassment, failure, and people's misunderstanding and hatred. What is important is that you follow the correct processing, and when you then do not get the expected results, don't worry. "You are going to get the mother of results." If you have thought the correct thoughts, spoken the right words, and done the right things, all you need to do is to be patient. The anointing rests on you for blessing, deliverance, and healing, and while God may allow you to go through sickness, God is actually only strengthening your desire for healing. God's purpose is that you become closer to God. It will make you strong in your faith. God is only concerned about your relationship with God. God will provide in your desires, as long as you do the right things.

tell it. This was supposedly revealed to Hagin by Jesus who appeared to him, and instructed him to write down: "1, 2, 3, 4." Jesus then said, "if anybody, anywhere, will take these four steps or put these four principles into operation, he will always receive whatever he wants from Me or from God the Father. That includes whatever you want financially."[51]

The foundation of these faith formulas is a deistic god, as John Fickett shows, and it represents the irony that prosperity teachers present an active, living God intervening in the lives of and for the sake of the interest of believers, while their hidden theology implies something completely different.[52] The faith formulas are in fact nothing else than ways to manipulate and use the presumed rules and principles laid down by a deistic god, and its application does not require a living, personal relationship with the God of the Bible who reveals Godself in unique personal ways to the individual, as Pentecostals believe. Any god who has to have faith in god's own faith, who is limited by god's word to act only according to "what is written in the Bible," or who can be manipulated by human endeavors is not the God and Father of our Lord Jesus Christ. In fact, such a god is no god at all but the impersonal "force" of the metaphysical cults, the "slavish puppet of anybody that knows the 'formulas' and 'spiritual laws' of how to control him."[53] While the formulas and laws are "faith" in the Faith movement, they are actually nothing more than recycled New Thought metaphysics, as explained in chapter 3. The cultist framework in which the prosperity message functions is clear.

Hank Hanegraff adds that the formulas closely resemble the principal beliefs of an occult worldview.[54] People in the world of the occult are told that the power to create their own reality lies within themselves. People have the inherent capacity to supernaturally change, create, or shape the world around them. They also believe that their words are imbued with creative power that directly and dramatically affect the real world in which they live. Occultists also believe that they can use creative visualization to speak things into existence. Although there may be agreement between some aspects of prosperity theology and the occult worldview, however, these same aspects also function in various other settings. Many psychologists use the same concepts and categories in their therapeutic

---

51. Hanegraaff, *Christianity in Crisis*, 105.
52. Fickett, *Confess it, Possess it*, 8.
53. McConnell, *Different Gospel*, 133.
54. Hanegraaff, *Christianity in Crisis*, 111.

practices. The implication is clear, that a mere agreement does not qualify to make an equation between different movements, and Hanegraaf's argument that the Faith movement is occultist in origin and functioning cannot be supported in all his implications. What should be kept in mind is that positive confession is also part of recognized cognitive therapy. Many people need to learn to be more optimistic about their lives and to see the bright side of things. To ascribe all references of positive confession to occultism is naïve.

Prosperity teachers tell their adherents that to have faith in one's own faith is to have faith in oneself, in this way replacing God with the self. This led to Charles Farah's charge that the Faith theology constitutes "charismatic humanism," because it is faith in a humanistic and anthropocentric god.[55] Biblical faith is qualified as theocentric or God-centered. Positive mental attitude (PMA) and positive confession are humanistic in the sense that they confer upon humans unrestrained powers to meet their own self-defined needs and desires, without any reference to God's will for humanity and individuals. The god of positive confession does not rule sovereignly over the work of God's hand but is the victim of the humans God was supposed to have made. Human desires are equated with God's will by the simple reasoning that it is God's will for humans to experience health, wealth, happiness, and prosperity without any exception. If they pursue these "blessings" then they are pursuing the will of God for them, it is taught. The humans who are positive and use the power of their spoken words of positive confession can manipulate the spiritual laws that limit the working of God in the world in order to control God. Human beings are in the driver's seat, not God any more.[56]

Prosperity teachers confess Jesus as their mediator, intercessor, advocate, shepherd, keeper, and the supplier of all their needs,[57] but at the same time they leave little in the hands of the living God but reduces God's involvement in the believers' lives to a mechanized way of dealing with divine provision. Everything God does is determined by God's established covenant on earth; this god is nothing else than a deistic god whose principles allow human beings to be masters of their own destiny and lives, manipulating god to serve their personal interests. In the words of Frederick Price, God has to be given permission to work in this earth

---

55. Farah, *From the Pinnacle*, 139.
56. McConnell, *Different Gospel*, 144.
57. Hagin, *Prevailing Prayer to Peace*, 28.

The Challenge

realm on behalf of humans. Humans are in control. When God gave Adam dominion, that meant that God no longer had dominion. So, God cannot do anything on earth unless humans let God do it. They give God permission through prayer.[58] You can make things work for you by applying possibility faith, teaches Hagin.[59] The god of prosperity theology is not the active and living God that determines what happens on earth and in the lives of God's children, but the god that one manipulates to do what one desires by means of one's faith, confession, and deeds in reaction to the positive confession.

In this sense, prosperity theology betrays its reliance on the theology of Kenyon who studied the ideas of the metaphysical cults and who remained sympathetic to these teachings all his life.[60] This leads Charles Farah to call Kenyon's writings a "treasure trove which all present Faith teachers mine."[61] Kenneth Hagin is not only literally dependent on Kenyon, but he actually plagiarized Kenyon in several of his publications, as happened in the books of other Faith teachers as well.[62]

Kenyon taught a cosmological theology of words, where faith-filled words brought the universe into existence, and faith-filled words are ruling the universe today. In this universe, believers have the power to speak reality into existence by way of their faith formulas. Faith formulas place the resources of the world at the disposal of human beings. The law of faith is the cosmological principle of the universe, leading to McConnell's conclusion that prosperity teaching provides a deistic system of spiritual laws.[63]

One such law is the law of sacrifice. In a sermon with the title, "Understanding the laws of success," David Oyedepo states that as natural

---

58. Price, "Prayer," 1178.

59. Hagin, *Prevailing Prayer to Peace*, 70.

60. McConnell, *Different Gospel*, 16 emphasizes that Kenyon was not a Pentecostal, contrary to popular opinion, nor is the prosperity gospel just another pentecostal perversion. The true origin of the Faith movement should be searched for outside the traditional Christian faith, and Pentecostalism. The equation between prosperity theology and Pentecostalism in the contemporary perception of many people should be explained for what is, the product of stereotyping and false perceptions. It is important enough that it should be repeated here as well.

61. Farah, *From the Pinnacle*, 4.

62. McConnell, *Kenyon Connection*, 30. See also McConnell, *Different Gospel*, 8-11 for a sampling of such plagiarism.

63. McConnell, *Kenyon Connection*, 20, 36. This study is important for its exposure of the connection between the works of Kenyon and several of the prosperity teachers, a connection that is never acknowledged by the teachers.

laws determine how our world operates, spiritual laws determine how the spiritual realm operates.[64] The spiritual laws make believers successful, let them get above their contemporaries, make them wealthy and healthy, and make them great. What is necessary is that they apply these laws in their lives. Some spiritual laws are superior to others, and one such superior spiritual law is the law of sacrifice. To apply the law of sacrifice you need to make your life a seed, but a seed that is planted because that is the prerequisite that the seed will bring forth a harvest and good fruit.[65] He mentions three examples: Abraham became the epitome of blessing because of his willingness to sacrifice his son, his dearest; Paul lived a sacrificial life and gave all in his commitment to the assignment entrusted to him by Jesus, and although he was the last of the apostles he ended first and wrote two-thirds of the New Testament; and Moses spent forty days and forty nights in God's presence without eating or drinking anything, and God called him a prophet like no other, with whom God talked face to face. What believers need, is an "enough is enough faith," that states that they do not accept their mishaps and difficult circumstances any more but they now believe God for a miracle. The preacher makes much of Matthew 9:29, with Jesus asking two blind men what they want and when they state that they need to be healed of their blindness, Jesus answers, "According to your faith be it unto you." It is faith that determines the answer to one's prayers. What is needed is that one is very specific in what one wants from God. God will answer faith by providing what God is believed for. The preacher emphasizes that the spiritual law of sacrifice always delivers, if one is willing to pay the price. The price may include long hours of fasting and prayer, and sacrificial and generous giving. The difference between diligence and sacrifice is that in diligence one is doing one's best but in sacrifice one is doing beyond one's best. You

---

64. https://www.youtube.com/watch?v=vaMSUwzTKco; accessed 2020-01-01. Oyedepo's Living Faith Church Worldwide Inc., better known as Winners Chapel, was founded in Lagos in 1983. It now has 400 branches in Nigeria and can be found in forty African countries. Its facility in Lagos seats 50,400 people. The network's leading pastors tend to be Nigerians, all fiercely loyal to Oyedepo (Gifford, "Expecting Miracles," 21).

65. See also Prophet Andrew Mutawunashe who in a sermon entitled, "Seven things you cannot do without" stated that if believers sow a seed, God will glorify them (https://www.youtube.com/watch?v=TwX6sloQ3uI; accessed 2020-01-12). What is needed is that they give all they have to God, like Abraham on the mountain sacrificing his only son to God. God will glorify such believers by breaking through new barriers in their lives and provide in new ways for all they dream about.

The Challenge

do not give what is expected of you; you give everything to God, and your sacrifice will always be honored by God who will provide what you desire from God. The emphasis is, however, on the motive for one's sacrifice, in order to gain something from God. If you sacrifice, God is compelled to answer your prayer and grant what you desire. The spiritual law serves as a means to acquire personal desires, of which at least some would be selfish and self-serving in intention.

Several other teachings of the prosperity movement also link up with the metaphysical cults, such as their anthropology that bears the mark of metaphysical pantheism, their worldview based on a dualistic epistemology, and their teaching of positive confession that correlates with the "Positive Mental Attitude" of New Thought.[66]

A deistic god provides the opportunity for believers to create their own circumstances by means of the manipulation of that god with their faith. Faith is then seen as a spiritual force, spiritual energy, and spiritual power that makes the laws of the spirit function.[67] No room is left for trust in the God who in God's sovereign power decides about human fate and destiny, whose thoughts are so incomprehensible that no human beings can understand them, as expressed in the words of the Deuteronomist historian, "The secret things belong to the Lord our God, but the revealed things belong to us and to our children forever, to observe all the words of this law." (Deut 29:29) For that reason, adherents of the prosperity gospel are encouraged never to end their prayers with the phrases, "Thy will be done" or "if it be Thy will," because it contradicts their faith formulas and positive confessions. The will of God is in reality negated and overruled by the faith formulas, putting the believer in the position to decide what will happen in their lives. Faith teaching has decided that health, wealth, prosperity, and happiness are God's will for all believers at all times, and they are providing believers with the formulas and recipes to attain these blessings from God by claiming it as their right and privilege in Christ. Prayer and trust in God to do God's unique will in the life of an individual believer lose their relevancy in this theology. It pre-decides the will of God and ignores God's sovereignty.[68]

---

66. McConnell, *Kenyon Connection*, 198-211. See also discussion later in chapter.
67. Copeland, *Laws of Prosperity*, 19.
68. Horn, *From Rags to Riches*, 95.

Prosperity Theology's View of Christ and Humankind

To understand the African understanding of prosperity, it is essential to understand the anthropology and Christology of neo-Pentecostal groups. The prosperity message has developed several of its theological loci but its Christology is not well developed, and for a good reason. The logical consequences of the prosperity gospel for the way Christians think about Christ is not clear. It argues in a certain manner about humans and for that reason Christ receives less emphasis, being replaced by human beings to a critical extent.

The debate about who and what Christ is also raged in the early church of the first three centuries CE and it was only in the fourth century, with the Council of Chalcedon (451 CE), that the church officially accepted the theology of the two natures of Christ. Today the Roman Catholic, Protestant, as well as Eastern Orthodox traditions abide by the doctrine that Christ had a divine and human nature. While the early Pentecostal movement also accepted it, in its early days a major split occurred over the trinity and a unitarian movement broke away from the Assemblies of God that supported a modalist doctrine of the trinity which states that there is only one God whose name is Jesus and who reveals Godself in three different forms.[69] In theory, prosperity teachers subscribe to the traditional doctrine of the two natures of Christ, understanding the person of Christ as one person who possesses two natures, a divine and a human nature. Each nature retains its unique properties, and the two natures remain distinct, though inseparably united in Christ's person. Thus, according to his divine nature, as the second person of the Trinity, the Son of God is omniscient, omnipotent, and so forth. According to his human nature, the incarnate Christ needed to eat food to survive, grew in knowledge, and so forth.[70] However, it does not feature in their exposition of the gospel and they emphasize a unitarian vision of Jesus as God that moves away from the traditional doctrine.[71] Although it does

---

69. Hollenweger, *Pentecostals*, 311.

70. https://www.ligonier.org/learn/devotionals/scripture-and-two-natures-christ/; accessed 2019-12-16.

71. According to McConnell, *Different Gospel*, 33 the transcendental and metaphysical movements arose in response to Unitarianism, and many Unitarians ended up in some form of New Thought. E.W. Kenyon regularly attended the services of Minot J. Savage, an outstanding minister and author in the Unitarian Church. Kenyon moved from Unitarianism to Transcendentalism to New Thought when he associated with a religious group that denied the fundamental doctrines of the Christian faith, such as the trinity.

not deny the deity of Christ, the emphasis on the upgrading of man is so prominent that it happens at the cost of the divinity of Christ. It is demonstrated by two popular doctrines in the movement, the "spiritual death" of Jesus, and his rebirth and "incarnation" in human beings.[72]

Although not all in the prosperity movement acknowledge the doctrine of the spiritual death of Christ, Kenneth Hagin and Kenneth Copeland accepted and taught it, and their publications are so influential that it became widely popular and in African neo-Pentecostalism it is taught widely. The teaching originated in the metaphysical arguments of E.W. Kenyon.[73] Kenyon teaches that Jesus left his divine nature in heaven when he became a human being. For that reason, Charles Capps argues, Jesus referred to himself as the "Son of man," as evidence that the Second Adam (a popular concept in the prosperity movement) did not take the nature of God but that of a human being.[74] The Second Adam with his human nature was not a revelation of God to humans, but was intended to serve as a restoration of the first Adam, resulting in the upgrading of human beings to super beings on a par with God. Adam was created as such a super being; he had the same light shining out of him and he was clothed with light because he was the very image of God, as Jesus had when he appeared to the apostle John on the island of Patmos.[75]

Jesus was only an empowered man by the Holy Spirit, and the most outstanding thing that was recorded about him was that he was a lay reader in the synagogue (Luke 4:16). For the first thirty years of his life he was without an identity.[76] He laid aside all of his God-powers when he came to earth and functioned on earth as a human being. If he had touched his God-given powers while living on the earth, he would have forfeited the right to be the Savior of the world. Adam, a human being, lost the rights and privileges of being a son of God when he sinned in

---

72. Horn, *From Rags to Riches*, 96. There are some problems with the notion that human beings are an incarnation in the same way that Jesus was, according to Hanegraaff, *Christianity in Crisis*, 192. One can only be incarnated if one existed prior to having a body; however, human pre-existence is foreign to biblical thinking. To state that we are as much an incarnation as Jesus was, is also to forge an unrealistic equality between creature and Creator. And the statement that God's reason for creating Adam was God's desire to reproduce Godself would indicate that God created a polytheistic planet with many gods living on earth.

73. Especially in Kenyon, *What Happened from the Cross*.

74. Capps, *Authority in Three Worlds*, 91-4.

75. Copeland, *Walking in the Realms*, 90.

76. David Oyedepo, quoted in Ntui-Abung, *Chaos of the Prosperity Gospel*, 28.

the Garden; Jesus, the second and last Adam, had to live totally as a human being (a son of man) to win it back so that all believers can become sons of God.[77] "Son of man" and "Second Adam" serve as more than mere technical terms in the prosperity movement. It explains that Jesus was stripped for a while of his deity in order that human beings may be adorned with it.

The death of Jesus Christ on the cross was not God's final work, according to this teaching. It was not even the most important or crucial part of the process of the atonement. The cross and death of Jesus served to demonstrate the defeat of Jesus. On the cross, he received the nature of Satan. It took his struggle in hell for three days after his death before he eventually conquered the powers of evil and victory was finally won.[78] Kenyon writes that the apostles did not know what happened on the cross, or during the three days and nights before Christ's resurrection, and that is why they did not reflect on it and why the New Testament does not refer to it. The mystery of the Messiah is hidden in these three days. It was only revealed in revelation knowledge to prosperity teachers. This new way of knowledge is now blazing a new path in constructive interpretation of the Pauline revelation and it uncovers "many new veins of primary truth long covered by sense knowledge interpretation of the Word. Now we can know about these three days, for this is the thing that will build faith in us".[79]

When he was resurrected from the dead, Jesus became the first human being to be born again. Hagin explains that Psalm 2:7, "You are my son; today I have begotten you," does not refer to the conception of Jesus nor to his birth, as the allusion or reference has been interpreted in most evangelical circles, but to Christ's resurrection.[80] For that reason, Paul in Acts 13:28–33 explains that when God says, "today I have begotten you,"

---

77. Henderson, *Operating in the Courts*, 50.

78. A related teaching is found in Paula White-Cain's book, *Something Greater*, that states that Jesus came to earth, not merely to reconcile humans to God by paying for sin and providing the eternal riches and glory of heaven to the poor, the rich, and the broken. He came to make humans wealthy, prosperous, and healthy. He came to bring abundant life to humankind, prosperity that consists of welfare, well-being, affluence, success, thrift, roaring trade, good fortune, smiles of fortune, blessings, and a godsend. To enjoy these blessings, it is important to be a tither. Only then can one expect to have a breakthrough. White is a world-renowned prosperity preacher and presidential advisor to Donald Trump.

79. Kenyon, *What Happened from the Cross*, 9.

80. Hagin, *Don't Blame God!*, 8-11.

it refers to when God raised Jesus from the dead, making Jesus the first person to be born again.[81] However, "born again" is then qualified to take on a new meaning, "to receive the nature of God."

Why would it have been necessary for Jesus to be born again and receive the nature of God? According to the traditional doctrine of the two natures of Christ, he was the son of God from the foundation of the world. The prosperity message explains it that Jesus left his divine nature, as God, in heaven. When he died on the cross, he did not only bear our sins but he also bore our sin, that is, our sinful nature. He had to bear our sinful nature as well as our sins; otherwise, we would only have been saved from our sins but not from our propensity or inclination to sin. We would have remained the same kinds of creatures. When he put away sin by his sacrifice, he changed the nature that caused us to sin. We lost our ability to sin. Prosperity believers live sinless lives.

The teaching goes back to Kenyon that explains that Jesus became obedient to Satan and because Satan is the author of death, Jesus had to die and he actually received a satanic spirit.[82] On the cross, Christ was stripped of his good human nature and received a sinful, or satanic nature. His divine nature did not feature at all because he left it in heaven. Gloria Copeland then concludes that Jesus experienced the same spiritual death that Adam experienced in the garden of Eden because of this "sin nature;" he did not only die physically on the cross, but he also died a second, spiritual death.[83] Because of this change in his nature, Jesus had to go to hell where he suffered for three days before God shouted from heaven, "That satisfied the Supreme Court of heaven. He is justified!"[84] Then God raised him from the dead and he became the first person to be born again, by receiving the nature of God, taking back his divine nature that he had left behind in heaven.

The fall of Jesus from perfect man to satanic and rejected being denies in effect that the redemption of man took place on the cross. It moves the redemption of man to the time after the supposed double death of

---

81. Hagin, *Don't Blame God!*, 9.
82. Kenyon, *What Happened from the Cross*.
83. Copeland, *God's Will for You is Healing*, 5.
84. Hagin, *Don't Blame God!*, 10. In the words of Hagin, *Zoe*, 35-6, 41, man was created on terms of equality with God, and he could stand in God's presence without any consciousness of inferiority. God has made us as much like Godself as possible. God made us the same class of being that God is. The believer is called Christ. This is who we are; we are Christs.

Jesus on the cross. Prosperity teachers assert that Jesus was the substitute for every human being in hell. What is also important in this theology is that knowledge hidden from others and also previously hidden from biblical authors as well, is now revealed to a specific group. This serves like secret knowledge, and illustrates the link between second-century Gnosticism and the mythological presentations of contemporary prosperity theology. Knowledge is the way to become and be like God. If one only knows this secret knowledge, that Jesus did not die on the cross to bear the price of one's sins but that he had to die a second death because he hung on the cross as a Satanic figure, then one will be restored, not only in one's relationship with God, but restored to become like Adam before the Fall. God intended for people to live like gods, as Adam did in the garden before the Fall. It took Jesus' fall to hell to restore the effects of the original Fall, in order that (some) believers can be restored to be like Adam, and be like God.

Faith teachers refer to two texts to shore up the notion that Christ suffered under Satan in hell: Matthew 12:40 that states that as Jonah was three days in the belly of a huge fish, so the Son of man would be three days in the heart of the earth, which is clearly an indication that Jesus would be buried in the tomb of Joseph of Arimathea, and Ephesians 4:9–10, with its idiomatic expression referring to Christ's incarnation on earth and not that Jesus was incarcerated in hell.[85] However, prosperity theology chooses to interpret the texts in another way, to be able to state that by knowing what happened to Jesus on the cross and in hell for the three days, one is able to realize one's equality with Jesus in all respects.[86]

In traditional theology, Jesus' death on the cross was interpreted as a sacrificial death. He was a holy, sinless substitute for sinners, as was expected of all sacrifices in the Old Testament, earning forgiveness for those who would have had to pay with their lives for the separation from God caused by their sins. The idea that Jesus physically became sin and for that reason had to die and go to hell, as propounded by prosperity teachers, is based neither on the New Testament's identification of Jesus Christ as the savior of humankind nor on the Old Testament concept of a holy sin-offering that reconciled humankind with God.[87] Nowhere

---

85. Hanegraaff, *Christianity in Crisis*, 182.

86. Matta, *Born Again Jesus*, 35, 37.

87. Lovemore Togarasei, "African Gospreneurship," 111 perceptively remarks that the prosperity gospel has mainly the Old Testament as source book, while those who criticize the movement mainly base their arguments on New Testament

in the New Testament is Jesus' death on the cross interpreted as Christ's identification with the sinful nature of sinners. He died because he served as a substitute for sinners, to pay the price of their sins, in their stead, and to overturn their resultant separation from God. His death acquired restoration in the relationship between humans and God who was also separated from each other because of humans' sins. His death did not serve to cancel their sinful nature and believers still struggle with the inclination to sin, as Paul clearly demonstrates when he explains in Romans 7:21–25 that although he delights in the law of God in his inmost self, he sees in himself another law at war with the law of his mind, making him captive to the law of sin that dwells in him. He concludes in verse 24–25, "Wretched man that I am! Who will rescue me from this body of death? Thanks be to God through Jesus Christ our Lord!" While he is a slave to the law of God, with his flesh he is still a slave to the law of sin.

The logical consequence of the teaching of the spiritual death of Christ is that Jesus was not a sinless substitute for sinners, but a substitutive sinner.[88] On the cross he received the nature of sin, or the nature of Satan, and for that reason he had to die spiritually as well because of his sinful nature. It implies that Satan had a part in the atonement; only because Jesus identified with him could his spiritual death and eventual born-again experience have been possible, enabling us to be born again.

An important consequence of the prosperity gospel of the atonement is that Jesus' death and resurrection, illustrating his victory over sin and the human sinful nature, makes of the believer a sinless creature who enjoys the divine privileges of health, wealth, happiness, and prosperity, as explained. And the further logical consequence of Jesus' complete identification with the sinful nature of humankind is that human beings are upgraded to the level of God, while Jesus is simultaneously downgraded. He became sin so that believers could become divine. Any believer who knows what the Bible teaches, understands intuitively the dangers of such reasoning. Our daily experiences demonstrate that we are not divine beings but *simul justus et peccator*, at the same time both righteous and sinners, a doctrine emphasized especially by Augustine and Calvin.

It was already stated that the prosperity message is not a unified message but that it is often presented in a diversified and contradictory way. What can be stated in terms of its Christology and anthropology,

---

teaching, particularly Jesus' teaching on material possessions and the necessity of carrying one's cross.

88. Horn, *From Rags to Riches*, 99.

however, is that a prominent part of African neo-Pentecostalism preaches the dogma of the spiritual death of Christ and his reincarnation in human beings, making them divine.

Pentecostalism traditionally taught that God did not abandon Christ on the cross even though Jesus experienced subjectively that God had abandoned him to the extreme suffering of crucifixion (Mark 15:34). Rather, God was in Christ on the cross of Calvary, and God's Spirit within him raised him from the grave after three days. Jesus also was not sinful during his stay on the cross and three days in hell; it implies that Jesus and God would have been completely separated during this period, because the result of sin is always separation from the presence of God. It was not possible for Jesus to be separated from God because Jesus was God. The Godhead cannot be divided because God is one God, in three co-eternal consubstantial persons or hypostases, as the Father, the Son, and the Holy Spirit, "one God in three divine persons." The three persons are distinct, yet are one "substance, essence or nature."[89]

That Jesus died twice, in a physical as well as spiritual death, is explained by prosperity teachers at the hand of the plural use of the noun "death" in the Hebrew text of Isaiah 53:9, something that occurs frequently because the plural in Hebrew language does not always signify numerical plurality but rather the extent of the association of the term. Jesus did not die two deaths; his death was so profound that he exorcised the demons of death when he died. The plural is used to show the full extent and implication of the death of the suffering servant. To state that Jesus died a second death, in his spirit, is to imply that the Holy Spirit abandoned him. The teaching that Jesus left his divine nature in heaven when he was incarnated might already have implied that he did his ministry on earth without the Spirit, an idea that the synoptic Gospels deny many times.

Pentecostals have been teaching for many years that sinners will have to die a physical death because of the brokenness of creation due to the first humans' disobedience to God, but that a second death awaits them when they receive their due before God's judgment throne if they did not put their trust in Christ's atoning death. However, when prosperity teachers refer to Jesus' spiritual death they do not say that his spirit died but rather that he became like a sinful human, a human being who can do no other than what is sinful before God.

---

89. See the Athanasian Creed or *Symbol Quicunque*.

The biggest problem with these teachings is that prosperity teachers claim revelation knowledge for their validity, implying that it surpasses what the New Testament clearly teaches about the atonement of Christ on the cross. Whenever believers would question the assumptions, they are told that one should not sin against the anointed one, the prophet, who has received the ability of revelation knowledge from God. Clearly the implication is that revelation knowledge surpasses what the New Testament teaches, an assumption that cannot be accepted at all. In this way, believers' consciences are curbed and guilt is incurred because they dared to question the authority of God's anointed man (or woman).

It was argued that the Christology of the movement is not well developed because of its overemphasis on the effects of the atonement for the believer. The light falls on believers rather than on Christ who identified with the sinful human on the cross to enable human beings to take up their new identity, in the place of Christ, and in order to exercise the rights Christ has earned for them. When Christ's sinful nature was expelled in hell and he was born again, the church was recreated as new creatures in him. Spiritual death, that consists of sin, sickness, and human needs in the world, was eradicated in the new birth. Where sins, sickness and poverty exist in the church, it is because believers have failed to realize their new identity in Christ.[90] Their new identity allows believers into a complete union with God; they became as much an incarnation of God as Jesus Christ. All Christians are gods.[91] David Oyedepo writes, "God was duplicated in man, leaving a man with all divine attributes to operate like the true son of his father. If sons of man are men, then it follows that sons of God are gods. Like, (sic) beget like," leading to the conclusion, "Ye are gods! This is the basis for the supernatural, that you are no longer an ordinary human being. You are superhuman, super extra-natural . . . The trust is that you are a son of God, so you are gods."[92] The devastating effects of original sin, as well the sinful nature of human inclination to sin, were completely neutralized in

90. McConnell, *Kenyon Connection*, 34.

91. Copeland, *Believers' Voice of Victory*, 9. Another more positive aspect of this new identity should also be mentioned, where believers come to see themselves as fulfilling a sacred mission in every context they live in, allowing a framing of one's life work or career as a sacred act, in line with the Calvinist emphasis on a career as a sacred way of living (Marti, "The Adaptability of Pentecostalism," 23).

92. Quoted in Ntui-Abung, *Chaos of the Prosperity Gospel*, 38-9. Oyedepo's calling narrative is deliberately related to that of Moses. Whereas Moses was demanded, "Go and set my people free," however, he was told, "Make my people rich!" (Gifford, "Expecting Miracles," 21).

the atonement. Humans who trust in Christ are reinstated in their original Adamic stance; the image of God is restored fully in their lives and they become like Adam and Eve before their act of disobedience led to their banishment from the garden of Eden.

The first Adam was perfect and therefore a god. He was not only the representative of God, as the image of God, but he was "god on earth." The Second Adam restored that capacity for contemporary believers; they were created to be gods over the earth and now they have received the ability to become what they were intended to be, and what Adam initially was. Christians do not have God living within them; they are gods. Christians are a God-kind of creature. God made humans gods under God.[93]

Prosperity teaching does not place humans on a par with God in the sense that they refer to believers as "gods" and they emphasize that as gods they are not "creator God." They are "gods under God" and "gods over the earth," and not over the universe. Although the distance between God and human beings is radically narrowed, it is still there. However, at the same time human beings are cast as super heroes reigning victoriously over the earth and its evil powers, claiming the privileges of gods in the form of prosperity and wealth.[94] Reference is made to Psalm 82:6, "I say, 'You are gods, children of the Most High, all of you,'" quoted according to John 10:34 by Jesus. However, the next verse that is still part of the same sentence is nearly never quoted as well: "nevertheless, you shall die like mortals, and fall like any prince (or: fall as one man, o princes)." The term "gods" should be qualified and explained in terms of the second denominator in the same sentence, "sons (or children) of the Most High," implying that it serves as honorable names for members of God's chosen people.[95]

93. See Hunt and McMahon, *Seduction of Christianity*, 84 for more quotations and explanations of prosperity teachers that illustrate this dangerous teaching.

94. Although some early Pentecostal preachers like John G. Lake also used the terms applied by the prosperity movement, including the idea that Christians become gods or God-men, the teaching was never accepted by majority Pentecostalism and the ideas died an early death in the movement.

95. To illustrate the point, Pastor Chris Oyakhilome in a sermon with the theme, "How to dominate your world through faith," based on Luke 18:1–8, Jude 3 and Luke 18:9–14, states that faith overcomes all adversaries, including sin, illness, poverty, and death (https://www.youtube.com/watch?v=0uvQNYRRy4E; accessed 2019-12-27). Faith is to be based on the word. Believers experience the same problems as non-Christians when they take their eyes from the word and put their trust in something else. For example, a Christian gets sick and then looks to the doctor or medicine for help. Before long, this Christian will experience difficulties in trusting God for all their other

If prosperity teachers used their teaching to emphasize that a close link exists between believers and God and that believers have an important role to play in creation, it would not be as heretical as it seems at first sight. However, at times it is stated in a more absolutist way, that humans are also destined to be creators, and they are able to create health, wealth and prosperity through the power of their words and positive confessions. "And since He created our spirits to be like Him, He expects us to be creators as well. This means He wants you to make things happened (*sic*) and change the world."[96] They are not putting their faith in Jesus for salvation but in Jesus' capacity to bring them money. The gospel is not primarily about the restoration of humans' relationship with God that was disturbed because of humans' sins; now all attention is taken up by an interest in daily life and its betterment in the here and now. The prosperity message focuses on what people have and do not have, what they want and what they can get through faith, and nothing is said about hope for an eternal life in the presence of God. It establishes dissatisfaction and discontent because it concentrates solely on material possessions and loses sight of eternal values.[97] Faith is not directed at God and its purpose is not to glorify God but it is directed at human desires and directed at satisfying those desires.

Most Pentecostals accept the Arminian theology that human beings were not banished from the garden of Eden as totally corrupted but that they were still able to choose to do some good. However, they do not accept that Spirit-filled believers can ever become perfect and sinless while still living on earth. They maintain the tension between the "already" and "not yet" of the establishment of the kingdom of God through the

---

problems. They give their tithes and still experience difficulties, and then they wonder about a good God who lets bad things happen to them. The reason why these bad things happen is because they look for the wrong culprit. They did not base their faith in the word and in that way they left the door open for the thief, the devil, to enter and steal their blessings. Fact is, "you were blessed before you were born and you are an heir of God, and only the best of blessings belong to you. You were meant to dominate your world through faith, and to speak only the best of circumstances into your life."

96. Chris Oyakhilome, quoted in Ntui-Abung, *Chaos of the Prosperity Gospel*, 18.

97. Prosper, *Prosperity Gospel*, 6. Not all prosperity teachers necessarily emphasize the same aspects all the time. For instance, in a sermon of Prophet T.B. Joshua entitled, "Value processing more than result," he states that to be a Christian is to be content with what you have (https://www.youtube.com/watch?v=obGhSHnHtYU; accessed 2020-01-04). He advises his audience to listen to their prayers and they will know whether they are Christians: if their prayers are characterized by gratitude. Christians leave everything for God to provide and they trust in God's provision.

incarnation, death, resurrection, and ascension of Jesus. The "not yet" will only be caught up in the "already" with the second coming of Christ. Although their relationship with God is restored, allowing them to enter into an intimate relationship with God as with a friend, human beings are not deified in any sense. They remain justified sinners who need to pray daily, "forgive us our debts," as taught by Jesus (Matt 6:12).

The Source of the Prosperity Message

One way to distinguish Pentecostals from most other Protestants is their view that God continues to reveal Godself in contemporary times in various ways, through the Spirit's explication of the Bible, a direct word of revelation in the form of prophecy, interpretation of tongues, a word of knowledge, a word of wisdom, an insight that develops in the mind, the sudden enlightenment of one's conscience, dreams and visions, signs and wonders, nature, and other means. God does speak through the Bible but not exclusively by means of the Bible. When God speaks, it is however imperative that the extra-biblical revelation should be tested at the hand of the revelation in the Bible. God would never contradict what God had revealed in the Bible.

Although extra-biblical revelation knowledge plays a significant role among Pentecostals, it is not clear what authority is granted to these revelations. Some churches write down all prophecies and study them further while other churches reject the writing down of prophecies and view it as temporary words directed at a specific audience in a specific situation and with limited value. The difference between these two approaches perhaps have to do with the way prophecy is viewed, in the first case as a direct word of God and in the second case as a confirmation of the revelation of God that the church had already received, also (and primarily) in the form of the Bible.

Very few classical Pentecostal denominations acknowledge the office of the prophet although they do not deny the ministry of the prophet.[98] When they do acknowledge the office of the prophet, they always emphasize the imperativeness that the office should be subjected at all times to the spiritual gift of the discernment of spirits (1 Cor 12:10).

---

98. This is probably in reaction to the Latter Rain movement that in the 1940s and 1950s led to various schisms in the Pentecostal movement with its emphasis on the office and authority of the prophet to lead and rule the church, much like the apostle is doing in some contemporary independent groups.

Prophecy and other revelations must be subjected to the judgment of the elders and other believers, and comparison with the revelation found in the Bible plays a primary role in its evaluation along with the gift of the discernment of spirits that allow Spirit-filled people to discern whether the revelation is from God or other competing spirits.[99]

What is important is that Pentecostals view the Bible as the authority when prophecies and other spiritual gifts or presumed direct words from God are judged, even though in practice they do not necessarily always succeed. Their history teaches them the dangerous situation the church created when prophecies were believed in a gullible manner, without critical judgment. The majority of Pentecostals accept a biblicist and literalist way of reading the Bible, in fundamentalist manner, as argued above,[100] and the positive asset of this way of interpretation is that it makes them more skeptical of the subjective risks inherent in any claims of revelation knowledge outside the Bible. Later it will be argued that the new pentecostal hermeneutic underlines this skepticism. While allowing room for such revelations it is clear that it should be viewed in terms of the contribution of the human participant in the revelation process that should be discounted before the word can be accepted as (partly) divine in origin.

Cessationists, whether hard or soft cessationists, see a problem in the view of a continuationist revelation of God. They argue that if newly revealed truths from God can be formulated by the contemporary church, it should be added to the canon of the Bible and disseminated as widely as possible, since it would constitute divinely given moral imperatives on a par with Scripture.[101] However, Pentecostals would argue that con-

---

99. Costi Hinn describes a practice and strategy among prosperity preachers, called shotgun prophecy, where the preacher-prophet fires off numerous predictions in the hope that one of the prophecies might hit the target, that would confirm their accurateness and reliability as prophets (Hinn, *God, Greed*, 78). This is demonstrated in a sermon by Prophet Enoch Adeboye on 16 October 2018 with the title, "Reversing the irreversible" (https://www.youtube.com/watch?v=85b-2ED388Q; accessed 2020-01-12). The sermon consisted of statements of what God can do, and these are then changed into prophecies containing the statements as promises for "someone in the audience." The audience consisted of a few hundred people who reacted enthusiastically to each promise.

100. Pentecostalism is implicated in fundamentalism when it shows certain doctrinal affirmations with fundamentalist use of the Bible, a literalist reading of the Bible, and a preoccupation with economic, social, and political power (Kalu, *African Pentecostalism*, 255). When it is characterized by intolerance toward believers of other Christian traditions and other faiths, it represents a hard fundamentalism.

101. Sarles, "Theological Evaluation of the Prosperity Gospel," 337.

temporary perceptions of revelation can never be on a par with the Bible because they constitute insights revealed to specific persons and limited to certain situations with relevance for no other persons or groups, and its value is always subjected to an evaluation in terms of the biblical revelation of Jesus Christ as God's final word. It can be stated that prophecy plays a role in Pentecostalism in the same terms as the historical creeds and confessions of established Protestant churches, such as, e.g., the Scots Confession (1560), the Westminster Confession of Faith (1646), Westminster Shorter Catechism (1649), Westminster Larger Catechism (1649), Confession of 1967, and the Book of Confessions (1983) play for the Presbyterians in their practice, as hermeneutical lenses through which the Bible is read and interpreted and to determine the boundaries of Scripture. The only difference in the authority of the Bible and the confessions formulated by the church is that the content of the Bible cannot be changed while it is theoretically possible that the confessions may be changed or added to, although it is highly improbable. The sermon serves the same function as described by the Lutheran tradition that is described as a word of God. Karl Barth argues that the word of God has three modes, the proclaimed word of God, the written word of God, and the revealed Word of God (in Christ).[102] Keener mentions that in its strictest form, hard cessationism fails to embrace the continuing relevance of a major aspect of the biblical message, namely, that we should expect God's continuing activity in history and in our lives.[103]

Prosperity teachers in Africa accept the basic pentecostal doctrine of revelation in theory.[104] While room is left for a direct "word from the Lord," they also accept the Bible as the last and final authority. Sometimes they refer to themselves as "Word teachers" because of the rather fundamentalist way in which they emphasize the Bible as their authority. For instance, Kenneth Hagin would have stated, according to Nico Horn, that he would not believe any vision, even of God, it if could not be proven from what God said in the Bible.[105]

However, in practice revelation serves a different function among prosperity teachers. They emphasize direct words from God much more strongly, according authority to it that implies that it does not allow

---

102. Barth, *KD* I/2, 87.
103. Keener, *Spirit Hermeneutics*, 199.
104. Horn, *From Rags to Riches*, 104.
105. Horn, *From Rags to Riches*, 103.

listeners to question or criticize their word and placing it on the exact same level as the revelation in the Bible. At the same time, they use and apply the Bible much more mechanically than Pentecostals.

They developed a theological structure for their understanding and use of the direct words from God, called revelation knowledge. At times they refer with the term to a supernatural understanding of certain parts of the Bible, as a function of the enlightenment by the Spirit of the human mind, while at other times they use the term to refer to direct revelations that individuals have received from God.[106] In this sense, Hagin called Kenyon's publications "the Word of God." Revelation knowledge turns those who had received it into a new class of men, the supermen, and the *illuminati* of the new type of Christianity, using the parlance of E.W. Kenyon.[107] The link with the metaphysical cults is clearly demonstrated. Supernatural revelations form a "wonderful new interpretation" of the Bible, the foundation of the new Christianity that brings healing and prosperity to all who possessed this revelation knowledge of the Bible. The cultic elements form the most distinctive and popular doctrines of the prosperity movement, and they owe their historical origins to E.W. Kenyon.[108]

The problem comes with the contents of some of the "new" revelations that prosperity teachers propound to their adherents, and their visions and revelations are sometimes described in terms that suggest that they heard from or saw God personally, containing the germ of the idea that its authoritativeness may not be doubted. Then the mechanical

106. See, e.g., Pastor Chris Oyakhilome's sermon on the theme, "How to pray effectively and receive answers" (https://www.youtube.com/watch?v=Hj7LxUeXWXM; accessed 2019-12-27). He calls David's words in Psalm 141:2, "Let my prayer be set forth before thee as incense; And the lifting up of my hands as the evening sacrifice," as a revelation that David had received, that our prayers are incense before God that needs to come before God every morning and evening, every blessed day of the year. "If you visit the house of God, it is important to remember to bring incense and offer sacrifices;" that was the reason why the temple was built, to offer sacrifices (from 2 Chron 7:12-14). All of the sacrifices in the Old Testament served as a shadow, or type of what is happening now. The incense in the tabernacle went up in the presence of God but God really wanted something better. Jesus Christ provided one sacrifice for all time, bringing the better sacrifice. David got revelation knowledge in the Spirit that our prayers are also incense and sacrifices.

107. Quoted in McConnell, *Different Gospel*, 47. "Now we are moving into the big things . . . We are going to see spiritual giants, supermen. They have God dwelling in them . . . They no longer walk as natural men. They belong to the love class, the miracle class. They are in the Jesus class. They have graduated from the lower class." (Kenyon, *Identification*, 60-61).

108. McConnell, *Different Gospel*, 50.

inspiration of their words need to be accepted and valued on the same level as when believers read the Bible.[109]

At times, these teachers go so far as to suggest that God told them that God would curse the ministries of those churches that did not accept their prosperity message because they were rejecting the word of God in an essentialist manner. This is a sectarian way to distinguish themselves from established churches and should be rejected with the contempt it earns. When a prophet or apostle claims authority for their ministries and revelations that brings the authority of the Bible into jeopardy without leaving room for its evaluation at the hand of the Bible, no Christian can submit to it. A second canon may never be created; the idea exists that some prosperity preachers use the works of other more prominent apostles like Kenneth Hagin, Kenneth Copeland, T.D. Jakes, and especially E.W. Kenyon in this way. Nothing may be equated with the word of God revealed in the Bible; as soon as it happens the church bows before a subjectivity that may lead to any form of heretical teaching without the means to evaluate and criticize it.

If revelation knowledge is defined as a higher knowledge which carries its adherents beyond ordinary Christians into a new realm of thinking which releases to them certain gifts that other Christians cannot access, as Charles Farah defines it, prosperity teachers are establishing a new form of Gnosticism.[110] People who claim to have "higher knowledge" than Christians can gain from a study of the Bible subject themselves to the judgment of the New Testament of similar trends in the time of the early church (see, e.g., 1 Cor 8:1; 1 Tim 6:20–21).[111]

---

109. See, for instance, the prophecy about Alph Lukau, a prominent prophet, that he is not a human, found on YouTube at https://www.youtube.com/watch?v=NkWChzbQm3A; accessed 2019-12-22. In another prophetic session, Lukau went to Lilongwe "in the Spirit," which he described "with an incredible level of accuracy" (https://www.youtube.com/watch?v=GhZzAhM4iVU; accessed 2019-12-22). These prophets and their antics find high levels of acceptance among gullible Africans, due to the authority ascribed to (and claimed by) the prophets.

110. Farah, *From the Pinnacle*, 15.

111. Charles Farah's book, *From the Pinnacle of the Temple*, was criticized backhandedly by prosperity teachers, even though some of them did not even read the book. E.g., Charles Capps admits that he has not read the book, and his comments are based on it from what he has heard from others. He concludes: "Here a good example for you of head knowledge. Here's a man who is very educated . . . he's so educated beyond his intellect that he don't (sic) know how to control what he's learned . . . He's put out of all revelation knowledge . . . This is what happens when people get highly educated . . . He's bordering on blasphemy" (quoted in McConnell, *Different Gospel*, 77).

The new revelation knowledge eventually becomes a new hermeneutical principle with which the Bible is interpreted. Prosperity teachers like to state that they are not victims of modern theological endeavors but participators in the knowledge received from God. When they read the Bible through the lenses of their particular revelation knowledge, that God intends every believer always to be healthy, rich, happy, and prosperous because Christ died on the cross to acquire these privileges for them, prosperity teachers ignore the results of scientific, or even just commonsense, exegesis of biblical texts. It is then that they arrive at some of the fabulous, fantastic, and incredible interpretations of biblical texts with which they support the structure of their theological fabrications.[112]

At times prosperity teachers claim that their revelation knowledge represents the final part of the pattern of salvation in the lives of Christians, following on their conversion, Spirit baptism, and a crisis experience of dedication with the impartation of health and wealth. This revelation knowledge then serves to "complete" the revelation initially provided in the Bible and furnishes them with a direct pipeline to truth.[113] The New Testament's revelation of God is then incomplete without this "new" revelation.

For instance, Paul's acknowledgement of his personal circumstances, for instance in 1 Corinthians 4:10–13, that he is weak and being held in disrepute, hungry and thirsty, poorly clothed, beaten and homeless, weary from the need to work with his own hands, becoming like the rubbish of the world, and the dregs of all things, is interpreted by the prosperity messengers as a negative confession that led to further difficult circumstances in Paul's life. If, however, Paul had the full faith message of prosperity (he did not because it was not revealed to believers of his generation), there would have been no need for his suffering and deprivation because he would have known to make a positive confession and create the best of circumstances through the power of his words.[114]

When some prosperity teachers are criticized for their theological extravagances, they use the argument that they would not respond to the critics because the critics do not possess any revelation knowledge and they base the authority of their teachings on the direct revelation of

---

112. See discussion later in chapter on their proof-texts.
113. Farah, *From the Pinnacle*, 18.
114. Farah, *From the Pinnacle*, 130.

the Spirit to them and other prominent prosperity teachers.[115] Charles Farah refers to one preacher who even stated that he was not spending any time in further devotional reading of the Bible because he was getting his knowledge directly from God, over and above the Bible.

A great problem for Pentecostals with this concept of revelation knowledge is that it is limited to specific individuals that God chose to reveal the word to, implying that not all believers have direct access to the revelation of the Spirit in their minds and lives. The sole authority then lies exclusively with the leaders, a teaching that is supported by the widespread notion that it is unpardonable and extremely dangerous to criticize the anointed leader of God. Pentecostals confess the idea propounded by Paul that all believers should strive for the spiritual gifts, and especially that they might prophesy (1 Cor 14:1), that to each is given the manifestation of the Spirit for the common good (1 Cor 12:7), and that in the one Spirit believers were all baptized into one body—Jews or Greeks, slaves or free—and they were all made to drink of one Spirit (1 Cor 12:13).

Prosperity preachers love to distinguish between two Greek terms for "word," with "*logos*" referring according to their opinion to a general revelation as found in the Bible and "*rhema*" as a specific word of revelation given to a believer outside the boundaries of the Bible. Such a linguistic distinction, however, cannot be maintained as it is not found consistently in the New Testament,[116] and it illustrates the gnostic element in the metaphysics of prosperity teachers.

Nico Horn asks, what is the agenda behind the teaching of revelation knowledge? He explains that prosperity preachers wish to acknowledge a superior knowledge possessed by only a few, of which they form a part.[117] It serves as an authoritarian way to prevent adherents from questioning their teachings and prevent them from listening to the valid criticism exercised by other parts of the Christian church of the heretical teachings of the prosperity gospel. Revelation knowledge has become a work of grace and a means of initiation into an elite group far superior to the rest of Christianity, marked by spiritual superiority and disdain for others.[118]

The radical realized eschatology of the prosperity movement is also demonstrated by their way of arguing about their superior knowledge.

---

115. Farah, *From the Pinnacle*, 18.
116. Contra Farah, *From the Pinnacle*.
117. Horn, *From Rags to Riches*, 108.
118. McNair Scott, *Apostles Today*, 271.

They claim to know completely, in contrast to the author of 1 Corinthians who states that earthly knowledge, even of believers, would one day come to an end because we only know in part, and prophesy only in part. However, the day will come when the complete comes, and the partial will come to an end (1 Cor 13:8–10). "Now I know only in part; then I will know fully, even as I have been fully known" (1 Cor 13:12). As stated above, the coming world does not feature in the practice of prosperity theology.

Prosperity teaching does not allow any room for its adherents to think for themselves, to have any doubts about the preaching of their leaders, to rethink certain Scriptures from other perspectives, or to evaluate different interpretations proposed by other believers outside their tradition. Revelation knowledge "guarantees" that the interpretation of the preacher of the text is correct and anyone who doubts it, exposes themselves to the danger of "grieving the Spirit" and earning the "wrath of God."

Authority is granted to some influential proponents within the prosperity movement who serve as "modern apostles" and who are quoted continually by preachers. The apostolic succession within the movement includes Kenneth Hagin, who prophetically sanctioned and anointed Kenneth Copeland, who in turn raised up Jerry Savelle. Other leaders who were influential were Reverend Ike (Frederick J. Eikerenkoetter),[119] Norvel Hayes, Charles Cowan, John Osteen, Robert Tilton, T.D. Jakes, Joel Osteen, Frederick Price, Charles Capps, Joyce Meyer, and several African apostles. These figures have gained the status of cult leaders within the movement and their writings and sermons have to a certain extent been canonized. Another feature is that the apostle or prophet sets himself up as the president and chief executive of the ministry, and his wife serves as the co-founder, deputy president, treasurer, and fellow pastor, while the children and relations of the "owner" and founder constitute members of the board of directors or trustees of the church or organization. This guarantees that the church remains as a family business with sole control over the finances.[120] The business model adopted by the prosperity preachers in order to ensure growth and profit underscores the underlying goal of the movement, which is to make money.[121]

---

119. His favourite phrase has become famous: "Don't wait for your pie in the sky by and by; have it now with ice cream and a cherry on top!" (Bowler, *Everything Happens*, 151).

120. Essien, "Ethical Audit of Prosperity Gospel," 62.

121. Essien, "Ethical Audit of Prosperity Gospel," 63.

Hermeneutical Angle and Key of the Prosperity Gospel

Hermeneutical Angle of Prosperity Theology, and Pentecostals

The wide influence and impact exercised by prosperity teachings on African Pentecostals can be explained at the hand of the touch points between their hermeneutical perspectives. Most African Pentecostals use an unsophisticated and rather biblicist and literalist-fundamentalist way of reading and interpreting the Bible, as is also true of a bigger part of the African Independent/Indigenous/Instituted Churches movement.[122] They read the Bible for its literal sense, with a high view of the authority of Scripture, emphasizing supernatural elements of Scripture, including miracles, visions, and healings, and venerating the Old Testament as much, or more, than the New Testament. To them, the Bible speaks to everyday, real world issues of poverty and debt, famine and urban crises, racial and gender oppression, and state brutality and persecution. Their ideas of supernatural warfare and healing serve to underline their biblical and theological conservatism.[123] This hermeneutic among Pentecostals is the result of historical cooperation with Evangelicals when Pentecostals since the 1930s and 1940s tried to shed their sectarian image.[124] The price they paid for acceptance by many established churches, and society and governments as well, was that they accepted many worship practices and other conventions of these established churches, as well as their hermeneutical angle. In the process, they freed themselves from the early pentecostal hermeneutic that read the Bible in the direction from the present revelation of the Spirit to the church and their experience, to the Bible in order to understand what God is telling them in their contemporary situation, taking that revelation back to their current context. What was important was not what the Bible was saying about a specific issue but what early Pentecostals perceived the Spirit was revealing to them in the Bible.

---

122. However, the diversity and variation on matters of theology, doctrine, and belief among African Pentecostals indicate a fissiparous dynamism and although they are scriptural literalists, they cannot be properly termed "fundamentalist" because they do not follow the pattern of doctrinal drilling and ideological inflexibility that characterize fundamentalism *per se* (also the opinion of Hefner, "Unexpected Modern-Gender," 9).

123. Jenkins, *New Faces*.

124. See chapter 2 for a fuller discussion.

The Challenge

In the early Pentecostal movement, members who served as elders, deacons, or missionaries with distinction and the perceived "anointing of the Spirit" were awarded with certificates that acknowledged their gifting that "licensed" them to take part in the ministry of local churches.[125] They did not have any formal or informal theological qualifications. At most, short-term Bible schools were held to introduce the new converts and train workers to the unique challenges, emphasis, ethos, and paradigm of pentecostal ministry. "Bible school training" consisted of a basic knowledge of the Bible and its focus was on the application of the content of the Bible in the practice of daily ministry. In most cases the only prescribed textbook was the Bible itself. The Bible was used at face value without complicating its historical data and it was literally interpreted before it was applied pragmatically. It avoided any critical or systematic thinking that was associated with theological or academic expertise because such knowledge was regarded by Pentecostals as endangering the individual's faith and corrupting the church.[126] What was needed was only a thorough knowledge of the Bible combined with the anointing with God's Spirit as the prerequisite to qualify to minister as an evangelist or teacher of the Word, and men as well as women, young and old qualified for the task. It has been suggested, perhaps with some justice, that Pentecostal people might have hidden their feelings of theological inferiority behind the impression of their superior spiritual qualities based on their strong faith in the Word of God, excluding the necessity of theological reflection and training.[127] Early Pentecostals were, in many cases, suspicious of the scholastic tendencies in the mainline Christian churches, seeing it as the reason for the "dead formality" and lack of numerical growth or impact they perceived as characterizing these churches. In the main, the mainline churches also looked down upon the leaders of Pentecostal assemblies as unlearnt and uncouth.[128] Why did Pentecostals during the first five decades develop a tradition of anti-intellectualism? This is important to note because it is easy to misunderstand pentecostal anti-intellectualism and ascribe it to ignorance and a lack of theological

---

125. For further discussion, see Nel, "Rather Spirit-Filled than Learnt!;" Burger and Nel, *Fire Falls*, 59-61.

126. Chan, *Pentecostal Theology*, 45.

127. Morton, "'The Devil Who Heals,'" 113.

128. Vondey, *Beyond Pentecostalism*, 88–98.

training while its motives are more complicated and related to the movement's initial restorationist and primitivist urges.[129]

A first reason for its anti-intellectualist sentiments can be found in the historical circumstances in which the movement started, mainly among the poor and dispossessed. Most of the early members were illiterate; seldom did professional people attend meetings of the early Pentecostal churches. Many members were from the poor classes and they held their meetings in members' houses and halls made from zinc, mainly in communities and inner cities that were characterized by difficult socio-economic circumstances. Early Pentecostals lacked the motivation to engage in intellectual activities and organizations. Many of their leaders can be described as "amateurs" compelled by their experience of the Spirit to speak and write rather than as trained academicians who obeyed literary and exegetical rules and scholarly inventions.

A further reason is in the urgency and determination of Pentecostals in their task of evangelization, a diligence motivated by an eschatological desire to proclaim the gospel of salvation to a world facing the imminent second coming with its judgement seat. The need to carry the message to the unreached was so urgent that there was literally no time for training and preparation. The gift of speaking in tongues was initially interpreted as the gift of speaking previously unknown foreign languages, enabling the receiver to preach the gospel to nations without the need to acquire the proficiency needed to speak the foreign language, and without the need for further theological or biblical training to equip the ordinary believers. Their missionary zeal was enthused by divine revelation and motivated by eschatological urgency. There was no time left for a formal educational process when the second coming of the Lord might happen at any moment! And the second coming was conditionally dependent on success that the gospel be proclaimed to all nations, requiring all the church's attention! However, they were quickly faced with the pragmatic reality that their new tongues showed no affinity with existing languages. In any case, missionaries received minimal training, bypassing college or seminar degree programs; even when Bible institutes became more prominent from the 1920s, many Pentecostal missionaries left for other countries without credentials or formal studies because of their declared "dependence on the Spirit."[130]

---

129. Refer also to the discussion in chapter 2 about pentecostal hermeneutics and early pentecostal anti-intellectualism.

130. By 1910, some 185 Azusa-inspired missionaries had set out from North

The Challenge

A last reason is found in the widespread negative perception found among early Pentecostals that an intellectualization of the Christian faith was resisting or even suppressing the work of the Holy Spirit, while the life of the Spirit and the demands of intellectual labors were seen as opposites that do not readily mix. According to a pentecostal evaluation of the history of the church, the early Christian church had eventually institutionalized and intellectualized by the fourth century at the cost of the dynamic power of the Spirit. The implication is that the Spirit was driven out of the church and replaced with a reliance on intellectual and speculative thinking leading to creeds, theological theories, and criticism that disempowered the gospel and paralyzed believers. Formal theological education was evaluated as liberal in contrast to the biblical conservatism of Pentecostals, unbiblical because it represents German higher criticism and historical critical methods, formal because it suppressed the spontaneous working of the Spirit, and out of touch with reality, specifically the unique demands that the mission fields set.[131]

The anti-intellectualist urge is still characterizing the African pentecostal scene to a certain extent, including the contemporary prosperity movement within independent network Christianity. Although their leaders are in many cases well-qualified, most of them still use a biblicist and literalist hermeneutic to interpret the Bible, characterized by a conservative theological stance that the Bible is the infallible and flawless word of God, a conception that views each word in the Bible on the same level, as a revelation of God self. It can also be called the proof-text method of interpreting the Bible; typically, the reader needs a biblical meaning for a real-life purpose, and goes in search for some scriptural texts that support the topical theme, ignoring the context in which the text occurs and the world in which it initially functioned.[132] The scriptural texts are

---

America for other mission fields. Pentecostal churches were up and running in Norway, England, India, China, and Chile by 1907; South Africa by 1908; Brazil by 1910; Russia by 1911; Mexico by 1914; the Netherlands East India (Indonesia) by 1921; and the Philippines by 1926 (Hefner, "Unexpected Modern-Gender," 4).

131. Vondey, *Pentecostalism*, 136.

132. Hanegraaff, *Christianity in Crisis*, 9 states that it is also a primary characteristic of cults in general that they take biblical texts out of context in order to develop pretexts for their theological perversions. They also use Christian terminology while pouring their own meanings into the words. However, it cannot be used as an argument to state that all groups that are guilty of such hermeneutical practices are cults; then an inordinate number of Christian groups and pastors would qualify to form a part of this definition.

valued more for their short, epigrammatic style of several key words that coincide with the topic or subject chosen than for the evidence that they actually bring from their own context.[133] This is a populist interpretation that string proof-texts together, reading predetermined beliefs into the Bible.[134] Their conservativeness is demonstrated by the nearly exclusive use of the King James translation (1611), with its unworldly use of the English language.[135]

A further effect of the anti-intellectualist urge is that improper hermeneutics led to a one-sided gospel in prosperity theology that marginalizes the poor and unprivileged, representing a gospel of neo-capitalist consumerism and a problem-free life alien to true biblical teaching.[136] It is another brand of positive thinking scrupulously cloaked in carefully selected biblical texts deficient of historic Christological focus and a diversion for humanistic hopefulness and self-achievement.[137]

It can be concluded that the hermeneutic used by many Pentecostals in interpreting the Bible coincides with the hermeneutic of prosperity teachers, effectively creating room for influences from the prosperity message to infiltrate pentecostal theology and practice. What is necessary, is my submission, is not that some of the doctrines of independent network Christianity be revisited but that Pentecostalism should reconsider its hermeneutics. A new pentecostal hermeneutics has been in the making since the 1970s, in continuity with the most significant elements that occurred in early pentecostal Bible reading practices and that reflects the ethos of Pentecostalism, with its emphasis on the experiential and the direct intervention of the Spirit. The implications of such a hermeneutics for the prosperity message will be discussed in the next chapter.

---

133. Kaiser and Silva, *Introduction to Biblical Hermeneutics*, 33.

134. Ayegboyin, "Rethinking of Prosperity Teaching," 82. The historical-critical objection to proof-texting is its assumption that the Bible is equally inspired throughout (Archer, *Pentecostal Hermeneutic*, 64). However, just as important is that popular users of proof-texting do not give attention to the texts' contexts. Proof-texting assumes that the Bible is equally inspired throughout and timeless in its teaching; any verse of Scripture could be used without distinction as a proof to support a doctrinal position (Archer, *Pentecostal Hermeneutic*, 64).

135. For that reason, the KJV or Authorised Version is used here when reference is made to neo-pentecostal use of texts, while in all other cases the NRSV is preferred.

136. In the opinion of Alfred Kodua, *Who is Disturbing the Nation?*, 121-45.

137. In the words of Quayesi-Amakye, "Prosperity and Prophecy," 295.

The Challenge

Hermeneutical Key of the Prosperity Message

It has been asserted several times that its radical realized eschatology not only serves as the prosperity message's proprium in terms of its pentecostal heritage but also as the hermeneutical key to their interpretation of the Bible. Prosperity teachers use the presupposition and assumption that God always wants believers to be healthy, happy, carefree, wealthy, and prosperous, and that believers' hope is established on the wonderful world created by their faith on earth. Copeland acknowledges that he always interprets the Bible in the light of the "absolute truth" of John 10:10, that Jesus came that believers may have life, and have it abundantly. For him, this absolute truth serves as a guideline and absolute hermeneutical key and lens through which he reads the entire Bible.[138] The "faith principle" of the name of Jesus is also used as a key to unlock the riches of health, wealth, and prosperity promised to every believer. When they read the Bible, they find proofs for this theological presupposition in everything they read. When the assumption is not found in a specific text, it is "interpreted with revelation knowledge" to explain the "deeper meaning of the text," that rather "accidentally" supports the presupposition. The way this hermeneutical key influences their understanding of the Bible is critically important.

For instance, Kenneth Hagin interprets the notion in Deuteronomy 28:15–68 that God would put sickness and affliction on God's people when they do not serve the Lord exclusively (the so-called Deuteronomistic theology) by stating that the verb should be translated in a permissive rather than causative sense.[139] He argues in the same manner to explain the statement in Isaiah 45:7—that God forms light and creates darkness, makes well and creates woe—that God could never do such a thing because then God would be a devil. He may permit evil but God never creates it. When 1 Samuel 16:14 states that the Spirit of the Lord departed from Saul, and an evil spirit from the Lord troubled him, Hagin "solves" what is for him a problem because the theology in the text does

---

138. Copeland, *Laws of Prosperity*, 63.

139. See, e.g., vv. 20–22, "The Lord will send upon you disaster, panic, and frustration in everything you attempt to do, until you are destroyed and perish quickly, on account of the evil of your deeds, because you have forsaken me. The Lord will make the pestilence cling to you until it has consumed you off the land that you are entering to possess. The Lord will afflict you with consumption, fever, inflammation, with fiery heat and drought, and with blight and mildew; they shall pursue you until you perish." See discussion of this theology when proof-texts are examined critically.

not agree with his own theology, by stating that God permitted the evil spirit from the devil to trouble Saul.[140] It should be emphasized that there is no exegetical basis for these suggestions. It is clearly the theological framework of the authors that is determining their interpretation and not the clear meaning or common sense reading of the text.[141]

A problem arises when a specific interpretation of the Bible is propped up by the claim that it is supported by "revelation knowledge" because the assertion does not allow room in principle for any disagreement with the interpretation. After all, God revealed the "real and true" meaning to the prophet or apostle! The preconception that God wants all believers to be healthy and prosperous and enjoy heaven on earth here and now has become the framework in which the Bible is interpreted, and the preconception is based on the "revelation" received by prosperity teachers. The hermeneutical key is not based on sound exegetical conclusions and it is supported by a theological construction that makes scientific exegesis impossible.

Some Remarks about Characteristics of the Prosperity Gospel in Africa

Unique Element of African Prosperity

The African emphasis on prosperity is diversified, with each different faction preaching a specific emphasis. Quayesi-Amakye suggests, for instance, that in the Ghanaian pentecostal scenario it is possible to distinguish between classical Pentecostals, charismatic (or independent) ministries, and peripheral prophetism, that refers to ministries that originated since the 1990s and led to the establishment of prophet-led churches within the charismatic ministries.[142] Such differentiation occurs across African Pentecostalism in various forms and in each different scenario in a unique way, making it possible to refer to different emphasis on prosperity. However, there are some elements that are inherent in all African emphasis on prosperity, and these are now described.

An important faction of an African emphasis on prosperity in prophet-led churches differs from the American gospel of prosperity

---

140. Hagin, *Redeemed from Poverty*, 12-3.
141. Horn, *From Rags to Riches*, 111.
142. Quayesi-Amakye, "Prosperity and Prophecy," 294.

in the following manner. The standard prosperity gospel, supported by charismatic ministries, reduces the concept of prosperity to the humanistic principles of self-effort and self-achievement, and interprets lack and failure as faithlessness and sin while the prophets' unique emphasis views the supernatural as the ultimate recourse for success and victory, including health and wealth.[143] In the prophets' teaching, the supernatural is facilitated through a prophetic word via a man or woman of God called a prophet, and the solution is to obey the prophetic direction of the prophet to the letter. A prophetic direction is defined as a word or counsel a prophet gives his or her clients to show how to deal with a problem, perpetuating the practice of African traditional *sangomas*, diviners, fortune tellers, shamans, medicine men, rainmakers, sorcerers, magicians, witches, and witchdoctors and explaining the link and association with African demonology and an enchanted worldview.[144] In the prophetic ministry, rituals are not adhered to in a mechanical or generalized way, as is the case in many other African churches, but they are individualized and personalized to suit each believer's unique needs and situation. The purpose of such rituals, as found in the use of worship, singing and music, is not only to assure the worshiper of divine benevolence but it is also used as a supernatural weapon that destroys the enemies of believers. Worship services are characterized by singing in the Spirit or tongues, at times leading to hitherto unknown songs emerging spontaneously during prayer or worship services, and believed to come directly from the Holy Spirit.[145]

David Oyedepo in a sermon entitled, "Vital keys to unlocking the supernatural," preaches that each Christian is ordained to operate in the supernatural and establish their dominion over the supernatural.[146] He provides four keys that will exalt the believer into the supernatural realm. These are: drinking in the word of God, engaging the force of prayer, exercising in spiritual exercises, and a commitment to engaging a biblical mentality. The good news is that the supernatural is at our mercy; all believers can unlock it. What is necessary, is that believers should discover that they are not spiritual people but spirit. They need the mentality of the supernatural; their mental state should shift to supernatural mode.

---

143. Quayesi-Amakye, "Prosperity and Prophecy," 295.
144. Mburu, *African Hermeneutics*, 33.
145. Quayesi-Amakye, "Prosperity and Prophecy," 296.
146. https://www.youtube.com/watch?v=Tgq33sCo25U; accessed 2020-01-02.

As a cellphone can be reset to factory settings, they should be reset by the Spirit and reprogrammed with the word of God in order to operate as God designed them to operate.

The African prophetic movement developed its own jargon directly related to the African worldview of an enchanted nature. It should be kept in mind that the majority of people in Africa rarely live exclusively in one system of thought or culture, and as a result various agencies of authority, such as those embodied in Western institutions, religious organizations, and indigenous leaders contribute to a generalized interpretation of reality.[147] Key in African theology is the personification of evil, with evil assuming a human face that requires a prophetic deflation for soteriological effects. To move forward in life and become healthy and wealthy requires that one is saved from one's physical and spiritual enemies. The enemies are defined as the devil, evil spirits, witchcraft, dissatisfied ancestors, and human enemies who threaten the individual for various reasons.[148] What is important is that misfortunes in this life are all explained in causative terms as the work of external forces which are more powerful than the one who suffers from their interference, requiring some outside help. David Oyedepo in a sermon referred to in the previous paragraph, for instance, states that as God placed a hedge around Job to protect him, he protects, secures, and defends spirit people from evil forces.[149] Nobody would be able to touch them or lay a hand on them and the devils will be subject to them, as Jesus promised in Luke 10:17–19. They will tread on their enemies. Their stewardship to God will be absolutely to their benefit and no enemy will be able to threaten them ever again. The condition is that the believers should learn to speak in faith, by breaking all curses and

---

147. Deacon and Lynch, "Allowing Satan in?," 111.

148. Neo-pentecostal teachings provide a means to respond to, but have also been closely associated with a resurgence of witchcraft and devil worship accusations across much of sub-Saharan Africa, according to Comaroff and Comaroff, "Occult Economies and the Violence of Abstraction." It is agreed that neo-Pentecostalism in Africa responds to the enchanted worldview underlying a part of the population's way of thinking about reality (and found also in the New Testament world) but the close association observed by the researchers is denied. Neo-pentecostal prosperity should rather be interpreted in terms of a conjunction of high levels of spiritual insecurity, globalization, economic liberalization, democratization, and raised and failed expectations of economic participation, with the possibility of rapid enrichment, and of amassing a fortune by largely invisible methods, pertaining to magic (see Deacon and Lynch, "Allowing Satan in?," 111).

149. https://www.youtube.com/watch?v=Tgq33sCo25U; accessed 2020-01-02.

engaging in spiritual warfare. The preacher then invites the audience to consult with him on how to gain their freedom from curses.[150]

In traditional African thinking, nothing happens without a spiritual cause. One is helpless in the failures of this life, emphasizing the need to find a means to negotiate with the culprits, the evil spirits, and angry ancestors. People are not responsible for their actions; misfortunes always have some spiritual explanation. Even people who act in an evil way are not to be held responsible for their actions because they are the victims of evil powers and persons, like witches and sorcerers, who envied and abused them. In this way, Africans do not accept responsibility for their own actions and its influence on their circumstances, like abuse of alcohol or drugs, but find convenient scapegoats that can be reproached and kept accountable for their own shortcomings, like bad habits, laziness or a lack of initiative. Drunkenness, social deviance, and abusive behavior are blamed on other powers than the individuals themselves, leaving them the opportunity to continue with their misconduct that is socially unacceptable and abusive. They are not held accountable for their behavior. This might also contribute to the way politicians' misdeeds and corrupt acts are viewed by many Africans, leading them not to hold the leaders accountable for the damage they are causing to the African economy and social fabric, and voting again and again for political parties paralyzed by endemic corruption.

Afflictions, it is asserted in sermons, testimonies, and confessions, often originate from jealous family members or selfish colleagues who use magic and the "witches in the village" to damage their enemies.[151] The influences of external factors and forces determining one's fate in life requires the help and intervention of the prophet who alone can subvert the evil machinations of powers greater than the individual or, to put it in sociological terms, to become immune to other persons' negative

---

150. It is interesting that although the preacher teaches his adherents that God would protect and secure all spirit people, the preacher himself seemingly needed body guards that watched the different sectors of the assembly during the course of the sermon, seemingly to ensure that no member would threaten the preacher's life or interests.

151. Meyer, "Pentecostalism and Neo-Liberal Capitalism," 14. Comaroff and Comaroff, "Millennial Capitalism," 27 state that magic is everywhere in Africa and it is aimed at making sense of and acting upon the world, especially among those who feel themselves disempowered, emasculated, and disadvantaged, although not exclusively to them.

intentions and actions, to develop a buffered self.[152] The prophet is a specialist in spiritual warfare, who can occupy and engage evil forces such as witchcraft, occult, magic, as well as systemic oppressions and suppressions.[153] They use a point of contact, a concept familiar from the faith healing ministry,[154] consisting of prophylactics and amulets such as blessed water, blessed cloth and handkerchiefs, blessed money, clothing worn by the prophet, olive oil, anointing oil, vow-making, and cane.[155] These items are sold as effective in neutralizing satanic or demonic attacks in the client's life, resulting in the full-scale commercialization of the gospel.[156]

The perceived influence of witchcraft and magic in the lives of African people explain the interest in generational curses in African Pentecostalism, and in the prosperity movement.[157] David Oyedepo, preaching about "Vital keys to unlocking the supernatural," teaches that one's stewardship to God is absolutely to one's own benefit.[158] One of the benefits

---

152. Taylor, *Secular Age*.

153. Akrong, "African Traditional Religion and Development," 40. There are many "accurate prophecies" of Prophet Shepherd Bushiri available on YouTube. In one of them, he confronts a man in the audience after the prophet stated that he (that is, the prophet) was born to demonstrate the power of God (https://www.youtube.com/watch?v=C-hWrDglgoA; accessed 2020-01-02). He was walking among the people, touching them and prophesying at random. When he got to this man, he asked him several questions, to all of which the man replied positively: Are you poor? Are there members of your family without a job? Has your wife left you? Is everybody in your house unhappy? Then he stated what he claimed the Spirit revealed to him, that the man had visited a *sangoma* which he paid to get some help. The man confessed that he had visited the *sangoma*, and that he paid two hundred (South African) rand for the services. The prophet then announced that the man would be delivered, along with his whole family. "As God raised Jesus from the dead, so he is raising you from poverty." What is important is that the man should never again pay for the services that employ evil forces to do their work but that he should pay God for the miracle of deliverance. All the while the audience partook with shouts of acclamation and clapping of their hands. Another video uploaded is dedicated to several instances where he "demolished" evil powers raised against families (https://www.youtube.com/watch?v=GobYUsIY2lU; 2020-01-02).

154. Chris Oyakhilome of Nigeria catapulted the concept of "faith healing" into the public eye when he supported faith healing as a means to cure HIV, earning much criticism (Ntui-Abung, *Chaos of the Prosperity Gospel*, 13).

155. Kgatle, "Unusual Practices."

156. In the words of Deyi Ayegboyin, "Rethinking of Prosperity Teaching," 78.

157. See Keener, *Spirit Hermeneutics*, 270–71.

158. https://www.youtube.com/watch?v=Tgq33sC025U; accessed 2020-01-02.

is that generational curses can be broken in the lives of spirit people, that is, those who have found the means to access the supernatural. He relates generational curses to the words in the Decalogue, in Exodus 20:5–6, that the Lord will be visiting the iniquity of the fathers upon the children unto the third and fourth generations of them that hate him while God will be shewing mercy unto thousands of them that love God, and keep God's commandments (in the exalted language of the KJV, preferred by all prosperity teachers).[159] Christ redeemed all believers from the curse of the law, as Galatians 3:13 states (without considering that the author of the epistle attaches a totally different meaning to the term, "the curse of the law," as shown by the literary context). Through his death and resurrection, Jesus cancelled all curses of enemies on the lives of believers. When they had accepted Christ, believers have come out of curse bondage. It is now their legal right to be free. When they still experience manifestations of curses, it is because of what the householder in the parable in Matthew 13:27 states, that an enemy has done it, illegally. The good news, however, is that the thief has been caught. Believers may establish their liberty today because they have the right to be free.[160] What qualifies as a curse? Oyedepo explains that anything of long continuance and endurance that brings discomfort is a curse, such as a chronic illness, poverty, difficulties in relationships, etc. No Christian needs to be bound by it. They may expect every diabolical and generational curse to be broken in their lives. What they need to do is to open their mouths and declare war on the enemy. They need to speak against it in faith, and their liberty shall be completely established. However, when the curse is broken, it must be replaced by a blessing. They will experience blessings when they obey and serve God diligently, as Exodus 23:25 explains.[161] Blessings

159. Nwoka, "Challenge of Nigerian Pentecostal Theology," 167 states correctly that for (Nigerian) Pentecostals the King James Authorised Version (KJV) is "the Bible." No other translation of the Bible is used and Pentecostals encourage their adherents to use only the KJV.

160. In a sermon on 16 October 2018 with the title, "Reversing the irreversible," Prophet Enoch Adeboye states that God can change any curse into a blessing (https://www.youtube.com/watch?v=85b-2ED388Q; accessed 2020-01-12). Joshua placed a curse on Jericho, and the curse continued until Elisha went into the past and replaced the curse with a blessing. Jacob pronounced a curse on his son Levi just before he died but the curse was changed into a blessing when God decided in God's sovereignty to make Levi's descendants the tribe responsible for the temple service. In referring to Ezekiel 7, he stated that God can breathe onto any dry bones and reverse the irreversible (Ezek 37).

161. The important role that experience fulfills in the discourse of the pentecostal

always follow on a commitment to serve God. Then in their lives those who curse them will be cursed and those who bless them will be blessed. No one will be able to curse them because those whom God has blessed will be blessed forever. The biblically specified solution, however, is not a prominent preacher's formulaic prayer of deliverance, but a turning from the ways of the ancestors to obey God's word.[162]

It is a valid question to ask to prosperity theology, that if it preaches that the curse of sin and Satan was prevailed over in the cross of Christ and that sin, sickness, and poverty have no hold over believers, then why do believers still die? If they are not supposed to suffer from the effects of the curse anymore, why is death not lifted and conquered on the cross along with sickness and poverty, leading to health, wealth, and longevity without end?

Clients are also encouraged to make monetary donations, claimed to release superhuman solutions to clients' problems. In some cases, consultations with the prophet are also possible only via specified donations. Prophets also prescribe and then sell their unique brand of blessed water or anointing oil in numbered bottles, and in some cases it is compulsory that clients buy some of these products before they are allowed into consultation with the prophet. The rituals prescribed by the prophet are often shrouded in mystery; clients are discouraged to refer to them before other people, and they are told that if these rituals are disclosed to other people they would become ineffective, while it at times also represents some unconventional injunctions.[163] In this way, African neo-pentecostal

---

worship service is demonstrated by Prophet Andrew Mutawunashe who preached about Joshua and the Israelites on the eve of their invasion of the promised land (https://www.youtube.com/watch?v=TwX6sloQ3uI; accessed 2020-01-12). As Israel awaited a new experience, so the preacher promised his audience that God is preparing God's people for a new experience. The new experience with God will include new things, when God will make God's people as prosperous as the people of Israel who inhabited the country God had promised them, a land of milk and honey.

162. Keener, *Spirit Hermeneutics*, 271.

163. In a message of Prophet T.B. Joshua read in a worship service, containing his new year's message for 2020 while he was on the mountain "waiting to understand the mind of God for 2020," it was stated that one knows a prophet is a man of God if his words come true (https://www.youtube.com/watch?v=L4zo8Uov-4E; accessed 2020-01-02). The authority of the prophet is thus seen in the truth of the words that he prophecies, and for that reason great emphasis is placed on the accuracy of the words of the prophets. Where prophets prophesied for people in the audience, asking each time whether they were stating the correct facts about the people, it was remarkable that all the prophets were supplied with earphones. Might it indicate that their

prophetism successfully contextualizes their version of the gospel to African traditional religion[164] and the prophet becomes a current substitute for the traditional African offices of the diviners, fortune tellers, and witchdoctors.[165]

Joseph Quayesi-Amakye's warning is valid, that such a personification of evil in Africa tends to invite clients to look for the solution to their challenges exclusively in the supernatural realm and to confer responsibility for the solution of their challenges and problems elsewhere, rather than to take responsibility for their own lives and behavior. They become over dependent on prophetic direction, obediently following the prophet's counsel even if it contributes to their financial woes by way of their support of the prophet's ministry, and it deprives them of own initiative and innovation to confront life's problems head on. It is easier to place the responsibility in a lazy manner on the shoulders of outside forces than to stand up and do something proactively about the problem.[166]

African Definition of Poverty

In traditional Africa, the community played an important role and communal effort in daily tasks of life was taken for granted. For instance, the bringing up of children was a community effort.[167] People did not work for themselves in the Western way, where they, rather selfishly, spend all their money on their own needs and desires. All work in Africa was geared towards providing for the family unit, and accumulation of personal wealth was unheard of. When parents grew too old to participate in work activities, the children were duty bound to provide for them. From an early age, children learned the value of hard work. Added to that,

---

"victims" were people chosen by hand and trained to answer the prophet correctly?

164. Akiri, "The Prosperity Gospel."

165. Bledsoe, "Prosperity Theology," 304 relates it to mediumistic religions, which commonly exist in fear-based societies where shamans go through rituals and distribute amulets for avoiding or ridding people of a malady and to receive a needed blessing. It is related to animism, that played an important role in traditional African thinking, consisting of the belief that personal spiritual beings and impersonal spiritual forces have power over human affairs, leading to the necessity that individuals should discover what beings and forces are influencing them in order to determine future action and to manipulate their powers.

166. Quayesi-Amakye, "Prosperity and Prophecy," 299.

167. Mburu, *African Hermeneutics*, 39.

when it came to work, getting the work done was secondary to maintaining good relationships within the work context. The same is partly true of a biblical worldview, where family and community were very important and the family was held together by traditional concerns that included employment and the education and socialization of children.[168]

As an example of the African way of thinking about failures and misfortunes, many accept that poverty is not just about a lack of finances. The solution is not necessarily to find a job (admittedly at times a difficult undertaking in parts of Africa) and generate enough money to provide in material provisions of a family. Poverty has a unique African connotation and definition; it is associated with any lack in a person's life that reduces their status in life and deprives them of the enjoyment of social acclamation and respect. Poverty removes its victim from society and disqualifies them from attending to other people, which is more significant than only its influence on the individual's life. In the words of Quayesi-Amakye in his Masters dissertation, poverty "dedefines" a person's socio-economic and political status and identity and leads to a "reidentification" of the person in new and depersonalizing social strata.[169] Poor people acquire a new name, a new face, and a new identity in society, associated with their invisibleness and vulnerability, especially to the rich and powerful. They are defaced, depreciated, depersonalized, downgraded, and humiliated, emphasizing the identification of poverty with a curse with spiritual consequences and causes. The unique impact and popularity of the prosperity message in the African context is clear when this view of poverty is held in perspective, leading to a unique definition of poverty in Africa.

In the prophetic ministry the curse of poverty is associated with sickness, disease, adversity, and any other experience that deprives persons of social acclamation and acceptance, and the only solution lies in deliverance from the evil forces responsible for the curse and its enactment in the life of an individual. One hears it repeatedly in sermons of African prosperity teachers that the faith heroes in the Bible were fabulously rich, including the patriarchs and Job, kings David and Solomon, and various others.[170] The curse causes a blockage that keeps people back

---

168. Mburu, *African Hermeneutics*, 39.

169. Quayesi-Amakye, "Ideas of the Divine and the Human," 33.

170. See, e.g., the reference in a sermon by Pastor Chris Oyakhilome that Job was one of the richest people living in his day on earth. Satan attacked Job on several fronts but he found there was no way to get into his house because he was faithful. Then Satan was given permission to take Job's possessions and valuable assets away. Job made the

from the success and wealth that are their rights and privileges as Christians, and only an anointed man of God could release the blockage.[171] The only solution for the victim of poverty, and including disease as part of the phenomenon of poverty, is to call on the name of Jesus with its magical powers. The only way to unlock the potential of the name of Jesus is to be channeled through the ministry of the prophet. One cannot do it on one's own, without the mediation of the anointed one.

Poverty is, however, not only a curse but also a sin, in the words of David Oyedepo.[172] He interprets 2 Corinthians 8:9 to say that sin brought material poverty, atonement restores material blessing, and the Christian that remains in material poverty is sinning against redemption. The prosperity gospel involves healing from sickness, exorcism, and deliverance from poverty for all believers and all the time.

The effect of this theological view of poverty is that the diversified causes of poverty in Africa are not necessarily addressed effectively by neo-Pentecostals. It offers believers (who faithfully pay for the prophet's service) the hope of liberation from their endangered existence without acknowledging that some forms of suffering are due to self-inflicted causes due to one's deliberate breach of God's laws. Others can be ascribed to abuse and corruption of those politicians elected by the people but not held accountable by people who ascribe their suffering rather to spiritual causes, while there are other types of suffering that are inflicted by individuals on their fellow human beings.[173]

On the other hand, prosperity is understood in the African cultural environment as having to do more with inner peace, social harmony, healing, health, liberation from evil spirits, witchcraft, and demons, than about getting rich in a material way.[174] Except for the new elite middle-class that characterizes the African democratization process and who are primarily the benefactors of Africa's vast resource deposits, economic liberalization, and corruption,[175] Africans have not sold their souls yet to Western materialism because the majority experience increasing poverty

---

mistake to blame God, calling God the cause of his mishaps. In the end he found out that the Giver of good gifts never take any gift away. It was the devil who was the thief (https://www.youtube.com/watch?v=yQppu1NnbuE; accessed 2019-12-27).

171. Gifford, "Persistence and Change," 172.
172. Quoted in Folarin, "Contemporary State," 81.
173. See, e.g., Magasa, "Christ the Liberator in Africa."
174. Kalu, *African Pentecostalism*.
175. Deacon and Lynch, "Allowing Satan in?," 110.

as national debts spiral out of control, and it should be kept in mind when the teachings of prosperity theology is proclaimed in the African context.

Long-Term Social Change

Another characteristic is concerned with what Pentecostalism traditionally viewed as one of the signs of a healthy and effective church, found in the life transformation of individuals due to their acceptance of the gospel.[176] What is the long-term social change brought about by independent charismatic networks representing neo-Pentecostals? How does its definition of poverty in terms of evil spirits as its cause, leading to adherents not concentrating on other man-made causes that can effectively be addressed (as discussed above), contribute to the movement's involvement, or lack of involvement, in social change in Africa?[177] Can their lack of institutional infrastructure and organizational capacity limit their ability to influence the African social scene?

Some of the neo-Pentecostal apostles' concern for the underprivileged and disenfranchised is evident. For instance, the involvement of controversial Prophet T.B. Joshua (of the Synagogue Church of All Nations, in Lagos, Nigeria) in issues of social justice has received much publicity and his relationship with African political leaders is also well-known, although he is to a large extent isolated and ostracized by most

---

176. Thiselton, *New Horizons*, 8 emphasizes the transforming character of biblical reading, with the potential to lead to a re-ranking of expectations, assumptions, and goals which readers initially bring to texts. The other side is that readers also have the ability to transform the texts they are reading, as the canonical context of the Bible given by the church proves (Kaiser and Silva, *Introduction to Biblical Hermeneutics*, 36).

177. Kalu, *African Pentecostalism*, 257 asserts that the Old Testament's diagnoses of poverty draws a distinction between external, internal, and moral causes. Causes of poverty in the Hebrew tradition are: the oppression of the rich, religious apostasy, social alienation, ecological causes, human factors, and self-alienation or lifestyle. Religious apostasy includes rebellion against God's will, Sabbath-breaking, neglect of civil responsibilities, and failure to tithe. Social alienation includes war, bad governance, bureaucratic and fiscal irresponsibility, excessive administrative costs, and burdensome taxation. Ecological causes include famine, drought, hurricanes, tornadoes, lightning, earthquakes, volcanic eruptions, and other forms of natural disasters. Human factors include emigration, environmental ethics and pollution, agricultural practices, depletion of natural resources, and a lack of ethics of replacement. Self-alienation is linked to laziness, sloth, drunkenness, a wasteful lifestyle, extravagance, love of wine and women, disobedience to parents, immorality, sexual orientation, and fraudulence. These may be good reasons for poverty, but it is not clear where the author finds all of his occurrences in the Old Testament.

other Nigerian Pentecostals.[178] It can be accepted that he influenced these leaders in a positive way by emphasizing issues related to social justice. Quite a few prominent African politicians and other leaders allow apostles and prophets to speak into their lives and provide social critique of norms and values such as political logic built on military force, energy generation by way of means that contribute to global warming and climate change, an economics of greed, an absence of truth from the political discourse, etc. This mostly happens in private and is not public knowledge. Poverty, economic inequality, violence, crime, HIV and Aids, state capture, and xenophobia have become an alternative epistemology that serves as a hermeneutical key with which these prophets and apostles read and interpret the Bible, in accordance with acceptable pentecostal hermeneutical practice,[179] operating on the assumption that God wants to meet the needs of God's people in a direct manner.

Pentecostal theology is not only word-based; it includes acts of healing and deliverance based on the belief in the intimate personal knowledge of and participation in God's anguished love for God's people and God's intervening power that can overcome any evil powers. The Bible is believed to contain answers for this-worldly needs and leaders in the independent movement operate on the assumption of immediacy, that God wants to meet people's needs.[180] Its pneumatological soteriology is expressed in interventionist and mediate terms. In this sense, Pentecostal prophets have become an innovative Christian alternative to traditional healers and diviners, as already explained.

C.J. Kaunda makes the important remark that any attempt by religious groups to change society involves creating new ways of being in the world and new possibilities for socio-economic transformation in order to find a remedy for the persistent social ills of the horrific and destructive phenomenon of xenophobia.[181] Some of the primary ways neo-Pentecostals react to social justice and the challenges that modern societies offer are through their involvement in schools, clinics and hospitals, labor unions, self-help groups, and development and relief organizations, and by influencing personal morality, nurturing civic responsibility, working

---

178. Anderson, "New African Initiated Pentecostalism," 84.
179. Anderson, "Hermeneutical Processes," 223.
180. Anderson, *Introduction to Pentecostalism*, 224.
181. Kaunda, "Enabling Liminality Prophetic Witness," 8.

for the alleviation of poverty, promoting education, and advocating for peace and justice.[182]

In analyzing the prosperity movement among neo-Pentecostal groups in Africa, David Ngong argues that they promote an African spiritualistic worldview that does not pay sufficient attention to the scientific imagination.[183] With its emphasis on physical healing it does not allow for the successes of medical science while at the same time its ascription in a wholesale manner of socio-economic and political challenges to the demonic cannot be upheld.[184] Previously, African traditional religion pacified evil deities and ghosts with animal sacrifices, necromancy, spiritism, and ritualism and some have asserted that the African Instituted Churches inappropriately and in syncretistic manner mix the Christian faith with African traditional religion by serving the same agenda. The African worldview traditionally explained misfortune in terms of the influence of evil spirits, necessitating their pacification. If neo-Pentecostalism indiscriminately intends to pacify evil spirits without an unapologetic commitment to biblical finality of authority, it would certainly degenerate into a syncretizing with questionable beliefs and practices.[185] However, Ngong's remarks generalize and he does not take into account that many neo-Pentecostal prophets do allow room for the contribution of medical science and the reality of sociopolitical and economic woes due to hardcore neo-capitalism and greedy politicians. And when they are faced with the challenge of xenophobia in their communities, they address the problems forcibly and practically. Still there is some truth in the remark; while providing in this-worldly needs of individuals, the causes of their challenges may not be spiritualized to such an extent that blame is shifted onto evil spirits, implying that human beings need not accept responsibility for their own lives, as seemingly taught by Derek Prince and the Nigerian Emeka Nwakpa.[186] It is not enough to cast out the demons of poverty, inequality, or xenophobia; believers need to hear the important gospel message again and again that they need to work hard and that all people are to be treated with dignity because they have been created in the image of God. K. Mana proposes that a bridge

---

182. Yong, *In the Days of Caesar*, 248.
183. Ngong, *Holy Spirit and Salvation*, 147.
184. Mana, *Christians and Churches of Africa*, 96.
185. Quayesi-Amakye, "'Nativizing' the Gospel," 287-303.
186. Quayesi-Amakye, J. "'Nativizing' the Gospel," 301.

should be erected by neo-Pentecostals between popular expectations of deliverance and theoretical analyses of liberation and reconstruction by the church in order to transform hearts and minds in the building of peaceful and flourishing societies that accommodate social justice.[187] What is needed is prophetic politics informed by pentecostal spirituality and piety that engages the public sphere boldly[188] and provides all kinds of counter-cultural and counter-conventional communities where the displaced experience companionship and solidarity in the form of "family," serving as a counter-history, counter-ethics, and counter-ontology to that of the myth of secularism.[189] According to Amos Yong, a prophetic politics recognizes and announces that allegiances to the state are secondary to allegiance to God, challenges the state to do what it is supposed to do, to uphold the law, and encourages Spirit-filled believers to explicitly witness in the public square, even and specifically in the "naked public square," characterized by the absence of religion from both the political and civic arena.[190] The result will be that communities function as alternative "cities" that intentionally set out to provide forms of sociopolitical and economic solidarity for people who otherwise find themselves on the margins of the city as conventionally defined.[191] Prophetic politics actualizes also in reflective participation in politics; Pentecostals were involved in the establishment of several conservative political parties in African states and Zambia has had two Pentecostal presidents,[192] with President Frederick Chiluba, who governed Zambia for two terms from 1991 to 2001, declaring the country a Christian nation in 1991 and the call of President Edgar Lungu, president of Zambia since 2015, to the nation to prayer, fasting and reconciliation and a National Day of Prayer and Fasting Service in 2015.[193]

What neo-Pentecostals lack, according to Christerson and Flory, is a clear vision of what social transformation should look like if they were

---

187. Mana, *Christians and Churches of Africa*, 97.
188. Bangura, "Charismatic Movements," 247.
189. Yong, *In the Days of Caesar*, 228.
190. Yong, *In the Days of Caesar*, 239-42, 248.
191. Yong, *In the Days of Caesar*, 13.
192. Anderson, "Deliverance and Exorcism," 104, 108.
193. http://www.times.co.zm/?p=66547; https://eliasmunshya.org/2015/10/15/after-we-have-said-amen-towards-a-Pentecostal-theology-of-politics-in-zambia/; accessed 2018-07-19.

to gain more influence, including the area of government.[194] In Africa some of the most dynamic and popular leaders of the movement lack a post-secondary education and cannot be expected to have a coherent and informed vision of social change and how to promote it. Their independent way of operating also excludes them from advice that would have been provided in an organizational setting where groups of leaders collectively define policies.

Another argument is that the emphasis on prosperity may disqualify it from reaching the disenfranchised and marginalized such as most immigrants are, because of the perception that it is a rich church and a rich man's church. Leaders of successful charismatic networks often portray themselves as blessed by God, with vast resources of finances available for their private consumption.[195] "Unfortunately, Christians, especially those from Pentecostal-charismatic circles, are not very keen to confront social and political causes of poverty on the continent," writes J. Kangwa.[196] Such a stereotyping is valid in some cases but not true for others, due to the diverse and changing participation of neo-Pentecostal groups in politics. Maria Frahm-Arp, for instance, discusses South African megachurches that initially did not participate in politics but in the end became involved.[197] For instance, Jacob Zuma as president of the ANC invited Ray McCauley of Rhema Bible Church to head the National Interfaith Leadership Council (NILC), and before the 2009 elections McCauley invited Zuma to Rhema to "preach" to his congregation.[198] Grace Bible Church invited political officials from different affiliations to address their congregations in the build-up to the 2014 elections. They motivated it by stating that the congregation should be informed about political choices in order to elect Christians into key political positions.[199]

What should be kept in mind is that when neo-Pentecostals concentrate on the this-worldly needs of believers their prophecies most of the time provide guidance derived from the Bible, although it must be admitted that Scripture might be misappropriated, as Quayesi-Amakye

---

194. Christerson and Flory, *Rise of Network Christianity*, 137.

195. Comaroff and Comaroff, "Privatizing the Millennium," 37 refer to the accumulation of wealth in prosperity theology as representing an act of sacral consumption.

196. Kangwa, "African Democracy and Political Exploitation," 544.

197. Frahm-Arp, "Rise of the Megachurches in South Africa," 279-80.

198. Frahm-Arp, "Rise of the Megachurches in South Africa," 267.

199. Frahm-Arp, "Rise of the Megachurches in South Africa," 271.

explains.[200] The worldly challenges then become the hermeneutical key to the interpretation of the Bible, in a historicist way where the social-historical background and horizon of the text is largely ignored and it is interpreted as though it were written exclusively for contemporary believers.[201] It also characterizes a large part of the sermons in neo-Pentecostal churches. One manner to address this issue is by bringing the importance of a sound theological training for all neo-Pentecostal pastors, prophets, and apostles to the attention of the movement's leaders, a difficult task since it is not organized into alliances or denominations, as is the case with classical Pentecostalism.

In most cases, neo-prophets do not have any or only loose connections with church mother bodies, implying that they are not answerable to anyone and they use any and all market techniques to ply their ministries.[202] The lack of accountability and transparency is harming the neo-Pentecostal movement and the behavior of a few prophets is discrediting the movement as a whole. For instance, a few cases have been reported of prophets who exploited the trust of their clients by abusing and assaulting them sexually or emotionally,[203] or requiring exorbitant payment for their healing prayers.[204] An example can be found in the Universal Church of the Kingdom of God (UCKG).[205] In 2000 the South African Human Rights Commission (SAHRC) found that the church exploited the poor financially and performed rituals that amounted to forms of

---

200. Quayesi-Amakye, J. "'Nativizing' the Gospel," 247.

201. See Nida's (*Message and Mission*, 33-58) remark that what is needed in relevant hermeneutics are three horizons that can accommodate the cross-cultural perspective. The first horizon is the culture of the Bible, the second is the culture of the interpreter, and the third is the culture of the receptor. Each of these horizons contain a circle of cultural baggage and understandings, and none of the cultures can be made normative for the others. Interpreters need to be aware of the way that their culture forces certain questions while leaving them blind to other, perhaps equally provocative questions (see also Kaiser and Silva, *Introduction to Biblical Hermeneutics*, 238).

202. Zulu, "'Sow a Seed' and Prosper?," 99-112.

203. In related sense, see Chris Oykhi Lome who propagates and promotes masturbation as part of his version of the prosperity message (Ntui-Abung, *Chaos of the Prosperity Gospel*, 14).

204. Mwale and Chita. "Religion and the Media," 41-63. See also Zulu, "'Sow a Seed' and Prosper?," 52-3.

205. Their motto is *pare de sofrir!* ("stop suffering!"), as related by Vásquez, "The Global Portability," 283.

psychological conditioning. After a legal battle the Commission had to retract its findings.[206]

Overselling the Miraculous in Africa

Pentecostalism has since its inception at the beginning of the twentieth century been characterized by its emphasis on direct contact with the supernatural in the form of miraculous "signs and wonders," such as *glossolalia*, deliverance from evil spirits, supernatural healing, and direct communication from God's side in the form of prophecy, interpretation of *glossolalia*, and words of wisdom and knowledge. It was argued that it is the element of emphasis on the miraculous and the expectation of divine intervention in the daily affairs of believers that guaranteed the enormous growth of African Pentecostalism.

The emphasis on the miraculous and supernatural leads to a product cycle within Pentecostalism that does not differ between the various manifestations of the movement. It starts with a charismatic leader who has the ability to produce and facilitate miraculous signs and wonders, and who breaks away from the constraints of traditionally organized and institutionalized denominational congregations. The leader's experimentation with direct contact with miraculous power and claims that he facilitates miraculous phenomena serving the interests of followers causes a rapid growth of those who follow him. The movement receives much criticism from the side of established churches, "proving" to its followers that it is God's unique revelation in their midst that threatens conventional Christianity marked by a dead formalism. In time the movement responds to the controversy and criticism by way of routinizing and regulating their practices of the miraculous, looking for respectability and the acceptance of the establishment, and loses the edge of its experimentation, eventually resulting in the emergence of new charismatic leaders who repeat the cycle, to escape from the routinizing movement with its growing institutional constraints to create a new movement.[207]

It was also argued that leaders of new independent charismatic or neo-Pentecostal networks apparently successfully escape this cycle by their continuous experimentation with the supernatural without the constraints of their new organizations and its inevitable routinizing trends by

---

206. See Van Wyk, *Universal Church of the Kingdom* for full details.
207. See Christerson and Flory, *Rise of Network Christianity*, 125-26.

acting without having accountability to any form of supervision. They see themselves as leaders in an absolute sense and their lack of accountability unfortunately includes the way they manage the organizations' finances. Their supposed direct connection with the divine allows them to manage their organizations without necessarily consulting anybody or reporting to anybody.

At times their prophecies are "overreaching" in terms of world events and create expectations with their followers that are impossible to achieve. They are overselling the miraculous. Such large-scale prophecies include, for instance, the transfer of wealth to Christian believers on a worldwide scale never seen before in history, with massive numbers of new converts, the rise of "kingdom-minded" (meaning, within the context of network Christianity, socially conservative, "born-again" Spirit-filled) Christian believers to top positions in government, education, media, arts, entertainment, and business, and the imminent return of Jesus Christ to the earth to rule the world in conjunction with believers.

Another problem is found in the sensationalized use of testimonies in the worship services and publications of prosperity teachers. Testimonies of claims of having received one's wealth or healing after applying the principles of the prosperity message of faith, positive confession, and consulting the prophet or apostle are recorded and publicized in both print and electronic media. Their services include ample opportunity for these testimonies that are supposed to build the faith of listeners, to trust God for their own miracle. Most testimonies focus on the material realm, of finances, a job, promotion at work, travel opportunities, the restoration of relationships in marriages, and the acquirement of children. Paul Gifford finds in his research that only a small fraction, perhaps ten percent, refer to moral reform, deliverance from laziness, or abuse of alcohol or drugs while the rest concentrate on material gains in their testimonies.[208]

The problem with "overselling" a product is that it creates disillusioned customers over time who might convince others of the improbability of the verity of leaders' claims and leave for other religious organizations with more modest claims. They may even abandon religion altogether. And although such movements may still show signs of growth because it reaches new markets with oversold claims of supernatural intervention, the markets will eventually diminish. The financial recipes provided by prosperity gurus do not bear fruit for all their disciples and

---

208. Gifford, "Persistence and Change," 173.

dissatisfied disciples may eventually lead to dissatisfaction with the way the gurus are spending the customers' hard-earned money.

The hype is generated by the expectation that sowing money will result in harvesting blessings in terms of business and private financial benefits. It also proclaims that even the businesses in which believers are employed will be blessed due to the believers' involvement. People respond to the message by giving generously, at times spending all their money in contributions to the organization and its projects. When they experience that "God is not showing up" and doing what the leader promised, their disappointment may cause disillusionment with the movement, or with religion. A Ugandan bishop at the Anglican Conference of Bishops in Jerusalem in 2018 warned that the prosperity message was sweeping Africa and the message did not deliver what it promised, leading to widespread disillusionment among Christians that he was already perceiving on a widespread scale.[209]

It seems that at least some people eventually tire of the hype that gets generated at conferences around the miraculous and money generated by contributing. However, it is also true that a majority of people keep the hype and excitement going by bouncing from one conference to the next, and from one boot camp to the next. Even though the events and their message are not financially viable and sustainable, it is clear that they are emotionally viable, even over longer periods.

Stability in Community Life

Various sociologists of religion explain the success of religious groups in reaching many people in terms of people's search for meaning and belonging.[210] Religion serves as a central source of the types of morally orienting collective identities that provide people with meaning and belonging. It can be said that prosperity theology instills a new morality in which wealth and status can accrue to a successful believer while elevating their social status with attendant privileges, power, and influence, and leads to a cleaning up of their lives and becoming more responsible.[211]

It is true of independent network charismatic Christianity as well; it provides meaning in compelling ways by involving participants in

---

209. Zaimov, "Prosperity Gospel Sweeping Africa."
210. See, e.g., Berger, *Sacred Canopy*; Emerson and Smith, *Divided by Faith*.
211. Marti, "The Adaptability of Pentecostalism," 23-4.

a supernatural battle on which the fate of the entire cosmos depends, bringing heaven to earth by accessing the supernatural power of the Spirit. Their apocalyptic worldview that views the future of the world in terms of a cataclysmic ending with God intervening and creating something entirely new provides a narrative that gives meaning to believers' lives and mission on earth.

A problem in the network movement identified by Christerson and Flory is that young people are much involved but once they get older, have families, and settle down, their involvement in the movement diminishes.[212] They suffer from a lack of continuous and stable community life in a movement where all the focus is on the charismatic leader, paralyzing the democratic character of the congregation as part of the body of Christ. A characteristic of the prosperity movement in Africa is its lack of stability in the life of the groups, with a constant change of faces over time, even more so than in other church groups.

Abuses in the Neo-Pentecostal Movement

It has become imperative that prophetic practices should be normalized and regulated to protect the Christian church *per se*. In chapter 1 reference was made to abuses found in the African prosperity movement and governments' reaction to it. Amos Yong writes that the church provides a site where Spirit-filled believers are emboldened to bear prophetic witness and learn how to live prophetically in the Spirit but also to engage the world external to the church, providing a prophetic alternative to the world's conventions of corruption, patronage and oligarchy. They are empowered by charitable works sensitive to larger socio-structural projects and tasks, even when it implies confrontation with the principalities and powers when necessary.[213] However, this ideal is not reached by some neo-Pentecostal groups, and conventions of corruption and patronage should be eradicated where it occurs in African neo-Pentecostalism.

That there are excesses and abuses within the neo-Pentecostal movement that are perpetuated by some prophets cannot be denied. Presumably turning water into wine, ordering believers to drink petrol and paraffin to prove their faith according to Mark 16:17-18, turning water

---

212. Christerson and Flory, *Rise of Network Christianity*, 133.
213. Yong, *In the Days of Caesar*, 250-51.

into petrol, turning a snake into chocolate,[214] walking on thin air, "healing" cancer, HIV and Aids,[215] "raising" the dead and predicting soccer and election results are some of the excesses that received wide and negative coverage in the daily African press.[216] These allegations damage the Pentecostal movement as a whole.

A tragic example is the Ngcobo killings of 21 February 2018 where five policemen and an off-duty soldier were shot during an attack on a police station in Ngcobo, between Mthatha and Komani (previously Queenstown) in the Eastern Cape, in South Africa. During the attack, ten firearms and a police van were stolen from the police station before an ATM a short distance from the police station was robbed.[217] Seven suspects were eventually killed and ten others arrested after a shootout with police at the town's Mancoba church, including one of the church's leaders. His brother confirmed his involvement with the gang who killed the policemen. Their motive was presumably to access funds because of the dire financial straits of the church. The South African Council of Churches responded that it had lodged a complaint with government over the Seven Angels Church but was ignored. The Commission for the Promotion and

---

214. Prophet Penuel Mnguni of End Time Disciples Ministries in Siyabuswa in Mpumalanga, South Africa, ordered church members to eat snakes in order to prove that nothing was impossible with his God. He also fed them live rats and locked some of them in a deep freezer, drove over them and walked on them. Women and men were ordered to strip half naked and started hissing like snakes. They called themselves pythons, mambas, cobras, or anacondas. He told his people that he had the authority to change anything into something else. Once he visited the beach with members of the congregation where he ordered the girls to strip naked; he kissed their behinds in order for them to find correct marriage partners. At another time he ordered members to undress in church and to start masturbating until they reached orgasm (like Chris Oykhi Lome also did). He stated that the holy fluid of masturbation would produce a sacrosanct fluid which would make the church floor as sacred as heaven (Kgatle, "Unusual Practices").

215. Daniel Smith, "Pentecostalism and Aids in Nigeria," 58, a medical anthropologist, expresses his surprise that while many African victims of Aids share the perception that the moral stigma associated with the illness is even worse than the illness itself, so many of them keep on visiting Pentecostal churches that teach that Aids is the result of widespread social immorality, and an individual problem most often because of the sin of the victim. A lure is the promise to HIV-positive people of a faith cure to the illness, although many sufferers do not disclose their illness to the church because of the stigma.

216. Mwale, and Chita, "Religion and the Media," 51. See also Zulu, "'Sow a Seed' and Prosper?," 104.

217. https://www.enca.com/south-africa/five-police-dead-in-attack-on-station; accessed 2018-02-26.

Protection of the Rights of Cultural, Religious, and Linguistic Communities (CRL) chairwoman, Thoko Mkhwanazi-Xaluva, reacted to the events at Ngcobo and said the church was probed already in 2016 and authorities were alerted to children living at the church and not attending school. The committee suggested that the government should regulate church leadership by way of registration. The co-operative governance and traditional affairs portfolio committee of Parliament responded to the committee's report by arguing that the state could not prescribe when it came to beliefs and religious convictions because of the value of religious liberty ensconced in the Constitution of the Republic of South Africa, but it unanimously condemned the abuse of vulnerability by religious leaders.[218] In another instance recorded in Kampala, Uganda a local prophet motivated his adherents to sell cattle, shops, plots of land, and all other house items they owed like fridges, television sets, and sofa sets, claiming that he would pay them back many times over and they would be enabled to live as rich people within a matter of months. Then the prophet disappeared and no word has been received about him as yet.[219]

Charismatic network Christianity has no other option than that its prominent leaders should be encouraged to organize the movement to such an extent that it can protect itself from swindlers and charlatans that damages its reputation with the public and governments.

These abuses led in July 2018 to a controversial decree by the government of Rwanda to close hundreds of Pentecostal prayer houses and about a third of all Catholic churches, in order to counter what it called "troubling behavior of unscrupulous individuals masquerading as religious leaders." In the Ivory Coast Catholic bishops opened a hotline against "swindlers and impostors," and advised their church members to be vigilant against "badly intentional individuals" who had solicited financial donations while claiming to be Catholic clergy.[220]

A negative feature of neo-pentecostal prophetism is the emphasis on the charisma and person of the individual prophet, also in advertisements of the ministry, and the accompanying adoration and veneration of the prophet. This is one of the important distinctions between the phenomenon of prophecy in the classical and neo-Pentecostal movements. The former emphasizes prophecy as a gift to the church by way of the participation of

---

218. http://www.enca.com/south-africa/parliament-slams-crl-chairs-comment-on-engcobo; accessed 2018-02-26.

219. Guyson, "Of False Prophets and Profits."

220. Luxmoore, "African Church Warns."

all believers, and the latter emphasizes the permanent office of the prophet functioning with absolute authority. The prophets' status might also lead to their enrichment and personal gain through gifts presented to them in order to secure their services, or as gratuity for supposed services;[221] Quayesi-Amakye refers to it as "prophetic monetization."[222]

Some of the positive benefits of neo-prophetism should also be described. Neo-Pentecostal churches purposefully do not take denominational political and doctrinal issues seriously, in consideration for the postmodern sentiment of respect for people with different opinions. Doctrinal differences play only a peripheral role because as part of the Pentecostal movement the emphasis is on people meeting the truth in the person of Christ rather than in the Bible. Perhaps the neo-Pentecostal movement may eventually serve as a catalyst for ecumenical engagement between Christians.

Corruption and Scandal as Part of Neo-Pentecostalism

Various references have already been made to abuses that have been occurring in the charismatic network community, scarring its reputation. It seems that these networks of apostles and prophets are more vulnerable to scandal and corruption than traditionally organized congregations and denominations and the reasons are clear. Apostles and prophets are not held accountable by anybody and transparency is not expected from them by their followers. Their enormous amount of authority and autonomy and their style of absolute leadership allow them the opportunity to make decisions without giving account to anybody, including reporting about their financial contributors. They do not have any oversight boards that may have protected them from financial practices that in the end make headlines. In many cases, the apostle reserves the right of exclusively taking all financial decisions, making them particularly fertile ground for financial excesses and abuses of power.

When an apostle becomes involved in a financial or sexual scandal, they are also restored in their position much quicker than would have happened in the established churches because they are not

---

221. Banda, "Prophets of God or Neo-Diviners?," 208-29.
222. Quayesi-Amakye, "'Nativizing' the Gospel," 303. Cf. also the critical work of Chitando, Gunda and Kügler, *Prophets, Profits*.

subjected to church laws and procedures. They decide about their ministries themselves.

At the same time, the "cost" of network apostles' scandals is much lower than in the traditional church, especially when it concerns high-profile leaders. Where an apostle is proven to be guilty of financial or other misbehavior, his followers join the following of another apostle. The network of which the apostle is a part (if he belongs to a network) also does not suffer because of the looseness and informality of the association. After a short while, in most instances the apostle involved gains another following, although perhaps not as big as before the incident.

Already in 1789, William Crabtree emphasized that the spiritual prosperity of a church is supported by the faithful and reputable character of those who serve as its leaders, requiring a deep spirituality, piety, diligence, and fidelity of them.[223]

In 2011, *Forbes* compiled a list of some of the world's richest preachers. Using only Nigeria in one of their reports, the top five preachers earned between $10 million and $150 million a year. Pastor Chris Oyakhilome disseminates his charismatic credo via *Facebook* to more than two million followers and thousands of subscribers on YouTube. Combined with three satellite television channels that he owns, this ensures that his reach extends far beyond Africa. For instance, in Britain he has a large following. With his own hotel, fast-food chain and several mansions, Oyakhilome has amassed a fortune estimated at $30 to $50 million.[224] T.B. Joshua's wealth is estimated at around $15 million.[225] Another report in 2017 listed the richest pastors in the world, and prosperity teachers topped the list, with Kenneth Copeland ($760 million), T.D. Jakes ($150 million), Benny Hinn ($42 million), Joel Osteen ($40 million), Creflo Dollar ($27 million), and Joyce Meyer ($25 million) among them.[226] In 2018, Benny Hinn received $89 million in donations with attendance at his crusades averaging 50,000 to 60,000 people, and a crusade in Kenya drawing 1.2 million worshippers.[227]

---

223. Crabtree, *Prosperity of a Gospel Church Reconsidered*, 20.
224. Kingsbury and Chesnut, "How Catholics are Falling."
225. Guyson, "Of False Prophets and Profits."
226. Hinn, *God, Greed*, 63.
227. Hinn, *God, Greed*, 67.

The same is true of African pastors such as Nigerian David O. Oyedepo of the Living Faith Church Worldwide (Winners' Chapel),[228] South African-based Malawian Shepherd Bushiri of the Enlightened Christian Gathering (ECG), televangelist Paseka Motsoeneng (Mboro) of Incredible Happenings, and Zimbabwean Prophet Walter Magaya.[229] The top six richest pastors in Africa, according to indapaper.com (2018), are all from Nigeria.[230] Dominic Umoh concludes that "religion appears to be the most lucrative business today" in terms of the Nigerian church scenario, that is applicable to other parts of Africa as well.[231]

"Proof-Texts" of the Prosperity Message

There are certain texts that one finds reference to repeatedly in die prosperity movement and these texts play a key role in defining prosperity and health. The literalist way of interpreting the Bible can also be called the proof-text method. [232] It relies on a naïve reading of the text, many times disregarding the purpose for which the text was written, the historical conditioning in which it is set, and the genre conventions that shaped it. As a result, the method is characterized by spiritualization, allegorization, psychologization, and other forms of easy adjustments of the words in the text to state what one wishes them to say in the contemporary context, and ignoring their intended purpose and usage as determined by context, grammar, and historical background.[233]

In this part I will refer to some of the most prominent of the texts that play a key role in defining prosperity theology's main teachings,

---

228. Ntui-Abung, *Chaos of the Prosperity Gospel*, 20 calls David Oyedepo "the highest proponent of the prosperity gospel teaching in sub-Saharan Africa, Europe, Latin America, South Africa, and Nigeria," and successor of Kenneth Hagin in Africa, that testifies to some exaggeration. However, Oyedepo's influence in Nigeria cannot be denied.

229. He pleaded guilty in 2009 on behalf of Aretha Medical, of which he is the managing director, after claiming that he created a herbal cure for HIV and Aids, and was fined $700 (https://www.news24.com/Africa/Zimbabwe/zim-prophet-walter-magaya-convicted-for-hiv-and-aids-cure-claim-20190206; accessed 2020-02-03).

230. Maxon, "Fake Pastors and Their Followers."

231. Umoh, "Prosperity Gospel and the Spirit," 656.

232. Hinn, *God, Greed*, 51 defines a proof-text as a passage taken out of context in order to prove a point. What the text or author intends to say is not important; what is important is that the author required a biblical text to "prove" a point.

233. Kaiser and Silva, *Introduction to Biblical Hermeneutics*, 33.

describe the way they are interpreted, and evaluate it from a pentecostal perspective. Although it is impossible to read the biblical text in an objective way, without one's background, education, cultural and social prejudices, and one's own religious tradition playing any role, it is still important to try to read the text as it stands, at face value. The intention should remain to ask, what did the original author intended the readers or listeners to hear, as far as it is possible to discern it? Why was it necessary to provide the information in the narrative? What was the intention?

Many contemporary exegetes argue that the authorial intention got lost in the mists of time and cultural changes. However, it is still possible in many cases to imagine something of the situation of the first readers or listeners by carefully reading the text and trying to understand what they probably heard when they read the words. The difficulty in reconstructing intention and meaning should encourage all Bible readers to study the text and supporting documents related to its historical situation, treat their own interpretation with the necessary humility, and keep their ears open to the insights and wisdom of fellow readers of the biblical text.

For Pentecostals it is imperative that the Bible should not be read only in an objective sense, as far as that is possible at all. They intentionally and deliberately leave room for the guidance and illumination of the Spirit and for that reason they emphasize that reading and interpretation of the biblical text should be done in an embodied and involved manner, with the reader listening to the text with mind and spirit (if "spirit" refers to the indefinable quality in human beings allowing them to stand in an intimate relationship with God). French Arrington, writing about the importance of the Spirit's activity in interpretation, writes that it requires submission of the mind to God so that the critical and analytical abilities are exercised under the guidance of the Holy Spirit, with a genuine openness to the witness of the Spirit as the text is examined, leading to the personal experience of faith as part of the entire interpretive process and a consequent response to the transforming call of God's word.[234] The implication is clear, that the Spirit can work through as well as beyond human cognitive faculties.

Responsible reading of the text also requires that Scripture should be used to interpret Scripture. After determining the genre of a text, the particular text should be compared to other texts of the similar genre, and the author's other thoughts about the subject should be compared

---

234. Arrington, "Use," 105.

to the thoughts in the present text, and an eye should be kept open for similar discussions of the same ideas in other passages. Paul Ricoeur asserts that literary genres do not only classify texts; they actually give a code that shapes the way a reader will interpret this text.[235]

The reader should also be sensitive to the fact that the original biblical text was written (or mostly spoken, in a primarily oral culture) in a different language. When the text cannot be read in its original language, the reader should remember that every translation also implies an interpretation. A different language is structured according to different cultural customs and thought patterns and these should also be studied. Fortunately, many commentaries provide such information and to do justice to a biblical text requires further study.

The rule should be that a text does not necessarily mean what the reader initially thinks after reading it the first time in a common sense way, and that a text may never be interpreted to mean what the reader wants to hear in it. Readers' minds should be applied to its interpretation before they tentatively decide what they think the intention of the author could have been. For that reason, it is also imperative that words, phrases, and even sentences should never be taken out of context or read without consideration for the immediate context, and the role the passage plays in terms of the greater argument and even book or epistle in which it is found should be kept in mind. For instance, when that does not happen, counsel in the book of Proverbs are for instance ascribed to God and not to the wisdom teacher where the context clearly shows that is not God who is speaking, according to the author.[236]

Second Corinthians 8:9

Christ died in poverty so that believers may be fabulously rich. There is a text that proves the point. 1 Corinthians 8:9 states, "For you know the generous act of our Lord Jesus Christ, that though he was rich, yet for your sakes he became poor, so that by his poverty you might become rich." We are intended to be rich because we put our trust in Christ and his generous act of atonement on the cross where he died in our stead!

235. Kaiser and Silva, *Introduction to Biblical Hermeneutics*, 31.

236. This happens repeatedly in a sermon by Chris Oyakhilome, "Use your tongue to give your life a meaning," for instance by ascribing Prov 15:4 to God's words and not the wisdom teacher's (https://www.youtube.com/watch?v=yQppu1NnbuE; accessed 2019-12-27).

The Challenge

The correct question is, what is the literary context in which this text occurs? Many adherents of the prosperity message have learnt the text by heart, repeating it in the course of each day as part of their regimen of positive confession. However, what is the author saying in this verse when it is compared to the rest of the argument? The context of 2 Corinthians is Paul's encouragement of believers to contribute generously to the need of others. Verse 1-2 states, "We want you to know, brothers and sisters, about the grace of God that has been granted to the churches of Macedonia; for during a severe ordeal of affliction, their abundant joy and their extreme poverty have overflowed in a wealth of generosity on their part." The poor Christians in Macedonia served as an example for the Corinthian believers; they shared with generosity what they had with the believers in Judea who were suffering greater material needs. The Macedonians voluntarily and sacrificially gave according to their means, and even beyond their means, although they also suffered extreme poverty (v. 2). It was so important for them to share what they had with believers they did not even know that they begged the apostle "earnestly for the privilege of sharing in this ministry to the saints" (v. 4).

Now Titus was visiting the believers in Corinth with the intention to take up an offering for the needs of the believers, and Paul was encouraging them to excel in their generosity, as they had excelled already in their faith, speech, knowledge, and utmost eagerness (v. 7). This is the context of verse 9. It is not about Christians getting wealthy because Christ sacrificed his life for them, rather, Christ's generous sacrifice serves as an encouragement for believers to contribute generously toward the needs of other Christian believers, even if they are poor themselves. The Macedonians, and Christ, did not find their joy in being wealthy but in sharing their poverty in a wealth of generosity (v. 3).

What were the riches that Jesus gave up for us so that we may share in it? Did he give up material wealth to become our Savior? Light is shed on the question when another passage of the same author about the giving up of Christ is compared (see note above about the importance of comparing Scripture with Scripture). In Philippians 2:1–11, Paul states that believers should do nothing from selfish ambition or conceit, but in humility regard others as better than themselves by looking not to their own interests only, but also to the interests of others. Their example is Christ Jesus who taught them how to put the interests of other people before their own. He was in the form of God, but did not regard equality with God as something to be exploited; he "emptied himself, taking the form of a slave, being born in human likeness. And being found in human form, he humbled himself and became obedient to the point of death—even death on a cross" (vv. 6–8). For that reason, God highly exalted him so that at the name of Jesus every knee should bend, and every tongue should confess that Jesus Christ is Lord (vv. 9–11).

Jesus was not rich while he was living as the Son of man on earth, as the prosperity message implies and as many prosperity teachers claim. On the contrary, Luke 9:58 suggests the opposite. When someone promises Jesus to follow him wherever he may go, Jesus responds, "Foxes have holes, and birds of the air have nests; but the Son of man has nowhere to lay his head." The riches he shared with others was in his incarnation, that implied that he left heaven and his intimate spiritual communion with his Father, sharing in the glory of God, in order to come to the earth and eventually die for the sake of others whose sins separated them from the presence of God. The riches that Christ temporarily gave up for human beings were heavenly and spiritual riches, and the riches that he died to win for us include reconciliation and communion with God, like Jesus enjoys in the presence of the throne of God.[237] In the words of Jesus' prayer in John 17:24, "Father, I desire that those also, whom you have given me, may be with me where I am, to see my glory, which you have given me because you loved me before the foundation of the world."

To come back to the author's argument in 2 Corinthians 8, he states that the generous act of Jesus serves to remind us to give with eagerness, because our willingness and eagerness to share in the needs of others make our gift acceptable. One should give according to what one has, not according to what one does not have (v. 12). Paul's motivation is that there should be a fair balance between believers because those with material provisions share with those in need, in order that no one is left without food or clothing. In this way, the communion of the Holy Spirit of believers across the world will experience a fair balance so that the one who has much does not have too much, and the one who has little does not have too little (v. 15).

Eternity is depicted in the New Testament in terms of fabulous riches, as the symbol of the streets of gold in Revelation 21 indicate, in which the prosperity message does not show much interest due to their nearly exclusive this-worldly concerns and realized eschatology. However, the Christians in the new city, the new Jerusalem, are not interested

---

237. Mbugua, "Misunderstanding the Bible," 18.

in the riches of the city with its twelve gates and with a wall built of jasper, and with the city built of pure gold, clear as glass, and the foundations adorned with every jewel, and the twelve gates being twelve pearls, and the street of pure gold, transparent as glass. What interest the inhabitants (and the author) is that there is no temple in the city, for its temple is the Lord God the Almighty, and the Lamb and the glory of God is its light, and its lamp is the Lamb (Rev 21:11–23). Believers aspire to reach this destination for the sake of being in the presence of God without ever being separated.

Believers who have seen the generosity of their Savior who shares his glory with them are encouraged to share what they own with others in need to ensure equality between all believers, so that no child will go to bed hungry, or attend school unable to attend to the teacher's words because of hunger. What greater motivation can there be for believers to become involved with poor people in a continent characterized by severe inequality as a product of neo-capitalism, consisting of those who fall in the spaces of exclusion created by the fact that the benefits of capitalism and modernity have not extended uniformly across the planet, with mainly the developing world as a victim?[238] Millions in the global south live in great uncertainty, yearning for the means necessary to survive, without any idea of the affluence that characterizes many Western people's lives.

Isaiah 53:5

A key proof text for the prosperity message (and faith healing movement) is Isaiah 53 that presumably links forgiveness of sins, healing, and wealth with the atonement of Christ on the cross. Literally verse 5 states, "Surely our sicknesses he himself bore and our pains he himself carried. Yet we ourselves esteemed him stricken, smitten of God, and afflicted."[239] The heart of the prosperity gospel is that God intends all believers to be born again, healthy, happy, wealthy, and prosperous. Verses 4–5 explain that the suffering servant was acquainted with infirmity and that he had borne our infirmities and carried our diseases. He was wounded for our transgressions, crushed for our iniquities. Upon him was the punishment

---

238. Kingsbury and Chesnut, "How Catholics are Falling."

239. The KJV translates vv. 4-5 as: "Surely he hath borne our griefs, And carried our sorrows: Yet we did esteem him stricken, Smitten of God, and afflicted. But he *was* wounded for our transgressions, *He was* bruised for our iniquities: The chastisement of our peace *was* upon him; And with his stripes we are healed."

that made us whole, and by his bruises we are healed. He did this to save us from sin, illness, and the brokenness that characterizes our world.

In the first place, it is important to note that prophecies in the Old Testament found their first and intended fulfillment within the world of the first readers and listeners. If the prophecy had no message of relevance for their own day, it would have been senseless to bring them the message in the first place.[240] Some of the prophecies also find further fulfillments, also in events in the New Testament, as demonstrated by the way the synoptic Gospels, John's Gospel, the epistles of Paul, and Luke's historiography of the early church appropriated them.[241]

Early Christians interpreted Isaiah 53 in terms of the suffering of the Messiah Jesus, in order to explain his sacrificial death. He died for our transgressions and iniquities, that is, for our sins. His life was characterized by infirmity so that he could bear out infirmities and diseases. What does it refer to? Within the context of the passage, with its explanation of the reason for the sacrifice of the servant, it seems that it refers to healing from the results of sins. Christians are healed of their sinful guilt by Christ's sacrifice on the cross.[242] This is confirmed by 1 Peter 2:24, "He himself bore our sins in his body on the cross, so that, free from sins, we might live for righteousness; by his wounds you have been healed." The wounds in terms of the literary context clearly refer to sins, as their effect.

Christ's work on the cross also dealt with the results of sin, which had corrupted the world. Suffering and brokenness that characterize our world in the form of illness and death will also be removed but the Bible makes it clear that the final victory over evil forces and their influence on the world will only occur when the new world dawns with the second coming of Christ. A part of redemption realized and the kingdom had already come in part with the establishment of the church as a creation of God; a part of redemption will, however, only realize when the kingdom is established in its finalized form, when the city of God will descend to become the center and temple of the new earth. Jesus' ministry of healing and deliverance, including resurrecting the dead, served as an announcement of what the new world will entail. However, his ministry did not include the resurrection of

---

240. See Chaney, *Peasants, Prophets, and Political Economy* for a discussion about the complexities involved in reconstructing the historical, social, agronomic, and religious contexts in which the different texts of the prophets in the Old Testament operate.

241. It should be kept in mind that these "fulfillments" were defined by the authors of the New Testament.

242. Mbugua, "Misunderstanding the Bible," 19.

all people; that will have to wait for the time of his second coming. The resurrection of Lazarus (John 11) served as a sign of what awaits humankind when the kingdom realizes completely.

For that reason, the author of Romans 8 explains that the sufferings of the present time did not cease with the death of Christ on the cross but will continue for the church in the form of persecution. However, the author continues that suffering does not discourage believers because they realize that their present suffering is not worth comparing with the glory about to be revealed to them (v. 18). The whole of creation is groaning because it shares in suffering and believers also groan while they wait for the redemption with patience (vv. 22–23). Some of the benefits of Christ's complete work are not to be enjoyed on earth already.

Signs of these benefits can be found in the ministry of Christ who healed many people, and the present church and its ministry of healing. However, as Jesus did not heal all people, as the narrative about the healing at the bath of Bethesda for example illustrates, the church's ministry of healing will always have limited success while it is still on earth. Healing is not the purpose; it is the means to the end. The kingdom that has come already will only realize fully when the earth is restored and death is banished. The same is true of prosperity. The cross of Jesus does not realize prosperity in this world for all people but contains the hope of a world where nobody would be hungry and without the necessary means to survive.

The Christian's hope is not to experience heaven on earth but the resurrection that will introduce them to the new earth where heaven will descend when God will come to stay in the midst of God's people (Rev 21:2). If we put our hope on Christ only for this world, we would have been the most hopeless of people!

Deuteronomistic Theology

Prosperity gospel relates to what is called the Deuteronomist theologians' way of explaining why the Assyrian exile banished the people of the Northern kingdom from the land in the eighth century BCE that eventually destroyed the identity of the ten tribes, and the Babylonian exile in the sixth century BCE that left the bigger part of Judah (and Benjamin) in Babylon took place. The reason given was that the people did not honor God by obeying his commandments. To prove the point, the Deuteronomist retells the narrative of Israel's history from the time they left Egypt to the time they lost the land in the exile. It happens in the books of Deuteronomy, Joshua, Judges, 1 and 2 Samuel, and 1 and 2 Kings. This perspective on Israel's history differs from the Chronicler's historical version of the same history in important aspects because the motives for providing the two historical works differ.

The Deuteronomist's retelling of the history emphasizes those aspects that serve the ideology to explain the theological principle while other aspects are underemphasized. For instance, for the Deuteronomist it was not important whether a king of the Northern or Southern kingdom was in military or strategic terms a good and successful king but whether he served God or not. Some kings are exalted for that reason as the nation's best kings although they were not necessarily very clever in political terms. A good example is Omri who reigned in the Northern kingdom and founded Samaria, and expanded the borders of his state even further than king David could do. The Deuteronomist spends only a few verses on him (1 Kgs 16:16-28); he did not serve the Lord and it was not worth mentioning any more about his long and prosperous reign.

In this context, Deuteronomy 28 can be called the constitution of the Deuteronomist's theological principle that states that, "If you will only obey the Lord your God, by diligently observing all his commandments that I am commanding you today, the Lord your God will set you high above all the nations of the earth" (28:1), and "... if you will not obey the Lord your God by diligently observing all his commandments and decrees, which I am commanding you today, then all these curses shall come upon you and overtake you" (28:15).

This is the context for several passages in Deuteronomy 28 that serve as favorite proof-texts of prosperity teachers, such as verses 4-6 that declares that the fruit of your womb, the fruit of your ground, and the fruit of your livestock, both the increase of your cattle and the issue of your flock, your basket and your kneading bowl shall be blessed.

The Deuteronomist's theological principle is also the context for Deuteronomy 15:4-6, that states that there will be no-one in need among Israel and they will lend to many nations, but not borrow from anyone. They will rule over many nations, but they will not be dominated by any. The reason is because the Lord is sure to bless them in the land that the Lord their God is giving them as a possession to occupy. The condition is that they obey the Lord their God by diligently observing all the commandments that God had commanded them. It is clear from history that while this principle was valid, it could not be stated in categorical terms that it happened consistently.

The prosperity message teaches that poverty was not what God had planned for God's people, and quotes the Deuteronomistic theology to prove their point. Believers are blessed by God to such an extent that they have enough to lend to others, making them the rulers over the people and of the earth and the wealth of the nations. However, when it is kept in mind that the Deuteronomist is applying the principle that God blesses those Israelites who serve God and curses those who disobey God, and that this principle is explained in terms of a generalization that is not applicable to every practical and individual situation, it warns us not to form a theological system on an ideology that the author utilized for a specific reason. To read it as a promise for contemporary people who are not even part of Israel is to ignore the historical, social, and theological context of the passage, the ideological purpose of the author, and the historical work of which it forms a part. It also requires of one to ignore the historical unreliability showed by some parts of the narrative.

The passage follows on the command to cancel any debt that Israelites may have each seventh year, so that all Israelites may start afresh on the same level, without any debts that might lead some to sell themselves as slaves to cover their debts. It was God's intention that no Israelite should be a slave or dirt poor. Even when it is not the seventh year when Israelites should cancel all debts, they were reminded to take care of their fellow Israelites in need. If there were among them anyone in need, Israelites were not to be hard-hearted or tight-fisted toward them but they should rather open their hand and willingly lend enough to meet their needs (Deut 15:7–8).

It is unlikely that the large scale cancellation of debts occurred in Israel at all, and for that reason one finds a realistic observation like the following, that there will never cease to be some in need, and for that reason Israelites were commanded to open their hand to the poor and needy neighbor (Deut 15:11). This observation is deliberately ignored by prosperity teachers.

It is a mistake to read Deuteronomistic theology that contains the absolute rule that sin results in punishment and repentance in reward, as a mechanistic application that operates without any exceptions. As is true of biblical promises, these theological statements served a purpose that should be taken in mind as part of the historical, social, ideological, and economic contexts that operate behind all biblical texts and provides the means to access the meaning for the first readers. Only then can the meaning be applied to a contemporary audience, if it is possible at all to bring it in connection with the current context or horizon. What Deuteronomistic theology portrays is a relationship with the living God; the element of retribution plays a subordinate role in this relationship and serves as an encouragement from the side of the author to encourage listeners to serve the God of their ancestors faithfully in the midst of the temptations of the other gods served by their neighbors.[243] Suffering, sickness and poverty is not always the result of sin. This is clear from the biblical witnesses but also from one's own empirical observations of the world. While Christians cannot explain all suffering, they can know and confess that God is reigning in the lives of believers and that suffering is part of a greater purpose with the creation of the world, and the existence of sin and brokenness in a world that is fast approaching its end is only temporary.

Africa is a poor continent with a majority of people suffering from one form of poverty or another. To proclaim that poverty is a curse and a visitation for one's sins should be seen as a criminal offence because it plunges poor people into an abyss of hopelessness.[244] However, as Elizabeth Mburu explains, traditional African interactions with the Supreme Being are transactional as opposed to relational, based on the widespread belief that if one lived wisely in the present, one would reap positive benefits in the future.[245] This led to the reality that the worship of God for many Africans was utilitarian, seeking God for the help they might receive, rather than for encountering God and extolling the greatness and goodness of God. Traditional African worship therefore largely focused not on God but on human needs and desires, explaining why the prosperity gospel has become so popular across the African continent. It presents a familiar way of relating to God in Africa.

Texts about Prayer and God's Provision

There are several texts about prayer and God's provision that are staple texts in the prosperity stall. For instance, John 14:12–14 states that Jesus promises that the one who believes in him will also do the works that he did and will do even greater works than these, because he is leaving for

---

243. Mburu, *African Hermeneutics*, 55.
244. Prosper, *Prosperity Message*, 86–9.
245. Mburu, *African Hermeneutics*, 28.

his Father. "I will do whatever you ask in my name, so that the Father may be glorified in the Son. If in my name you ask me for anything, I will do it" (vv. 13–14). The promise is repeated in John 16:23–24, that if believers ask anything of the Father in Jesus' name, he will give it to them. "Ask and you will receive, so that your joy may be complete". It seems as if believers can get what they want just by asking the Father in Jesus' name for it.

However, the promises in the Bible are neither unconditional nor applicable to all people at all times. For instance, John 15:7 contains the same promise, within the context of Jesus' teaching about the importance that believers should remain a part of the community to bear fruit. He uses the image of a true vine, with his Father as the vine grower who removes every branch in Christ that bears no fruit. For that reason, it is important to abide in Christ as Christ abides in us (v. 4). The branch can only bear fruit as long as it abides in the vine. This is the context for the promise, "If you abide in me, and my words abide in you, ask for whatever you wish, and it will be done for you." Jesus continues that his Father is glorified when believers bear much fruit. To abide in Christ is to keep his commandments (v 10). When they do so, the joy of Jesus will be in them, and their joy will be complete (v. 11).

Believers who live in Christ and let his words live in them find that God does answer their prayers, because they are sanctified by the presence of Christ and his words in them. They understand the will of God because the Spirit of God reveals Christ and his heart to them, sanctifying their desires. Their prayers are concerned with the interests of the kingdom and its establishment on earth; their primary interest in life is to glorify God and serve God's kingdom. When God's words live in them, their desires start reflecting God's will, they desire and pray for what God wants, and they experience that their prayers are consistently answered.

This does not imply that God will give believers everything they desire, as good parents do not grant all the wishes of their children, even if they are financially able to do so. God does as God pleases, as Psalm 135, a psalm of praise, explains, "Whatever the Lord pleases he does, in heaven and on earth, in the seas and all deeps" (v. 6). God makes the clouds, lightning, the wind, and did signs and wonders when God saved Israel from Egypt.

Another text used (or rather, abused) in this context is Romans 8:28, "We know that all things work together for good for those who love God, who are called according to his purpose." The impression is created that God gives people everything they want; God's interest is what serves

God's children the best. However, the statement is also qualified, by limiting God's involvement to "those who love God," live for God's glory, and are eager to do God's will in their lives more than anything else.

In teaching his disciples how to pray, according to Matthew's report, Jesus instructs them not to pray like the hypocrites, who desire to turn people's attention to their piety by praying in public, or like the gentiles, who use lots of words in the hope that they will be heard. "When you are praying, do not heap up empty phrases as the Gentiles do; for they think that they will be heard because of their many words. Be not ye therefore like unto them: for your Father knoweth what things ye have need of, before ye ask him" (Matt 6:7–8). If the Father knows what our needs are before we ask him, then the primary purpose of prayer cannot be to tell God what we desire but rather to listen to God's instructions on how to pray so that we can be effective collaborators in serving the interests of God's kingdom on earth.

When believers are interpreting texts concerned with prayer and God's provision, they should always keep the bigger picture in mind, a principle that applies to all interpretation of Scriptures. They should never lose sight of the one addressed in prayer, the God who rules sovereignly over the works of God's hands. Then their main interest will not be to serve their own interests by way of religious manipulation, but rather to glorify God and serve God's interests. If Jesus served only his own interests when he was praying in the garden of Gethsemane, his prayer would have ended with the words, "remove this cup from me;" yet he did not stop there but added, "not what I want, but what you want" (Mark 14:36).

Principle of Sowing and Reaping

Two verses are used in particular to demonstrate what is defined as an important principle in the world of faith. The first is 2 Corinthians 9:6 that states, "He which soweth sparingly shall reap also sparingly; and he which soweth bountifully shall reap also bountifully," and the second is Galatians 6:7, "Be not deceived; God is not mocked: for whatsoever a man soweth, that shall he also reap." Both texts are connected to and use images from the world of agriculture, that to reap a harvest it is first necessary to sow the necessary seed. The same applies to many other areas of life, including relationships, referring to the hard work required to make a success of studies or a profession, personal habits that one requires to form one's moral and personal character and that allows one to live alongside other people, etc.

The problem with the prosperity message starts when it defines the harvest of Christian reaping only in terms of temporary benefits, as Kenneth Mbugua explains.[246] If they should read verse 8 alongside Galatians 6:7, prosperity teachers would have found that the benefits extend beyond this world when believers sow to the Spirit: "he that soweth to his flesh shall of the flesh reap corruption; but he that soweth to the Spirit shall of the Spirit reap life everlasting". The purpose of the encouragement not to grow weary in doing what is right so that we will reap at harvest time is contained in the statement that God will grant us entrance into God's eternal presence and glory. The text functions in Paul's corpus within the ideal found in, *inter alia*, 2 Corinthians 9 where, as explained above, the context is the offering that the apostles were taking up for the poor believers in Judea, and the apostle encourages the readers to sow in abundance as far as it is possible for them, because as Christians we care for each other so much that we aspire to equality in the daily provisions of life for all of us. Paul is dreaming of an equal world where no Christian suffers from extreme hunger and poverty because Christians take mutual care of each other. It is probable that this will be the economic status of the new world that believers await. It also forms the background against which Galatians 6 functions.

When we invest our time, energy, talents, and money, our perspective as believers should not only be on what we can gain from God in terms of temporary benefits, because we are instructed not to store up for ourselves treasures on earth, but rather in heaven, where it will be safe. The reason for the instruction is motivated by Jesus' words in Matthew 6:19–21, not to lay up for ourselves treasures upon earth, where moth and rust corrupt, and where thieves break through and steal. We should rather lay up for ourselves treasures in heaven, "where neither moth nor rust doth corrupt, and where thieves do not break through nor steal: For where your treasure is, there will your heart be also."

Believers' prayers betray where their hearts are. If their prayers are focused exclusively on their earthly, temporary existence and their own this-worldly desires, it serves as a clear sign that they are living only for this world and what they can get from it. However, with their hearts in heaven their focus will be on the eternal, the glory of God, and the

---

246. Mbugua, "Misunderstanding the Bible," 25.

interests of the kingdom on earth, and persecution and suffering will not be able to put their treasure at risk. They will not be overcome by doubt when they suffer afflictions, ordeals, and trials because they realize that their existence on earth only serves to prepare them for eternal life with God (see Heb 10:34 for one example of such faith).

The prosperity message awards a connotation to money and possessions that coincides with the current cultural perspective as a result of capitalism and the consumer mentality it produces, viewing money and what it can buy as the highest good and value in life. Its success in reaching many Africans is connected to their desire to enjoy the finer things in life that cost a lot of money, or at least, to survive in a world without jobs and job opportunities. The principle of sowing and reaping is supposed to unlock the world of material benefits for them, creating an appreciation and love for money that is clearly not in line with several other instructions found in the New Testament, such as 1 Timothy 6 where the author encourages his readers to strive for godliness because there is great gain in godliness combined with contentment (v. 6). Contentment is then defined in terms of having food and clothing, with the warning that those who want to be rich may fall into temptation and they may become trapped by many senseless and harmful desires that plunge people into ruin and destruction (vv. 8–9). Verse 10 states that "the love of money is the root of all evil: which while some coveted after, they have erred from the faith, and pierced themselves through with many sorrows." Timothy is then encouraged to shun the acquirement of riches but rather to pursue righteousness, godliness, faith, love, endurance, and gentleness.

A further perspective on the pursuit of money is found in Mark 10:17–31, telling of a young man inquiring what he must do to inherit eternal life. Jesus responds that he should sell all that he owns and give the money to the poor, and his generosity will store up for him treasure in heaven. He could not follow Jesus as long as his possessions and his love for it stand in his way (v. 21). The rich young man is shocked and goes away grieving because he is very rich and not willing to part with the benefits of wealth. Then Jesus states, "How hard it will be for those who have wealth to enter the kingdom of God!" (v. 23). When his disciples are perplexed at his words, he explains what he means by stating, "It is easier for a camel to go through the eye of a needle than for someone who is rich to enter the kingdom of God" (v. 25). In discussing prosperity teachers' view of God, reference was made to how Copeland interprets the text. He argues that the ruler was rich because he observed the biblical laws of prosperity from his youth. The only reason Jesus wanted him to give all his money to the poor was that he may receive it back a hundredfold, and then he would have been fabulously rich!

Money and possessions can easily become an idol, as Luke in his version of Jesus' teaching on Mammon explains, associating and personificating wealth with the Syrian deity called Mammon (see also Matt 6:24, where the reference does not personify a god). Wealth easily engulfs its victim with many possessions and means to spend time so that it easily becomes a god that claims exclusive loyalty from human beings.[247]

It is not implied that God does not provide for God's children and that their prayers are nothing else than a waste of breath. The heavenly Father does provide although there are also many Christians worldwide who suffer from economic inequality and a lack of material provisions, apart from others who are persecuted and even killed for their faith. One of the biggest problems for the prosperity message is created by this reality, that some African people's needs are so great that they and their children face the daily possibility of extermination by famine. What benefits do the prosperity gospel offer them? While first world people probably spend more money in paying for one meal at a restaurant than many Africans earn in a week or a month, does the prosperity message for Americans promising Cadillacs, expensive houses, and designer clothes imply for poor Africans the means just to survive? The practicalities of the results of the prosperity message are culturally and economically determined, implying that it is not valid at all places and for all people at the same time. This is not a valid version of the gospel, that distinguishes between people based on their socio-economic status.

Power of the Spoken Word

The prosperity message was explained already in terms of the instruction to speak words of faith and positive confessions, with the implication

---

247. In African liberation theologies, interestingly enough, the struggle against Mammon, evaluated in Marxist and materialist terms, is seen as the main task for theology. Africa is to a large extent characterized as an integral part of the current globalized neo-liberal capitalist economic climate. For Julius Nyerere, the first president of a liberated Tanzania, it was an imperative in the theological task to recognize that the god of "profit" must be replaced by the people of God, humanity (in West, *Stolen Bible*, 355-356). In contrast, African prosperity theology resignifies Mammon into financial blessing (Heuser, "Charting African Prosperity Gospel Economies," 3).

that words are so powerful that they create realities. Believers can speak health and wealth into existence with their positive confession of their desires for it; at the same time, it is possible to speak illness, death, and poverty into existence by negative words. When continuous positive confession does not lead to the desired results, the blame is placed on the believers' lack of faith.

Several texts are used repetitively by various prosperity teachers to explain the principle. The first is the definition of "faith" provided in Hebrews 11:1, "faith is the assurance of things hoped for, the conviction of things not seen." Because of their literalist leanings, most prosperity preachers use the King James Version translation of the Bible that translates the text as, "faith is the substance of things hoped for, the evidence of things not seen." "Substance" is then seized upon and the conclusion is reached that faith creates substance, that believers become co-creators of their world and circumstances by their faith in the things they cannot yet see, but trust that God, the cosmic banker, will bless them with in response to their faith (and usually seed money, first fruits or donations as well). We speak our will into existence by our words of faith.

Readers just have to continue with the rest of the chapter (Heb 11) to find why this definition of faith as creating substance is not valid. The chapter, describing the faith heroes in the Old Testament, explains how believers in the past acted on the basis of a future reality they could not see because it was not material or earthly. However, their faith did not realize but they rather believed in the hope that God's promises about a future world would realize. Some of them were tortured, others suffered mocking and flogging, and even chains and imprisonment, they were stoned to death, they were sawn in half, they were killed by the sword, etc., but all of them eventually received their reward, the eternal glory that awaited them. They desired a better country, that is, a heavenly one, and their hope kept their faith alive vv.39–40).

The important question is, how many prosperity believers' faith was undermined when the desired material benefits of their belief in the power of words did not realize, at least not as it realized in the bank balances of the wealthy leaders of the prosperity movement? Their eyes were put on earthly, temporary benefits and now they might be losing the eternal benefits of those who stayed faithful to God, even through times of hopeless poverty, illness, unjust discrimination, and death because they were not living for what this world offers but for eternal gain.

The Challenge

Other proof-texts of the power of words can be found in, *inter alia*, Proverbs 3:9-10; 10:22; 18:21, Mark 4:24; Luke 6:38; Jeremiah 9:8, James 3:5-6, and 2 Corinthians 8:9 (as discussed above).

John 10:31-39

Faith teachers love to cite this text to prove that humans are indeed gods. In the passage, Jesus is about to be stoned for claiming that he is God. He defends himself by quoting from Psalm 82:6, and in ironic fashion he asks, "Is it not written in your law, 'I have said that you are gods?'" (v. 4). Faith teachers state that "Jesus said it, we believe it, and that settles it—we are little gods!"

Christ held the Jewish basic assumption that there is only one God, as Mark 12:29 explains (in reference to Deut 6:4). Why would Jesus contradict himself by stating that human beings are also gods? In Psalm 82, God holds court in the great assembly of God's presence, and God is pronouncing sentence on human judges who are supposed to defend the weak but instead favor the wicked, showing partiality to weak and poor righteous people. This is the context of the Psalm that is ignored by a careless reading such as found among prosperity teachers. God ridicules the human judges who have the audacity to think of themselves as gods in terms of the authority assigned to them as judges, with the implied power of life and death over those who appear in their courts as the accused. God tells the judges, "So you think you are gods? The grave will prove that you are mere human beings. When you die, you will forever know the infinite difference between God and even the mightiest of mortals."[248]

A literal interpretation of the term "god" in Psalm 82:6 is ruled out by the context. The passage is determined by a renunciation of the injustices perpetrated by the judges of Israel (v. 2) who acted dishonestly and in an unrighteous manner. God says, "I said, 'You are gods, you are sons of the Most High, but you will die like mere men, you will fall like any other human ruler'" (vv. 6-7). The judges were no different from other human beings, even if they pretended to be. They were subject to the same frailties and weaknesses; they were far from gods. To interpret the text as to state that the judges were gods in a literal fashion is to imply that Israel accepted the existence of more than one God, while a reading of the text in terms of the context of the psalm reveals the opposite.

248. Hanegraaff, *Christianity in Crisis*, 136.

In addition, it should be kept in mind that the term "gods" (*elohim*) is used in different contexts. Moses is called a god-like judge over the pharaoh (Ex 4:16) as the Israelite judges are called "gods" in Exodus 21—22, in that they held the power of life and death over men. However, both the immediate and broader contexts of the Bible make it clear that neither Moses nor Israel's judges were gods by nature or essence; it is only in their function that they are so designated.[249] Satan is also referred to as a "god" in 2 Corinthians 4:4, yet no one assumes that Satan serves as a duplicate or on equal terms with the holy God.

As stated above, a further consideration is that in the parallelism that Hebrew poetry prefers, the respective terms "gods . . . sons of the Most High" and "men . . . any other human ruler" serve as substitutes of each other. The "gods" are also the "sons of God," a term that is applied to Israel as such, as the elect people of God, while "gods . . . sons of the Most High" is supplemented by "men . . . any other human ruler," explicating its meaning further. In conclusion, it is not possible to call frail human beings "gods" by using this psalm.

Conclusion

We packed out the theological presuppositions of the prosperity message in this chapter, explaining how and why its view of God, human beings, Christ and his atonement, blessings, and poverty differ from those of classical Pentecostalism, and Protestantism in general. Prosperity preachers differ on many points from each other but they agree on the way they view and describe God. Although they subscribe to almost all of the traditionally accepted Christian teachings on God, in practice they portray God in terms that differ from the pentecostal and Protestant view in several critical aspects. Prosperity is the right and heritage of all believers because God laid down certain rules and principles to govern every single thing into existence. These rules are found in God's Word, described as a textbook for success because it works in an almost magical way when the laws are applied. The implication is that their concept is that God is a good God who intends believers to have all the best things in life, and that God made promises in the Bible that God is compelled to comply with. God is the owner of a heavenly storehouse with unlimited supplies and believers are invited to claim their share of the riches by

---

249. Hanegraaff, *Christianity in Crisis*, 138.

applying the right formulas and recipes. The foundation of these faith formulas is a deistic god because the faith formulas are ways to manipulate and use the presumed rules and principles laid down by a deistic god. Their god has faith in god's own faith, and god is limited and compelled by god's word to act according to the promises in the Bible.

Their Christology states that Jesus had left his divine nature in heaven when he became a human being. For that reason, Jesus referred to himself as the "Son of man." As the Second Adam, his human nature was not a revelation of God to humans, but was intended to serve as a restoration of the first Adam. Adam was created as such a super being but he lost his divine nature in the Fall. Jesus had to live totally as a human being to win back divine nature for human beings so that they can become sons of God. The death on the cross was not God's final work, but on the cross Jesus received the nature of Satan, requiring three days in hell to conquer the powers of evil. Jesus' death on the cross is interpreted as Christ's identification with the sinful nature of sinners; he was a substitutive sinner and not a holy, sinless substitute for sinners. When he was resurrected from the dead, Jesus became the first human being to be born again, and now believers receive back the divine nature God intended for them, and live as gods.

We also showed how and why African prosperity has a unique focus and emphasis that differ in several respects from that used in the Western prosperity message. Poverty has a unique African connotation and definition; it is associated with any lack in a person's life that reduces their status in life and deprives them of the enjoyment of social acclamation and respect. African traditional religion and an African worldview define prosperity in a specific way that differs from the definition that serves the American version of the prosperity gospel. In Africa it is related to an enchanted worldview where evil spirits and angry ancestors cause poverty and illness. At the same time, it is clear that the prosperity gospel and classical Pentecostals use different hermeneutical angles when they read the Bible, and that it leads to widely differing interpretations of key biblical doctrines. In confronting abuses in their ministry and heretical teachings in their doctrine, prosperity preachers should be confronted with their hermeneutical angle and lenses because they function as a result of these choices before concentrating on the contents of their doctrines.

Some of the most prominent characteristics of the prosperity message as it is proclaimed in Africa were also described, including the tragedy of some abuses that marred the movement and damages the reputation of African Pentecostalism *per se,* such as claims to have resurrected the dead, of being able to turn water into wine, ordering believers to drink petrol and paraffin to prove their faith and healing cancer, HIV and Aids. Scandals also follow some of the neo-Pentecostal pastors, such as financial and sexual misconduct. It was argued that prosperity teachers in an effort to escape the cycle of institutionalization that threatens any ministry, they are overselling the miraculous. The problem with "overselling" something is that it creates disillusioned customers and dissatisfied disciples may eventually lead to dissatisfaction with the way the gurus are spending the customers' hard-earned money.

Lastly, the popularity of the proof-text method among prosperity teachers was discussed, that uses a naïve reading of the text without regard for its purpose, context, or genre conventions. The purpose is to find words in the text that state what one wishes them to say in the contemporary context. The most popular proof-texts that prosperity teachers quote in their exposition of the message were visited and discussed, explaining what a classical pentecostal perspective on these texts would be, and how it differs from the prosperity message.

After looking at the prosperity message in terms of its origins and theology, and how Africa received this message, changing some of its essential elements and applying it to a context with a different worldview, it is now time to evaluate African prosperity theology in terms of a new pentecostal hermeneutic, that was developed in chapter 2. This is the task of the last chapter.

5

The Solution

An Evaluation of African Charismatic Prosperity Theology from a New African Pentecostal Hermeneutical Perspective

Introduction

IN THIS CHAPTER, THE African version of the prosperity gospel is evaluated in terms of some practical and theological considerations from a classical pentecostal perspective. In terms of the practice of the prosperity movement, its leadership styles, financial models, involvement (or lack of involvement) in economic, societal, and ecological challenges, and its complicity in subjugating women in the traditional African patriarchal society will be investigated and evaluated, among other elements. Then its theological content will also be evaluated as far as it differs from the pentecostal (and Protestant) theological standards. First it is important to describe the hermeneutic and underlying epistemology, in the form of unique revelation knowledge as contrasted to the pentecostal hermeneutic, before other important issues such as the definition of faith, prosperity, knowledge, supernatural involvement, and giving are discussed and evaluated. In each case, the angle of evaluation is a pentecostal hermeneutical perspective.

What is the unique pentecostal hermeneutical angle? In the first part of the chapter, it is discussed in terms of the proprium of pentecostal theology in order to define it more clearly, after discussing the history of hermeneutical shifts in Pentecostalism in chapter 2.

Proprium of Pentecostal Theology

Theology is not the strength of the movement that propagates prosperity theology. As in the rest of the Pentecostal movement, practice and experience play the bigger role. When Pentecostals get involved in theological endeavors, the implication is that it would be introduced by an experiential encounter with God. "Second-hand" theology has never been trusted by them. Because of this focus on experience, the prosperity movement is often unpredictable and its theological statement at times contradictory. For the reason that the movement did not start with a founding father (or mother) and is not centered on a single person or group, the different teachers contradict each other at times on the most prominent themes. To evaluate the theology underlying the prosperity gospel is for that reason difficult and open for difference of opinion from other observers. What binds the movement together is an allegiance to the main teachings propounded by E.W. Kenyon, as expounded by Kenneth Hagin and Kenneth Copeland.

One can ask, what is the proprium of prosperity theology, that is, what is unique, typical, distinctive, or characteristic to this form of theology in comparison with other traditions? What distinguishes it from other theologies? Is it possible to describe it? It seems to me to be the case, even though one should allow for diversity of opinion on some matters.

Henry Lederle makes an important distinction between different elements of the proprium of any theological tradition.[1] A first element consists of what is at times described as the proprium but which is based on a caricature of the theological tradition. Such a caricature is found frequently in the way the media popularly depicts it, for instance, that the prosperity message is focused on some individuals using the proclamation of the gospel for selfish financial gain, that they are misleading gullible and sincere but ignorant believers, that poor people who are attending the meetings and who are joining the churches are "deprived" people who are trying to better their situation by applying the recipes for financial success provided by prosperity preachers, etc.[2] The implications of seeing the prosperity movement in these terms is that it is

---

1. Lederle, "Ecumenical Investigation," 4-9.

2. Horn, *From Rags to Riches*, 114. See, e.g., the remark of Akiri, "The Prosperity Gospel" that he is amazed that those who attend the prosperity churches are not bothered at all by the level of wealth enjoyed by most prosperity teachers, the promotion of a personality cult, and the idolatry of money although they are dirt poor themselves.

The Solution

evaluated in a prejudiced manner as an heretical teaching that should be excluded from the Christian community of churches because of the great damage that it is doing, leading believers "far away from the Lord Jesus Christ and the genuine gospel,"[3] and as an object for evangelization by the established church.[4] It is not denied that some of these accusations may be true; however, it is generalized opinions that do not apply in all cases. J. Matta concludes on the basis of these and similar caricatures and generalizations that the movement is a modern-day recurrence of Gnosticism and she argues that the movement should be treated by the Christian church in the way the second century CE church father, Irenaeus, treated Gnostics in his day, by exorcising them from the community of believers.[5] Other examples of such evaluations based on caricatures abound, e.g., in the press and social media. They all share the conclusion that the prosperity movement's teaching on poverty, prosperity, and suffering encourages contempt for the poor and abandonment of any responsibility for poor people.

Kenneth Mbugua, pastor of a Baptist church in Nairobi, Kenya, introduces a book written in conjunction between Africa Christian Textbooks and the Gospel Coalition and provides a good example of such a distorted caricature.[6] He writes that the prosperity message is marred by four crucial distortions that explain its difference from the "true" gospel. Prosperity preachers call people to turn to Jesus with the wrong motivation, so that they might receive health, wealth, husbands, wives, jobs, and promotions. Jesus is regarded as merely the way to get the material things our worldly hearts hunger for, establishing human desires as a false god in the place of the living God. Jesus suffered and died in order that he might bring human beings to God but the prosperity gospel reduces God to a sugar daddy by treating material gifts as the purpose of the gospel, reducing God to littleness. However, Jesus did not die for temporal benefits but to gain for us eternal life (John 17:3).[7]

---

3. This is the presupposition on which the contribution of Michael O. Maura *et al.*, "True and False Prosperity" is based.

4. See, in contrast, the description of how the money aspect in the prosperity teaching forms a fundamental factor in evangelizing the current world, in Gathogo, "Challenge of Money," 133.

5. Matta, *Born Again Jesus*, 12-4.

6. See Mbugua, "Introduction," 1-14.

7. Mbugua, "Introduction," 3-5. See, e.g., the remark of David Oyedepo Jnr. in a sermon entitled, "Vital keys to unlocking the supernatural," that stewardship

A second distortion is that prosperity preachers point people to their physical, financial, and relational struggles as the main problem that requires fixing in their lives, ignoring humanity's biggest problem, its sinfulness that separates it from God. Mbugua refers to the crowds that wanted to make Jesus their king in John 6:15, seeking Jesus but for the wrong reason, because they ate your fill of the loaves. Jesus, however, encouraged them not work for the food that perishes, but for the food that endures for eternal life, which he alone can give.[8]

A third distortion is that its message preaches that the purpose of Jesus' death was our healing and prosperity, with the invitation to "come to Jesus and have your best life now." The gospel is reduced to providing in human beings' godless desires, missing the point of the gospel and robbing the gospel message of its essential power and purpose.[9]

A last distortion is that it robs God of God's glory by putting human beings in the center of the universe. Instead of glorifying God, the prosperity gospel obscures the understanding of sin, do not lead people to repentance and teaches them just to think of what they will get from God. It misunderstands the design of the gospel, which is to glorify God by reconciling humans to God. The prosperity gospel robs God of God's glory by redefining the blessings received in Christ by desiring earthly treasure more than God and by turning people away from Christ's sufficiency.[10] It claims that rituals like anointing oil, holy water, prayers, as well as specific apostles are channels of blessings from God outside of Christ Jesus.

However, in the better part of the prosperity gospel the message of salvation through faith leading to a restored relationship with God is emphasized and invitations to interested persons are given at many of the services held within the movement. These distortions betray the prejudices of the author without providing ample evidence of its widespread occurrence in the prosperity movement.

This is the tenor of all the contributions in this specific book, written from a neo-Calvinist perspective. It sets up a mark created by the authors without relating it to specific prosperity teachers, and without acknowledging the diversity represented by the movement, and then shoots

---

to God absolutely benefits the interests of believers (https://www.youtube.com/watch?v=Tgq33sCo25U; accessed 2020-01-02).

8. Mbugua, "Introduction," 6.
9. Mbugua, "Introduction," 7-8.
10. Mbugua, "Introduction," 10-11.

its caricature effectively down. Fact is that nearly all prosperity teachers also strongly emphasize a personal conversion experience of new birth, as well as Spirit baptism. The difference is that for them it refers to holistic salvation, with the influence of the cross of Christ not only resulting in forgiveness of sins but with implications for the believer's whole life, including ethical and moral transformation, healing and prosperity, peace and joy, etc. Atonement is not exclusively limited in its sufficiency to human sinfulness but includes the wholeness of the believer, an emphasis that neo-Pentecostalism shares with Africa's traditional religion; the relation between holiness and health, and "wholeness" is recognized.[11]

In presenting Christ as the solution to the human problem, it does not emphasize health or prosperity at the expense of salvation of the soul. It was suggested that the prosperity movement is linked to the Pentecostal movement in the sense that it also emphasizes the essence of the gospel as Christ preached as savior, Spirit-baptizer, sanctifier, and healer. It differs from that tradition by its realized eschatology (Pentecostals had added the "coming King" as a further element) and the assertion that the gospel claims freedom from all sickness, all suffering, and all poverty on the basis of Christ's death on the cross. It does not teach that human beings' biggest problem is relational, physical, and financial challenges but preaches that the basic human predicament is sinfulness and the resultant separation from God, as Protestants do. The purpose of Christ's death was not healing and prosperity, but wholeness of which a restored relationship with God is the precondition. And the human desire for healing and the means to survive materially cannot be described as godless *per se,* as Mbugua asserts. Prosperity theology also teaches that the gospel glorifies God, by saving sinners from a certain eternal death, but adds that divine healing and God's provision in our daily needs keep on glorifying God in our lives.

The basic difference between a part of Protestantism and the Pentecostal movement, including the prosperity movement, is that it accepts a cessationist viewpoint, that God's direct dealings and immediate involvement with humankind and direct "dictation" ceased somewhere during the course of the first century, perhaps with the death of the last apostle who was an eyewitness of Jesus' ministry, leaving no room for divine intervention, signs, wonders, and other miracles. The prosperity movement, like Pentecostalism, is based on a continuationist perspective

---

11. The words use the same root, in wholeness, health, healing, and holiness (Kabat-Zinn, *Mindfulness for Beginners,* 74).

and reads the Bible with the expectation that the same God who revealed God's power and grace to people in Israel and the early church, still works in the same way in the contemporary lives of people and nations.[12]

It cannot be denied that the prosperity movement holds many theological challenges and that their questionable doctrines and ethics pose a threat to doctrinal purity and the lifestyle of its members. However, in deciding about what the proprium of prosperity theology is, such caricatures cannot provide the final answer.

Secondly, Lederle suggests that the proprium of any movement can also be defined in terms of what is the essence or core of its faith. What do adherents view as the heart of their faith? The fourfold or fivefold full gospel (Christ as savior, healer, Spirit-baptizer, sanctifier, and coming King) probably serves as the proprium of classical pentecostal theology. The distinctive elements can be described as the necessity that each member of the church is able to testify of conviction of sin as a function of the Spirit, leading to a personal encounter with God, and the experience that one's sins have been forgiven. A sign of a personal meeting with God is the wish to witness of salvation. Secondly, another distinctive is the experience of sanctification, as preparation for Spirit baptism, that leads to the transformation and empowerment of the first group of disciples into a missionary fellowship that boldly carried the gospel throughout the world, with speaking in tongues as the (initial) evidence, among other signs. Thirdly, its emphasis on healings, exorcisms, and other miracles as proof that the modern church succeeds as Christ's body on earth serves as distinctive. Lastly, a distinctive is an eschatological expectation of Christ's imminent second coming.

To limit the pentecostal distinctive to Spirit baptism with speaking in tongues is not sufficient, as some critics do. The movement is about much more than speaking in tongues and should rather be described in terms of an affective and embodied epistemology, a holistic spirituality, and a non-reductionist worldview, as a criticism on what it perceived as the pretentiousness of the scientific mind and modernism.

Prosperity theology shares all these emphasis, except the last one, of Christ as coming King, and its emphasis on glossolalia as a sign of Spirit-baptism is also reduced. Their realized eschatology that forms an essential element of prosperity theology prevents them from placing the same emphasis on eschatology as confessed among Pentecostals. The

---

12. Mashau and Kgatle. "Prosperity Gospel and the Culture of Greed."

common ground between the two groups, then, seems to be substantial enough to guarantee and require cooperation between the two groups and an ongoing dialogue.[13]

What then distinguishes prosperity theology from the theology of the Pentecostal movement? What can be defined as the proprium, when "proprium" is limited to those element or elements which specifically distinguish the movement from other related and similar theologies, in this case pentecostal theology? Defined in this (the third) way, the proprium of prosperity theology is a specific emphasis on faith as a mechanism at the disposal of the believer that promises to make believers healthy, wealthy, and victorious, because healing and prosperity are provided for in the atonement, according to Isaiah 53:4-5 that states that the suffering servant would bear humanity's infirmities and carry their diseases because he would be wounded for their transgressions and crushed for their iniquities. He would carry the punishment that would make them whole, and by his bruises they would be healed. From this teaching, the faith formulas and doctrine of positive confession were developed that affects the sovereignty of God and changes God into a deistic and manipulable god. Its final implication is also that it deifies the believers at the cost of and by denying the deity of Jesus Christ.[14]

It is true that many of the metaphysical elements of prosperity theology's perspective on God were also evident in the early years of the Pentecostal movement when several prominent leaders like Charles Parham and John G. Lake propounded it. However, in the case of John G. Lake, for example, time provided some better perspectives. Where he preached that God would heal all believers and in all situations, the message was tempered later in his life when he was faced with the reality of illnesses that did not leave the bodies of believers, including his own. A more realistic and biblical view of healing left room for the mysteriousness in all God's dealings with humankind, implying the incomprehensibility of at least some situations that occur in the lives of believers.

Although the prosperity movement took over most of the elements that Pentecostals had been emphasizing for many years, in some instances prosperity teachers radicalized some elements, like the doctrine that the gift of healing functions in the sphere of faith. They teach that the lives of Christians are fully determined by their faith that God would heal, make

13. Horn, *From Rags to Riches*, 117.
14. For a full discussion, the reader may refer to the previous chapter.

successful and rich. Salvation for them includes guaranteed bodily and material well-being as well. Even though Pentecostals also traditionally emphasized faith, their definition of faith and its operation differed.[15]

Within Pentecostalism the teaching that healing was provided for in the atonement on the same level as forgiveness of sins with time shifted to leave room for the realization that although all who accepted the work of the cross were restored in their relationship with God, not all were healed in equal terms. Then healing evangelists functioning on the fringes and outside of classical Pentecostalism since the 1950s responded by "restoring" the initial emphasis on healing, claiming that no Spirit-filled believers should accept any form of illness in their bodies, but fight the struggle of faith to regain their healing. They preached the original message although many of their contemporaries in Pentecostal circles did not accept their absolutized form of the doctrine. To a great extent, the healing evangelists were the forerunners of the prosperity movement, which added prosperity to the list of benefits gained in the process of atonement in the same absolutist manner, along with forgiveness of sins and healing. The breach between the prosperity movement and classical Pentecostalism was caused by their unorthodox style of ministry, but also by their emphasis on divine prosperity as part of the will of God for all believers, coupled with their extraordinary fundraising methods, and their strong emphasis on divine healing without exception.[16] Prosperity teachers have to admit that the prosperity gospel does not work equally well in affluent and poor societies, such as the USA and Africa, and this can be seen as a first step in realizing that prosperity is not consistently a biblical promise applicable to all people and in all situations.

Network Christianity represents the fastest-growing niche in African Christianity, influencing not only their followers but also classical Pentecostalism as well as other established mainline churches through the ongoing process of pentecostalization that these older churches experience. Before looking at theological implications of prosperity theology, some practical considerations need to be highlighted.[17]

---

15. Horn, *From Rags to Riches*, 70.

16. Horn, *From Rags to Riches*, 5.

17. The work of Christerson and Flory, *Rise of Network Christianity*, 159-65 proved valuable in its discussion of some of these issues.

Some Practical Considerations

Public Expression of Beliefs and Practices

A positive factor of the prosperity movement is that its practices are for public consumption, with leaders healing the sick, offering words of prophecy, as well as prayer walks and prayer rallies aimed at the public market rather than the church service limited mainly to believers. Faith is not relegated exclusively to the individual, home, family, or local church but conveys the message that neo-Pentecostals are involved in social transformation, bringing heaven to earth in ways that traditional congregations did not dream of. Traditionally, classical Pentecostals spent most of their time saving individual souls for heaven and building institutional congregations, excluding their involvement in prophetically challenging society's ills and wrongs. The supernatural expression of neo-Pentecostals is ideally shared in public because of wide interest in these phenomena among the people of Africa, and the same is true of other expression of their faith, such as social services, political action, and commitment to social reform. A new generation is interested in and gets enthusiastic about participating in a project that has public, world-changing implications. However, to widen their influence neo-Pentecostal leaders should revisit their social vision of changes, especially their views of poverty and its varied causes, as argued above. At the same time, they should take care not to be compromised by relationships and cooperation with conservative politicians who might manipulate them to serve their own political interests.

Leadership among Neo-Pentecostals

Most of early Pentecostalism was characterized by democratic practices where anyone anointed with the Spirit might participate in any activity in the church, or initiate an activity. This is due to their belief in the Spirit that is poured upon all believers, enabling them to be empowered and to speak and proclaim the gospel to the ends of the earth.[18] That included women and young people, as well as physically or mentally challenged people.[19] In the new apostolic movement, the idea of permanent apostleship with near absolute powers disempowers believers because of the emphasis on the apostle's nearly absolute authority to speak on behalf

---

18. Dube, "Between the Spirit and the Word," 2.
19. However, it is also true that it excluded people of different sexual orientations.

of God, robbing them of the opportunity to practice the *charismata* they have received from the Spirit.

At the same time, Pentecostals affirmed that the Spirit was the chief interpreter of the Bible while the Bible was sufficiently clear in and of itself for believers to understand, implying the principle of the perspicuity of Scriptures. The principle implies that the Bible is clear enough for the simplest person to live by and deep enough to form an inexhaustible mine for readers of the highest intellectual ability, because God intended all Scripture to be a revelation of Godself to humankind.[20] However, the prosperity movement accords and endows the apostles and prophets with the exclusive right to interpret Scriptures in terms of their exclusive access to revelation knowledge, disempowering other Christians to interpret the Bible.

The other side of network Christianity is that the constraints of many denominations on ministry can be sidestepped by prosperity leaders who can encourage and allow lay people to participate in the diverse ministries without getting bogged down in bureaucratic administrative issues. In the traditional established mainline churches, the congregation were spectators of the worship service that unfolds before their eyes. In a ministry designed to serve the public and society, however, there are many opportunities for young leaders to emerge. The social context of experiential consuming is built on the expectation that consumers will interact with and personally shape the information and products they consume, and in religious practices that contain few opportunities to shape the direction of the practice few will be satisfied.

New Financial Models

While traditional churches survived financially through Sunday service donations by members to fund their operations, charismatic Christianity has developed new models for financing their often expensive ministry outreaches as well as the at times sumptuous lifestyles of their leaders, with interns and ministry school students paying to participate in programs, other leaders required to fund their own ministries by way of donors, the sale of media products, conference tickets, curriculum material, and live-streaming of sermons and other teaching.

---

20. Nwoka, "Challenge of Nigerian Pentecostal Theology," 168.

As explained above, in many instances apostles or prophets reserved the right to take all financial decisions without any oversight from established bodies, leading to various financial abuses in the past. A new financial model of financial oversight of these ministries is critically necessary. The movement needs individuals with the necessary skills and experience who can become involved through the practice of financial oversight of the different ministries, facilitating much required financial accountability within the movement.

In the end, the important question is: who holds the ultimate power to make decisions in a religious group, an individual or (representatives of) the group itself? When dynamic and charismatic religious entrepreneurs have too much power, their beliefs and practices can drift far outside the realm of what is theologically and ethically acceptable, leading to abuses of power and wealth in some cases in the near past. On the other hand, giving too much power to formal bureaucracies often leads to a process of decision (rather, indecision) making, crippled by overcautiousness and without a compelling vision of the future.

New Work Ethic

Tiza Nyirenda, a Zambian economist and Pentecostal believer, provides a timely warning to African Pentecostals about fanaticism in terms of the practices of divine healing and the teaching of prosperity.[21] He writes that at a time when prophets have gone viral and believers see them as authority figures whom they believe implicitly, some of the prophets teach a miraculous supply of daily needs from God without emphasizing the importance and biblical requirement of a sound moral work ethic. Some even teach what they call "miracle money," that is, money that mysteriously appears in a believer's bank account after prayer for a financial breakthrough, or money that gets mysteriously stashed into hip pockets or magically appears in people's bags. These teachings about the miraculous supplying of material needs may (and do) result in laziness and kill an entrepreneurial spirit. Instead, Africans should be taught that God honors hard work, dedication, creativity, perseverance, and responsibility and that it adds value to their societies. The author does not imply that God cannot provide money or a job miraculously, as God had provided for Israel during their desert

---

21. Nyirenda, *Misconceptions of Healing, Blessings and Miracles*, 98-106.

journey (Ex 16), for Elijah at Kerith (1 Ki 17:2–6), or for the widow of Zarephath (1 Ki 17:7–16). Although God may provide miraculously in specific circumstances, working is the biblical standard by which God provides for the material needs of people, as Psalm 128:2 teaches (that those who fear the Lord and walk in God's ways, will eat the fruit of the labor of their hands and that it will go well with them).

The Bible warns repeatedly against laziness (see, e.g., Prov 6:10—11; 20:13; also 2 Thess 3:6–12 that urges believers to earn the food they eat). It seems that some Pentecostals operate from a theology of prayer that expects God to bless only in miraculous ways and provide in magical manners, without realizing that a sound work ethic plays the most important role in people's success stories. It is not good enough to state that "poverty is not my portion," as some prophets teach, or rebuke the "spirit or demon of poverty," without backing up positive declarations of faith with hard work. The financial blessing asked from God requires hard work and good planning to realize it.

Israel was to rest on the seventh day and consecrate the day to worshiping God, but they were to spend the other six days cultivating fields, raising animals, and engaging in trade (Judg 5:16–18). Prayer does not work like a magic spell; biblical principles of success need to be followed to realize God's blessings. Mere talk leads to poverty (Prov 14:23); neo-Pentecostals need a healthy and balanced work ethic. Religious activities will not cause God to miraculously achieve what hard work alone can realize. It is fanatical to expect God to provide in our daily needs without hard work from our side, is the contention of Nyirenda. Christians can expect that God would bless them spiritually when they are baptized in the Spirit but provision of daily needs still require from them good time management and giving the best in their callings that they realize in their daily jobs. Neo-Pentecostals need to be taught that their professions are the ways and means that God prepared for them to serve the world and God, as John Calvin emphasized.

Kay Musonda argues that African pastors who teach the prosperity message at times tell their adherents that the only way to prosper is by paying their tithes and "seeds" to the church.[22] They will never talk about people who have placed themselves on the world map through hard work and dedication. They would rather tell about sister Agatha who got a job, although she was not the most qualified for it, because she prayed and

---

22. Musonda, "African Pentecostalism Has Given Birth."

fasted in line with their church program, or about brother John, a millionaire, because he used all his salary as a seed in the church, or how Mama Esther paid her tithes and then her business started growing everywhere across the nation without any business plan. This could have led to a new breed of mentally lazy young people who now see God as a rewarder of mediocrity, in Musonda's opinion. "The African God abhors hard work and creative thinking, he only gives to those who sow seeds and offerings . . . and those who shout: 'I am a millionaire' every morning and do nothing the rest of the day."[23]

The other side of the coin is, however, that many African people are without any job opportunities. Some qualified people cannot get any jobs while others are unemployable due to a lack of adequate training. Unemployment levels in Africa are unacceptably high, and it is especially the youth that suffer because of a lack of opportunities to exercise their energies in establishing themselves in a profession.[24] Christians should pray for their political leaders for divine wisdom to create an economy attractive to national and international investors while they should also campaign for responsible and accountable political leadership in their countries.

The Poor in Africa

Prosperity theology teaches that poverty is a curse on humanity due to the first people's sin of disobedience to God, and demonic powers' attempts to undermine the good of God's creation. It also teaches that no believers should be poor; it is God's will that all should be prosperous and experience good health and wealth because Jesus died on the cross to turn the curse into a blessing. To reach that position, it is important that they should contribute to the ministries of the prophets and apostles. A favorite verse is Malachi 3:8-11, that presumably teaches that people should pay tithes "to God" or "the storehouse . . . so that there may be food in my house," and when they are disobedient, they are robbing God.[25] The prophet invites the people to put God to the test; when they

23. Musonda, "African Pentecostalism Has Given Birth."

24. In South Africa, e.g., the current (2020) unemployment rate among the youth 15-24 years old is 55.2 percent (http://www.statssa.gov.za/?p=12121; 2020-02-03).

25. The context for the reference to tithing in Mal 3:10-11 is a long chastisement of Israel because their hearts had grown cold toward God, and they envied the evil ways of living that characterized their neighbors. The elect people had turned away from God's ordinances, as shown when they presented animals at the temple as sacrifices

obey God's command they will be blessed with blessing, but when they are disobedient they will experience the destruction of their assets.

Some prophets and apostles put an excessive premium on giving money to their ministries, at times even using tactics that include manipulation and threats that are ethically questionable. They forget that 2 Corinthians 9:7 in the context of Paul's call to give generously for the needs of believers in Judea who were suffering due to a famine teaches that people should give what they have decided and made up their mind, not reluctantly or under compulsion, for God loves a cheerful giver.[26] For that reason, they are encouraged to give generously because the one who sows sparingly will also reap sparingly, and the one who sows bountifully will also reap bountifully (2 Cor 9:6).

In many cases it is the prophet or pastor who is getting wealthy while the majority of church members are still wallowing in poverty.[27] It seems that church members are coerced into giving so that the pastor could continue living lavishly at the expense of the poor; they are fleecing the flock for their selfish interests.

In an important study, Essien Essien finds that there exists a significant correlation between the prosperity teaching in Africa and psychological manipulation.[28] While a majority of the adherents of prosperity preachers are desperately poor people in search of economic deliverance from poverty, they believe the promise that God would reward them a hundredfold for their monetary donations, even though they may be aware of its unlikelihood. The teachers are responsible for the welfare of their followers, and a good ethics will have a positive effect upon behavior, decision making, activities, and results of those to whom the action is addressed.[29]

---

that were stolen, lame, or sick. The prophet calls on the people to return to God, in the hope that God would return to them. One way of returning would be to bring all the withheld tithes and offerings to the storehouse in the temple, as practical evidence of their obedience to and reverence for God. Because the people withheld their sacrifices, first fruits, and tithes, some Levites had to turn to farming to sustain themselves, even though the Levitical laws determined that they should live from the offerings, because all their dedication should be given to the temple service. The prophet is reiterating the original instructions given to Moses (Ntui-Abung, *Chaos of the Prosperity Gospel*, 47).

26. See the discussion of this proof-text in the previous chapter.
27. Nyirenda, *Misconceptions of Healing*, 119.
28. Essien, "Ethical Audit of Prosperity Gospel."
29. Essien, "Ethical Audit of Prosperity Gospel," 61.

A principle implied by the author of 2 Corinthians is that the goal of giving should be that there might be equality between believers in a situation where some are hard-pressed while others have more than enough to supply in their needs, as suggested above. The argument in 2 Corinthians 8 is that undue pressure should not be put on some believers, but that a fair balance between some who experience present abundance and others who experience dire needs could be established. The purpose is that there may be a fair balance between Christians so that, "(t)he one who had much did not have too much, and the one who had little did not have too little" (2 Cor 8:13–15). It might be the case also with the communion in the congregation of the Corinthians, that believers enjoyed a daily love (*agape*) meal together where those with more than enough food shared it with those without any food, establishing a balance between believers' daily needs, and which ended with celebrating the communion (1 Cor 11:17–22).

The implication is clear, that a good portion of funds contributed to the church should be used to assist the poor, widows, orphans, and those without any income. The help should be for fellow believers although it does not exclude other people in need (Gal 6:9–10 explains that believers should not grow weary in doing what is right, but whenever they have the opportunity, work for the good of all, and especially for those of the family of faith). When pastors and prophets get excessively rich, buying helicopters, expensive cars, penthouses, and designer clothes through their ministries, believers have the right and should be taught to question their priorities. Especially in cases where these leaders do not subject themselves or their ministries' financial earnings to financial scrutiny, red lights should be flashing for well-meaning believers. A considerable portion of the church's funds should be spent on effectively spreading the gospel to the unreached and believers should question to what extent this is happening in the ministries that they contribute to, while the extreme poor should also benefit from the church's presence in their communities.[30]

In Africa many people are without any job opportunities and without good prospects of acquiring any job that might generate an income to live from. What do prosperity teachers tell these people? It seems that they imply that it is these people's own fault that they find themselves in

---

30. According to Christine Schliesser, "On a Long Neglected Player," this is already happening to a certain extent, and in her comparison with secular NGOs, some neo-Pentecostal churches emerge as more effective agents of change.

such dire circumstances. To put even more blame on people experiencing the hopelessness of their situation, the poor who continue to hope against hope, even in their hopelessness,[31] is irresponsible. The prophets' ministries should rather take co-responsibility along with their members to create an entrepreneurial climate where jobs can be generated and to invest in projects that might serve to provide opportunities for the unemployed to earn a livable income by tackling what has been dubbed the triple unholy alliance of poverty, unemployment, and inequality, while at the same time providing in the most urgent needs of these poor people.

Ecological Concerns

Ecological concerns have become critical in terms of the current crises that the world faces due to climate change. An important question that needs to be answered is, how sustainable is the extreme wealth-seeking mission of prosperity preachers in Africa, in view of the finite nature of the earth's resources? Bennie-Willie Golo of Ghana refers to the inability of most African countries to recycle solid waste that is already causing an environmental catastrophe.[32] Many cities in Africa are characterized by mountains of heaped garbage, in many instances not even removed from where people stay and work, and the same is true of rural areas, causing hazardous living conditions for the poor. The continent faces countless ecological challenges without the burden of a theology that is widespread and influential among many Africans that propagate affluent consumption that in Western countries had already contributed to environmental unsustainability. Three factors are cause for concern: the message of unqualified consumerism preached by the prosperity movement, the lavish lifestyles of the leaders consisting of profligate acquisitiveness, consumption, and extravagance that serve as models for their adherents, and their salvation theology that asserts that poverty is caused exclusively by the existence of evil and evil spirits in this-worldly structures. Affluence and consumerism reduce the earth to a warehouse of natural resources and raw materials without considering the longer-term effects of an over-utilization of such resources. And the consequence of a theology that negates the existence of systemic poverty and suffering due to human interventions leads to a "neo-Puritan flight-from-the-earth" attitude, characterized by the perception

---

31. Umoh, "Prosperity Gospel and the Spirit," 665.
32. Golo, "Africa's Poverty," 376.

that the natural world is permeated by evil forces that are always at war with the redeemed.[33] Golo defines it as neo-Puritan because their flight from the world is not a complete retreat into holiness enclaves or monasteries, as happened through the centuries. Rather, they adopt the same attitude as the Puritans who shied away from the demonic world and refused to show concern for the health and well-being of creation. At the same time, however, they are extremely interested in material goods and resources that the natural world provides. As a result, they desacralize creation because they assert that as believers they have been given the mandate to exert dominion over creation as a right and privilege earned on the cross of Golgotha. As a result, they participate in spiritual warfare to fight the enemy consisting of the principalities and powers inhabiting the natural world and with the natural world itself, in order to harness their "divinely bequeathed" goods and resources that the enemy "illegitimately withheld from them." At the basis of neo-pentecostal theology is a superficial and simplistic dominion theology in which Genesis 1:26–8 features as a divine mantra for living beyond the limits that nature and other aspects of creation impose on humankind.[34]

Definition of Prosperity

An important reason why pastors, prophets and apostles are exploiting believers is because their perspective on kingdom prosperity has been narrowly defined. Prosperity is limited to the accumulation of wealth, as proven in expensive homes and cars, living lavishly, and buying jets and designer clothes. They have become obsessed with acquiring wealth, rather than using a kingdom perspective to prioritize the way their ministries and congregations spend the money donated to them. Their Jesus wore designer robes, since the New Testament states that his robe was seamless and that the soldiers at the foot of the cross gambled for it when they saw its quality, and he used the ancient equivalent of a Cadillac or Mercedes-Benz when he entered Jerusalem on the back of a donkey. In this way, greed and covetousness is sacralized.[35]

When Jesus was confronted by someone asking him to encourage his brother to divide the family inheritance with him, Jesus responded

---

33. In the words of Golo, "Africa's Poverty," 377.
34. Golo, "Africa's Poverty," 377, fn. 46.
35. Asamoah-Gyadu, "Did Jesus Wear Designer Robes," 41.

by refusing to act as a judge or arbitrator but he told the man to take care and be on his guard against all kinds of greed, for one's life does not consist in the abundance of possessions (Luk 12:13–21). In current times, greed still tempts people to claim the best for themselves, including some prosperity teachers.

Success in spiritual terms rather implies that a believer's life impacts positively on the lives of the less privileged in society by carrying out humanitarian work that realizes the command to love one's neighbor as one is to love oneself, by providing in the needs of the poor (Gal 2:10), and looking after widows and orphans (Jas 1:27). A successful pastor is not one with expensive material assets and a lavish lifestyle, but one who introduces people to the King and brings them into God's kingdom.[36]

The implication is clear, that Christians should live generously and hospitably, taking care of people in need, and their generous giving should help in spreading the gospel in their communities and other countries. They should contribute to the sharing of resources with other believers to ensure their survival in a world characterized by extreme financial and social inequalities. Poor people are not exempted from having a generous spirit as well, as demonstrated by Jesus when he commends a poor widow for her generosity (Mark 12:41–4), and even though the poor cannot contribute money, they can give in other ways, through their time, service, and prayers (Luke 60:20–1 calls them the blessed ones). The author of 1 Timothy 6:17–19 commands those who are rich among believers in his audience not to be haughty, or to set their hopes on the uncertainty of riches, but rather on God who richly provides with everything for people's enjoyment. "They are to do good, to be rich in good works, generous, and ready to share." In this way, they will store up for themselves the treasure of a good foundation for the future.

Nyirenda uses the Puritans in America as an example of God-honoring people who made a difference in their societies by working hard.[37] They believed that Christian principles should mold their whole lives and they saw honorable work as a means to glorify God. They made no distinction between sacred and secular work but argued that God called each person to a particular vocation or occupation, and that God expects of Christians to act as careful stewards of the talents and gifts God had given them. They considered idleness a big sin and diligence in one's

---

36. Nyirenda, *Misconceptions of Healing*, 122.
37. Nyirenda, *Misconceptions of Healing*, 135-36.

calling a virtue. These values and beliefs had a great and inordinate influence in terms of their relatively small numbers in America's subsequent development into becoming a leader in innovation and technology.[38]

In the contemporary world, the Third or Majority World is sometimes considered as a byword for poverty and economic failure, driven as some of them are by unsuccessful economic policies, corruption, state capture, and economic crimes. Christians have the opportunity to take the lead in Africa, following the example or the Puritans, in developing the African continent with its enormous resources waiting to be tapped in a responsible and ecologically viable manner, by emphasizing the values of hard work, entrepreneurialism, perseverance, honesty, and endurance. It is time that Pentecostals should take hands with investors and entrepreneurs in their midst and develop a policy that might drastically change the lives of Africans.[39] They should not only pray for the politicians to take the lead, but take the lead themselves.

In that sense, the prosperity gospel can help with poverty alleviation in Africa because it considers basic necessities as a sign of God's blessing, and not necessarily what Western teachers imply by the concept of prosperity.[40] Poverty in Africa is malnourished babies, plastic houses or shacks, food cooked using plastic paper for fuel, an entire family sharing a single blanket, and children crying themselves to sleep from hunger. Poverty is indeed a hindrance to true worship of God.[41] What is needed is that the prosperity gospel becomes some form of entrepreneurship ("gospreneurship," as Lovemore Togarasei suggests), and it happens when Pentecostal churches teach their followers the need to create their own employment. Believers need to be taught entrepreneurship skills for survival, in order to prove the prosperity gospel true that the Father does provide in believers' needs.[42] Entrepreneurship is one way to promote

---

38. Nyirenda, *Misconceptions of Healing*, 136.

39. Gifford, "Expecting Miracles," 20 acknowledges that the determination and persistence to succeed in being successful and getting rich, as motivated by the prosperity gospel, focuses on entrepreneurship. In some churches, members are encouraged to turn to their neighbors and ask, "Have you started your own business yet?" Entrepreneurs such as Bill Gates are held up as models (Gifford, "Expecting Miracles," 22).

40. See the description in Akoko, "Ask and You Shall Be Given," of the impact of a church such as the Full Gospel Mission in Cameroon in changed business practices, that led to a new capacity in poverty alleviation programs and that, in turn, created more wealth for both members of the church and the church itself.

41. Togarasei, "Pentecostal Gospel of Prosperity."

42. Togarasei, "African Gospreneurship," 121 refers in this context to Dr Enock

sustainable development in contexts where unemployment is rampant. Many neo-Pentecostals have already taken lead roles in establishing business enterprises that provide employment opportunities and much-needed private sector development in Africa. Their involvement in economic activities is motivated by their understanding of the command to do business until Christ's return (see Luke 19:13), because they are not informed by the older premillennial eschatological expectation of classical Pentecostalism, of a world that will progressively descend into turmoil and end with the rapture. Neo-Pentecostals' renewed understanding of eschatology inspires them to be economically productive.[43] At the same time, believers should also be encouraged to work hard for the sake of self-sustenance, and not out of greed.

Women in the African Prosperity Movement

Some women serve as prophets in the African prosperity movement, although they are an exception and in the minority. Few women serve (or are allowed to serve) as apostles because in the New Testament the position is limited to males. Seen as a whole, the movement in its practices and rituals might be contributing to the degrading of African women, given its uncritical acceptance and support of traditional patriarchy, based on traditional African values and the prevailing view of the Bible, and some practices that amount to the abuse of female adherents of the movement by way of manipulation, cultural violence, financial exploitation, stringent control measures for members, coercive practices, and power abuse where women are ordered, or only allowed to do demeaning tasks. While women form the majority of adherents, they are not allowed in leadership positions within the oppressive and saliently draconian nature of neo-pentecostal spaces.[44]

Pentecostals traditionally believed that the Spirit was poured upon all believers, and that all Spirit-filled people are empowered to minister with the individual spiritual gifts each are endowed with, with the result

---

Sitima of Bible Life Ministries in Gaborone, Botswana who helps believers discover the operative for wealth and financial intelligence. Sitima attributes poverty to an African nomadic mentality, the inability to focus on one thing, a consumer mentality, a civil servant and salary mentality that seeks employment instead of creating employment, and a materialism mentality, rather than evil spirits and angry ancestors as its cause.

43. Bangura, "Charismatic Movements," 249.
44. Khanyile, "The Virtualization of the Church."

that women in the early movement served in all positions. However, as explained above, the truce with Evangelicals led to the eventual exclusion of women from leadership roles in the Pentecostal movement, except in cases of women working with children, prisoners, and other women. As a result of the acceptance of Evangelical hermeneutics, Pentecostals also experienced the tension between the revelation of the Spirit to all believers, and the biblical injunctions about women and ministry ascribed to Paul. In following the Evangelical redemptive-historical approach that views the Bible as the inerrant "Word of God," they also had to accept the patriarchal undercurrent that determines the better part of the Bible's perspective on women in leadership positions, based in contemporary times on a literalist interpretation of the so-called creation ordinances supposedly established in Genesis 1—2. Believing in the inerrancy of the biblical witnesses makes it a necessity to side-line women.[45] Prosperity churches use the Bible as a law code and this leads to a legalistic theology. They accept that the Bible is unerring in every single detail, never contradicts itself, and is to be taken literally.[46] Their hermeneutics contributes to their discriminatory behavior toward women. They embrace the household codes in the New Testament that prescribe silence of women in worship services and absence in teaching positions, applying them literally in practice.[47] The oppression of women in the movement is vindicated by their taking the Bible as normative without the acknowledgement that it is a patriarchal document. At the same time, it should be held in mind that Africa still functions to a certain degree as mainly patriarchal societies that show considerable resistance to new developments based on an international emphasis on human rights including the rights of women. The widespread physical and emotional abuse of women by men and discrimination by employers that is endemic can be ascribed to Africa's patriarchal basis. The tension between the liberating Spirit that caused the early Pentecostal movement to accept the Spirit's anointing and empowerment of women in leadership positions and the patriarchal oppressive written "word of God" requires prosperity teachers to reconsider the Bible as a "double-edged sword" in revisiting the gendered role of the Bible and prosperity theology.[48] Musa Dube refers

45. Dube, "Between the Spirit and the Word," 2.
46. Maura and Parsitau, "Perceptions of Women's Health," 177.
47. Maura and Parsitau, "Perceptions of Women's Health," 180.
48. The excellent article of Dube, "Between the Spirit and the Word," 2 discusses this tension in more detail and suggests ways to resolve it.

to the space between the Spirit and the Word as the borderlands where the perpetual battle for gender justice is to be fought in the Pentecostal movement. It is also true of a part of Pentecostalism's acceptance of the prosperity gospel that requires reconsideration.

A remark by Tomas Dronen deserves attention, to close the discussion, that although men are most often the pastors and leaders of prosperity churches, believing women take leadership roles within the family by "domesticating" their husbands and by making sure their children are educated,[49] something that Peter Berger calls a comparative cultural advantage in terms of social mobility and economic development.[50] Berger sees a positive correlation between their social mobility and the growth of an economically productive Protestant middle class. He refers to the situation in Latin America but although it cannot be applied in an unqualified manner to the dire economic circumstances that characterize a large part of Africans, it might be beneficial to test the thesis here as well.

Some Theological Considerations

Hermeneutical Angle

It was argued that it is not enough that only some doctrines of the prosperity message, concerned with its Christology, anthropology, and eschatology, should be revisited but that Pentecostalism as a movement that accommodates the prosperity message should reconsider its hermeneutics. The challenge is not concerned with some elements in the teaching but in the way a part of the movement, probably the majority, read and interpret the Bible. They consider that the Bible gets its authority from being a book containing the words of God, clear and understandable for the average person, and with each text on the same level as all other texts. Anyone can understand the basic meaning and what the Bible teaches about different subjects, and there are no contradictions or human mistakes reflected in the Bible. Understanding it does not require complex academic analysis or specialized knowledge about the cultural world that characterized the biblical world or the languages in which the Bible was written. The Bible is read at face value and in a common sense manner, ignoring the literary, social, economic, political, and ideological contexts

---

49. Dronen, "Weber, Prosperity and the Protestant Ethic," 323. See also discussion in Hefner, "Unexpected Modern-Gender," 11-2.

50. Berger, "Max Weber is Alive and Well," 5.

of specific texts. The Old Testament does not contain different traditions, some of which clash with the others, but it is a seamless text reflecting high standards of historiography.

In reading the Bible in a literalist sense, they interpret statements in the Bible literally,[51] except when it is clear from the text that the author utilizes allegory, parable, poetry, or other literary instruments that require another reading. Even in interpreting parables, they accept that even though the parable is not literally true, it refers to circumstances that are. For that reason, they accept that there is a great chasm that has been fixed between paradise and Hades where sinners are tormented because the parable about Lazarus and the rich man pictures it, and that all people who die immediately go to an intermediate place where believers already experience the bliss of paradise while unbelievers are subjected to suffering and pain (Luke 16:19—31). The narratives in Genesis 1—11, consisting of two different creation narratives (normally read as one narrative that is harmonized with each other), the narrative about the first humans in the garden of Eden and their Fall, of the first sons of Adam and Eve having wives and children without explaining where their wives came from, the longevity of the ancient people, the flood that blotted out all living things from the whole earth except those surviving in Noah's ark, all the nations of the earth descending from Noah and his sons, and the tower of Babel are also accepted as historical facts. They are read as simple history of facts, according to its plain sense, and the findings of modern science are subjected to its conclusions, leading, *inter alia*, to the widespread rejection of the theory of evolution. The same is true for other historical accounts, even though there are contradictions between different accounts, for example, between the Deuteronomist's and the Chronicler's accounts. When these accounts tell about supernatural inventions, including the sun stopping for a whole day (Judges 10-12-13) and the going back of the sun with ten intervals at behest of the prophet Isaiah (2 Kings 20:11), they are accepted as literal facts. The same is true of Jesus' birth from a virgin without any earthly father, his miracles, and his resurrection. Although it accepts that the Bible uses metaphors and

---

51. The difference between a literal and literalist reading is important. Literal comprehension refers to the understanding of information and facts directly stated in the text. It is the first and most basic level of comprehension in reading. Literalist reading of the Bible accepts that, unless a passage is clearly intended by the writer as allegory, poetry, or some other genre, the Bible should be interpreted as literal statements by the author. The literal sense refers to the grammatical-historical sense, that is, the meaning which the writer expressed.

parables, all other texts are read in terms of a contextual interpretation based on what the reader perceives as the apparent authorial intention.[52]

At most, they apply the grammatical-historical method of exegeting the biblical text. The *Chicago Statement on Biblical Inerrancy,* formulated by more than 200 evangelical leaders at a conference convened by the International Council on Biblical Inerrancy held in Chicago in October 1978, explains that the literal sense of a text is its grammatical-historical sense, that is, the meaning which the author expressed, implying that it does not accept the attributing of a meaning which the literal sense does not support, except in case of figures of speech.[53]

When the Bible is read from a fundamentalist angle, as infallible and flawless, all texts are given equal weight and value as words of God. When it is interpreted in a literalist sense, adhering to the exact letter or the literal sense, without considering the existence of the different traditions that were combined by early redactors for different ideological reasons, texts are read without any historical and social consciousness of its function in the lives of its first readers. When the text is ascribed authority as though it contains the words of God without distinguishing between different elements in the Book, such as wisdom literature, historical narratives retold to support specific theological and ideological perspectives, and occasional documents linked to specific and unrepeatable historical circumstances, then the human element found in the Bible is lost. "The Bible is God's word in human language and thought" then becomes, "The Bible is the authoritative word of God that is applicable in all situations without any exceptions."

Kenyon goes a step further and coined the term "revelation knowledge," and distinguishes it from "sense knowledge."[54] Sense knowledge refers to knowledge that one gains through one's five physical senses and it serves as the source of all human observational, rational, as well as scientific knowledge. The physical senses are the "parents of all this

---

52. Many times Pentecostals do not give enough consideration to the wide arrays of rhetorical devices and figures of comparison found in the pages of the Bible, including emblematic symbolism and climactic parallelism, simile, metaphor, parable, allegory, pleonasm, paronomasia, hyperbole, hendiadys, hendiatris, metonymy and synecdoche, irony, litotes, euphemism, zeugma, and ellipsis (Kaiser and Silva, *Introduction to Biblical Hermeneutics,* 143-50).

53. http://www.danielakin.com/wp-content/uploads/old/Resource_545/Book%20 2,%20Sec%2023.pdf; accessed 2020-01-08.

54. Kenyon's book, *Two Kinds of Knowledge,* is dedicated to this distinction.

knowledge."⁵⁵ Sense knowledge contributes to technological innovations that ease the lives of modern people but it is limited; it fails to answer the deepest and oldest questions of human existence. It is unable to shed light on the ultimate issues in life, and cannot satisfy the "God hunger" that all people share.⁵⁶ "Sense knowledge cannot find God and would not know God if it found Him."⁵⁷ To know God, one must transcend sensory and scientific knowledge in order to act upon the knowledge provided in the Bible. That requires another type of knowledge, revelation knowledge. Revelation knowledge is transcendent, ultra-sensory, and supra-sensory knowledge that exists in the realm above sense knowledge.⁵⁸ It reveals the "reality" of the spiritual realm, and illustrates the illusory character of the physical and sensory realm. McConnell suggests as a working definition for revelation knowledge the following: Revelation knowledge is that supernatural knowledge of God and the spiritual realm revealed in the Bible, particularly in Paul's epistles, which enables human beings to transcend the limitations of sense knowledge and act in faith.⁵⁹

The doctrine of revelation knowledge is the epistemology of the prosperity message. With "epistemology" is meant a theory about the nature of knowledge. How does one gain knowledge, and how much can be known? Epistemology is the backbone of one's hermeneutics. How one acquires knowledge determines what rules one applies when interpreting sources of knowledge and it determines what and how one responds to sources of knowledge to acquire knowledge. An acquisition of knowledge can take place only by following the dictates of the "hermeneutical circle," which commences with the projective anticipation of meaning and proceeds through the dialogical-dialectical mediation of subject and object, in the thought of Josef Bleicher.⁶⁰

In theology, epistemology is important because it determines how one attempts to know God and the world. One's knowledge of God and the world, and human beings is limited by what one's epistemology determines as sources of knowledge. Kenyon's epistemology is determined by his radical distinction between revelation knowledge and

---

55. Kenyon, *Two Kinds of Knowledge*, 11.
56. Kenyon, *Two Kinds of Knowledge*, 25.
57. Kenyon, *Two Kinds of Knowledge*, 34.
58. Kenyon, *Two Kinds of Knowledge*, 20.
59. McConnell, *Different Gospel*, 102.
60. Bleicher, *Contemporary Hermeneutics*, 3.

sense knowledge. His distinction produces two results in epistemological terms. In the first place, it produces a radical dualism that reduces all of reality to two opposite principles, with little or nothing in between. Reality consists for him in the distinction between light and darkness, spirit and matter, good and evil, and these two parts of reality are known by different methods of acquiring knowledge. One cannot gain knowledge of the reality represented by revelation by way of one's senses and one cannot gain knowledge of the sense world by way of revelation knowledge. A second result is that it produces fideism, that is, the belief that religious truth is based solely on faith rather than reasoning or sensory evidence. Science and common sense are not sources of revelation knowledge at all.

McConnell argues that Kenyon's epistemology reveals strong parallels with metaphysical cults in that both epistemologies are dualistic,[61] both teach that to possess one type of knowledge demands denial of the other type, both teach that perfect knowledge of God is attainable in this life, both claim to teach a way of knowing that will enable one to transcend physical limitations, and both teach a way of knowing that creates classes of Christians, with the elites distinguished from "ordinary" Christians of a lower class in terms of their knowledge of God and enjoyment of privileges and rights that Christ earned for them.[62]

The prosperity message shares an anthropology with much of Pentecostalism that compartmentalizes humankind into three radically distinct and mutually exclusive parts: spirit, soul, and body.[63] The human's spirit is the fundamental identity and sole means to receiving and perceiving revelation knowledge and it has little or even nothing to do with the intellect, which can only process sense knowledge. What is necessary is that the human spirit should gain ascendancy over the thinking faculties so that the senses can take their proper place, with the spirit being the master of the person's being. The human spirit must subjugate the physical senses because God cannot normally communicate through the

---

61. See, e.g., the remark of Mary Baker Eddy, Phineas P. Quimby's chief disciple and founder of Christian Science, that knowledge of the matter through the physical senses represented an "error" and "false belief" of the mind. She defines knowledge as evidence obtained from the five corporeal physical senses which is not divine and serves as the origin of sin, sickness, and death, and forms the opposite of spiritual truth and understanding (Eddy, *Science and Health*, 590).

62. McConnell, *Different Gospel*, 103.

63. Although the distinction is borrowed from Paul's epistles (e.g., 1 Thess 5:23), it is rather based on the Greek idea of such a radical distinction while Paul held to the unitary and holistic view of the human being that characterized Hebrew thinking.

senses. God can only communicate with humans' spirit because God is Spirit.[64] Later Hagin would write that one almost has to by-pass the brain and operate from the inner man, the heart or spirit, to really progress in the things of God.[65]

The definition of faith is then defined in terms of the epistemology: real faith is acting upon the Word independently of any sense evidence.[66] Faith demands that the believer acts solely upon revelation knowledge to the total exclusion of sense knowledge. In terms of prayer for healing, it requires that the believer confesses the healing because of its promise in the Word, without listening to the senses and reacting to symptoms of the illness. People with sense knowledge faith do not believe they are healed until the pain has left the body, but real faith denies the physical evidence of pain and listens only to the Word.[67] Some adherents of the Faith movement denied their physical symptoms to the point of death.[68]

In hermeneutical terms, Pentecostalism differs from the other Christian traditions in the sense that it leaves room for the work of the Spirit, not only in illuminating the interpretation of the Bible for the believing reader and hearer, but also in revealing extra-biblical insights and other knowledge. Pentecostals believe that words of knowledge or wisdom, interpretation of tongues, or prophecy still operate today and that knowledge of God and God's will can be further explicated, although it will always be in line and agree with the revelation in the Bible. This view has implications for pentecostal epistemology. In reading and interpreting the Bible, a new pentecostal hermeneutics operates with the expectation that the Spirit would reveal the word of God in the Bible when it is read and meditated upon in a prayerful manner.

Pentecostal hermeneutics differ from the hermeneutics underlying the prosperity movement in the sense that the prosperity hermeneutic

64. Kenyon, *Two Kinds of Knowledge*, 18.
65. Hagin, *Right and Wrong Thinking*, 27.
66. Kenyon, *Two Kinds of Knowledge*, 34.
67. Kenyon, *Jesus the Healer*, 26.
68. For instance, a good friend that became a Christian late in life, a retired chemical engineer, once visited the campaign of an American faith healer in Johannesburg, South Africa where he was prayed for. He came back home, convinced that he was healed of deafness and removed his hearing apparatuses. After two weeks he had to confess that even though he kept on believing that he could hear, his hearing had not improved at all. During the two weeks we all had to contend with a friend who partook in our conversations without hearing anything that we had said. It was a disappointing experience in his faith life that caused much anguish and pain for him and his wife.

starts with the presupposition that God intends all believers to be saved and restored in their relationship with God, but also to be healthy, wealthy, happy, and prosperous. Their definition of salvation includes the healing of the soul, healing of the body, and the well-being of the person. Their heaven starts already on earth. It is based on supposed revealed knowledge that serves as the hermeneutical angle from which the Bible is read and interpreted, that consists of knowledge of the origin and destiny of humankind that is hidden from other believers, by means of which an elect group of believers can receive redemption. Redemption is then defined in their own terms. The main difference between pentecostal and prosperity hermeneutics is the Gnostic element found in prosperity hermeneutics.

Rudolf Bultmann explained that three central aspects define the concept of knowledge in Gnosticism, an epistemological way of thinking that goes back to the second century CE and that also characterizes the so-called revelation knowledge found in the prosperity movement.[69] These aspects also define the epistemology found in the metaphysical cults and consist of dualism, with knowledge of God absolutely distinct from and mutually exclusive of all other kinds of knowledge; anti-rationalism, that knowledge of God is radically distinguished from rational thought, based on an esoteric illumination rather than an objective, historical revelation; and classification, that is, that knowledge classifies believers into classes or categories, the highest of which is divine. Knowledge invests Gnostics with the divine nature through which they were supposed to be transformed from a human being into God.

These three aspects agree with the doctrine of revelation knowledge as developed by Kenyon and form the essence of his hermeneutics. Revelation knowledge is based on the spiritual as its origin, denying that the physical senses can contribute anything in understanding it or using it. It teaches that the human is a "spirit being" who happens to have a body, but the value of the body is devaluated because only the "spirit man" has the capacity to receive revelation directly from the Holy Spirit.[70]

---

69. Bultmann, "*ginosko*," *TDNT* 1:692-96. The Gnostics classified believers in terms of what degree of knowledge they possessed. Gnostics consisted of three "classes," the *pneumatikoi*, the spiritual ones who possessed perfect knowledge; the *psychichoi*, the psychic ones who possessed partial knowledge; and the *sarkikoi*, consisting of those who possessed no spiritual knowledge, but instead led carnal lives.

70. The prosperity message is rather sexist, especially in Africa, in terms of its language. It is also supported by its leadership, which is largely exclusively male. The issue was discussed earlier in the chapter.

The Bible does not contain such a dualistic view of revelation. All biblical revelation and its definition of salvation contains physical as well as spiritual elements. The best proof is found in God's final revelation, in Jesus Christ.[71] The incarnation of Jesus implies that he took on a body of flesh, and through the sacrifice of his body on the cross we are reconciled with God (Col 1:22; 2:9). The Bible does not allow for a spiritualization of salvation, limited to the spirit man and extended to include health, wealth, and prosperity as essential elements of salvation. Christ's incarnation, death, resurrection, and ascension are decidedly physical in nature.[72]

Biblical revelation was also perceived and understood through physical means. The apostles used their five physical senses to understand the incarnation and ministry of the Christ. In the words of John 1:14, "the Word became flesh and lived among us, and we have seen his glory, the glory as of a father's only son, full of grace and truth." The God who revealed Godself in Christ, also revealed Godself in the beauty and intricacies of nature, the work of God's hands, emphasizing the physical elements that exist within revelation, apart from but also in conjunction with the work of the Holy Spirit.

The prosperity message represents fideism, implying that it rejects reason because of its belief that revelation is spiritual and can only be perceived by spiritual means. However, the Bible shows that the human mind is just as much an instrument of revelation as the human spirit. For that reason, Jesus according to Mark 12:30 states that the first of the commandments is to "love the Lord your God with all your heart, and with all your soul, and with all your mind, and with all your strength," and to love your neighbor as yourself (see also Col 3:2; 1 Pet 1:13). The mind is just as necessary in knowing and loving God as the human spirit, and reason is not the enemy of faith because God is not an irrational being. In God's revelation through God's Spirit, the believer perceives and understands the will of God also in rational terms, although the encounter is not limited only to

---

71. The idea of Christ as final revelation of God is based on Heb 1:1–4, that states that long ago God spoke to our ancestors in many and various ways through the prophets, but in these last days he has spoken to us through a Son, whom he appointed heir of all things, through whom he also created the worlds. Jesus is then qualified as the reflection of God's glory and the exact imprint of God's very being, who sustains all things by his powerful word.

72. McConnell, *Different Gospel*, 108.

a cerebral experience but includes emotional, volitional, and charismatic elements. "Christianity may transcend reason, but it does not reject it."[73]

A result of revelation knowledge is the belief that one can receive perfect knowledge of God. "It goes without argument that God has the ability to give us exact knowledge in regard to spiritual things."[74] Revelation knowledge opens one to direct knowledge of God, making one's spirit open to unerring guidance from the Spirit. However, the Bible is clear that our knowledge of God would always be dependent on God's gracious initiative, and while we are on earth that knowledge will always be partial. Human beings cannot know God as God is; the symbol of God living in a light so intense that no human beings can survive when they are exposed to God's direct presence or glory and holiness attributed to God symbolize the unknowability of God. Creation can never comprehend its Creator. God's holiness and eternal existence are other symbols of God's unknowability.

When prosperity teachers claim that they have discovered the way to a perfect knowledge of God, they confess in fact that their deistic god can be comprehended in terms of certain laws or principles according to which their god operates. When human beings apply these laws, their god is compelled to react in a prescribed way, described in the Bible (actually, read into the Bible by the hermeneutical process that characterizes prosperity theology, and that shows affinities with the way Gnostics like the metaphysical cults through the ages read the Bible).

The Bible denies that a perfect knowledge of God is attainable in this life. Perfect knowledge of God and human beings will only be attainable when human beings encounter the perfect One, when Christ returns on the clouds to prepare his body for living on the new earth. In the words of 1 Corinthians 13:8–12, while love never ends, prophecies, tongues, and knowledge that reveal God will come to an end because it represents only partial knowledge about God. "For we know only in part . . . but when the complete comes, the partial will come to an end . . . For now we see in a mirror, dimly, but then we will see face to face. Now I know only in part; then I will know fully, even as I have been fully known."

Prosperity preachers teach that the believer does not only gain perfect knowledge of God as they learn to deny their physical senses, but they also transcend all physical limitations and walk in continual revelation.

---

73. McConnell, *Different Gospel*, 109.
74. Kenyon, *Hidden Man*, 167.

"I am no longer hemmed in by limitations because I am united with the limitless One."[75] It is no longer necessary that believers live under the domination of any physical agent; they may have absolute control over their own environment. They can write their own ticket, with a god who responds in predictable ways in providing in their desires and needs. Through revelation knowledge, the believer can transcend and conquer any evil or deficiency in life.

Reference was made to the classification that is one of the results of revelation knowledge that draws class lines between those who possess knowledge and others who do not. The one class of supermen and superheroes, the miracle class, also consists of a further distinction, with a few elect who become "god men." Kenyon writes that revelation knowledge lifts believers out of the common place where other believers are, in the second class, into the super-realm. They have gone outside of the realm of the senses, outside the realm of sense knowledge, and they have passed over into the realm of God, the spirit realm. They have become supermen and superwomen, the saviors of lesser people.[76] Those who possess revelation knowledge constitute a higher class of Christians than those who rely merely on sense knowledge. They can even become gods through this knowledge, acquiring perfect knowledge. To the degree that persons cultivate their inner spiritual sense, they are opened to the direct revelation and knowledge of God, and the secrets of nature and life.[77] They realize their own deific nature and supremacy as sons of God. For this reason, it is dangerous to oppose or criticize such persons, because it represents the "sin against the Holy Spirit (see, e.g. Matt 12:31). The high regard that prosperity teachers claim for themselves because of their exclusive access to revelation knowledge leads to uncritical acceptance of all that they teach, even if it is not biblical in nature. The idea is created that the preacher has saving knowledge as though it were resident in their own person, accommodating a messiah complex in some of these leadership figures. They pose as new Messiah figures.

75. Kenyon, *Two Kinds of Life*, 58.
76. Kenyon, *Hidden Man*, 158.

77. In this regard, David Oyedepo Jnr. in a sermon entitled, "Vital keys to unlocking the supernatural," defines "revelation" as that which must be done to take into possession what we have received at redemption (https://www.youtube.com/watch?v=Tgq33sCo25U; accessed 2020-01-02). Christians need knowledge, that is, knowing what God has provided; revelation is knowing how to access it. In order to command the supernatural, we need revelation, as the spiritual keys that will unlock the full potential of what God has intended believers to enjoy.

This sectarian element in the prosperity movement should be resisted by all means as it creates a classification of Christians that is unbiblical and affects the dignity of persons. In Christ all are equal, whether Jew or Greek, slave or free, male and female; "for all of you are one in Christ Jesus" (Gal 3:28). The Bible does not allow the notion that some believers could attain to the status of a savior or redeemer; the prophets in the Old Testament and the apostles in the New Testament were harbingers of the revelation of God but they were at the same time fallible beings, as illustrated by all the disciples' forsaking of the Lord in his hour of greatest need.

Prosperity epistemology is based on revelation knowledge, granted only to a select few, in contrast to pentecostal epistemology that leaves room for extra-biblical revelation, but subjected to the confines of biblical teaching. Prosperity teaches that one's faith determines what one's status is. Faith is measured by the type and amount of knowledge one has. If one has received the "secret knowledge" of which even the New Testament apostles and Paul were excluded, that God's intention is for all Christian believers to be healthy and wealthy and that Jesus had to go to hell for three days to earn our salvation, one has reached the exalted elite status. However, in the Bible faith is not measured by knowledge, but love. See, for instance, the reference in 1 Corinthians 8, where the author is writing about food sacrificed to idols, and some members in the church who rely on their knowledge about the issue. Paul then states that knowledge easily puffs up, but love builds up. "Anyone who claims to know something does not yet have the necessary knowledge; but anyone who loves God is known by him" (vv. 2–3). If knowledge about God does not lead to love, the knowledge is worthless. In the argument in Galatians 5 about circumcision, the author also states that in Christ Jesus neither circumcision nor uncircumcision counts for anything; the only thing that counts is faith working through love (v. 6). Love demands the democratic perspective that all believers have the same status in Christ, as the new creation intended to inherit the new earth.

What is clear is that Pentecostalism is vulnerable to a certain extent to heretical teachings and that it does not always succeed in responding timely to the matter. It is submitted that its hermeneutics, of a biblicist nature, should be replaced by the vibrant new hermeneutics developed in theological circles to strengthen its abilities to resist such heretical teachings as those found in the Toronto Blessing in Ontario, Canada of the 1990s, a neo-charismatic church; the "discipleship" or shepherding movement within some British, Australian and American charismatic churched; and the prosperity message.

The Goal of Revelation Knowledge

Revelation knowledge about God's will in terms of prosperity and wealth has been described as the essence of the prosperity epistemology. The goal of prosperity theology is the transformation of the human being into a god. The epistemology of revelation knowledge leads to a hermeneutical angle with which the Bible is read, including the important doctrine of Identification in the prosperity message that also forms a significant perspective with which the Bible is read.

The concept of Identification became popular during the nineteenth century in the "Deeper Life" Conventions, the first of which was held in Keswick, England, in 1875. A South African Reformed reverend, Andrew Murray, played a major part in the conventions and brought its teachings also effectively to Africa with his many publications which are still widely available, after a century and a half. The Keswick movement taught that believers can, in part, overcome their inherent tendency toward sin through personal identification with various aspects of Christ's redemptive act, specifically his suffering, death, resurrection, ascendancy, and exaltation. It reminds of the Roman Catholic custom of identification with Christ's passion, for example, in the Stations of the Cross, and some extreme examples where mystics identified with Christ's five wounds to such an extent that they received the *stigmata* themselves.

Identification serves an experiential bridge between anthropology and Christology.[78] To identify with his life and death is seen as a prerequisite to be "in Christ," where his vicarious redemptive act becomes the human's current experience.

The angle of prosperity theology differs radically from that of the Keswick movement that used biblical doctrines about Christ and human beings to form its doctrine of identification. Faith theology uses cultic, metaphysical concepts that deny the physical nature of the atonement, with Christ's supposed spiritual death as the crucial element, asserting that Christ became a demoniac and needed to be "born again" in hell. The purpose of their doctrine is that believers can be transformed into incarnations of God that implies that they are deified. Identification is the

---

78. McConnell, *Different Gospel*, 114.

critical element in prosperity theology because it serves as the basis for its claims that the believer is an incarnation of God.[79]

To understand the doctrine, it is necessary to comprehend prosperity theology's anthropology. The human being is viewed as a unique species in God's class of being.[80] The human being and God possess a common nature, in that both are spirit beings, or spirits. The human is not primarily a physical being but a spirit.[81] The difference between God and the human being is of degree, not kind. The human as spirit possesses a soul and inhabits a body. The spirit is the real human being. This is a pantheistic idea of God, widely used in metaphysical cults, that states that God is in everything, and everything (especially human beings) is God. They also state that there is no difference in quality between God and human beings.

Another important aspect is that humans do not have an independent nature of their own. They are always dependent upon a higher power than themselves for their spiritual life. They either partake in God's nature or Satan's nature. Their nature was divine before the Fall in the garden of Eden, and demonic after the Fall. The transformation from the divine to demonic nature represents a spiritual death, that is, the death of the human nature. Now human beings were not qualified to live with a divine nature anymore. Spiritual death means having Satan's intrinsic nature. Another part of spiritual death implies that human beings' corporate dominion over creation, granted by God, was transferred to Satan. Adam had betrayed God by giving to Satan that which God had given to him. This is Adam's "High Treason,"[82] resulting in Satan becoming a god and ruling creation by "legal right." In order to recapture creation, God had to deal with Satan "justly" by paying him a ransom.[83]

As explained, this required that Jesus died two deaths on the cross, a spiritual and physical death. He had to die a spiritual death because sickness and sin are spiritual in origin, not physical. It is not physical because it comes from the same source; Satan is the author of both sickness and sin. Christ's physical death could not eradicate sin and sickness and could not restore the divine nature to humankind. To achieve that goal, he had

---

79. See Kenyon, *Identification*, as well as the more expansive *What Happened from the Cross*.

80. Kenyon, *Hidden Man*, 7.

81. Hagin, *Redeemed*, 27.

82. Hagin, *Authority of the Believer*, 15.

83. Kenyon, *Bible*, 43.

to die a spiritual death. For that reason, his physical death was but just the beginning of his redemptive work.

To die a spiritual death implies that Christ's spirit had to be made sin, and that his spirit suffered the torments of judgment and hell on behalf of humanity. It was also his spirit that was eventually declared righteous. It was the resurrection of his spirit that has given humanity its redemption. We are so tied up with our sense knowledge that we have only seen the physical suffering of Christ on the cross, and that includes the Evangelists. They did not know that there was something infinite beyond that.[84]

The implication is clear, that the agonies and suffering on the cross and the triumph of his resurrection were not the true redemptive work of Christ. It was his spiritual death and spirit resurrection that were his true redemptive acts. His physical death was but a means to an end and had no intrinsic meaning for Christians without reference to what followed on it.

Fred Price explains that if the punishment for our sins was to die on a cross, the two thieves could have paid the price for us. The punishment was much more; it required that Christ had to go to hell itself and serve time in hell, separated from God. Satan and his cohorts realized that they had Christ bound when they dragged him down to the pit of hell to serve his sentence.[85] Jesus had to go to hell to free mankind from the penalty of Adam's high treason. His blood did not atone our sins. He had to spend "three horrible days and nights in the bowels of the earth getting back for you and me our rights with God."[86] He went to hell in order to take us to heaven.[87] It was needed that he died a spiritual death to regain the divine nature for himself, and us.

The spiritualization of Christ's death destroys the core of the gospel, of Christ's propitiatory death for us. It is related to a Christology that is heretical, that Christ had left his divine nature in heaven when he came to earth, and that he had to suffer in hell to regain the divine nature, now not only for himself but also for us. The teaching states that when Jesus died spiritually he experienced an internal transformation in his nature, just like what happened to Adam when he died

---

84. Kenyon, *Hidden Man*, 47.

85. Price, *Ever Increasing Faith*, 7.

86. Copeland, quoted in McConnell, *Different Gospel*. See also Irene B. Faulkes, "Was Jesus born again?" (http://revirene.org/Was%20Jesus%20Born%20Again.htm; accessed 2020-02-14).

87. Kenyon, *Identification*, 8.

spiritually. On the cross, when man's sin and spiritual death were imputed to him, Jesus became a satanic creation, a demoniac. He became sin, representing the demonic human nature, and it separated him from God. The separation was more than just alienation; his spiritual death transformed him into a satanic man, severing him from God. His death did not serve as a substitute for sin in any vicarious sense; he was transformed into a demoniac.[88] He went to hell a demon-possessed man, and emerged from hell a born-again, resurrected man. As a born-again man he defeated Satan and his forces in hell, serving as an example for believers of their authority over evil forces.

There are two sides to our identification with Christ. The legal side consists of Christ's complete identification with us in our fallen and demoniacal state, and our complete identification with him in his sacrifice, and shows us what Christ did for us when he went to the cross and hell. It is legal because it fulfills the justice of God towards Satan, in order to buy back creation from Satan's rule after Adam's high treason handed Satan the legal right to rule over creation. To do so, Christ had to experience spiritual death, which consisted of taking up the satanic nature and the curse of the law, which is sin, sickness, and poverty. The vital side consists in the faith actualization of the redemption of Christ already credited to humans in the legal side of the identification, and results in the believer experiencing perfect victory over sin, sickness, and poverty. The ultimate end of the vital side of identification is deification of the believer, the process whereby human beings are transformed into gods. Through rebirth, the human is again infused with the divine nature that was lost when Adam received the satanic nature.

The strangeness of these ideas that do not conform to the information provided in the Bible or the teachings of the rest of the Christian church has to do with the assertion in prosperity theology that it possesses special knowledge that no other believers knew about. It demonstrates the direct links with Christian Science, Theosophy, New Thought, and Modern Unitarianism that commonly share the ideal that human beings will be incarnated to become divine.[89]

Believers are Christ,[90] and for that reason they are able to transcend all physical limitations. They are elevated above all sickness, pain,

---

88. Kenyon, *What Happened from the Cross*, 12.
89. Kenyon, *Hidden Man*, 26.
90. Hagin, *Zoe*, 41.

accidents, negative circumstances, and imperfections. If these things still exist among believers, it is because they have failed to realize their identification with Christ. [91]

It is clear that prosperity theology represents a view of man, the Fall and its results, and Christ and his death that is not biblical. The Bible as a whole supports the Hebrew concept of a holistic human person, an integrated being with a mind, emotions, body, and spiritual abilities that cannot be separated from one another. The body was just as important in Hebrew anthropology as any other aspect of the human nature.

To state that fallen humanity as a result of the Fall became filled with satanic nature and that human beings became a new satanic creation is also unbiblical. Satan does not have any creative powers; he is a created being of God, subject to God's sovereign rule over the universe. Pentecostals realize that demon possession among believers may occur in rare cases, while demon oppression is much more prevalent, but they do not believe that Satan has the power to alter the nature of humankind on a cosmic scale. It is unbiblical to subscribe so much power to Satan. It is also a questionable assertion to identify the snake in the garden of Eden in an unqualified sense with Satan. In Hebrew thinking, God's sovereignty requires that all powers are subjected to God, and most of the Old Testament does not know of a concept that can be equated with the New Testament concept of Satan. Even in the book of Job, "the satan" (used with the definite article) depicts the figure as an employee in God's courts, reporting to God about his doings, and allowed to interact with human beings and their circumstances only to the extent that God allowed it.

It is also a false anthropological assertion that human beings do not have a nature of their own but can only exist in terms of having a divine or satanic nature. Human beings are created in the image of God, but it is a distinctly human nature. They can reflect God's glory and they may have some of God's capabilities, but they are not gods and they were not created to be gods.[92] For the sake of the argument, I accept that being created in the image of God implies, *inter alia*, that humans have the capacity and need to live in a restored relationship of friendship with God, a characteristic that only human beings possess of all created beings on

---

91. Kenyon, *Jesus the Healer*, 54.

92. The discourse about what the image of God in humankind implies is an ongoing debate with various opinions, and it does not serve the purpose of the research to discuss these views extensively.

the planet, as far as we can ascertain. When believers' relationship with God is restored through Christ, they become more like God and reflect something of God's glory in their altruistic behavior, but that does not change them into gods. With the Fall, the image of God was shattered within human beings, and even if their relationship with God is restored, the broken mirror is not repaired completely. That will only happen in eternity when human beings will live in the direct presence of God and represent or reflect God's glory in fullness (see Eph 1:3–14).

Christ was also not sacrificed to Satan, as prosperity teachers proclaim. Satan does not own human beings "by legal right" and a ransom was not needed to be paid to him for humans' redemption. The "ransom theory" of the atonement had surfaced many times in the past in the church but it was rebutted each time. As a mediator, Christ's ransom was to God. His death served as a sacrifice to God (see Eph 5:2; 1 Tim 2:5–6). Although Satan is called the god of this world (in 2 Cor 4:4) and the ruler of the world (in John 14:30), Christ destroyed his power on the cross. Satan owns nothing by legal right because his dominion is a usurped one. He stole it and he maintains it by accusation, deception, enslavement to sin, fear of death, and the power of death. God owes Satan nothing; God can destroy him if God so wishes. Christ did not destroy Satan's dominion by paying a ransom to him but by fulfilling the law of God, freeing human beings from the law of sin and death, and destroying sin and death at the same time.[93]

The idea that Christ became sinful, taking on a satanic nature is derived from one verse, in 2 Corinthians 5:21, that states that for our sake God made Christ to be sin who knew no sin, so that in him we might become the righteousness of God. Prosperity teachers say that Christ ransomed humanity's sin, not by dying on the cross, but by taking on the human nature which had become satanic in the Fall. However, the context suggests another interpretation of the verse that has also characterized the Christian church's theology over the millennia. The context is God's redeeming action in the bodily crucifixion of Christ. Believers in Christ are a new creation because God reconciled them to Godself through Christ, not counting their trespasses against them. Now they are ambassadors for Christ who proclaim that all people should be reconciled to God. The next verse then states that God made Christ sin for our sake. God was clearly the primary player in the atonement, not the devil.

---

93. See full discussion in McConnell, *Different Gospel*, 123-4.

God made Christ sin in the forensic sense, as payment for our sin. In other words, God treated Christ who was without sin as though he were a sinner by delivering him up to the cross, to pay the price for humanity's sin. "Made sin" cannot be changed into "took upon himself the human nature" without violating all the principles of exegesis.

The background of Christ's atonement is the Levitical concept of substitution, based on the requirement of the perfection and holiness of the sacrificial victim (see Lev 4:3; 23; 32). The transfer of sin and guilt happened when the sinner laid their hands on the lamb in a symbolic sense (Lev 4:4, 24, 33). At that moment of transference, the sacrifice became holy to God, and anyone who touched or ate the sin offering also became holy (Lev 6:25-7, 29). The sacrificial animal did not become sin and therefore unholy, as prosperity teachers assert. Sin was symbolically imputed to it. It served as a substitute for sin and atoned for sin because it was perfect and consecrated, and being acceptable before God. In the same way, Jesus did not literally become sin but our sin was imputed to him. He was a fit substitutionary offering precisely because he was sinless and acceptable to his Father.

He also did not die a second death before he could work atonement for us with God. The double death theory of Jesus is built exclusively on one verse, in Isaiah 53:9, that states that he made his grave with the wicked, and with the rich in his death. Prosperity theology interprets Isaiah 53 as a messianic prophecy and interprets the plural "deaths" in verse 9 as proof that Jesus died twice. As explained in the previous chapter, plural nouns are commonly used in Hebrew, not to denote a plurality of objects but to emphasize a particular meaning of the noun, such as majesty, rank, excellence, magnitude, and intensity. The same happens when Hebrews referred to God as *Elohim,* a plural of "God." It does not signify that they served many gods, but that their God was so majestic that God encompasses everything that is signified by the term "God." "Death" as a plural noun is used in Isaiah 53:9 to indicate that the death mentioned was a particularly violent one; the servant (in the historical context) did not die two deaths but a death that was terrible because the Lord had laid on him the iniquity of us all (see v. 6).

Jesus commended his spirit to God at the moment of his death (Matt 27:50; John 19:30). Nowhere is there any indication in the New Testament that he died twice. However, such a statement does not hold water with prosperity theology because its proponents claim that they have received revelation knowledge that revealed to them what happened during and after Christ's death. One cannot argue with their knowledge because it is attributed to a source alongside the Bible, making their epistemological and hermeneutical angle completely unacceptable for Pentecostals who accept the Bible as the one and only source for their theology and practice (in line with the Protestant *sola Scriptura*).

If Jesus was taken to hell immediately after his death, how is it possible that he told the repenting thief on the cross, "today you will join me in paradise" (Luk 23:43)? We do not know "what happened from the cross to the throne" (because we do not have access to the revelation knowledge that prosperity teachers claim to have but only the New Testament to refer to), but we do know that Satan played no role in what happened to Jesus when he died.[94]

Another aspect of prosperity atonement that is very alarming is their assertion that Christ's physical death alone could not atone our sins. However, the Bible is clear that Christ defeated Satan on the cross through his physical death, when he also paid the sacrifice for our sin. The author of Colossians 2 states that believers were buried with Christ in baptism, and raised with him through faith in the power of God. This was due to God forgiving them their trespasses and erasing the record that stood against them with its legal demands. "He set this aside, nailing it to the cross. He disarmed the rulers and authorities and made a public example of them, triumphing over them in it" (vv. 14–15). Humans were liberated from the law and the dominion and authority of the devil on the cross at the same time.

It was also not his spiritual sufferings, death, and resurrection that defeated Satan. Christ suffered and died in the flesh (1 Pet 4:1), defeating death and the devil. His blood was shed on the cross as the victim of sacrifice, cleansing us and bringing forgiveness of our sins (see Heb 9:22). For that reason, we are redeemed "with the precious blood of Christ, like that of a lamb without defect or blemish" (1 Pet 1:19). Jesus died a physical death, like any live sacrifice brought in the Old Testament to the tabernacle or temple, releasing us from our sins by his blood (Rev 1:5).

Faith in God or Faith in Faith?

The prosperity movement is characterized by its emphasis on faith that believers need to unlock heavenly riches of health, wealth, and happiness.

---

94. See Kenyon, *What Happened from the Cross*.

The question needs to be asked, is it the same concept that the Bible uses? Religious faith is determined by its subject, the person who believes, and the object of faith, God. Christian faith is centered on Jesus Christ as the way to the Father. In the words of Peter in his sermon before the Sanhedrin in Acts 4:12, "There is salvation in no one else, for there is no other name under heaven given among mortals by which we must be saved."

The faith proclaimed in the prosperity message states that faith provides you with the opportunity to write your own ticket with God. By following certain steps, you can get what you desire from God. Hagin, for instance, claims that God gave him four steps that one should follow to always receive from the Father whatever you want. Follow these four steps and your every desire will be fulfilled by God. The four steps are: say it, do it, receive it, and tell it.[95]

The formulas used to define and realize "faith" is based on a specific worldview that sees in the creation narrative the means of God's creating act, by speaking a word, as the way that believers also should call all things into being. God is a faith God; God had faith in God's faith, demonstrated by the fact that God spoke words of faith and God's words came to pass. Believers should follow God's example, by having faith in their own words to create. To have faith in your words is nothing else than to have faith in your faith. We need to learn from God how to have faith in our own faith.[96] Faith-filled words brought the creation into being and holds everything together, and believers can rule the universe today with their faith-filled words. Their words have immense power. If one has discovered the spiritual laws established and used by God at the creation and which God uses to run the universe, one can put these laws to work for one's own use. The law of faith is a spiritual law because God put that law into motion, and when one comes into contact with that law it will always work for one.[97]

Spiritual laws work in a mechanical and automatic way, which implies that when sinners or unbelievers apply them, they will receive the same results as believers. When they have learnt to speak words of faith, in positive confessions, there is no end to the wealth they can create, even without any faith in God. Fred Price teaches in this regard that Romans 10:10–12 is a formula that applies to all people when it states that one

---

95. Hagin, *How to Write*, 5, 20-21, 32.
96. Hagin, *Having Faith*, 4-5.
97. Kenyon, *Two Kinds of Faith*, 20.

believes with the heart and so is justified, and one confesses with the mouth and so is saved, because the Bible teaches that no one who believes in him will be put to shame. And this is valid for all people, for Jew and Greek.[98] Faith places the resources of the heavens and universe at our disposal.

What kind of god can be manipulated by spiritual laws that compel that god do certain things? How does the god look like that needs to believe in the god's own faith? Such a god is not a personal god who speaks and acts in unique ways in the lives of individuals or rules sovereignly over the work of God's hands and decides about the fate of nations and powers in the world. The god of formulas is an impersonal force, called the Intelligence, Infinite Power, and Spirit by the metaphysical cults. The Force, made famous by science fiction utilizing the same concept, rules the universe indirectly through immutable laws and principles, as in the case of scientific laws controlling the natural world. It is a deistic god that was spiritualized, consisting of great laws and forces that govern the world and people's lives.[99] In this regard, H. Emily Cady of the Unity School of Christianity, a metaphysical cult, writes that laws govern the mental and spiritual world, and they are just as real and unfailing as the laws that govern the natural world.[100] There is a cause-and-effect relationship between the spiritual laws and the human mind; every human thought has an effect in the universe because of the operation of the spiritual laws. The implication is clear, that it becomes possible to manipulate these laws to one's own advantage. It is not necessary to take into account that God decides about the life of each individual, and reveals Godself through the Spirit in a unique manner to those who seek God with their whole hearts.

Prosperity faith manifests in positive confession, that can be defined as affirming something people believe, testifying to something they know, and witnessing to a truth that they have embraced, without seeing it.[101] The secret to effective confession is to know what one's rights and privileges as a child of God are, and to confess publicly and verbally that Christ provides in all our needs and desires. What one believes and confesses is what one gets from God. That is why it so important to think the right thoughts. This is called positive mental attitude, already referred to.

---

98. Price, *How Faith Works*, 110-111; Hagin, *Four Steps*, 7.
99. McConnell, *Different Gospel*, 134.
100. Cady, *Lessons in Truth*, 64-5.
101. Hagin, *New Thresholds*, 40.

Reality is the sum total of what we think it to be; we possess the innate power to shape and reshape reality through the power of our positive thinking and our powerful words.

It is important not to wait for the results but that one should keep on believing and confessing, until reality changes according to one's designs. Sense knowledge may not overpower us; we should learn to rely on revelation knowledge to inform our mental attitude. It is important because unbelief is not defined as the absence of belief, but as a destructive belief that expresses itself in negative confessions, changing reality for the negative. Belief and unbelief is the difference between fear and faith that creates our reality. The moment we fear something we have opened the door for the fear to be realized, and what we feared will be actualized in our lives. "For the thing which I greatly feared is come upon me, And that which I was afraid of is come unto me" (Job 3:25). Joyce Meyer refers to fear is a self-fulfilling emotion.[102] This is so because the Bible says it will be unto us as we believe (Matt 9:29). That principle works in the negative as well as the positive: we can receive by fear as well as by faith.

Faith teachers emphasize the power of the Word of God to influence our thoughts and create the reality God intended for believers to experience. However, what is at stake is not the power of the word but the power of our thoughts that is supposed to draw unseen, impersonal forces into play.[103] Our thoughts lead to positive confession, in which we use God's formula for creation, "let there be," to create our own reality. Faith has creative powers; speaking the Word will bring what you desire.[104] It unlocks the faith force that moves and changes things and circumstances. Believers can grow in their faith force to possess more power and move bigger obstacles in the spirit realm.[105]

This faith is also designated as the God-kind of faith, with Mark 11:22's "Have faith in God" being translated with a subjective genitive as "Have the faith of God." The faith of God is produced in believers by the living Word; it is the same kind of faith that spoke the universe into existence.[106] The God-kind of faith prays once, speaks the words into existence, and then confesses what it expects even despite contradictory

---

102. Meyer, *Approval Addiction*, 9-10.
103. McConnell, *Different Gospel*, 137.
104. Capps, *God's Creative Power*, 5-6.
105. Price, *Faith, Foolishness*, 46-7.
106. Hagin, *New Thresholds*, 74.

evidence of our physical senses. Hebrews 11:3 is also used in this relation, when prosperity teachers interpret the text as that God, by God's faith, created the world, implying that God is thus a faith being. However, rather than stating that God by God's faith created the world, Hebrews 11:3 states that we by faith understand that God created the world. The same sentence construction is used in verses 3, 4, 7, 8, 20, and 24–25, each time implying that Moses, Jacob, Abraham, Noah, Abel, and the present readers were responsible for the described action.

In evaluating the doctrine of faith as applied in the prosperity movement, the most important question is, what kind of god is supposed by this type of faith? It was argued that it represents a deistic, impersonal god who cannot operate independently of the laws that hold the universe together. The god of the faith movement is not the sovereign ruler of the universe because it denies God's personality; in other words, what makes God a person that relates to human beings through Christ and the Spirit. The use of God's name, and especially the name of Jesus, in a near magical way to unlock all the promises given in the Bible is an attempt to manipulate and control the Most High who accomplishes all things according to God's counsel and will (Eph 1:11), without needing any human assistance. It blurs the distance between God and human beings by using the holy name for magical purposes.

The concept of creative power in faith is also a denigration of the Creator's exclusive power and existence as trinity. It distorts the relationship between God and the Bible, using biblical phrases without considering their literary or historical context and applying them to situations that the biblical authors in most cases did not foresee. Fact is, the universe is the handiwork of God who also maintains it. It is not spiritual laws that hold everything together, and our knowledge and application of spiritual laws do not change us into creative powers comparable to God. Pentecostals believe that the word of God has power to realize God's will in our lives. However, the biblical words in themselves do not have power apart from the application of these words in the lives of believers through the Spirit. They are not concerned primarily with the Bible as the word of God, but with God who exists in holiness, love, grace, and sovereignty. By believing the revelation of God in Christ, the final word of God, as proclaimed in the New Testament, one gets saved. It is not the Bible that saves one but God's saving grace. When the words of the Bible are mechanically repeated they do not automatically represent words uttered by

God; only when the Spirit reveals Christ, which is the Spirit's main task, do the words in the Bible become powerful.

It was already asserted that the prosperity movement's theology is human-centered instead of theocentric, and the definition of faith that it utilizes proves the assertion. To state that one needs the God-kind of faith, the faith that belongs to God, is to claim that believers can receive a characteristic that is unique to God. Even though I do not think that God has faith (in what would the Creator God have faith, and for what and in what would the sovereign Ruler of the universe need to believe?), the prosperity definition of faith confers godhood upon those human beings with the correct faith. No serious exegete of the New Testament accepts that Mark 11:22 uses a subjective genitive; even though the term "faith" (*pistis*) occurs many times in the New Testament and it is frequently followed by the genitive, it is consistently translated with an objective genitive. To reduce faith to positive confession or a positive mental attitude is to divorce it from God, who is the sole object of Christian faith but also the subject, as the source of our faith.

The tendency in prosperity theology to build a doctrine on one proof-text, as happens for instance with its interpretation of Mark 11:22, Isaiah 53:5, or Isaiah 53:9, is an unacceptable practice. The majority of their proof-texts are from the Old Testament, and they are read without considering what the rest of the Bible teaches about the same subject.[107] The rule is that the Bible should primarily be used to interpret itself, and in each case there are other references about the same subject that do not support the specific interpretation.[108]

---

107. Many African Christians spend a lot of time reading the Old Testament and they describe their experiences in the language and categories of the Old Testament. Jenkins, *New Faces*, 43 asserts that the Bible of the South is a good deal larger than its Northern counterpart, because the Old Testament lost its appeal for many Western believers. The portrayal in the Old Testament of a world of nomadism, polygamy, sacrificial rituals, etc., results in many Africans sharing a deep affection for the Old Testament; they recognize their own realities in its pages. See the discussion of proof-texts at the end of the previous chapter, and especially the discussion of the importance of Deuteronomistic theology for prosperity theology.

108. Asamoah-Gyadu, "Learning to Prosper," 70 judges that up to about 60 percent of all sermons in African Pentecostalism center either on the patriarchs or some Old Testament narrative involving figures like Moses, Joshua, Samuel, or David and Goliath. Even when some of these figures acted in ways that are clearly morally wrong, their actions are reinterpreted by prosperity teachers as "smart moves" or "skillful negotiations" needed today to succeed in a turbulent, capitalist, consumerist, and competitive world, reflecting the disproportionate stress on and hermeneutics of positives,

It is the anthropocentric focus of prosperity theology that led to Charles Farah's seemingly contradictory remark that it constitutes "charismatic humanism" because it is faith in a humanistic and anthropocentric god.[109] To have faith in one's own faith also demonstrates the humanistic nature of the definition of faith utilized by the prosperity teachers. To have faith in your own faith is nothing else than to have faith in yourself, and it is understandable if the human being is equated with God, as is the case in prosperity theology. It attempts to confer upon believers unrestrained power to meet their own self-defined desires without any reference to God's sovereign will, expressing the anthropocentric and selfish nature of the theology. Anyone who has learnt to be positive and confess the positive thinking in words can manipulate the spiritual laws to manipulate God, and it is true even for unbelievers!

Prosperity as the Goal of Faith

The charismatic renewal movement that originated in the 1960s and led to the charismatization of established churches emphasized healing, and especially inner healing in its early history, while early Pentecostals were characterized by their addition of holiness alongside healing. The emphasis has since shifted, with the doctrine of prosperity getting nearly as much attention as in independent network Christianity, and to a lesser extent in the rest of African Pentecostalism. D.R. McConnell suggests that prosperity teaching falls into two types, an egocentric teaching that promises success and prosperity from God to those who contribute generously, especially to the apostle, prophet, or evangelist's ministry, and a cosmic teaching of prosperity.[110] The last type promises success and prosperity from God to those who know the spiritual laws of the universe that govern the spiritual realm, including financial prosperity that functions essentially in the spiritual realm. The first type centers on the personality of the preacher and the motive is to enrich themselves and serve the interests of their own ministry, and constitutes nothing else than personal self-enrichment and abuse of gullible believing people. The second type is cosmic because it centers on universal principles that God has set up in

---

possibilities, empowerment, and prosperity (Asamoah-Gyadu, "Learning to Prosper," 68).

109. See also the discussion in chapter 4.
110. McConnell, *Different Gospel*, 170.

the cosmos. McConnell's distinction is significant because it does justice to the diversity that characterizes the prosperity movement, with proponents serving different motives.

At first, most prosperity teachers fell into the first class; they bankrolled their ministries in a lucrative manner by their teaching. Today, most teachers may sound egocentric at times when they appeal for more money, using all kinds of emotional tricks to convince their audiences to contribute to a specific cause, like keeping the doors of a specific ministry or television station open. In my observations, and those of several other researchers, this is not true in Africa. The first type of prosperity teaching, emphasizing the significance of the apostle and grounded in human egocentric desires, occurs the most. In further evaluation of African prosperity gospel, it is this rather crude form of the prosperity message that will be criticized.

In general, however, both types teach prosperity on a cosmic scale, utilizing formulas and laws to define their teaching. They want their audience to share in knowledge of the spiritual laws that supposedly govern prosperity in the universe, in the hope that is usually not mentioned, that the realized prosperity shall be shared with the minister who taught the principles. One such success formula is the hundredfold return, based on Mark 10:30 and discussed in chapter 3. It is supposed to be a universal spiritual law because it works for anybody who knows it, even unbelievers. "God has a certain law of prosperity and when you get into contact with that law and those rules, it just works for you—*whoever you are.*"[111]

The same teaching about prosperity occurred already in the Unity School of Christianity, where Charles Fillmore insisted that all men who had prospered in this world had used the law that governs the manifestation of supply, demonstrating that there is no other way to unlock personal prosperity.[112] To operate the law of prosperity it is required that one should understand the law, have faith in it, and apply it to one's need.[113] Prosperity is the result of knowledge of how to manipulate spiritual laws, without any mention of personal trust in a sovereign God providing for God's children because God is their Father.

Applied by prosperity preachers, it becomes: "*You can have what you say!* In fact, what you are saying is exactly what you are getting

---

111. Copeland, *God's Will is Prosperity*, 54.
112. Fillmore, *Prosperity*, 33.
113. Fillmore, *Prosperity*, 50-51.

now."[114] For that reason, it is important that believers discipline their vocabulary and their thoughts in order to agree with what God says and thinks. Then God is obliged to meet their needs because God's word compels God to do what God had promised.[115] This is true because God is not asking believers to serve God for free and does not expect them to serve God for free.[116]

Because thoughts and words are powerful and creative, it is critical for believers to use their faith to unlock these powers by way of positive mental attitude, positive confession, and visualization through mental suggestion and verbal affirmation. Dave Hunt and T.A. McMahon in a work that provides a distorted image of prosperity theology in my opinion asserts that the practice of visualization is based in the occult and Eastern religions.[117] I do not think that its origins necessarily explain its widespread use in psychological and religious practice, and it does not necessarily introduce an occult practice as a substitute for biblical faith.[118]

To do justice to some preachers in the prosperity movement, not everyone teaches a selfish doctrine of prosperity. Some also warn against the dangers of greed and the powerful hold that money can get over a person.[119] Kenyon, for instance, defines prosperity as not just the ability to make a success of your life but emphasizes that it always includes the ability to serve humanity better.[120]

Experience of Supernatural

It is clear that African Pentecostals in their diversity share the dissatisfaction with religion that only engages one's mind with theologies and

---

114. Copeland, *Laws of Prosperity*, 98.
115. Copeland, *Laws of Prosperity*, 101.
116. Price, *Faith, Foolishness*, 7.
117. Hunt, *Seduction of Christianity*, 43.
118. *Contra* McConnell, *Different Gospel*, 173.
119. For instance, in a sermon of Prophet T.B. Joshua entitled, "Value processing more than result," he states that God hears your desire that God should bless your business but God knows that perhaps when your business is blessed you will not find time for God and the faith community (https://www.youtube.com/watch?v=obGhSHnHtYU; accessed 2020-01-04). Your money will then start to control you. What is important is that God wants to engage with you so that you acknowledge God. Therefore, discuss with God whatever you are doing.
120. Kennedy, *Advanced Bible Course*, 59.

concepts about God without an experience of the direct experience and intervention of God. In Africa primal spirituality requires an engagement with the spirit world because of the direct effect of the invisible world upon the daily affairs of human beings. When individuals accrue wealth, enjoy good health and possess material well-being, they are believed to be living in harmony with the spirit world.[121] At the same time, a religious group structured around passive imparting of information about God will probably not succeed anymore in an information-saturated, experience-hungry social context. A holistic approach is required that engages the body, senses, emotions, and spirit of participants. A long sermon consisting of a theoretical exposition of some aspect unrelated to daily life by a theological expert has lost a large section of the market share already. Effective preaching in Africa engages people's bodies, senses, and emotions while at the same time it stimulates their minds.

While the experience of God in an encounter with God is non-negotiable for Pentecostals, the image of God presented by the prosperity message should be elucidated so that believers can understand what is so alluring about this version of the gospel. The traits that characterize the contemporary Western world has to a certain extent been accepted and integrated in African thinking, like its individualism, materialism, self-centeredness, urge to search for all pleasures possible for humankind, etc. The God picture created by prosperity preachers is a supernatural deity that exists for the exclusive pleasure and benefit of humankind, linking directly to some of these aspects. God resides in the heavenly realm for our utility and benefit. Today's human beings have noticed that true power is accessed not by looking upward but by turning inward, and for this reason the prosperity message identifies the believer with the deity, implying that the faith message is able to change one's consciousness about oneself. Chris Oyakhilome utilizes the words in 2 Corinthians 5:17 that the person in Christ is a new creature for whom the old things have passed away and all things have become new, and then states that even if one were born with an illness or into a poor family, the person in Christ does not have it anymore. Illness and poverty have passed away and believers live in perfect health and wealth. The consciousness God wants the person to have excludes any belief in or allowance for illness and poverty. "This is how He wants you to think about yourself."[122] At the same

---

121. Bangura, "Charismatic Movements," 243.
122. Quoted in Ntui-Abung, *Chaos of the Prosperity Gospel*, 17.

time, many other prosperity teachers have taken the concept further in a negative sense. Where early teachers preached about prosperity in terms of the believers' fundamental needs, now the preachers claim that God wants to grant every desire of the believer as well. God does not only want to rescue God's children from poverty; God wants them to drive the most expensive car, stay in the best neighborhood in the largest houses, eat only the best food, and wear the most expensive designer clothes.[123] As children of royalty and king's kids they are destined to live in a manner befitting their exalted status in Christ.

While it is true that the Bible states unequivocally that the Father knows what the needs of God's children are, even before they ask, and that God provides in it (Matt 6:8), it is also true that Christ teaches his disciples not to be anxious about their life, about what they will eat or drink, or about their body, what they will wear because life is more than food, and the body more than clothing. Their heavenly Father knows that they need all these things, and God cares for them. What is important, instead, is that they strive first for the kingdom of God and its righteousness, and all these other things will be given to them as well (Matt 6:25–33).

In referring to "needs," the New Testament employs the Greek term *chreia* which refers to "that which is necessary, without which no one can survive." The Sermon on the Mount states that human needs consist of food, drink, and clothing, while Paul teaches in 1 Timothy 6:8 that one's needs are limited to food and clothing, and Jesus tells Martha in Luke 10:42 that there is only thing a believer needs, and that is to sit at Jesus' feet and listen to his teaching. The definition of "need" that God promises to supply is important because it limits our basic needs to that which we need in order to be able to function and survive. It does not include the menu of "needs" that prosperity teachers propagate as the heritage and rights of all believers, earned by Jesus on the cross for them, including big houses, cars that serve as status symbols, expensive clothes, and dining at restaurants that cost more than most Africans can ever pay.

Prosperity teaching does not make a distinction between needs and wants or desires, and they define it in many cases as selfish and self-seeking lusts.[124] It seems that God's answer to such desires and lusts is to offer to crucify them for the believer who trusts God for all needs (Rom 6:1–14; 8:12–3; Gal 5:16–24). The cross of Jesus is not just an event

---

123. Hagin, *New Thresholds*, 54-5.
124. McConnell, *Different Gospel*, 175.

that the believer should believe and trust in. In a crucial sense, the cross should become a personal way of life for the believer. To believe in the cross implies that one dies to one's claims on one's own life, to stop living for one's own interests, and to pursue the interests of God's kingdom. The cross implies that one has also died to the law, and that explains why our relationship with God could never have been restored if it were dependent on our own good works. In the words of Galatians 2:20, it is no longer "I who live, but it is Christ who lives in me. And the life I now live in the flesh I live by faith in the Son of God, who loved me and gave himself for me."

The cross holds eternal benefits for the believer but that does not include all earthly benefits. In contrast, identification with the cross implies that one declares one's willingness to get crucified in terms of one's relation to the world and its interests and lusts (Gal 6:14). Because prosperity theology misunderstands the cross and resurrection of Jesus in a way that serves their interests, they interpret it nearly exclusively in terms of what benefits a believer can gain in terms of their earthly existence from the cross. I explained my viewpoint that Isaiah 53 cannot be used to connect healing with the cross of Jesus, and the same is true of prosperity, happiness, and wealth. In claiming the cross for their own selfish pursuance of desires, prosperity teachers are creating a mind-set among believers which is entirely antithetical to the true meaning of the cross.[125] This is done when it contradicts the meaning of the cross by subverting the demands of the cross for self-denial, by reducing God to a means to an end, which is prosperity, and by focusing on the material things of this world as the sign of God's approval and the means of God's blessing. In this way, they disqualify believers to become followers of Jesus, who deny themselves and take up their cross and follow Jesus. It is only in losing one's life for Jesus' sake, and for the sake of the gospel, that one gets saved. The danger Jesus depicts is that one can gain the whole world and forfeit their life (Mark 8:34–36).

What should believers' attitude toward prosperity and wealth be? Gordon Fee writes that one should on the one hand avoid rejecting all prosperity in the belief that money is inherently evil, and on the other hand guard against accommodating oneself to worldly cultural values without considering Jesus' demands to carry one's cross in the world.[126]

---

125. McConnell, *Different Gospel*, 178.
126. Fee, "New Testament View," 8.

All Christians should take note, in my opinion, of the enormous inequalities created by a neo-liberal capitalist economy and its implications for upsetting and denying the dignity of all people. I believe that Pentecostals should reconsider their implicit approval of an economic system that discriminates against a majority of people, in order to effectively serve the interests of a small minority. Their model should be taken from the life of the early believers of which Acts 2 tells, who lived together in community and had all things in common. They would sell their possessions and goods and distribute the proceeds to all, as any had need (vv. 44–45). In following this model, they should form an alternative *polis* representing counter-cultural and counter-conventional communities where all people are invited to experience companionship and solidarity in the form of "family."[127]

As far as prosperity theology contributes to degrading the poor by claiming that their poverty is the result of their dishonoring of God and that the curse of poverty is a sign that God's pleasure does not rest on them, it must be rejected with all the contempt that such behavior demands.

Emphasis on the Sovereignty of God

The prosperity message uses as a premise that prosperity (and healing) is an integral part of the gains Jesus won for believers in the atonement and that faith is the key to realize the promise. It does not allow for exceptions; God's intention and wish is that all people should be wealthy and prosperous. It does not allow room for God's individual will for the situation believers find themselves in. In the prosperity gospel, there is nothing mysterious in God's dealings with human beings. God is in effect forced and manipulated to do what the believer desires.

Believers at times experience lightning flashes of God's sovereign love in the form of the answers to their prayers for healing and provision, while they accept the incurability of some diseases and the inevitability that some sicknesses are unto death. After all, the great giants of faith portrayed in the Bible all had to die to reach the realization of their hope. Paul left Trophimus sick (2 Tim 4:20) and enjoined Timothy to use a little wine for his stomach's sake (1 Tim 5:23), and Paul prayed three times without receiving an answer about a thorn in the flesh that he justified as necessary to harass him in order not to become too elated

---

127. See also discussion in chapter 4.

about the abundance of revelations he had received (2 Cor 12:7–9). Why all believers do not receive the same provision in their needs as others who also pray, or all are not healed is a mystery that believers cannot fathom because it has to do with the character and work of God, which is unfathomable to human beings. God cannot be boxed in with our syllogisms; God refuses to dance to believers' tunes (or faith and positive confessions, even if they are based on the Bible). There is a mystery in humans' dealings with God and humility is our best approach to unraveling some answers. The mystery of God's sovereignty requires believers to wait before God to reveal God's will for their lives and situations.

When their answers for provision and blessing on their finances and businesses are answered, it serves as a sign of the impending coming of the kingdom of God. That kingdom comes each time someone repents of sin and accepts the forgiveness available in the atonement. Other benefits presumably linked to the atonement do not necessarily realize on earth, requiring believers to keep on trusting in the God whose kingdom is still realizing.

A theological system (or prayer) that makes demands on God that are causative, in other words, that guarantees that God will always act in such and such a way due to humans who follow the correct "recipes" or formulas, is bound to eventual failure. Pentecostals emphasize and believe that theology is only possible when it is based on embodied belief, as the result of personal encounters with God and the experience of the Spirit's guidance and revelation. True theology (that also sounds true or authentic) is based on worship and adoration of the God that is met in worship. However, they confess that such encounters are taken at the initiative of God, and the same is true of answers to their prayers. There is nothing mechanistic or guaranteed in the relationship with God; as sovereign God it is God's initiative and privilege to intervene in human beings' lives.

The problem with formulas is that they are generic. However, there is nothing generic about the unique situations that characterize each human being's life. These formulas are nothing more than clichés. God may be universal, but our lives are very specific, requiring specific questions to be asked.[128]

If the supposed answers to prayers sound magical, it is nothing but magic. It is human presumption trying to force God's hand. Theological

---

128. Bowler, *Everything Happens*, 124–5.

formulas that teach that prosperity and wealth is the privilege and right of all believers deny that Paul many times went hungry and experienced shipwrecks in his pursuit to preach the gospel across many regions and that he suffered from continuous persecution. A theology that teaches that God is forced to heal all believers denies that Paul left Trophimus sick or that an aged Paul was ill at times. A theology that teaches that poverty is part of the curse of the Fall that was nullified on the cross denies that the apostles and the early church, especially in Judea, experienced poverty.

Galatians 3:1–14, containing a discussion of the law or faith, explains that people who rely on the works of the law are under a curse but Christ redeemed us from the curse of the law by becoming a curse for us in order that in Christ Jesus the blessing of Abraham might come to the Gentiles, so that we might receive the promise of the Spirit through faith (vv. 13–14). Being redeemed from the curse of the law implies being freed from sin, sickness, and poverty. The way prosperity teachers get from the curse of the law to their teaching about the inclusiveness of healing and wealth in the blessing of Abraham is by linking Galatians 3 with Deuteronomy 28. The curses mentioned in Deuteronomy 28 are identified with the curses of the law that are mentioned in Galatians 3 while the blessings of Deuteronomy are identified with the blessing mentioned by Galatians, without any good theological grounds for doing so. The curse of the law consists mainly of poverty and disease, in prosperity theology, while health and wealth are the marks of the blessing of Abraham.[129] The atonement is then brought into direct connection with healing and prosperity in this way because it brought deliverance from the curse of the law, defined as sickness, poverty, and death.

A theology of triumphalism is human-centered (and therefore popular among humans), and not centered on God and God's glory. Such theology focuses on human beings and their needs and desires, centering the self as the focus of life on earth. It consists of acquiring what humans desire rather than seeking for the glory of God, forgetting what Jesus according to Matthew 6:33 teaches: "strive first for the kingdom of God and his righteousness, and all these things will be given to you as well." It does not attend to God's plan for the lives of humans other than what God is supposed to do for the freedom from illness, poverty, disease, and death of each and every believer. Because it is based on the recitation of certain formulas that are alleged to work in all cases, it judges the amount and quality of faith by

---

129. Horn, *From Rags to Riches*, 25.

its results and consequences.[130] Because God's word is true, it must be due to a lack of faith when prayer for provision is not answered.

The prosperity message is characterized by an implied dualism with God and the devil seen as about even, although God enjoys a slight advantage over evil forces. As a good God, the Lord provides all the beautiful things in life. Everything good comes from God and every bad thing is the result of the devil's interference in God's creation and work. All trials and tribulations are ascribed to the devil and should be resisted in faith. By utilizing faith, right thinking, and positive confession, believers can live free from trials and tribulations and control their world. They rule sovereignly over their world and take control of their circumstances. What is necessary is that they know about two mutually exclusive sources of knowledge, as part of the radical dualism of the metaphysical cults that Kenyon introduced into prosperity thinking. Sense knowledge originated from the physical realm below while revelation knowledge is from the spiritual realm above.[131] Knowledge from one realm is of no value to the other realm.[132] The curse of Adam was nullified on the cross and believers reign over creation by applying the "blessings of Abraham." Such a theology does not discount the suffering and persecuted church in parts of the world where governments and other faith traditions do not allow Christians freedom of religious expression, or Christians who live in dire circumstances, not of their own choosing but for historical, political, and economic reasons. The prosperity gospel should by all rights be confined to a few countries, where populations experience a high standard of living. It is a local message applicable to only the most privileged parts of the world (if it is a privilege to be wealthy). Because it is based on materialism and consumerism, providing in the selfish desires of human beings, its God is the author of all that is good, while the devil is the author of all that is bad. And it is a religion that does not offer hope any further than

---

130. Farah, *From the Pinnacle*, 144.

131. Kenyon (*What Happened from the Cross*, 9, 12) writes that, "This book will blaze a new path . . . It uncovers many new veins of primary truth long covered by sense knowledge interpretation of the Word . . . They (the apostles) did not know what happened on the cross, or during the three days and nights before His resurrection, but we must know of these three days, for this is the thing that will build faith in us. The mystery is hidden in these three days." Kenyon continues to explain that such knowledge as he purveys originates from his revelation knowledge, that stands in direct contrast to the apostles' and evangelists' sense knowledge, as described in the New Testament.

132. McConnell, *Different Gospel*, 103.

life on earth. Its realized eschatology does not contain any elements that provide Christians with hope for eternity and it does not contain any explanation for death except as part of the curse of humanity due to their disobedience in the garden of Eden. The expectation of life after death, the resurrection and post-resurrection bodies with which believers will serve God on the new earth are absent in this theological system.

That God is sovereign means that God is supreme, all powerful, and that God possesses complete authority. It implies that Christians may trust God that the promised future would realize. In God's sovereignty, God cannot be manipulated to do anything; God controls and maintains the universe that represents the work of God's hands. God is divinely infinite and beyond human comprehension and exists outside humanity's frame of reference. Any human attempt to bring God's character under words always contains a germ of idolatry; our views of God are subject to change and the day humans' may see God will probably change their views of God completely. Our descriptions of God can become idolatrous when we create picture of God and assign characteristics to God that only exists in our minds.[133]

God cannot be made into a formula. Speaking smoothly and easily about God is nothing else than speaking easily about our views of who and what God is, that is, the God who is the creation of our minds. One can only speak about one's experience of an encounter with God with any authority, and in the encounter one always meets God as the indescribable One, emphasizing the need of the gift of speaking in tongues when one wants to relate verbally with God. God also cannot be manipulated in any way. As the holy one, God is the definition of perfection that humanity cannot express. As the eternal one, time cannot hold God and no one understands what "eternity" implies. As the sovereign one, God is the majestic ruler of the universe.

---

133. An instance of this is found in a sermon entitled, "Reversing the irreversible" by Pastor Enoch Adeboye on 16 October 2018 (https://www.youtube.com/watch?v=85b-2ED388Q; accessed 2020-01-12). He stated that one of God's attributes is God's sovereign power to control times and seasons, to stop time or turn it back, to go into the past and bring something from the past and restore it in the present, or go into the future and realize something of the future in the present. God can suspend each and every law established by God if God so wishes. This is then brought into direct relation to the audience's needs. If somebody had displaced anyone in the audience, the pastor then prophesied and proclaimed loudly that they would be displaced themselves. If an opportunity of the past was lost in the lives of the audience, God would replace it in the course of the sermon. This becomes a manipulation of God to provide in believers' needs.

Faith as Presumption

In an important early contribution to the discourse about the prosperity message, Charles Farah, who served as professor at Oral Roberts University and pastor of a charismatic church, made an important distinction between faith and presumption.[134] He asserts that a lot of what passes as faith in the Faith movement is actually presumption, an overstepping of boundaries with a forwardness that does not honor or trust God who in sovereignty rules over the world, without being confined to what people stated about God in the Bible. In terms of healing, presumption consists in the effrontery of confronting God with the claim that God promised healing in the Bible and it is claimed by the believer because God is compelled to do what God promised. That God would heal all people at all times as God's word promised and that such healing is based on Christ's act of atonement on the cross is perceived as the word or direct revelation of God. Because Christ's death on Golgotha is a historical fact, it becomes possible to "hold God to God's word," that believers would always be healed from of all their illnesses. Such a way of reasoning does not allow room that God wants to decide in each individual case how the prayer for healing is answered, whether by healing the person immediately, after a period, or gradually, or using other means to bring healing to the person, or even deciding that the illness is the way to prepare the person for entrance into the presence of God, by way of death.

In his discussion of eleven biblical references to presumption, he concludes that these texts all describe presumption as a deadly sin, in most cases so deadly that it was punishable by death, as a sin against God. For instance, in claiming that one's words were the revelation of God when that is not the case, one was liable to be punished by death (Deut 18:20). When Israel overstepped God's words and went out against their enemies when God had not them told them to do so, they were destroyed (Num 14:44).

In terms of the current church, presumption can be defined as the sin that particularly tempts bold, courageous people with faith who in their eagerness to accomplish great things for God overstep the boundaries, claiming falsely (in many cases, because they deceive themselves as well) that they have received a revelation from God.[135] Even Jesus was tempted to act presumptuously, when the devil took him to the pinnacle

---

134. Farah, *From the Pinnacle*, 4.
135. Farah, *From the Pinnacle*, 21.

of the temple and dared him to throw himself down, because it would have served as an excellent publicity stunt. "You can do it because you trust in God, and God will carry you down safely." Farah emphasizes that God never performs miracles to prove that God is God, but to meet the needs of believers and for God's own glory.

In conversation with the devil, Jesus demonstrates according to Matthew 4:4–10 the importance of never reading a specific Scripture without comparing it to the rest.[136] The best way to explicate the Bible is to compare the Bible with itself. In the case of each individual temptation, Jesus answers the devil's arguments, in one case even based on a quotation from Scripture, with a balanced view of Scripture. He emphasizes the importance not to test God, even though he is the son of God. Presumption would have implied that he takes a general provision of the Bible quoted by the devil, "for it is written, 'He will command his angels concerning you,' and 'On their hands they will bear you up, so that you will not dash your foot against a stone'" (Matt 4:6), and applies it to a specific situation where God had not spoken.

An example of how prosperity teachers' abuse the Bible is in their interpretation of Hebrews 1:14 as referring to ministering angels placed at the disposal of believers and subject to their command. The context, however, clearly explains that "sent to render service for" should rather be rendered "sent to render service for the benefit of."[137]

Farah makes a distinction in line with pentecostal thinking between a general word of God as found in the Bible, and a specific word of God received by the individual through an insight generated by the mysterious work on the Spirit in the person, and applicable to a specific situation.[138] The first refers to a specific provision in Scripture

---

136. If only a few verses are used to form the basis of a specific doctrine, polygamy or polyandry can be justified from the Bible. Israel's patriarchs without exception were, after all, polygamists. When the apparent acceptance of polygamy by parts of the Old Testament is compared to the rest, for instance, the creation narratives, and Jesus' and Paul's teaching about marriage, it is clear that monogamy represents the biblical ideal. It is important that the Bible should be read as a whole, and from a Christological perspective because Christians confess that Jesus is to be Lord of their lives; they are striving to understand and do his will. Humility is needed to do so; pride in thinking that one has found the final truth is presumptuous. Many African Christians found it difficult to understand why missionaries prohibited polygamy that was prevalent in African culture if their God allowed the patriarchs to do so.

137. Keener, *Spirit Hermeneutics*, 272.

138. Farah, *From the Pinnacle*, 25. Farah refers to the first as *logos* and the second as *rhema*, a distinction between two terms that in New Testament usage does not hold

The Solution

and applicable to a specific historical situation, and the second to an experiential, existentialist appropriation of that word in an individual sense. While Pentecostals believe that the Bible contains God's words, they also teach that a specific revelation in the Bible first needs to be applied to their situation through the work of the Spirit before it becomes God's specific revelation for their circumstances.

To claim that everything promised in Isaiah 53 in relation to the atonement of Christ is applicable to all believers in all situations, is to deny that God in God's sovereignty has a specific will for the life of each individual believer (and human being) that God unfolds with or without the cooperation of the individual involved. The believer's task is not to tell God what to do, based on the promises found in the Bible, but to wait upon the Lord to reveal God's will in order to appropriate it and cooperate with God as far as it is possible.

Farah compares the benefits in the atonement to medication designed to be released at properly spaced intervals to be effective.[139] In the current dispensation, the benefit of salvation is universal for those who repent and receive Jesus as Savior and Lord. The other benefits are released at times, but most will have to await the arrival of the new age to realize for all people. The kingdom has come, bringing salvation to all who call on the name of the Lord, but it is also still coming, bringing perfect wholeness to all only when the new heaven and earth will dawn. For some, the medication for healing and wholeness has not been released, and without exception all believers would have to die, except those who will be alive at the moment of Christ's second coming.

When God is held captive to the promises found in the Bible and encapsulated in a word-trap in an attempt to manipulate God to do what the believer desires, as prosperity preachers do, God is no longer the Lord of the universe. To use the words of the song of praise ascribed to Nebuchadnezzar in Daniel 4 after the king ignored the interpretation of his dream by Daniel and he was humiliated to live like an animal: The Most High's sovereignty is an everlasting sovereignty, and God's kingdom endures from generation to generation. Before God all the inhabitants of the earth are accounted as nothing. This God does what God wills with the host of heaven, how much more with the inhabitants of the earth, and there is no one who can stay God's hand or ask God, "What are you

---

water. See also discussion in chapters 3 and 4.

139. Farah, *From the Pinnacle*, 35.

doing?" (vv. 34–35). Important is that the king confesses that his presumption was based on pride, and he had to learn the hard way that God was able to bring low those who walk in pride (v. 36).

God cannot be held captive to some words written about God or ascribed to God by human beings, even though the words are found in the Bible. As Creator of the universe, God's decisions determine everything that exists in the temporary, visible and the eternal, invisible world. It is not doubted that the Bible contains some words of God (as well as words about God), but these words need to be enlivened by the energizing power of the Spirit before believers can build their faith for God's intervention in their current situation on it. God is Lord of the Bible as well.

A Caring Church

Africa views prosperity and poverty as spiritual phenomena, as it does with all other aspects of life. When one is prosperous, it is due to spiritual forces looking favorably on one; the prosperous are experiencing God's blessings. When one suffers from poverty, it is due to the same forces that are bound to destroy one's status and value in society. What is needed is that one should consult someone who can negotiate a process to appease the spiritual forces and convince them to act favorably to the benefit of the victim. In the past African traditional religion offered such services (and still offers them) at a price, in the form of the practice of witchdoctors and medicine men. In some parts of African Pentecostalism this practice was appropriated and applied to the ministry of the prophet, ministering prosperity and healing (sometimes also at a price) through the ministry and rituals of deliverance and exorcism that require the cooperation of the victim. The effect is that victims are not (partly or wholly) responsible for the circumstances in which they find themselves and they do not have to take responsibility for and are not held accountable for their own contribution to these circumstances and its solution. Responsibility is shifted onto the shoulders of the prophet who would take care of the scapegoats of poverty and ensure a prosperous future.

A further effect of this practice is that the Christian church is deprived of the opportunity to take responsibility for the poor and underprivileged but contributes to their further marginalization and disenfranchisement by its contribution to the institutionalization of poverty. Prosperity teachers do not respond in any proactive way to the existential needs of the societies in which they exist, and for which they are responsible, if the example of the early Christian church is to be followed. At the same time, its emphasis on individual success implies and requires its silence about economic injustices built into the neo-capitalist economic policies *per se* and the social marginalization as its result, and it does not develop a theological analysis of society and the inequalities that it breeds.[140] Some non-Christian traditions that it took over from Africa and that probably contributed to its success by contextualizing Pentecostalism to the African mind and accommodating African primal spirituality have also become a stumbling block in the realization of one of the important reasons why the church exists, to take care of the needy in its midst in practical ways.

It is submitted that the African prosperity movement in its diversified forms needs to revisit some of their theological perspectives and re-examine their traditions and practices in order to identify, recognize, and overhaul whatever is non-Christian and irreconcilable with the gospel but has gained access to the movement's theology.[141] To refer to one instance, its personalization of all evil, including poverty and illness, and that leads to further impoverishment of Africans with its inhibiting tendencies and beliefs and that tends to create conditions for idleness, laziness, and inefficiency in people urgently needs to be reconsidered.[142]

Thinandavha Mashau and Mookgo Kgatle suggest that in its reconsideration of its theology, the prosperity movement may consider *ubuntu* as an alternative to their prosperity theology.[143] *Ubuntu* as a form of indigenous knowledge and traditional African philosophy is an excellent resource in their opinion for bolstering African identity and empowerment, in the context of globalization and glocalization. Africans need to rediscover their own voice and use it to contribute to their own well-being as well as the well-being of their countries, the African continent, and the planet. In contrast, in preaching the prosperity message and applying its principles, it is only the prosperity teachers who benefit, at the cost of their adherents.

The concept *ubuntu* became famous after retired Archbishop Desmond Tutu utilized it. It is a unifying vision or worldview enshrined in

---

140. Mashau and Kgatle, "Prosperity Gospel and the Culture of Greed."
141. Quayesi-Amakye, "Prosperity and Prophecy," 304.
142. Quayesi-Amakye, "Prosperity and Prophecy," 305.
143. Mashau and Kgatle. "Prosperity Gospel and the Culture of Greed."

African philosophy in different ways and languages. The Nguni people teach that *umuntu ngumuntu ngabantu*, or "a person is a person through other persons;" the Kikuyu equivalent is *mundu ni mundu ni undu wa andu*, or "a human being is a person because of the other people;" the Sotho idiom is *motho ke motho ka batho ba bang*; or *munhu munhu nekuda kwevanhu* in the language of the Shona people of Zimbabwe.

The principle is the same, that it is only through interaction with fellow human beings that one discovers one's humanity and human qualities. Humanity is affirmed when there is acknowledgement of others' humanity. One's humanity is inextricably caught up in other people. We are human beings because we belong.[144] In governance the implication is that the ruler can only rule in consultation with the people, and in Christian ministry it implies that all people should be welcomed and heard because the pastor can only lead the congregation in consultation with the congregants. When this becomes the case, and the other principles of *ubuntu* like benevolence, thoughtfulness, compassion, and caring for others are applied, *ubuntu* becomes an excellent antidote to the culture of greed and selfish enrichment of a few individuals established in the prosperity gospel.[145] *Ubuntu* encourages persons to open themselves to others, to learn from them, to stand in their shoes and imagine their life situation, and to reach out and care for them. It highlights other values than the prosperity message with its values of capital, self-interest, and individual autonomy. It defines the abundant life (John 10:10) in other terms than the accumulation of capital, monopolization, hoarding, and concentration of wealth, power and economic possibilities, when the group gets priority over the individual while at the same time establishing the climate for the blossoming of the individual.[146] The thief that comes to steal, kill, and destroy is not specifically the devil but rather anyone who exploits the sheep for their own interest (see John 10:1, 8, 12). The context of the passage is the Pharisees who expelled a believer from the synagogue (9:34-41) and their behavior exemplified the thief referred to in John 10.[147]

The prosperity movement needs a theology of social and economic justice to quicken its conscience because, as has been argued, its exclusive

---

144. Munyaneza, "'Ubuntu'", 101.

145. The Christian church needs to further develop an African theology and prophetic politics of *ubuntu* as an antidote to the greed displayed by many politicians in Africa as well.

146. Mashau and Kgatle. "Prosperity Gospel and the Culture of Greed."

147. Keener, *Spirit Hermeneutics*, 272.

interest in wealth and prosperity deafens its ears for the desperate cries of the poor in Africa, some of whom are the victims of systemic political, social and economic injustices and inequalities. It has the potential to do so and it has occurred in some cases, as Isabelle Barker explains.[148] In developing countries some neo-Pentecostal churches have come to function as non-state sites addressing social needs that have gone unmet by the state due to a combination of factors. Only when this becomes the rule will neo-pentecostal theology become infused with hope for the future, an eschatological hope that accepts responsibility to establish conditions for the survival of the planet in the face of the crisis of global warming and the possibility that the planet might become uninhabitable for some (or even all) of its citizens.[149] This eschatological hope will also stretch across the chasm of the present and the coming age; it was suggested that the absolute realized eschatology of the prosperity message provides no hope for believers in terms of the certainty of death. Instead of taking from their adherents, prosperity teachers need to give them real hope by being compassionate and attending to their needs, in the spirit of *ubuntu*.[150] Then the prosperity movement will be empowered to dedicate its energies and finances to social and structural transformation and overcoming the evils of capitalism, because it has discovered a desire and passion for social justice.[151]

This is already happening to a certain extent, as Barker shows, with many African neo-Pentecostal churches having become involved in education, skills training programs, and the development of an ethics of hard work as imperative factors to address social misery.[152] In recognition of these contributions, Peter Berger refers to Pentecostalism as a potential positive resource for modern economic development.[153] See, for example, the PEACE program initiated by Rick Warren of Saddleback Church in

148. Barker, "Charismatic Economies," 409.

149. In dozens of countries, heatwaves are bringing the highest temperatures since measurements began while Arctic freezes bring the lowest. Tropical storms, unprecedented in frequency and strength, are displacing a record number of people. Ecosystems are collapsing at a terrifying rate while carbon emissions, the root cause of the devastation, continue to peak (https://mail.google.com/mail/u/0/#inbox/FMfcgxwGCQfqNfGjRFZwGMGsvgPkccJC; accessed 2019-12-24).

150. Mashau, "Reimagining Mission," 7.

151. Nyengele, "Cultivating Ubuntu," 19.

152. Barker, "Charismatic Economies;" Heuser, "Charting African Prosperity Gospel Economies," 6.

153. Berger, *Faith and Development*, 5.

California in 2005 (that empowers believers to plant a church or partner with an existing one, equip local leaders, assist the poor, care for the sick, and educate the next generation). Another example is the empowerment of participants with entrepreneurial skills, modern management techniques, and marketing strategies, in the cooperation between American televangelist Bill Winston of Living Word Christian Center (Chicago) and Nigerian mega-church ministry of Samuel Adeyemi of Daystar Christian Center in Lagos.[154] Donald Miller and Tetsunao Yamamori assert that some of the most innovative social programs in the world are being initiated by fast-growing Pentecostal churches, and refer to Prophet T.B. Joshua's ministry that cares for orphans, widows, elderly and physically challenged people, persons afflicted with disease, including HIV and Aids; offers educational scholarships; establishes rehabilitation centers for criminals and ex-militants from Niger Delta, and other humanitarian activities.[155] In 1988 Joshua was awarded with the Order of the Federal Republic for his initiatives.

These actions are usually "under the radar," to use the title of a study of the Centre for Development and Enterprise, situated in Johannesburg, South Africa in which Peter Berger and James Hunter participated to research the influence of Pentecostalism on economic development.[156] The authors assert that these churches are leading a silent revolution associated with attitudes, habits, and dispositions that promote market-led growth, serving as an unacknowledged social force.[157] They promote drive and determination that create a change in members' attitudes, encouraging and empowering entrepreneurship and practical life skills with a focus on hard work, savings, investment, organizing skills, etc.[158] However, Dronen is correct in observing that it cannot be stated as yet whether the Pentecostal movement as a whole will bring economic growth through capital ventures to struggling economies in Africa because it is too early to evaluate its potential positive influence.[159]

---

154. Heuser, "Charting African Prosperity Gospel Economies," 8.

155. Miller and Yamamori, *Global Pentecostalism*, 6.

156. "Under the Radar: Pentecostalism in South Africa and its Potential Social and Economic Role," 2008. https://www.cde.org.za/under-the-radar-Pentecostalism-in-south-africa-and-its-potential-social-and-economic-role/; accessed 2020-01-22.

157. "Under the Radar," 9.

158. See also Gifford and Nogueira-Godsey, "Protestant Ethic," 11-2.

159. Dronen, "Weber, Prosperity and the Protestant Ethic," 334.

There are some prosperity teachers in Africa that preach what Nimi Wariboko calls the "excellence model," although they are in the minority.[160] Their prosperity gospel stresses the importance of human efforts in the process, while attributing poverty to mismanagement and laziness.[161] That Peter Berger is positive about the prosperity movement can be ascribed to the influence of these leaders that he calls "intentional Weberians," whose faith in divine success is always paired with an emphasis on doing one's best.[162]

Christians and Giving

Most Pentecostals support the theological stance that Christians do not keep all the laws contained in the *Torah* of Moses. Their lives as believers are not qualified by keeping the moral, ceremonial, and purity requirements that Israel was supposed to maintain to illustrate God's holiness with their lifestyle that set them apart from their neighbors. However, traditionally the "principle" of tithing, one of the cultural provisions on the Mosaic law, was taught by Pentecostals since its earliest years, and many times tithing was motivated by using Malachi 3 without considering its historical and textual context. Malachi 3 is interpreted to teach that by not giving one's tithes, believers rob God with the result that God curses their possessions and provisions, and they are impoverished as a result. On the contrary, believers are invited to test God. When they bring the full tithe into the storehouse, so that there may be food in God's house, they find that God opens the windows of heaven for them and pour down for them an overflowing blessing. Many testimonies among Pentecostals emphasize the blessings that people experienced who put the "principle" of Malachi 3 to the test. However, the Malachian tithe is a part of the Mosaic lawgiving concerned with the ceremonial regulation of the tabernacle service; if Christians are taught to obey this command they should also be empowered to obey the rest of the ceremonial lawgiving in order to be consistent.

While it is true that no congregation can survive without access to financial resources, however, it is suggested that Pentecostals should revisit the way believers are taught to donate generously to the ministry of the

---

160. Wariboko, "Pentecostal Paradigms," 41-4.
161. Haynes, "'Zambia Shall Be Saved!,'" 18-9.
162. Berger, "'You Can Do It!'"

congregation. It is probably true to state that Pentecostals with their traditional emphasis on tithing as a means to unlock God's blessings partly established the climate in which the prosperity message would flourish since the 1970s. And an important reason why many Pentecostals accept the prosperity teaching without further consideration is that the motif of giving sounds the same as in their classical pentecostal tradition.

Hebrews 7 is a good starting point in reconsidering financial donations to the work of the ministry. Melchizedek received Abraham's tithe of the spoils of war, but it should be kept in mind that this was a one-time event. It is probably true that Abraham gave the tithe as a way to show his reverence for the king of the city state under whose jurisdiction he fell. It might even be true that it was expected of him while he was staying as a visitor of, and at the mercy of the king. To make of Abraham's tithe to Melchizedek a principle that all believers through the ages should apply is to abuse the text for own reasons, and in the process to ignore the unique historical context of the specific text (in Gen 14:16–20).

There is no biblical command that Christians are to pay tithes to the Melchizedek priesthood. All Christians, like Jesus Christ, are the Melchizedek priesthood (according to Heb 5:6, 10; 6:20; 7:11, 15, 17, 21; 1 Pet 2:5–9). Hebrews 7 contains no evidence to support the injunction that Christians must tithe. The author's intention is not to provide any regulation concerning tithing among Christian believers but to show the superiority of the Melchizedek priesthood, as developed by the author, over the Levitical priesthood, and the superiority of God's revelation in Christ to the revelation in the giving of the law at Sinai. The New Testament does not contain any regulations concerning tithing, and even Paul who had a lot to say about donations for the sake of the poor in Judea did not say anything about tithing or even giving to the church. Giving to him was exclusively for the sake of the poor and impoverished.

Tithing may be a workable and practical principle of giving in order to help the local congregation to survive, contribute to the care of the poor and needy, and finance the church's outreach with the gospel to the unreached. However, it cannot be presented as a part of the new covenant brought about by Christ's death. It cannot be motivated from the New Testament when Christians are taught to tithe. Preaching tithing as a way to earn eternal life or as a means to get rich is to abuse the Bible for what it did not intend to say.

It can be stated that the injunctions in the Old Testament about tithing are not valid for Christians, unless they accept that Christian believers should maintain the Mosaic law in all its aspects, including the rest of the laws determining the priestly service at the temple as well as all the other cultic and purity regulations. Teaching the Old Testament custom of tithing is not consistent with pentecostal teaching about the law in the Old Testament; it is not acceptable that one regulation that suits the church can be taught while the rest are simply ignored. This is not consistent theology.

The laws in the Old Testament concerning tithes do not have the intention to motivate believers to give generously. Christian giving is not a legal obligation but a matter of living generously in terms of one's time, energy, and finances as a means of expressing one's gratitude toward God for the gifts provided generously for believers in Christ and the Spirit. Christians share their lives with other people, showing a predilection for investing in the lives of the poor and needy people, because they love God who through Christ provided the means for them in pursuing the only goal in life that brings happiness that is temporary as well as eternal, to live for the glory of God.[163] Christians use Christ as their example of generosity and offer themselves and what they own to Christ and the service of others, sharing in his prejudice to be with and provide for the marginalized and disenfranchised, the poor and needy.

John Wesley states that Christians should not fall short of Pharisees when it comes to doing good to other people. "Give alms of all thou dost possess. Is any hungry? Feed them. Is he athirst? Give him drink. Naked? Cover him with a garment. If thou hast this world's goods, do not limit thy beneficence to a scanty proportion. Be merciful to the uttermost of thy power."[164] Christians respond like Zacchaeus to Christ's love for them, by giving half of their goods to the poor and restoring whatever they took from others fourfold (Luke 19:8). Giving stems as an instinctual reaction to the needs of others from a heart that is dedicated to God. It does not need the persuasions of men with self-seeking tricks to motivate the involvement of believers with the poor, and giving is not only tailored to the needs of the local congregation. "Giving is done through a heart

---

163. Especially the Gospel of Luke is characterized by its option and predilection for the poor, as liberation theology in Africa emphasizes. Prosperity teaching de-spiritualizes poverty and money has become a dominant part of the imagery and a legitimate aspect in neo-pentecostal church structures (Heuser, "Charting African Prosperity Gospel Economies," 3).

164. See also 1 John 3:17. Quoted in Ntui-Abung, *Chaos of the Prosperity Gospel*, 49-50 from the Authorised Version.

that is always ready with a loving desire to lose even its most precious goods and kindred for Him alone. This is the kind of giving that is recommended for Christians."[165]

Conclusion

In this chapter, the proprium of the prosperity message was first described, in their faith theology of formulas and recipes that enables believers to "manipulate" God to provide in their desires. It is this proprium in its hermeneutics that is being applied in the evaluation of the proclamation of the prosperity gospel in Africa. Some practical and theological considerations from a classical pentecostal perspective were then evaluated in terms of the practice of the prosperity movement, its leadership styles, financial models, involvement (or lack of involvement) in economic, societal, and ecological challenges, work ethics, ecological concerns, and its complicity in subjugating women in the traditional African patriarchal society.

This then led to theological considerations that were evaluated as far as it differs from the pentecostal (and Protestant) theological standards, such as the movement's hermeneutical angle, its teaching of revelation knowledge, lack of emphasis on the sovereignty of God, a discussion of definitions of faith and prosperity, and the importance of generous giving that the New Testament seemingly expects of Christians in general. First and foremost, it was important to describe the hermeneutic and underlying epistemology of prosperity theology, in the form of unique revelation knowledge. It was argued that it is not enough that only some doctrines of the prosperity message should be revisited but the question should be asked, why does a part of Pentecostalism support the prosperity message of neo-Pentecostals at all, since it seems to be foreign to the better part of classical pentecostal theology? Several reasons can be given but it is argued that the most important of these reasons is because of a new pentecostal hermeneutics that sneaked into the movement when Pentecostalism and Evangelicalism joined forces during the 1940s and 1950s. Today probably the majority of Pentecostals interpret the Bible in a biblicist and literalist manner, implying that texts are at times lifted out of their literary and historical contexts and applied to the current situation without considering its validity for a new situation in a world that differs radically in some respects from the biblical world. Because the

---

165. Ntui-Abung, *Chaos of the Prosperity Gospel*, 50.

Bible is viewed as authoritative, with all texts valued on the same level, it becomes possible to read texts into current situations without necessarily realizing its appropriateness and applicability for the new context.

Prosperity theology accepts this hermeneutic of literalism and emphasizes it in its preaching and teaching, but then goes further and establishes the possibility of revelation knowledge, that refers to transcendent, ultra-sensory, and supra-sensory knowledge that is supposed to exist in the realm above sense knowledge, and which enables human beings to transcend the limitations of sense knowledge and act in faith. The doctrine of revelation knowledge represents the epistemology of the prosperity message. Its definition of faith is also defined in terms of its epistemology: real faith is acting upon the Word independently of any sense evidence—that is, believing without seeing. Faith demands that the believer acts solely upon revelation knowledge to the total exclusion of sense knowledge. A result of revelation knowledge is the belief that one can receive perfect knowledge of God and unerring guidance from the Spirit. God can be comprehended in terms of certain laws or principles according to which God operates and when human beings apply these laws, their desires will all be met consistently. The goal of prosperity theology is the transformation of the human being into a god; believers can be transformed into incarnations of God, that implies that believers are deified. While human nature was divine before the Fall in the garden of Eden, it became demonic after the Fall. Humans' Fall resulted in Satan becoming a god and ruling creation by legal right. In order to recapture creation, God had to deal with Satan justly by paying him a ransom. This required that Jesus died two deaths on the cross, a spiritual and physical death. Prosperity theology clearly represents a view of man, the Fall and its results, and Christ and his death that is not biblical and acceptable to pentecostal theology.

Prosperity teaching consists on the one hand of an egocentric type that promises success and prosperity from God to those who contribute generously, promising success and prosperity to those who know the spiritual laws of the universe that govern the spiritual realm; and on the other hand a cosmic type that centers on universal principles that God has set up in the cosmos. However, all prosperity teachers share in the message that there are spiritual laws that govern prosperity in the universe, and those with knowledge of the laws can ensure enormous prosperity and wealth as a result of applying it. By using faith as a means to speak wealth into reality, believers write their own ticket because God is compelled to provide in whatever they desire from God. This is the God-kind of faith, applying the principle that God spoke creation into existence by the power of God's words and positive confession.

The God of prosperity preachers is a supernatural deity that exists for the exclusive pleasure and benefit of humankind, linking directly to individualism, materialism, self-centeredness, the urge to search for all pleasures possible for humankind, etc., that characterize the mind-set of some Western consumers. The God of prosperity resides in heavens as a cosmic banker, to exclusively serve the interests of human beings. True power is accessed not by looking upward but by turning inward; the believer gets identified with the deity, implying that the faith message is also able to change one's consciousness about oneself.

What passes as faith in the Faith movement is actually presumption, representing an overstepping of boundaries It states that because Christ's death on Golgotha is a historical fact, it becomes possible to hold God to God's word, that believers would always be healed from of all their illnesses and would always be prosperous and wealthy. Such a way of reasoning does not allow room that the sovereign God deals with each individual case in unique manner.

It was also suggested that the prosperity movement should consider *ubuntu* as an alternative to their prosperity theology. *Ubuntu* states that it is only through interaction with fellow human beings that one discovers one's humanity and human qualities. Humanity is affirmed when there is acknowledgement of others' humanity. One's humanity is inextricably caught up in other people. We are human beings because we belong. What is needed is a theology of social and economic justice because its exclusive interest in wealth and prosperity deafens the movement's ears for the desperate cries of the poor and impoverished in Africa, and disqualifies it from addressing systemic political, social and economic injustices and inequalities. A new philosophy will also lead to a new emphasis on the church as a caring community that exists for the sake of the poor and needy, as well as a new motivation for giving, not primarily to serve the interests of leaders and their ministries, but to facilitate social and economic equality between believers as a sign of the coming of the kingdom and to reach the ends of the world with the good message of Jesus Christ who died so that human beings may live.

Concluding Summary and Recommendations

Summary

THE STUDY LOOKED AT the widespread proclamation and acceptance of the prosperity message in Africa due to several reasons. One of the most important of these reasons is that pentecostal spirituality and African traditional religion share certain features that define primal spirituality, resulting in the acceptance of Pentecostalism by many Africans and the establishment of certain practices that contain Africans' spiritual needs. Pentecostalism's emphasis on a holistic spirituality accommodates an African feature. The prophet in both traditions plays an important role and the modern prophet facilitates reconciliation with evil forces and angry ancestors that cause natural catastrophes and personal problems, as the diviners and witchdoctors did (and still do) in traditional Africa. Lastly, the emphasis on prosperity in neo-Pentecostalism also has a unique African flavor, where an enchanted worldview relates poverty and prosperity to a visible and invisible world, which are influencing each other. The essence of neo-Pentecostalism consists of the spiritual, with an emphasis on the Holy Spirit and spirit beings that directly influence the circumstances of people living in Africa, and the necessity for mediation and appropriation of these forces. African pentecostal spirituality also links with the New Testament's enchanted worldview.

The angle used in the study is the new pentecostal hermeneutics that developed in the last half century. Initially, in early Pentecostalism most believers had no theological training and they read the Bible as literally as possible, taking it at face value, in the process at times collapsing the distance between the original context of Scripture and their own context. Significantly, however, their interpretation was informed by their encounters with God and charismatic experiences so that the language of the Bible determined their discourse in testimonies about their adventures with God. They did not ascribe authority to the Bible due to its inerrancy or infallibility, but to its utility of showing the way to a personal encounter with God. The Bible served to provide them with an indication of ways that God still intervened in the lives of present-day believers (continuationism). They used their experiential lens to interpret the Bible. In the process they did not move from the Bible to their context, but from their context of encounters with the Spirit of God to the Bible, in order to find what God did for people of faith in the past, and taking it back to their context with the expectation that those biblical experiences would be repeated in their lives in some form or another.

Since the 1930s and 1940s, however, many classical Pentecostals joined hands with Evangelicalism, accepting also its more conservative hermeneutical values and principles, and resulting in the view that the Bible presents believers with changeless commands and timeless truths that should be read literally and that are valid for all times. All texts were placed on the same level and accorded with the same authority, as words that came from the mouth of God, to be taken at face value and containing historical and existential truth. The Bible was viewed as the infallible and inerrant word of God.

Since the 1970s, pentecostal scholarship started defining a new pentecostal hermeneutic in terms of the preferences found among early Pentecostals, accepting that the Spirit still speaks today, and has more to say than just Scripture, although it is consistently emphasized that the Spirit will always echo, confirm, and cite Scripture. Their epistemology was not based primarily in the Bible but in knowing God and directly experiencing God. This hermeneutic is based on the anticipation that the Spirit can be discovered in all of life, and the Bible is seen as a performative book, with the expectation that the events in the Bible is to be re-enacted today. The present is interpreted in terms of the past, Christian life in terms of biblical narratives, and charismatic experiences in terms of the earliest church and their encounters with the power of God.

The prosperity message originated in the non-pentecostal world of mind-cure, positive thinking, self-help, and success literature as part of the New Thought movement. There is no direct historical link between Pentecostalism and prosperity theology, despite widespread equation between the two in current perceptions. Faith theology and the prosperity movement can be traced historically to cultic sources, with E.W. Kenyon, a non-Pentecostal Methodist minister who left the church and founded

Concluding Summary and Recommendations 273

several churches which he linked to the Baptist church. In his many publications he combined New Thought with the help of Ralph Waldo Emerson's philosophical idealism, Swedish mystic Emmanuel Swedenborg's Neoplatonic theory of correspondence, Helena Blavatsky's theosophical quest for uniform spiritual laws, Phineas Parkhurst Quimby's mind thought ideas and its relation to healing, and Mary Baker Eddy's insight of the power of the mind over the body in Christian Science.

The prosperity gospel teaches that to produce the required results, in the form of what one desires in terms of health, wealth, success, and well-being, one should make contact with the power of God, to turn it on, and to believe that the power is coming into use. One should accept this power by faith, acting as though it has already happened. One needs to confess one's faith that the power of God can be accessed to provide in everything the believer may need and desire. For that reason, what we think and express in words bring about in our life and affairs whatever we put into them. The law of faith is the contract that secured the Christian benefits earned on the cross for Christians, providing all the rights and privileges that Adam had initially enjoyed in the Garden, and serving as the warranty deed that everything believers can hope for is at last theirs. The believer's faith has the divine right to "compel" God to give them their hearts' desires, even if God would not want to. Prosperity gospel added that invisible faith can also be transformed into financial rewards; in fact, prosperity is God's will for all believers, in the same sense that God provided for a restored relationship of the believers with God, through Christ's act of atonement. Prosperity and health are two sides of the same coin. The rules of prosperity are: pay tithes and first fruits; expect financial miracles on a daily basis; and think positively. Prosperity must follow one when one applies these spiritual laws consistently.

Since the 1970s, the neo-Pentecostal independent churches movement originated, centered around prophets and apostles as an authoritarian form of governance, and eventually leading to Network Christianity with its emphasis on the reinstitution of the office of the apostle, influencing Christianity on a wide front today, including African Pentecostalism. This successful movement also accepted the prosperity gospel. It is necessary for the Pentecostal movement to rethink its viewpoint on the current office of prophet and apostle in the light of the influence that the New Apostolic Reformation is exercising on it, and evaluate the practice from a classical pentecostal perspective. Although Pentecostals traditionally believe that the gift of apostle is still given to the church with the purpose to facilitate the missional nature of the church, if it implies a new form of governance with ultimate powers given to the individual, then the office cannot be accepted as a continuation of the New Testament occurrence of apostles. The office of the apostle was already emphasized in a movement, the Latter Rain in the 1940s, that led to a schism in many Pentecostal denominations. Apostles in New Testament terms were anointed by the Spirit, recognized by the local church and empowered by the church to take the gospel to the unreached. It was suggested that the designation "apostle" should rather be avoided because of its use in the Latter Rain movement, the Catholic Apostolic Church, the New Apostolic Church, the Apostolic Church, and the New Apostolic Reformation, although the function should be maintained.

The prosperity movement agrees with most of the doctrines of the Pentecostal movement (and Protestantism as such). Here attention will be given to those aspects in which they differ from both the pentecostal and broader Protestant traditions. These differences are critical because it is directly related to what can be described as the heart of the gospel. Firstly, prosperity teachers' view of God and the Bible differs from the pentecostal and Protestant views in several critical aspects in the application of their faith, although their theoretical confessions about God largely agree with Protestant orthodoxy. The relationship between God and the Bible is described in almost pantheistic terms. God and God's word is one. The Bible is not a history or testimony of revelation, but a textbook of laws and rules for success that works in an almost magical way when they are applied. The main view of God is that God intends believers to have all the best things in life, including health and wealth. God is the owner of a heavenly storehouse with unlimited supplies and God has passed the key to believers. What believers should do, is to appropriate these riches that belong to them by speaking, living, and acting like rich and healthy people of longevity. The faith formulas are ways to manipulate and use the presumed rules and principles laid down by a deistic god, to be identified with the impersonal force of the metaphysical cults, who becomes nothing more than a puppet of those who know the formulas and spiritual laws of how to control god. A deistic god provides the opportunity for believers to create their own circumstances by means of the manipulation of that god with their faith.

A second theological presupposition of neo-Pentecostals is found in their anthropology and Christology. The doctrine of the spiritual death of Christ originated with E.W. Kenyon who teaches that Jesus had left his

Concluding Summary and Recommendations 275

divine nature in heaven when he became a human being, implying that he was nothing more than an empowered man by the Holy Spirit. His death on the cross was not God's final work of atonement, but only served to demonstrate his defeat because he received the nature of Satan and it took a struggle for three days in hell before he eventually conquered the powers of evil and God declared him righteous. When he was resurrected from the dead, be became the first human being to be born again. The logical consequence of the teaching of the spiritual death of Christ is that Jesus was not a sinless substitute for sinners, but a substitutive sinner. As a result of his death and victory, the believer now becomes a sinless creature who enjoys the divine privileges of health, wealth, happiness, and prosperity, and human beings are upgraded to the level of God, while Jesus is simultaneously downgraded. He became sin so that believers could become divine. Its Christology is not well developed because of an overemphasis in the movement on the effects of the atonement for the believer, with all light falling on believers and their rights and privileges on earth, rather than on Christ. Their new identity allows believers into a complete union with God; they become as much an incarnation of God as Jesus Christ was. All Christians are gods.

A last theological presupposition is concerned with the basic pentecostal doctrine of revelation that prosperity preachers in theory accept. Pentecostals leave room for a direct "word from the Lord," but also accept the Bible as the last and final authority, subjecting extra-biblical revelations to the Bible. In prosperity teachers' practice, however, revelation serves a different function and direct words from God received by the prophets are overemphasized, according authority to prophets that do not leave room for any questioning or criticizing of their teaching and behavior from the side of their adherents. Their words are placed on the exact same level as the revelation in the Bible, and their interpretation of passages from Scripture is viewed as authoritative, while they apply the Bible in a mechanical manner. Revelation knowledge has become the hermeneutical principle with which they interpret the Bible, found, for instance, in their idea of what the final part of the pattern of salvation consisted of, in the spiritual death of Jesus and his stay in hell, that was not revealed to any of the authors of the New Testament. The teachings that deviate from traditional theology are ascribed to revelation knowledge and its "accuracy" is guaranteed by the prophets' and apostles' claim to have received it directly from God.

The African prosperity gospel is characterized by a unique definition of poverty in terms of a traditional African enchanted worldview, where evil spirits serve as the sole cause of poverty, paralyzing adherents to face and address the real causes of poverty and causing a lack of any contribution to social change in Africa, and an overselling of the miraculous. This emphasis results in a potential disillusionment among prosperity's adherents; a destabilization of community life as a result of the exclusive focus on the preacher as a sole recipient of revelation; and the potential of abuses, scandals, and corruption, due to a lack of ethical accountability.

The basic difference between Protestantism and the Pentecostal movement, including the prosperity movement, is that Protestantism accepts a cessationist viewpoint, that God's direct dealings and immediate involvement with humankind and direct dictation ceased somewhere during the course of the first century, leaving no room for divine intervention, signs, wonders, healings, deliverances, and other miracles. The pentecostal continuationist perspective, in contrast, reads the Bible with the expectation that the same God who revealed God's power and grace still works in the same way in the contemporary world. It was suggested that the proprium, consisting of the essence or core of its faith, is the fourfold or fivefold full gospel, of Christ as savior, healer, Spirit-baptizer, sanctifier, and coming King. Prosperity theology shares all these emphasis, except the last one, of Christ as coming King, and its emphasis on *glossolalia* as a sign of Spirit-baptism is also reduced. Prosperity's realized eschatology that forms an essential element of prosperity theology prevents them from placing the same emphasis on eschatology as confessed among Pentecostals. The common ground between the two groups, however, it was submitted, seems to be substantial enough to guarantee and require cooperation between the two groups and an ongoing dialogue.

Prosperity theology's proprium also contains a specific emphasis on faith as a mechanism at the disposal of believers that promises to make believers healthy, wealthy, and victorious, because healing and prosperity are provided for in the atonement, alongside forgiveness of sin, as a prerequisite for a restored relationship with God, and it is the will of God for all believers without exception. However, the teaching of faith formulas and positive confession affects one's concept of the sovereignty of God, changing God into a deistic and manipulable god, and deifies the believers at the cost of and by denying the deity of Jesus Christ.

Concluding Summary and Recommendations

Some theological considerations from a pentecostal hermeneutical perspective that seriously need attention have been identified. The epistemology of prosperity theology teaches that to know God, one must transcend sensory and scientific knowledge in order to act upon the knowledge provided in the Bible. That requires another type of knowledge, revelation knowledge. Revelation knowledge is transcendent, ultra-sensory, and supra-sensory knowledge that exists in the realm above sense knowledge, consisting of supernatural knowledge of God and the spiritual realm revealed in the Bible, which enables human beings to transcend the limitations of sense knowledge and act in faith. Faith demands that the believer acts solely upon revelation knowledge to the total exclusion of sense knowledge. A result of revelation knowledge is the belief that one can receive perfect knowledge of God, consisting of spiritual laws and principles that give the privileged few who had become recipients of revelation knowledge access to God's vast riches. These principles unlock prosperity, wealth, success, health, and longevity for its practitioners. When prosperity teachers claim that they have discovered the way to such perfect knowledge, they confess in fact that their deistic god can be comprehended in terms of certain laws or principles according to which their god operates. Revelation knowledge lifts believers out of the common place where other believers are, in the second class, into the super-realm. The high regard that prosperity teachers claim for themselves because of their exclusive access to revelation knowledge also leads to the requirements that their adherents uncritically accept all that they teach, even if it is not biblical in nature, because of the direct access the leader has to God's revelation. The idea is established that these preachers have saving knowledge as though it were resident in their own person, accommodating a messiah complex that is perceived in some of these leadership figures. The goal of acquiring revelation knowledge is the transformation of human beings into a god. The transformation from the divine to demonic nature in the Fall in the garden of Eden represents a spiritual death, that is, the death of the human nature. Now human beings were not qualified to live with a divine nature anymore because they now had Satan's intrinsic nature. At the same time, human beings' dominion over creation was transferred to Satan, resulting in Satan becoming a god and ruling creation by legal right. In order to recapture creation, God had to deal with Satan justly by paying him a ransom. This required that Jesus died two deaths on the cross, a spiritual and physical death. Christ's physical death could not eradicate sin and sickness and could not restore the divine nature to humankind. To achieve that goal, he had to die a spiritual death because he had left his divine nature in heaven when he was incarnated, and he had to die as a sinner. He was not the perfect sacrifice that brought atonement for the sinner; he was a sinner like all other people. It was argued that the spiritualization of Christ's death destroys the core of the gospel, claiming that Christ had to suffer in hell to regain and reclaim his own and our "divine" nature. Jesus went to hell a demon-possessed man, and emerged from hell a born-again, resurrected man who had defeated Satan and his forces in hell. Now his disciples become little Christs, gods in their own right, exercising dominion over the earth and its wealth. These teachings require Pentecostals' continuous attention because of its dangers in misleading believers.

Recommendations

It has become imperative for the Pentecostal movement to distance itself from some elements of prosperity theology preached in neo-Pentecostal and independent churches and movements that are abusive and unacceptable to other Christian churches as well. These practices resulted in a bad press affecting also the reputation of Pentecostalism that is identified with the practices of some of the neo-Pentecostal groups. Such identification is a cause of great concern. For many researchers and most journalists and participators on social media, the classical Pentecostal as well as the charismatic movements (described as the first two of three waves of Pentecostalism) are equated deliberately with prosperity theology, including its negative aspects. Classical Pentecostal churches should teach their members more consistently how important it is to understand the historical and theological differences between these movements, and what the heretical implications of some of the teachings of prosperity gospel are, in order to equip them to face the challenges when they are confronted by the lure of successful prosperity teachers who are literally promising them heaven on earth. The leaders of Pentecostal churches should also be vocal about the incompatibility of such prosperity teachings with the ethos and theology of the Pentecostal movement. The secular press as well as members of Pentecostal churches should take note of the deep differences between Pentecostalism and prosperity teachings; not all groups and churches that pentecostalize their liturgy of worship and preaching can be included as part of the classical Pentecostal movement.

Concluding Summary and Recommendations

The pentecostal ethos and unique theological emphasis should be retained at all costs. Greater understanding of what is referred to as the prosperity, Faith, or Word of Faith movement is also necessary to assess the movement in its diversity. Although some publications condemn all their teachings as false and cultic, a balanced view shows that while some of the affected prosperity teachers are guilty of abusing Scriptures and emotionally manipulating and abusing their adherents, that is not true for most others and all their teachings.

At the same time, leaders of neo-Pentecostal networks should be encouraged to ensure that leaders who join their networks as leaders are theologically qualified, to ensure that the gospel they preach has a solid biblical foundation. Several prosperity teachers and networks have established theological schools and they should also be encouraged to study traditional Christian theology in comparison to some of their own viewpoints. Pentecostal theological schools should also be encouraged to include prosperity studies in their curriculum to expose candidate ministers to its teachings and empower them to expose those elements that are harmful to their members and the reputation of the Pentecostal movement as a whole, and to facilitate understanding and the potential for ecumenical contact between historic Christianity and new (and very popular, in the case of prosperity) forms of faith.

The question of what faith is should also be revisited. Pentecostals had always emphasized faith, as a means to find justification through the atonement brought by the cross of Christ, and to pray for healing and other divine interventions in their lives. There is an element of truth in the assertion that one creates the reality in which one lives through the perspective one holds on whatever is happening in one's life and circumstances. The implication is that when Christians are positive about the events that transpire in their lives, ascribing it to God's involvement in their lives, they will be more positive and mentally healthy. However, when faith is described as a means to compel God to provide in whatever human beings desire because believers use the so-called eternal spiritual laws of faith, positive thinking, and positive confession, then the biblical definition of faith as trust in God when events in one's life have become incomprehensible, and that God is still in control is denied.

The observation that the prosperity message is largely based on the Old Testament and prosperity teachers mainly use the Old Testament in their preaching requires the restoration of a balance between a reading of the Old Testament informed by faith in Christ's atonement and the New Testament notion of faith in Christ.

The challenges that prosperity theology present to classical Pentecostalism are concerned with its origins in the metaphysical theories of New Thought, but also its notion of revelation knowledge, consisting of a direct word from the Lord, leaving no room for anyone to question the authority of the preacher. Teachings that deviate from traditional theology are ascribed to revelation knowledge, including their view of the relationship between God and the Bible, of God described in deistic terms, of the spiritual death of Jesus, of the downgrading of Christology and accompanying exaltation of believers to gods, etc. The epistemology of the prosperity gospel should be reconsidered by Pentecostals in terms of their perspective on ongoing and extra-biblical revelation.

Lastly, the lack of accountability in the neo-pentecostal form of governance, with the leader being the sole person who makes decisions, including how finances are spend, and leading to abuses and widespread media coverage of such scandals, implying the reputation of the Pentecostal movement as a whole, should be addressed by classical Pentecostals. Their leaders should in their contact with prosperity preachers emphasize the need for the establishment of structures for responsible decision-making and accountable financial practices, as well as training in financial management and a solid theological foundation for neo-Pentecostal leaders. A new financial model of financial oversight of these ministries is critically necessary, facilitating much required financial accountability within the movement.

Bibliography

Akiri, Mwita. "The Prosperity Gospel: Its Concise Theology, Challenges and Opportunities." *GAFCON: Global Anglicans*, 25 January 2019. https://www.gafcon.org/resources/the-prosperity-gospel-its-concise-theology-challenges-and-opportunities

Akoko, Robert M. *"Ask and You Shall Be Given:" Pentecostalism and the Economic Crisis in Cameroon*. Leiden: African Studies Centre, 2007.

Akrong, Abraham. "African Traditional Religion and Development: Clash of Two Worlds of Discourse and Values." *Trinity Journal of Church and Theology* 13.3 (2003) 36-50.

Allen, A. A. *The Secret to Scriptural Financial Success*. Denver, CO: Allen, 1953.

Anderson, Allan H. "African Independent Churches and Pentecostalism: Historical Connections and Common Identities." *Ogbomoso Journal of Theology* 13.1 (2008) 22-42.

———. "African Pentecostalism." In *Handbook of Pentecostal Christianity*, edited by Alan Stewart, 27–31. DeKalb, IL: Northern Illinois University Press, 2012.

———. *African Reformation: African Initiated Christianity in the 20th Century*. Trenton, NJ: Africa World Press, 2001.

———. "Deliverance and Exorcism in Majority World Pentecostalism." In *Exorcism and Deliverance: Multi-Disciplinary Studies*, edited by W.K. Kay and R. Parry, 101-19. Milton Keynes: Paternoster, 2011.

———. "The Hermeneutical Processes of Pentecostal-Type African Initiated Churches in South Africa." *Missionalia* 24.2 (1996) 171-85.

———. *An Introduction to Pentecostalism*. Second edition. Cambridge: Cambridge University Press, 2013.

———. "New African Initiated Pentecostalism and Charismatics in South Africa." *Journal of Religion in Africa* 35.1 (2005) 66-92.

Anderson, Allan H., and Gerald J. Pillay. "The Segregated Spirit: The Pentecostals." In *Christianity in South Africa: A Political, Social, and Cultural History*, edited by Richard Elphick and Rodney Davenport, 227–41. Berkeley: University of California Press, 1997.

Anderson, Robert M. *Vision of the Disinherited: The Making of American Pentecostalism*. New York: Oxford University Press, 1979.

Archer, Kenneth. *A Pentecostal Hermeneutic: Spirit, Scripture and Community*. Cleveland, OH: CPT, 2009.

Arrington, French L. "The Use of the Bible by Pentecostals." *Pneuma* 16.1 (1994) 101-7.

Asamoah-Gyadu, J. K. *African Charismatics: Current Developments Within Independent Indigenous Pentecostalism in Ghana*. Leiden: Brill, 2005.

———. *Contemporary Pentecostal Christianity: Interpretations from an African Context*. Eugene, OR: Wipf & Stock, 2013.

———. "Did Jesus Wear Designer Robes." *Christianity Today* (November 2009) 3841. https://www.christianitytoday.com/ct/2009/november/main.html

———. "In Search of a Better Country: Migration and Prosperity Hermeneutics in Contemporary African Pentecostalism." *PentecoStudies* 17.2 (January 2018) 158-79. http://oi.org/10.1558/ptcs.34880

———. "Learning to Prosper by Wrestling and by Negotiation: Jacob and Esau in Contemporary African Pentecostal Hermeneutics." *Journal of Pentecostal Theology* 21 (2012) 64-86. DOI 10.aa63.174552512x633303

Avanzini, John. *The Wealth of the World: The Proven Wealth Transfer System*. Tulsa, OK: Harrison House, 1989.

Ayegboyin, Deji. "A Rethinking of Prosperity Teaching in the New Pentecostal Churches in Nigeria." *Black Theology* 4.1 (2006) 70-86. https://doi.org/10.1558/blth.2006.4.1.70

Ayegboyin, Deji, and F. K. Asonzeh Ukah, "Taxonomy of Churches in Africa: The Case of Nigeria." *Ogbomoso Journal of Theology* 13.1 (2008) 1-21.

Bafford, Douglas. "The Prosperity Gospel and an Unprosperous Reality in Post-Apartheid South Africa: Conservative Evangelical Responses to Charismatic Christianity." Paper Presented at the Wits Interdisciplinary Seminar in the Humanities, Wits Institute for Social and Economic Research, University of the Witwatersrand, Johannesburg (March 4, 2019).

Bakker, Jim. *I Was Wrong: The Untold Story of the Shocking Journey from PTL Power to Prison and Beyond*. Nashville, TN: Thomas Nelson, 1997.

Banda, L. "Prophets of God or Neo-Diviners? A Theological Assessment of Prophecy in Zambia Today." In *Prophecy Today: Reflections from a Southern African Context*, edited by Herman Kroesbergen, 208-29. Wellington: Christian Literature Fund, 2016.

Bangura, Joseph B. "Charismatic Movements, State Relations and Public Governance in Sierra Leone." *Studies in World Christianity* 23.3 (2017) 237-56.

Banjo, Temi. "Aftermath of Eating Grass: Pastor Lesego Daniel's Church Members Fall Sick." *Nigerian Monitor* (16 Jan 2014). http://www.nigerianmonitor.com/photos-aftermath-of-eating-grass-pastor-lesego-daniels-church-members-fall-sick\

Barker, Isabelle V. "Charismatic Economies: Pentecostalism, Economic Restructuring, and Social Reproduction." *New Political Science* 29.4 (December 2007) 407-27.

Barrett, David B. "AD 2000: 350 Million Christians in Africa?" *International Review of Mission* 59 (1970) 39-54.

———. "The Worldwide Holy Spirit Renewal." In *The Century of the Holy Spirit: 100 Years of Pentecostal and Charismatic Renewal*, edited by Vinson Synan, 381–414. Nashville, TN: Thomas Nelson, 2001.

Barron, Bruce. *The Health and Wealth Gospel*. Illinois, MI: InterVarsity, 1987.

Barth, Karl. *KD: Die Lehre vom Wort Gottes* I/2. Zürich: Evangelischer Verlag, 1944.

Bartholomew, Craig C. *Introducing Biblical Hermeneutics: A Comprehensive Framework for Hearing God in Scripture*. Grand Rapids, MI: Eerdmans, 2015.

Benjamin, Walter. "Das Kunstwerk im Zeitalter Seiner Technischen Reproduzierbarkeit." In *Gesammelte Schriften* 1/2, edited by Walter Benjamin, 136-69. Frankfurt am Main: Suhrkamp, 1977.

Berger, Peter L. *Faith and Development: A Global Perspective*. Centre for Development and Enterprise Public Lectures, 2008. http:/www.cde.org.za/wp-content/uploads/2013/02/Faith_and_Development.pdf

———. "Four Faces of Global Culture." In *Globalization and the Challenges of a New Century: A Reader*, edited by Patrick O'Meara, Howard D. Melinger, and Matthew Krain, 419–27. Bloomington, IND: Indiana University Press, 2000.

———. "Max Weber is Alive and Well, and Living in Guatemala: The Protestant Ethic Today." *Review of Faith and International Affairs* 8.4 (2010) 3-9.

———. "'You Can Do It!' Two Cheers for the Prosperity Gospel." *Books and Culture* 14.5 (2008) 14-5.

———. *The Sacred Canopy: Elements of a Sociological Theory of Religion*. Garden City, NY: Doubleday, 1967.

Bitrus, Ibrahim. "The Means of Prosperity: The Neo-Pentecostal Interpretation of the Lord's Supper in Nigeria." *Dialog* 55.4 (2016) 334-42.

Bledsoe, David A. "Prosperity Theology: Mere Symptom of Graver Problems in Neo-Pentecostalism." *Revista Batista Pioneira* 3.2 (2014) 301-7.

Bleicher, Josef. *Contemporary Hermeneutics: Hermeneutics as Method, Philosophy and Critique*. Abingdon, OR: Routledge, 2018.

Bosworth, Fred F. *Christ the Healer*. Old Tappan, NJ: Fleming H. Revell, 1973.

———. *Christ the Healer; Sermons on Divine Healing*. Miami Beach, FL: F.F. Bosworth, 1948.

Bourdieu, P. "The Forms of Capital." In *Handbook of Theory and Research for the Sociology of Education*, edited by J.G. Richardson. Westport, CT: Greenwood, 1986.

Bowler, Kate. *Everything Happens for a Reason and Other Lies I've Loved*. New York: Random House, 2018.

———. *Blessed: A History of the American Prosperity Gospel*. Oxford: Oxford University Press, 2013.

Bryant, Antony, and Kathy Charmaz. "Grounded Theory Research: Methods and Practices." In *The SAGE Handbook of Grounded Theory*, edited by Antony Bryant and Kathy Charmaz, 1-28. London: SAGE, 2007.

Bultmann, Rudolf. "ginosko." In *TDNT*, edited by Gerhard Kittel and Gerhard Friedrich, translated by Geoffrey W. Bromiley, 1:692-96. Grand Rapids, MI: Eerdmans, 1964.

Burger, Isak, and Marius Nel. *The Fire Falls in Africa: A History of the Apostolic Faith Mission of South Africa*. Vereeniging: Christian Art, 2008.

Butler, Anthea. "Media, Pentecost and Prosperity: The Racial Meaning Behind the Aesthetic Message." *Pneuma* 33 (2011) 271-6. DOI: 10.1163/027209611X575050

Cady, H. Emily. *Lessons in Truth*. Lee's Summit, Mo: Unity, 1955.

Capps, Charles. *Authority in Three Worlds*. Tulsa, OK: Harrison House, 1982.

———. *God's Creative Power Will Work for You*. Tulsa, OK: Harrison House, 1976.

———. *The Tongue: A Creative Force*. England, AR: Capps, 1976.

Capps, Charles, and Annette Capps. *God's Creative Power for Finances*. Tulsa, OK: Harrison House, 2004.

Cartledge, Mark J. "Glossolalia." In *Handbook of Pentecostal Christianity*, edited by Adam Stewart, 94–7. DeKalb, IL: Northern Illinois University Press, 2012.

Castells, Manuel. *The Network Society: A Cross Cultural Perspective*. Cheltenham: Elgar, 2004.

Castells, Manuel. *The Rise of the Network Society: The Information Age: Economy Society and Culture 1.* Second edition. West Sussex: Wiley, 2000.

Castelo, Daniel. *Pentecostalism as a Christian Mythical Tradition.* Grand Rapids, MI: Eerdmans, 2017.

Chan, Simon. *Pentecostal Theology and the Christian Spiritual Tradition.* JPT 21. Sheffield: Sheffield Academic Press, 2000.

Chaney, Marvin L. *Peasants, Prophets, and Political Economy: The Hebrew Bible and Social Analysis.* Eugene, OR: Cascade, 2017.

Chitando, Ezra, Masiiwa Gunda, and Joachim Kügler. *Prophets, Profits, and the Bible in Zimbabwe.* Bamberg: University of Bamberg Press, 2013.

Clarke, Clifton R. "Pan-Africanism and Pentecostalism in Africa: Strange Bedfellows or Perfect Partners? A Pentecostal Assist Towards a Pan-African Political Theology." *Black Theology* 11.2 (2013) 152-84. DOI 10.1179/1476994813Z.00000000001

Comaroff, Jean. *Body of Power, Spirit of Resistance: The Culture and History of a South African People.* Chicago, ILL: University of Chicago Press, 1985.

Comaroff, Jean, and John L. Comaroff. "Millennial Capitalism: First Thoughts on a Second Coming." *Public Culture* 12.2 (2000) 291-343.

———. "Occult Economies and the Violence of Abstraction: Notes from the South African Postcolony." *American Ethnologist* 26 (1999) 279-303.

———. "Privatizing the Millennium: New Protestant Ethics and Spirits of Capitalism in Africa and Elsewhere," in *Religion, Politics, and Identity in a Changing South Africa,* edited by David Chidester, Abdulkader Tayob and Wolfram Weisse, 24-43. Waxmann: Münster, 2004.

Copeland, Gloria. *God's Will is Prosperity.* Fort Worth, TX: Kenneth Copeland, 1972.

———. *God's Will for You is Healing.* Fort Worth, TX: Kenneth Copeland, 1972.

Copeland, Kenneth. *Believers' Voice of Victory.* Fort Worth, TX: Kenneth Copeland, 1987.

———. *Don't Blame God!* Tulsa, OK: Faith Library, 1979.

———. *Poverty: The Choice is Yours.* Fort Worth, TX: Kenneth Copeland, 1985.

———. *The Laws of Prosperity.* Fort Worth, TX: Kenneth Copeland, 1974.

———. *Walking in the Realms of the Miraculous.* Fort Worth, TX: Kenneth Copeland, 1979.

Cox, Harvey. *Fire from Heaven: The Rise of Pentecostal Spirituality and the Reshaping of Religion in the Twenty-First Century.* New York: Addison-Wesley, 1995.

Crabtree, William. *The Prosperity of a Gospel Church Reconsidered: In a Sermon, Delivered at the Ebenezer-Chapel, at Leeds, January 14, 1789.* London: Bradford, 1789. Reprinted by Ecco Print Editions, n.d.

Cross, F.L., and Elizabeth A. Livingstone, eds., *The Oxford Dictionary of the Christian Church.* Oxford: Oxford University Press, 2005.

Daniels, D.D. "'Wonder and Scholarship:' Reflecting on Jacobsen and Jacobsen's Scholarship and Christian Faith: Enlarging the Conversation." *Pneuma* 27.1 (2005) 110–14. http://dx.doi.org/10.1163/157007405774270356

Deacon, Gregory, and Gabrielle Lynch. "Allowing Satan in? Moving Toward a Political Economy of Neo-Pentecostalism in Kenya." *Journal of Religion in Africa* 43 (2013) 108-30. DOI: 10.1164/15700666-123412467

Droogers, André. *Identity, Religious Pluralism and Ritual in Brazil: Pluralism and Identity: Studies in Ritual Behaviour.* Leiden: Brill, 1995.

Dronen, Tomas S. "Weber, Prosperity and the Protestant Ethic: Some Reflections on Pentecostalism and Economic Development." *Swedish Missiological Themes* 10.3 (2012) 321-5.

Dubarry, Thibaut, and Retief Müller. "Pentecostal Churches and Capitalism in a South African Township: Towards a Communism of the Market?" *The Journal of Religion in Africa* (2019) 1-34. doi 10.13140/RG.2.2.24583.55202

Dube, Musa. "Between the Spirit and the Word: Reading the Gendered African Pentecostal Bible." *HTS Teologiese Studies/Theological Studies* 70.1 (2014) 1-7. http://dx.doi.org/10.4102/hts.v70i1.2651

Editorial, "New Role for Swaggart?" *Charisma* (June 1987) 60.

Egan, Anthony. *The Politics of a South African Catholic Student Movement, 1960-1987*. Cape Town: University of Cape Town, 1990.

Eddy, Mary Baker. *Science and Health with Key to the Scriptures*. Boston, MA: Trustees, 1934.

Ellington, Dustin W. "Is the Prosperity Gospel Biblical? A Critique in Light of Literary Context and Union with Christ." In *In Search of Health and Wealth*, edited by Hermen Kroesbergen, 29-46. Eugene, OR: Wipf & Stock, 2014.

Ellington, Scott A. "Pentecostalism and the Authority of Scriptures." In *Pentecostal Hermeneutics: A Reader*, edited by Lee Roy Martin, 149-70. Leiden: Brill, 2013.

Emerson, Michael O., and Christian Smith. *Divided by Faith: Evangelical Religion and the Problem of Race in America*. New York: Oxford University Press, 2000.

Ervin, Howard M. "Hermeneutics: A Pentecostal Option." *Pneuma* 2.2 (1981) 11-25.

Essien, Essien D. "Ethical Audit of Prosperity Gospel: Psychological Manipulation or Social Ministry." *International Journal of Knowledge-Based Organizations* 8.2 (2018) 53-66. DOI: 10.4018/IJKBO.2018040105

Farah, Charles. *From the Pinnacle of the Temple: Faith or Presumption?* Plainfield, NJ: Logos International, 1980.

Fee, Gordon D. *The Disease of the Health and Wealth Gospel*. Costa Mesa, CA: Word for Today, 1979.

———. *God's Empowering Presence: The Holy Spirit in the Letters of Paul*. Peabody, MA: Hendrickson, 1994.

———. "The New Testament View of Wealth and Possessions." *New Oxford Review* (May 1981) 8.

Fickett, John D. *Confess it, Possess it: Reflection on Faith-Formula Theology*. Oklahoma City, OK: Presbyterian and Reformed Renewal Ministries, 1984.

Fillmore, Charles. *Prosperity*. Unity Village, MI: Unity School of Christianity, 1981.

Finke, Roger, and Rodney Start. *The Churching of America 1776-1990: Winners and Losers in Our Religious Economy*. New Brunswick, NJ: Rutgers University Press, 1992.

Flory, Richard, and Donald E. Miller. *Finding Faith: The Spiritual Quest of the Post-Boomer Generation*. New Brunswick, NJ: Rutgers University Press, 2009.

Folarin, George O. "Contemporary State of the Prosperity Gospel in Nigeria." *Asia Journal of Theology* 21.1 (2007) 69-95.

———. "Prosperity Gospel in Nigeria: Examination of the Concept, Impact, and Evaluation." *African Journal of Biblical Studies* 23.2 (2006) 79-97.

Fowl, Stephen E. *Engaging Scripture: A Model for Theological Interpretation*. Malden, MA: Blackwell, 1998.

Frahm-Arp, Maria. "Pentecostalism, Politics, and Prosperity in South Africa." *Religions* 9.298 (2018) 1-16. DOI: 10.3390/rel9100298

———. "The Rise of the Megachurches in South Africa." In *Global Renewal Christianity: Spirit-Empowered Movements Past, Present, and Future,* edited by Vinson Synan, Amos Yong, and J. K. Asamoah-Gyadu, 3:263-84. Lake Mary, FL: Charisma House, 2016.

———. "Understanding the Rise of Cult Churches in SA." *Financial Mail* (30 May 2019). https://www.businesslive.co.za/fm/opinion/on-my-mind/2019-05-30-maria-frahm-arp-understanding-the-rise-of-cult-churches-in-sa/

Gaffin, Richard B. "The Redemptive-Historical View." In *Biblical Hermeneutics: Five Views,* edited by Stanley E. Porter and Beth M. Stowell, 89-110. Downers Grove, IL: InterVarsity, 2012.

Gaiya, Musa A.B. "Charismatic and Pentecostal Social Orientations in Nigeria." *Nova Religio: The Journal of Alternative and Emergent Religions* 18.3 (2015) 63-79. DOI: 10.1525/nr.2015.18.3.63

Ganiel, Gladys. "Pentecostal and Charismatic Christianity in South Africa and Zimbabwe: A Review." *Religion Compass* 4.3 (2010) 130-43.

Gathogo, Julius. "The Challenge of Money and Wealth in Some East African Pentecostal Churches." *Studia Historiae Ecclesiasticae* 37.2 (2011) 133-51.

Geschiere, Peter. *The Modernity of Witchcraft, Politics, and the Occult in Postcolonial Africa.* Charlottesville, VA: University of Virginia Press, 1997.

Gifford, Paul. "Persistence and Change in Contemporary African Religion." *Social Compass* 51.2 (2004) 169-76. https://doi.org/10.1177/0037768604043004

———. "Expecting Miracles: The Prosperity Gospel in Africa." *Christian Century* (10 July 2007) 20-24.

———. *Ghana's New Christianity: Pentecostalism in a Globalizing African Economy.* Bloomington, IN: Indiana University Press, 2004.

———. "Prosperity: A New and Foreign Element in African Christianity." *Religion* 20 (1990) 373-88.

Gifford, Paul, and Trad Nogueira-Godsey. "The Protestant Ethic and African Pentecostalism: A Case Study." *Journal for the Study of Religion* 24.1 (2011) 5-22.

Golo, Ben-Willie K. "Africa's Poverty and Its Neo-Pentecostal 'Liberators:' An Ecotheological Assessment of Africa's Prosperity Gospellers." *Pneuma* 35 (2013) 366-84. DOI: 10.1163/15700747-1234566

Gossett, Don. *What You Say is What You Get.* Blaine, WA: Whitaker House, 1976.

Grbich, Natasha. *Repentance: Cleansing Your Generational Bloodline.* Helderkruin: Ariel Gate Africa, 2013.

Grenz, Stanley J. *A Primer on Postmodernism.* Grand Rapids, MI: Eerdmans, 1996.

Guinness, Os. *Fit Bodies, Fit Minds: Why Evangelicals Don't Think and What to Do About It.* London: Hodder & Stoughton, 1995.

Gukurume, Simbarashe. "Singing Positivity: Prosperity Gospel in the Musical Discourse of Popular Youth Hip-Hop Gospel in Zimbabwe." *Muziki* 14.2 (2017) 36-54. DOI: org/10.1080/18125980.2017.1403862

Guyson, Nangayi. "Of False Prophets and Profits: Meet the Pentecostal Preacher Taking on the Prosperity Gospel." *African Arguments* (12 September 2016). https://africanarguments.org/2016/09/12/of-false-prophets-and-profits-meet-the-Pentecostal-preacher-taking-on-the-prosperity-gospel/

Hackett, R. I. "Charismatic/Pentecostal Appropriation of Media Technologies in Nigeria and Ghana," *Journal of Religion in Africa* 28.3 (1991) 258-77.

Hagin, Kenneth E. *Authority of the Believer.* Tulsa, OK: Faith Library, 1967.

———. *The Biblical Keys to Financial Prosperity*. Tulsa, OK: Kenneth Hagin, 2005.
———. *El Shaddai: The God Who is More than Enough*. Tulsa, OK: Kenneth Hagin, 1987.
———. *Four Steps to Answered Prayer*. Tulsa, OK: Faith Library, 1980.
———. *Godliness is Profitable*. Tulsa, OK: Kenneth Hagin, 1982.
———. *Having Faith in Your Faith*. Tulsa, OK: Faith Library, 1980.
———. *How to Keep your Healing*. Tulsa, OK: Faith Library, 1980.
———. *How to Write Your Ticket with God*. Tulsa, OK: Faith Library, 1983.
———. *In Him*. Tulsa, OK: Kenneth Hagin, 2006.
———. *The Midas Touch*. Tulsa, OK: Kenneth Hagin, 2000.
———. *The Name of Jesus*. Tulsa, OK: Faith Library, 1979.
———. *New Thresholds of Faith*. Tulsa, OK: Faith Library, 1980.
———. *Prevailing Prayer to Peace*. Tulsa, OK: Faith Library, 1979.
———. *Redeemed from Poverty, Sickness and Death*. Tulsa, OK: Faith Library, 1983.
———. *Right and Wrong Thinking*. Tulsa, OK: Faith Library, 1966.
———. *Zoe: The God-Kind of Life*. Tulsa, OK: Faith Library, 1982.
Hanegraaff, Hank. *Christianity in Crisis 21st Century*. Nashville, TE: Thomas Nelson, 2009.
Haynes, Naomi. *Moving by the Spirit: Pentecostal Social Life on the Zambian Copperbelt*. Oakland, CA: University of California Press, 2017.
———. "On the Potential and Problems of Pentecostal Exchange." *American Anthropologist* 115.1 (2013) 85-95. DOI: 10.1111/j.1548-1433.2012.01537.x
———. "Pentecostalism and the Morality of Money: Prosperity, Inequality, and Religious Sociality on the Zambian Copperbelt." *Journal of the Royal Anthropological Institute* 18 (2012) 123-39.
———. "'Zambia Shall Be Saved!' Prosperity Gospel Politics in a Self-Proclaimed Christian Nation." *Nova Religio: The Journal of Alternative and Emergent Religions* 19.1 (2015) 5-24. DOI: 10.1525/nr.2015.19.1.5
Hefner, Robert W. "The Unexpected Modern-Gender, Piety, and Politics in the Global Pentecostal Surge." In *Global Pentecostalism in the 21st Century*, edited by Robert W. Hefner, 1-36. Bloomington, IN: Indiana University Press, 2013.
Henderson, Robert. *Operating in the Courts of Heaven: Granting God the Legal Right to Fulfill His Passion and Answer Our Prayers*. Helderkruin: Ariel Gate Africa, 2013.
Herskovits, Melville J. *The Myth of the Negro Past*. New York: Harper & Brothers, 1941.
Heuser, Andreas. "Charting African Prosperity Gospel Economies." *HTS Teologiese Studies/Theological Studies* 72.1 (2016) 1-9. http:/dx.doi,org/10.4102/hts.v72i.3823
Hinn, Costi W. *God, Greed, and the (Prosperity) Gospel: How Truth Overwhelms a Life Built on Lies*. Grand Rapids: MI: Zondervan, 2019.
Hollenweger, Walter. "From Azusa Street to Toronto Phenomenon: Historical Roots of Pentecostalism." *Concilium* 3.6 (1993) 3-14.
———. *The Pentecostals*. Minneapolis, MN: Augsburg, 1977.
Horn, J. Nico. *From Rags to Riches: An Analysis of the Faith Movement and its Relation to the Classical Pentecostal Movement*. Pretoria: University of South Africa, 1989.
Horsfield, Peter G. *Religious Television: The American Experience*. New York: Longman, 1984.
Hunt, Dave, and T. A. McMahon, *The Seduction of Christianity: Spiritual Discernment in the Last Days*. Eugene, OR: Harvest House, 1985.

Hunter, Harold D. "Introduction: Global Pentecostals are not 'Protestant' and are not 'Western.'" In *The Many Faces of Global Pentecostalism,* edited by Harold D. Hunter and Neil Ormerod, 1-5. Cleveland, OH: CPT, 2013.

Hutchinson, Mark. "'Fools and Fundamentalists': The Institutional Dilemmas of Australian Pentecostalism." In *The Many Faces of Global Pentecostalism,* edited by Harold D. Hunter and Neil Ormerod, 219-42. Cleveland, OH: CPT, 2013.

Jackson, B. *The Quest for the Radical Middle: A History of the Vineyard.* Cape Town: Vineyard International, 2006.

Jacobsen, Douglas. *Global Gospel: An Introduction to Christianity on Five Continents.* Grand Rapids, MI: Baker, 2015.

Jakes, T. D. *Reposition Yourself: Living Life Without Limits.* New York: Atria, 2008.

Jenkins, Philip. *The New Faces of Christianity: Believing the Bible in the Global South.* New York: Oxford University Press, 2006.

Jones, Candace S., William S. Hesterly, and Stephen P. Borgati. "A General Theory of Network Governance: Exchange Conditions and Social Mechanisms." *Academy of Management Review* 22.4 (1997) 911-45.

Kabat-Zinn, Jon. *Mindfulness for Beginners: Reclaiming the Present Moment . . . And Your Life.* Boulder, CO: Sounds True, 2012.

Kaiser, Walter C., and Moisés Silva. *Introduction to Biblical Hermeneutics.* Revised edition. Grand Rapids, MI: Zondervan, 2007.

Kalu, Ogbu U. *African Pentecostalism: An Introduction.* New York: Oxford University Press, 2008.

———. "A Discursive Interpretation of African Pentecostalism." *Fides et Historia* 41.1 (2009) 71-90.

———. "'Globecalisation' and Religion: The Pentecostal Model in Contemporary Africa." In *Uniquely African? African Christian Identity from Cultural and Historical Perspectives,* edited by James L. Cox and Gerrie Ter Haar. Trenton, NJ: Africa World Press, 2003.

Kangwa, J. "African Democracy and Political Exploitation: An Appraisal of Xenophobia and the Removal of the Rhodes Statue in South Africa. *The Expository Times* 127.11 (2016) 534-45. DOI: 10.1177/0014524616630702

Kärkkäinen, Velli-Matti. "Pentecostal Hermeneutics in the Making: On the Way from Fundamentalism to Postmodernism." *Journal of the European Pentecostal Theological Association* 18 (1998) 76–115. http://dx.doi.org/10.1179/jep.1998.18.1.006

Kay, William K., and Anne E. Dyer, eds. *Pentecostal and Charismatic Studies: A Reader.* London: SCM, 2004.

Katsaura, Obvious. "Theo-Urbanism: Pastoral Power and Pentecostals in Johannesburg." *Culture and Religion* 18.3 (2017) 232-62.

Kaufman, Joanne. "The Fall of Jimmy Swaggart." *People* (March 1988) 35-6. http://www.people.com/people/archive/article/0,,20098413,00.html

Kaunda, Chammah J. "Enabling Liminality Prophetic Witness to Xenophobia: Proposing a Missiological Spirit Response for the Church in South Africa." *KOERS* 81.1 (2016) 1-9. http://dx.doi.org/10.19108/ KOERS.81.1.2217

Keener, Craig S. "Pentecostal Biblical Interpretation/Spirit Hermeneutics." In *Scripture and its Interpretation: A Global, Ecumenical Introduction to the Bible,* edited by Michael J. Horman, 270–83. Grand Rapids, MI: Baker Academic, 2017.

———. *Spirit Hermeneutics: Reading Scripture in Light of Pentecost.* Grand Rapids, MI: Eerdmans, 2016.

Keener, Craig S., and M. Daniel Carroll. "Introduction." In *Global Voices: Reading the Bible in the Majority World*, edited by Craig Keener and M. Daniel Carroll, 1-4. Peabody, MA: Hendrickson, 2013.

Kennedy, John W. "The Crusader." *Christianity Today* (November 2013) 51-4.

Kenyon, E. W. *Advanced Bible Course: Studies in the Deeper Life*. Seattle, WA: Kenyon's Gospel Publishing Society, 1970.

———. *The Bible in the Light of Our Redemption*. Second edition. Lynnwood, WA: Kenyon's Gospel Publishing Society, 1969.

———. *The Hidden Man: An Unveiling of the Subconscious Mind*. Seattle, WA: Kenyon's Gospel Publishing Society, 1970.

———. *Identification: A Romance in Redemption*. Seattle, WA: Kenyon's Gospel Publishing Society, 1968.

———. *Jesus the Healer*. Seattle, WA: Kenyon's Gospel Publishing Society, 1943.

———. *The Two Kinds of Faith: Faith's Secret Revealed*. Lynnwood, WA: Kenyon's Gospel Publishing Society, 1998 (1942).

———. *The Two Kinds of Knowledge*. Seattle, WA: Kenyon's Gospel Publishing Society, 1942.

———. *The Two Kinds of Life*. Seattle, WA: Kenyon's Gospel Publishing Society, 1971.

———. *What Happened from the Cross to the Throne*. Lynnwood, WA: Kenyon's Gospel Publishing Society, 1969.

Kgatle, Mookgo S. "Social Media and Religion: Missiological perspective on the Link Between Facebook and the Emergence of Prophetic Churches in Southern Africa." *Verbum et Ecclesia* 39.1 (2018). https://doi.org/10.4102/ve.v39i1.1848

———. "The Unusual Practices Within Some Neo-Pentecostal Churches in South Africa: Reflections and Recommendations." *HTS Teologiese Studies/Theological Studies* 73.3 (2017). https://doi.org/10.4102/hts.v73i3.4656

Khanyile, Sphesihle B. "The Virtualization of the Church: New Media Representations of Neo-Pentecostal Performance(s) in South Africa." MA diss., University of the Witwatersrand, 2016.

Kingsbury, Kate, and Andrew Chesnut. "How Catholics are Falling for the Prosperity Gospel." *Catholic Herald* (29 November 2018). https://catholicherald.co.uk/magazine/the-liturgy-of-money/

Kodua, Alfred. *Who is Disturbing the Nation?* Accra: Advocate Publishing, 2008.

Kroesbergen, Hermen. "The Prosperity Gospel: A Way to Reclaim Dignity?" In *In Search of Health and Wealth*, edited by Hermen Kroesbergen, 74-84. Eugene, OR: Wipf & Stock, 2014.

Lake, John G. *The John G. Lake Sermons on Dominion over Demons, Disease, and Death*. Dallas, TX: Christ for the Nations, 1982 (1950).

———. *John G. Lake: The Complete Collection of His Life Teachings*. Edited by Richard Liardon. Blaine, WA: Whitaker House, 2005.

———. *Spiritual Hunger and Other Sermons*, edited by Gordon Lindsay. Dallas, TX: Christ for the Nations, 1994.

Land, Steven J. *Pentecostal Spirituality: A Passion for the Kingdom*. JPT 10. Sheffield: Sheffield Academic Press, 1993.

Lederle, Henry I. "An Ecumenical Investigation into the Proprium or Distinctive Element of Pentecostal Theology." Paper read at the Seventh Annual Meeting of the Society for Pentecostal Studies, Virginia Beach, VA, 1987. http://uir.unisa.ac.za/bitstream/handle/10500/19535/Clark__SM__0869816969__Section4.pdf?sequence=4&isAllowed=y

Lee, Moonyang. "Future of Global Christianity." In *Atlas of Global Christianity, 1910–2010*, edited by Todd M. Johnson and Kenneth R. Ross, 104–5. Edinburgh: Center for the Study of Global Christianity, 2009.

Lewis, Gordon R. *Confronting the Cults*. Grand Rapids, MI: Baker, 1975.

Long, Thomas G. "Living with the Bible." In *Homosexuality and Christian Community*, edited by C. L. Seow, 64-73. Louisville, KY: Westminster John Knox, 1996.

Louw, Johannes P., and Eugene A. Nida. *Greek-English Lexicon of the New Testament: Based on Semantic Domains*. New York: United Bible Societies, 1996.

Luxmoore, Jonathan. "African Church Warns Against Illusions of 'Prosperity Gospel.'" *The Tablet* (29 October 2018). https://www.thetablet.co.uk/news/10933/african-church-warns-against-illusions-of-prosperity-gospel-

Maclean, Ruth, and Eromo Egbejule. "Gospel Glamour: How Nigeria's Pastors Wield Political Power." *The Guardian* (14 February 2019). https://www.theguardian.com/world/2019/feb/13/gospel-glamour-how-nigerias-pastors-wield-political-power

Magasa, Laurenti. "Christ the Liberator in Africa Today." In *Faces of Jesus in Africa*, edited by Robert J. Shreiter, 151-63. Maryknoll, NY: Orbis, 1997.

Mana, K. *Christians and Churches of Africa: Salvation in Christ and Building a New African Society*. Maryknoll, NY: Orbis, 2004.

Marshall, Ruth. *Political Spiritualities: The Pentecostal Revolution in Nigeria*. Chicago, IL: University of Chicago Press, 2009.

Marti, Gerardo. "The Adaptability of Pentecostalism: The Fit between Prosperity Theology and Globalized Individualization in a Los Angeles Church." *Pneuma* 34 (2015) 5-25. DOI: 10.1163/157007412X621662

Martin, Lee R. "Introduction to Pentecostal Biblical Hermeneutics." In *Pentecostal Hermeneutics: A Reader*, edited by Lee Roy Martin, 1-10. Leiden: Brill, 2013.

Mashau, Thinandavha D. "Reimagining Mission in the Public Square: Engaging Hills and Valleys in the African City of Tshwane." *HTS Theological Studies* 70.3 (2014) 1-11. https://doi.org/10.4102/hts.v70i3.2774

Mashau, Thinandavha D., and Mookgo S. Kgatle. "Prosperity Gospel and the Culture of Greed in Post-Colonial Africa: Constructing an Alternative African Christian Theology of Ubuntu." *Verbum et Ecclesia* 40.1 (2019). https://doi.org/10.4102/ve.v40i1.1901

Matta, J. *The Born Again Jesus of the Word-Faith Teaching*. Fullerton, CA: Spirit of Truth Ministries, 1987.

Maura, Michael O. "True and False Prosperity." In *Prosperity? Seeking the True Gospel*, edited by Michael O. Maura, Conrad Mbewe, Ken Mbugua, John Piper, and Wayne Grudem, 33-47. Nairobi: Africa Christian Textbooks, 2015.

Maura, Philomena N., and Damaris Parsitau. "Perceptions of Women's Health and Rights in Christian New Religious Movements in Kenya." In *Christianity in Africa and the Diaspora: The Appropriation of a Scattered Heritage*, edited by A. Adogame, 175-86. London: Continuum, 2008.

Maxon, Chris. "Fake Pastors and Their Followers: This is Why the 'God Business' is Thriving in SA." *City Press* (7 March 2019). https://city-press.news24.com/Voices/fake-pastors-and-their-followers-this-is-why-the-god-business-is-thriving-in-sa-20190307

Maxwell, David. "'Delivered from the Spirit of Poverty?' Pentecostalism, Prosperity and Modernity in Zimbabwe." *Journal of Religion in Africa* 28.3 (1998) 350-73.

Mbewe, Conrad. 2011. "Nigerian Religious Junk!" *A Letter from Kabwata* (20 February 2011). http://www.conradmbewe.com/2011/02/nigerian-religious-junk.html

Mbugua, Kenneth. "Introduction: A False Gospel." In *Prosperity? Seeking the True Gospel*, edited by Michael O. Mbugua et al., 1-14. Nairobi: Africa Christian Textbooks, 2015.

———. "Misunderstanding the Bible." In *Prosperity? Seeking the True Gospel*, edited by Michael O. Mbugua et al., 15-32. Nairobi: Africa Christian Textbooks, 2015.

———. "Suffering." In *Prosperity? Seeking the True Gospel*, edited by Michael O. Mbugua et al., 65-78. Nairobi: Africa Christian Textbooks, 2015.

Mburu, Elizabeth. *African Hermeneutics*. Bukuru, Nigeria: HippoBooks, 2019.

McCauley, John. "Pentecostal Politics in Ghana." In *Atlas of Pentecostalism: An Expanding Record of the Fastest Growing Religion in the World*, 68-9 (29 July 2018). www.atlasofPentecostalism.net

McConnell, Dan R. *A Different Gospel: A Bold and Revealing Look at the Biblical and Historical Basis of the Word of Faith Ministries*. Peabody, MA: Hendrickson, 1988.

———. *The Kenyon Connection: A Theological and Historical Analysis of the Cultic Origins of the Faith Movement*. MA diss., Oral Roberts University, 1982.

McQueen, Larry R. *Joel and the Spirit: The Cry of a Prophetic Hermeneutic*. Cleveland, OH: CPT, 2009.

Mensch, James. "The Hermeneutics of Fundamentalism." https://www.academia.edu/309359/The_Hermeneutics_of_Fundamentalism

Meyer, Birgit. "Pentecostalism and Neo-Liberal Capitalism: Faith, Prosperity and Vision in African Pentecostal-Charismatic Churches." *Journal for the Study of Religion* 20.2 (2007) 5-26. DOI: 10.4314/jsr.v20i2.47769

Meyer, Joyce. *Approval Addiction: Overcoming Your Need to Please Everyone*. New York: Faith Words, 2005.

Miller, Donald E. *Reinventing American Protestantism: Christianity in the New Millennium*. Berkeley, CA: University of California Press, 1997.

Miller, Donald, and Tetsunao Yamamori, *Global Pentecostalism: The New Face of Christian Social Engagement*. Berkeley, CA: University of California, 2007.

Moltmann, Jürgen. "The Destruction and Healing of the Earth." In *God and Globalization: The Spirit and the Modern Authorities* 2, edited by Max L. Stackhouse, 166-90. Harrisburg, PA: Trinity, 2001.

Morton, B. "'The Devil Who Heals:' Fraud and Falsification in the Evangelical Career of John G Lake, Missionary to South Africa 1908–1913." *African Historical Review* 44.2 (2012) 98–118. http://dx.doi.org/10.1080/17532523.2012.739752

Munroe, Myles. "Praise the Lord." Trinity Broadcasting Network (11 December 2000).

Munyaneza, A. "'Ubuntu' and Mother's Old Black Bible." *Cultural Encounters* 51.1 (2009) 99-102.

Musonda, Kay. "African Pentecostalism Has Given Birth to A New Breed of Mentally Lazy Christians Who See God as A Rewarder of Mediocrity." *Modern Ghana* (1 April 2017). https://www.modernghana.com/news/765993/african-Pentecostalism-has-given-birth-to-a-new-breed-of-men.html

Mwale, N., and J. Chita. "Religion and the Media: The Portrayal of Prophecy in the Zambian Media." In *Prophecy Today: Reflections from a Southern African Context*, edited by Herman Kroesbergen, 99-112. Wellington: Christian Literature Fund, 2016.

Nel, Marius. *An African Pentecostal Hermeneutics: A Distinctive Contribution to Hermeneutics*. Eugene, OR: Wipf & Stock, 2018.

———. *African Pentecostalism and Eschatological Expectations: He is Coming Back Again!* London: Cambridge Scholars, 2019.

———. *Pacifism and Pentecostals in South Africa: A New Hermeneutic of Nonviolence*. London: Routledge, 2018.

———. "The Pentecostal Movement's view of the continuity of tongues in Acts and 1 Corinthians." *In die Skriflig* 51.1 (2017). https://doi. org/10.4102/ids.v51i1.2198

———. "Pentecostals' Reading of the Old Testament." *Verbum et Ecclesia* 28.2 (2007) 524-41.

———. "Rather Spirit-Filled than Learned! Pentecostalism's Tradition of Anti-Intellectualism and Pentecostal Theological Scholarship." *Verbum et Ecclesia* 37.1 (2016). a1533. http:// dx.doi.org/10.4102/ve. v37i1.1533

Nida, Eugene A. *Message and Mission*. New York: Harper & Row, 1960.

Ngong, David T. *The Holy Spirit and Salvation in African Christian Theology: Imagining a New Hopeful Future for Africa*. Oxford: Peter Lang, 2010.

Ntui-Abung, John. *The Chaos of the Prosperity Gospel: A Case Study of Two Prominent Nigerian Pastors*. Bloomington, IN: WestBow, 2017.

Nwoka, A. O. "The Challenge of Nigerian Pentecostal Theology and the Perspicuity of Scripture." *Alternative* 2 (2005) 164-77.

Nyengele, M. Fulgence. "Cultivating Ubuntu: An African Postcolonial Pastoral Theological Engagement with Positive Psychology." *Journal of Pastoral Theology* 24.2 (2014) 4.1-4.35. https://doi.org/10.1179/jpt.2014.24.2.004

Nyirenda, Tiza J. *Misconceptions of Healing, Blessings and Miracles*. Scotts Valley, CA: Createspace, 2018.

Obadare, Ebenezer. "'Raising Righteous Billionaires:' The Prosperity Gospel Reconsidered." *HTS Theologiese Studies/Theological Studies* 72.4 (2016) 1-8. http:// dx.doi.org/10.4102/hts.v72i4.3571

Oliverio, L. William. "Introduction: Pentecostal Hermeneutics and the Hermeneutical Tradition." In *Constructive Pneumatological Hermeneutics in Pentecostal Christianity*, edited by Kenneth J. Archer and L. William Oliverio, 1–14. New York: Palgrave Macmillan, 2016.

———. *Theological Hermeneutics in the Classical Pentecostal Tradition: A Typological Account*. Leiden: Brill, 2012.

Omenyo, Cephas N., and Wonderful A. Arthur. "The Bible Says! Neo-Prophetic Hermeneutics in Africa." *Studies in World Christianity* 19.1 (2013) 50–70.

Oosthuizen, Gerhardus C. *The Healer-Prophet in Afro-Christian Churches*. Leiden: Brill, 1992.

Osborn, T. L. *Miracles: Proofs of God's Love*. Tulsa, OK: Osborn, 2003.

Osteen, Joel. *Become a Better You: 7 Keys to Improving Your Life Every Day*. New York: Free, 2007.

Paas, Steven. *Christianity in Eurafrica: A History of the Church in Europe and Africa*. Washington, DC: New Academia, 2017.

Parker, Larry. *We Let Our Son Die*. Irvine, CA: Harvest House, 1980.

Pawson, David. *Unlocking the Bible Omnibus: A Unique Overview of the Whole Bible*. London: HarperCollins, 2003.

Peale, Norman V. *The Power of Positive Thinking*. New York: Touchstone, 1952.

Phiri, Isaac, and Joe Maxwell, "Gospel Riches: Africa's Embrace of Prosperity Pentecostalism Provokes Concern—and Hope." *Christianity Today* (July 2007) 23-29.

Pinnock, Clark H. "The Work of the Holy Spirit in the Interpretation of Holy Scripture from the Perspective of a Charismatic Biblical Theologian." In *Pentecostal Hermeneutics: A Reader*, edited by Lee Roy Martin, 233-48. Leiden: Brill, 2013.

Piper, John. "Appendix I: Twelve Appeals to Prosperity Teachers." In *Prosperity? Seeking the True Gospel*, edited by Michael O. Mbugua et al., 107-22. Nairobi: Africa Christian Textbooks, 2015.

Plüss, Jean-Daniel. "Azusa and Other Myths: The Long and Winding Road from Experience to Stated Belief and Back Again." *Pneuma* 15.2 (1993) 189-201.

Pretorius, Stephanus P. "The Toronto Blessing: An Expression of Christian Spirituality in the Charismatic Movement?" DTh diss., University of South Africa, 2002.

Price, Frederick K. C. *Faith, Foolishness, or Presumption?* Tulsa, OK: Harrison, 1979.

———. *How Faith Works*. Tulsa, OK: Harrison, 1976.

———. *Ever Increasing Faith Messenger*. Crenshaw, LA: Crenshaw Christian Centre, June 1980.

———. "Prayer: Do You Know What Prayer Is . . . And How to Pray?" In *The Word Study Bible*, 1178. Tulsa, OK: Harrison, 1990.

Prosper, Jean M. *The Prosperity Gospel Truth or Lie? Reviewing the "Wealth Gospel."* Bloomington, IN: WestBow, 2012.

Quayesi-Amakye, J. Kwabena. "Ideas of the Divine and the Human in Ghanaian Pentecostal Songs." MA diss., Vrije Universiteit, Amsterdam, 2008.

———. "'Nativizing' the Gospel: Pentecostalism and Theology in Africa." In *Global Renewal Christianity: Spirit-Empowered Movements Past, Present, and Future*, edited by Vinson Synan, Amos Yong and J.Kwabena Asamoah-Gyadu, vol. 3: Africa, 287-303. Lake Mary, FL: Charisma House, 2016.

———. "Pentecostalism and the Transformation of the African Christian Landscape." In *Pentecostalism in Africa: Presence and Impact of Pneumatic Christianity in Postcolonial Societies*, edited by Martin Lindhardt, 100-114. Leiden: Brill, 2015.

———. "Prosperity and Prophecy in African Pentecostalism." *Journal of Pentecostal Theology* 20 (2011) 291-305. DOI 10.1163/174552511X597161

Resane, K. T. "The Ecclesiology of the Emerging Apostolic Churches: Fivefold Ministry." PhD diss., University of Pretoria, 2008.

Ricoeur, Paul. *Hermeneutics: Writings and Lectures 2*. Translated by David Pellauer. Cambridge: Polity, 2013.

Robeck, Cecil M. "National Association of Evangelicals (NAE)." In *Dictionary of Pentecostal and Charismatic Movements*, edited by Stanley M. Burgess and Gary B. McGee, 634-36. Grand Rapids, MI: Zondervan, 1988.

Roberts, Oral. *Holy Spirit in the Now*. Tulsa, OK: Oral Roberts University, 1974.

Ruthven, Jon. *On the Cessation of the Charismata: Protestant Polemic on Postbiblical Miracles*. Sheffield, UK: Sheffield Academic Press, 1993.

———. "The 'Foundational Gifts' of Ephesians 2:20." http://hopefaithprayer.com/books/The%20Foundational%20Gifts%20Ephesians202-20.pdf

Sanford, Agnes. *The Healing Light*. St. Paul, MN: Macalester Park, 1947.

Sarles, Ken L. "A Theological Evaluation of the Prosperity Gospel." *Bibliotheca Sacra* 143 (1986) 329-52.

Schliesser, Christine. "On a Long Neglected Player: The Religious Factor in Poverty Alleviation: The Example of the So-Called 'Prosperity Gospel' in Africa." *Exchange* 43.4 (2014) 339-59.

Schmidgall, Paul. *European Pentecostalism: Its Origins, Development, and Future.* Cleveland, TN: CPT, 2013.

Scott, Benjamin G. McNair. *Apostles Today: Making Sense of Contemporary Charismatic Apostolates: A Historical and Theological Appraisal.* Eugene, OR: Pickwick, 2014.

Sherket, Darren E., and Christopher G. Ellison. "Recent Developments and Current Controversies in the Sociology of Religion." *Annual Review of Sociology* 25 (1999) 363-94.

Sider, Ronald. *Rich Christians in an Age of Hunger.* Nashville, TN: Thomas Nelson, 1978.

Smith, Daniel J. "Pentecostalism and Aids in Nigeria." In *Atlas of Pentecostalism: An Expanding Record of the Fastest Growing Religion in the World* (29 July 2018) 58-61. www.atlasofPentecostalism.net

Smith, James K. A. *Thinking in Tongues: Pentecostal Contributions to Christian Philosophy.* Grand Rapids, MI: Eerdmans, 2010.

Steele, Ron. *Destined to Win: A Biography of Ray McCauley.* Johannesburg: Conquest, 1986.

Stibbe, Mark. "This is That: Some Thoughts Concerning Charismatic Hermeneutics." *Anvil* 13.3 (1998) 181-93.

Stronstad, Roger. "Pentecostal Experience and Hermeneutics." *Paraclete* 26.1 (Winter 1992) 14-30.

Sundkler, Bengt. *Bantu Prophets in South Africa.* Second edition. London: Oxford University Press, 1961.

Sutton, Matthew A. *American Apocalypse: A History of Modern Evangelicalism.* Cambridge, MA: Belknap, 2014.

Swaggart, Jimmy. *The Confession Principle and the Course of Nature.* Baton Rouge, LA: Jimmy Swaggart, 1981.

Swaggart, Jimmy, and Marvin E. Solum. *The Balanced Faith Life.* Baton Rouge, LA: Jimmy Swaggart, 1981.

Taylor, Charles. *A Secular Age.* Cambridge, MA: Harvard University Press, 2007.

Taylor, John V. *The Primal Vision: Christian Presence Amid African Religion.* London: SCM, 1963.

Thiselton, Anthony C. *New Horizons in Hermeneutics.* Grand Rapids, MI: Eerdmans, 1992.

Togarasei, Lovemore. "African Gospreneurship: Assessing the Possible Contribution of the Gospel of Prosperity to Entrepreneurship in Light of Jesus' Teaching on Earthly Possessions." In *In Search of Health and Wealth*, edited by Hermen Kroesbergen, 110-25. Eugene, OR: Wipf & Stock, 2014.

———. "The Pentecostal Gospel of Prosperity in African Contexts of Poverty." *Exchange* 40 (2011) 336-50.

Trine, Ralph W. *In Tune with the Infinite.* New York: Bobbs-Merrill, 1970.

Ukah, Asonzeh. "The Redeemed Church of God in Nigeria." In *Atlas of Pentecostalism: An Expanding Record of the Fastest Growing Religion in the World* (29 July 2018), 16-9. www.atlasofPentecostalism.net

Umoh, Dominic. "Prosperity Gospel and the Spirit of Capitalism: The Nigerian Story." *African Journal of Scientific Research* 12.1 (2013) 654-66.

Van Wyk, Ilana. *The Universal Church of the Kingdom of God in South Africa: A Church of Strangers*. Cambridge: Cambridge University Press, 2014.

———. "Why 'Money' Gospel Followers Aren't Simply Credulous Dupes." *The Conversation* (21 February 2019). https://theconversation.com/why-money-gospel-followers-arent-simply-credulous-dupes-111838

Vásquez, Manuel A. "The Global Portability of Pneumatic Christianity: Comparing African and Latin American Pentecostalisms." *African Studies* 68 (2009) 273-86.

Verweij, André C. *Positioning Jesus' Suffering: A Grounded Theory of Lenten Preaching in Local Parishes*. Delft: Eburon, 2014.

Vondey, Wolfgang. *Beyond Pentecostalism: The Crisis of Global Christianity and the Renewal of the Theological Agenda*. Grand Rapids, MI: Eerdmans, 2010.

———. *Pentecostalism*. London: Bloomsbury, 2013.

Waddell, Robby. *The Spirit of the Book of Revelation*. Blandford Forum: Deo, 2006.

Wagner, C. Peter. *Wrestling with Alligators, Prophets, and Theologians: Lessons from a Lifetime in the Church*. Ventura, CA; Regal, 2010.

———. *Apostles Today: Biblical Government for Biblical Power*. Ventura, CA: Regal, 2006.

Waltke, Bruce K. *The Dance Between God and Humanity: Reading the Bible Today as the People of God*. Grand Rapids, MI: Eerdmans, 2013.

Walton, Jonathan L. *Watch This! The Ethics and Aesthetics of Black Televangelism*. New York: New York University Press, 2009.

Wariboko, Nimi. "Pentecostal Paradigms of National Economic Prosperity in Africa." In *Pentecostalism and Prosperity: The Socio-Economics of the Global Charismatic Movement*, edited by Katherine Attanasi and Amos Yong, 41-44. New York: Palgrave Macmillan, 2012.

———. *The Pentecostal Principle: Ethical Methodology in New Spirit*. Grand Rapids, MI: Eerdmans, 2011.

Weber, Max. *Economy and Society: An Outline of Interpretive Sociology*. Guenther Roth and Claus Wittich, eds. Berkeley, CA: University of California Press, 1978.

———. *The Protestant Ethic and the Spirit of Capitalism*. London: George Allen and Unwin, 1971 (1905).

West, Gerald. *The Stolen Bible: From Tool of Imperialism to African Icon*. Pietermaritzburg: Cluster, 2016.

White-Cain, Paula. *Something Greater: Finding Triumph over Trials*. New York: FaithWords, 2019.

Wilkerson, Bruce. *The Prayer of Jabez*. London: Penguin, 2005.

Wink, Walter. *Bible in Human Transformation: Toward a New Paradigm for Biblical Study*. Minneapolis, MN: Fortress, 2010.

Yong, Amos. *In the Days of Caesar: Pentecostalism and Political Theology*. Grand Rapids, MI: Eerdmans, 2010.

———. *Spirit-Word-Community: Theological Hermeneutics in Trinitarian Perspective*. Aldershot: Ashgate, 2002.

Zaimov, Stoyan. "Evangelical Pastor Accused of Running Slave Labor: 'It Was Hell, Not Paradise,' Says Former Worker." *The Christian Post* (16 April 2018). https://www.christianpost.com/news/evangelical-pastor-accused-of-running-slave-labor-it-was-hell-not-paradise-says-former-worker.html

———. "Prosperity Gospel Sweeping Africa, Pentecostals Ignores Jesus: Anglican Conference Bishops." *The Christian Post* (26 June 2018). https://www.christianpost.com/news/prosperity-gospel-sweeping-africa-Pentecostals-ignores-jesus-global-anglican-future-conference-bishops.html

Zulu, E. "'Fipelwa na ba Yaweh': A Critical Examination on Prosperity Theology in the Old Testament from a Zambian Perspective." In *In Search of Health and Wealth*, edited by Hermen Kroesbergen, 21-28. Eugene, OR: Wipf & Stock, 2014.

———. "'Sow a Seed' and Prosper? A Critical Examination of the Trends, Practices of 'Prophecy' in a Zambian Context." In *Prophecy Today: Reflections from a Southern African Context*, edited by Herman Kroesbergen, 99-112. Wellington: Christian Literature Fund, 2016.

www.ingramcontent.com/pod-product-compliance
Lightning Source LLC
Chambersburg PA
CBHW050838230426
43667CB00012B/2053